SEOUL

SEOUL

*Memory, Reinvention,
and the Korean Wave*

ROSS KING

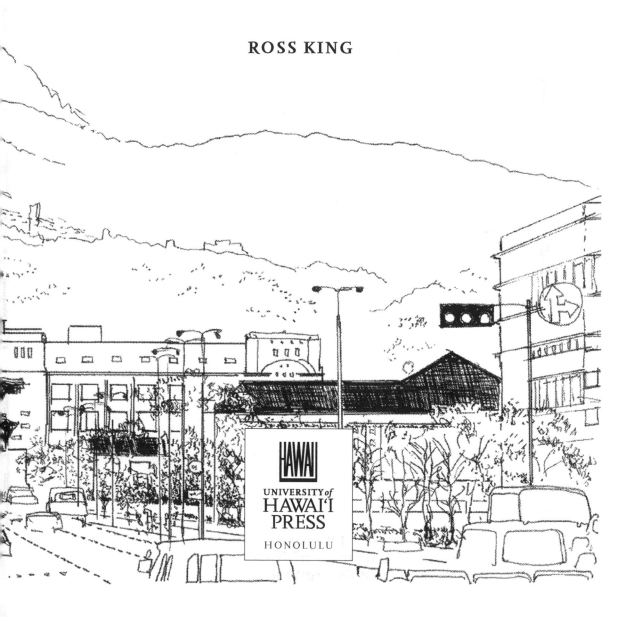

UNIVERSITY *of*
HAWAI'I
PRESS
HONOLULU

23 22 21 20 19 18   6 5 4 3 2 1

Library of Congress Cataloging-in-Publication Data

Names: King, Ross, author.
Title: Seoul : memory, reinvention, and the Korean wave / Ross King.
Description: Honolulu : University of Hawai'i Press, [2018] | Includes
    bibliographical references and index.
Identifiers: LCCN 2017036841 | ISBN 9780824872052 (cloth alk. paper)
Subjects: LCSH: Seoul (Korea)—History. | Architecture—Korea (South)—Seoul.
Classification: LCC DS925.S457 K59 2018 | DDC 951.95—dc23
LC record available at https://lccn.loc.gov/2017036841

University of Hawai'i Press books are printed on acid-free paper and meet the guidelines for permanence and durability of the Council on Library Resources.

Designed by Mardee Melton
All photos, maps, and drawings are by the author unless otherwise indicated.

For Heidi and Edward

Contents

Preface

In the 1990s one's first glimpse of Seoul would typically be from the air, circling to the old Gimpo airport. At night this could be decidedly disorienting: overwhelming the usual twinkling display of the nighttime city would be a forest of giant, illuminated red crosses, seemingly on all manner of sites and buildings, in an incomprehensible display of Christian witness. One would have heard of Korea's proliferation of sects; however, the realization that proliferation could so transform the fabric of the city would beggar understanding. A second impression, from the ground and in the light of day, would reveal that these crosses were in the main atop the most nondescript of boxes, most frequently also adorned with a bewildering display of advertisement boards for brands and businesses, from the global to the most local. Seoul presents as a city of boxes: even the National Assembly Building, monument to the Fourth Republic and ultimate symbol of the Sixth Republic, reads as a box that would seem to represent nothing, though here without advertisement boards. A further impression would come with the view from the air by day, also from the highway into the city, from the old Gimpo or the new Incheon airport or almost any point in the city: serried arrays of high-rise apartment towers inserted into a disheveled city of boxes and stretching across immense distances. The entry to the city from the new airport can be exceptionally disorienting—it is across seemingly limitless mudflats, alluvial plains, with no clear horizon line, visually bleak and desolate, empty, with distant and disconnected mountains seemingly floating on the mud; there are glimpses of high-rise cities, also disconnected and distanced both from each other and from the traveling observer, presenting as dispersed assemblages of concrete towers. These also arise from a world of mud and motionless water.

Old Seoul is a seemingly disordered city of nondescript boxes; new Seoul presents as a place of regimented, undifferentiated order. It will be argued in what follows that the ambiguity of seemingly opposed urban realms is a consequence of Seoul's cultural history, most notably of the obliterations of the twentieth century—colonialism, war, decolonization, recolonization in the name of liberation, and then ambivalent revolution in the midst of rampant developmentalism. Korea is the paradigm case of both surviving and reconstructed cultural memory intersecting with the imagining—or is it the reality?—of cultural erasure. It is into this ambiguity of perceptions and experiences that there flooded the "economic miracle," a fury of creativity and invention in an age of electronic fadism but distorted memories, the explosion of Korean video art and the phenomenon of "the Korean Wave" in global pop culture. Whereas Benedict Anderson (1991) has argued that print capitalism was an enabling condition for the rise of the classic nation-state, it became necessary to imagine the new, postrevolutionary (post-1987) Korean nation to fill the void of twentieth-century destructions and contested memories in a later age of electronic communication and digital imagery.

The argument to be addressed in this book concerns two sets of dialectical relationships. The first is between destruction and creativity—disruption, even erasure, as a condition of possibility underlying the explosion of creativity and new invention. It is akin to the argument of creative destruction variously linked to the ideas of Nietzsche, Walter Benjamin, and Joseph Schumpeter.[1] It will be suggested that the imagining of a new form of nation to follow the 1910 Japanese annexation of Korea was always already immanent in the culture and was certainly finding expression by the time of the abortive 1919 anti-Japanese uprising and establishment of the Provisional Government of the Republic of Korea in Shanghai.

The second dialectic is that of the local and the "hyperspatial," the stretching of space and time to accommodate the ever-accelerating flows of capital, information, ideas, and desires that characterize the world of "late capitalism."[2] It is the space of undifferentiated jetliners and international airports that are ultimately interchangeable despite all efforts at national or city "identity"; likewise hotel lobbies and shopping malls with their identical sets of franchised outlets marketing identical sets of products—the same logos, imagery, and automobiles, the Cineplex with the same instant-release movies the world over. It is also the space of the mobile phone, the Internet, Facebook, CNN, BBC World, Al Jazeera. Yet the hyperspace also rests on hypertraditionalism—on the exaggeration of the local and its "difference" as each city competes with all others for global tourists, entrepreneurs, and investors. Places frenetically compete for tourist consumption, expertise, and investment by demonstrating their specialness and, they hope, their uniqueness. Local ambience and its alterity constitute the necessary obverse of the hyperspace.

It is not difficult to locate Seoul in this dialectic of the local and the hyperspatial. The global intrusions are here all in place, as in other world cities; additionally, Korean brands are also now global, such as Samsung, LG, and Hyundai. Korea's cultural production has also broken free from the restrictions of nation and language. However, on first glance, there is something missing in Seoul. It seems all too modern; certainly the erased palaces are being rebuilt, the old rituals restaged, and the production of new antiquity proceeds apace, yet the continuities of history seem more elusive than in other great cities. The pervading, beguiling, physical (architectural, landscapal) sense of difference is more difficult to discern here, although to discern it and reflect upon it is the fundamental task of this book. The tourists are far less evident in Seoul than they are in Beijing, Shanghai, or Tokyo, although this may be illusory, as Seoul's tourists are more likely to be from China and increasingly from Japan.[3]

Is it possible, however, that Seoul has leaped ahead of that stage in late capitalism theorized by Fredric Jameson, to a new era of pervading cyberpresence? Has Seoul finally disappeared (self-erased) into a virtual world of an electronic antiquity (the Korea-sourced historical dramas that sweep Asia and beyond, claiming a new form of difference)? Is it now no longer the *postmodern* hyperspace but a condition in which the hyperspace is in some senses *posturban*—transiting to a new understanding of the urban—and, more powerfully, *postnation?*

This book's argument will unfold as a sequence of four interlinked themes. First there is ancient Seoul, a city of symbols, transgressed and distorted in modern colonization and war but whose memory continues to haunt. Second is the reimagining of the nation and the city after modernity's obliterations. This is the Seoul of dictatorship, the rush forward of the tiger economy, the "Miracle on the Han," delayed revolution, and a space of nondescript boxes, advertising boards, and the reimagining of contents. The third theme relates to how history is to be read from a space characterized by such distortions (destruction, erased memories, sense of loss) and in a relative absence of explicit historical referencing—the concern is with obliteration's heritage. How do we "read" the present Seoul? The fourth theme takes this questioning further: how do we explain the rise of the present city of *digital* contents, its cyberpolitics and the global spread of its imagery? We enter the age of Hallyu, the Korean Wave and its increasingly global subversive power. It is also an age and a city in which, it seems, identity and its genealogy are reconstructed in the virtual realm of TV drama and digital imagery. The physical and the virtual cities merge.

Although these four themes must be seen as intersecting and mutually explanatory, they are prized apart here and explored consecutively, in chapters 2, 3, 4, and 5, respectively. These chapters are framed by two others: chapter 1 introduces the vexed issue of contested Korean historiography, ideas such as forgetting and imagining, authenticity and nostalgia, which, it is argued, are inescapable in any attempt to understand the tortured past of Seoul and its present brilliance. Chapter 6, the final chapter, seeks to conclude the narrative, albeit in a sense of some speculation: What might be the conditions that have made such a counterintuitive (post-)urbanism possible, and how are we to understand this new urban condition? Even further, do we foresee, in Korea, some replacement of the hitherto treasured dream of the nation-state, albeit in a context of pride in a reconstituted idea of nation?

The casual reader who simply wants to "read about Seoul" will bypass these framing chapters 1 and 6 and simply go to the story of the city told in the "internal" chapters 2 through 5. Any deeper reading of the city, however, will rest on the somewhat more abstract issues and conceptual frameworks introduced in chapter 1, which weave their way variously through the narrative of the succeeding chapters and then are reflected upon in chapter 6. Stated otherwise, the book, like Seoul itself, can be read at multiple levels.

A note on method: the book's approach is based on an interweaving of themes and ideas—historiography, architecture, urban form, literature, film, religion, television, and popular culture. The purpose is to invoke reflection on challenging juxtapositions in which diverse ideas mutually interact, are thrown into doubt, and deconstruct, thereby forcing the city and society to be seen anew. As if to reinforce the point that a city's story inevitably has overlapping—even fragmentary— themes, there is a partial chronology of Seoul's story as an appendix following the final chapter.

CHAPTER 1

INTRODUCTION

Contested Memory

Memory fastens upon sites, whereas history fastens upon events.
— **Pierre Nora,** *Realms of Memory*

P ierre Nora's aphorism might help to clear the mind, yet it simultaneously obfuscates, for memory will also dwell on events, albeit distorted with time, just as historiography will also write of places. The focus of the chapters that follow is the city of Seoul (sites, therefore memory and its consequence in identity); however, no consideration of the spaces of the city can escape from the messages and meanings that might be conveyed by them to a present observer, or therefore from events and the contestations over how they are to be interpreted.

The immediate purpose of the present chapter is to interrogate what might be meant by "memory" in the context of Seoul's bitter past and the dilemma of its selective memorializing. It will be in four parts: the first will address the issue of Korea's often bitterly contested historiography—how is the past presently to be seen? Second, there is the question of memory in the context of such contested historiography —memory itself becomes a field of contestation, also of manipulation and officially sanctioned distortion, forgetting and imagining. The third part will turn to the city—to Seoul itself—in this context of memory, both lost and reconstructed; the fourth will introduce the place of new media in the distortion of memory and thereby of the city.

First, however, a clarification: this book is not intended to be read as a history. My concern is with memory rather than history, in the sense of Nora's aphorism, and the intrusions here into the contested field of history are in the search for insights into how the spaces of the city are to be read and how we are to make sense of their uses and of the memories seeming to attach to them. Where have these things come from?

Part 1

KOREA AND HISTORIOGRAPHY

At issue is the question of the place of the 1910–1945 Japanese colonization of Korea in any explanation of the emergence of modern (South) Korea and the brilliance of its emblematic capital: Is it continuity? Or is it instead the radical, enabling break? Or is it rather that the Japanese era is to be seen more as one of suppression, even of erasure, yielding something of a tabula rasa on which a new economy and culture might be written? Or are we to see the convergence of different effusions of modernity, variously rivaling, contradictory, clashing, striking sparks off each other, as it were? What are the historical origins of both nation and city? It is the issue of Korean (and Japanese) historiography.

Seoul space seems to speak more of present consumption than of origins or histories or the past. Where the past does manage to emerge, it seems often a Japanese past—colonial-era buildings for colonial institutions, also a very few precolonial buildings, albeit designed by Japanese architects in the period of precolonial Japanese infiltration. Certainly there are the old palaces—Changgyeonggung, Changdeokgung, Deoksugung—but the grandest and most prominently displayed, Gyeongbokgung Palace, is a reconstruction from the 2000s of the vast complex obliterated in the Japanese era.[1] There are other modern evocations of the past: on the ceremonial axis to approach the reimagined palace there is a monumental statue in honor of Admiral Yi Sun-sin and his confrontation with an earlier Japanese invasion, and another honoring King Sejong the Great as representative of the achievements of a long-distant past.[2] King Sejong sits in majesty in front of the US Embassy, to many a neocolonial emblem, his gaze disdainfully averted from it.

While the statue of Admiral Yi might be seen as invoked memory, its provision likely evokes a wished-for forgetting: it was erected by the dictator Park Chung-hee. Incompatible historiographies intersect. The long military dictatorship will commonly be recollected as an era of oppression, violence, and national shame, too recent to be forgotten, yet it was also the era of the tiger economy, the "Miracle on the Han," and the reimagining of the nation.

Colonial historiography

In their introduction to *Colonial Modernity in Korea,* Shin Gi-Wook and Michael Robinson observe that, at the time of Japan's insertion into Korea, contradictory historical narratives were being conjured up in support of rival nationalist agendas.[3]

> Concurrently, Korean nationalist historians constructed a nation from the repository of traditional historical narratives and cultural memories in order to have the Korean people think their way toward a new collective identity. After 1910, Japanese colonialist historians countered with elaborate justifications for seeing Korea as a part of Japan in order to legitimate Japanese political, economic, and cultural domination. Both the Korean and the Japanese narratives produced a prodigious amount of information and presented Korea, in effect, to the gaze of the global community. In their fidelity to dominating causal theories, however, they also began an equally powerful process of obfuscation. (Shin Gi-Wook and Robinson 1999, 3)

The reductionism of such narratives was characterized by a variety of binaries: failed tradition versus the advances of modernity, national pride erased by alien domination, backwardness overcome by progress, rapacious collaborationists against the impoverished masses, colonial repression and exploitation versus Korean resistance, Korean squalor against Japanese advancements in health and education.[4]

In 1925 the Japanese Government-General established the Joseonsa Pyeonsuhoe, or Korean History Compilation Committee, charged with the collection of Korean historical materials and the compilation of Korean history. The massive output from this exercise was a historiography from a Japanese colonialist perspective. Henry H. Em (2013, 12–13) has observed that, among Korean historians trained at Japanese universities, many adopted the framework of colonialist historiography, specifically *mansenshi,* a Manchurian-Korean spatial conception negating Korea's historical sovereignty, as well as the idea of *toyoshi* (Oriental history) whereby Japan is seen as uniquely capable, in contrast with moribund societies such as China and Korea. *Toyoshi* could legitimize Japan's imperial expansion. Against these schools of historiographic thought, Em sets colonial-era historian Paek Nam-un, who saw Korean society and economy developing in accordance with universal stages of development and as a result of socioeconomic forces internal to the society—that Koreans are sovereign subjects of their own history and thus there is a historiography "that does not know despair."[5]

Post-1945 Korean historiography then bifurcates: North and South present opposed accounts of both antiquity and the more recent colonial past to justify rival claims to legitimacy as the "true" Korea. Both claims are nationalist and both states resort to force to suppress rival or dissident narratives. Shin Gi-Wook and Robinson (1999, 4) suggest a third master narrative in that post-1945 era, engineered by the United States, that would place Korean history in the context of America's own Cold War struggle. While this further problematizes the disconnection between North and South accounts, it too is to be seen as politicized, nationalist myth obfuscating history.

Nowhere is historiographic conflict more confronting than over the tragedy of the "comfort women." Korean accounts of the 1937–1945 war period share a close to universal fixation on women coerced into prostitution to service the Japanese military; Japanese history writing and teaching is for the most part silent on the subject, although it will occasionally revert to revisionist denial.[6] The division is bitter and continuing, as will be recounted in chapter 2. Challenging irreconcilable histories there is now C. Sarah Soh's *The Comfort Women* (2008), forcing open the sociocultural context within which such a tragedy could occur. It provides an anthropological interpretation of both Japanese and Korean patriarchy as the context of the tragedy: "gendered structural violence" prevailed in both cultures. There is also Yoshimi Yoshiaki's *Comfort Women* (2002). Where Soh exposed unreflective, centuries-old patriarchy as a structural condition, Yoshiaki exposed the agency of the Japanese government in the atrocity, effectively redirecting the current Japanese focus on public memory and arguments about the writing and teaching of history. Both reveal the fragility of historiography.[7]

George Akita and Brandon Palmer, in their *The Japanese Colonial Legacy in Korea, 1910–1945* (2015), comment on the polarity of present reductionist arguments: historical remembrance in South Korea unabashedly portrays the colonial era negatively. The Japanese colonial regime is presented as a fascist, authoritarian regime that exploited the innocent Korean people. In some cases, academic circles in Asia and America have taken up positions that mirror this extreme Korean stand. However, Akita and Palmer's account challenges the pro-Korean nationalist narrative, declaring that a different view emerges when colonialism is considered in the light of Japan's strong legalist tradition, even more so when the Japanese colonial record is compared with that of European colonizing powers in that era.

Colonialism and modernization

Present debates range around the relationships between colonialism and modernization in particular. Brandon Palmer has argued that, since the 1970s, South Korea's "collective national memory" has been dominated by a nationalist paradigm, also called "internal development theory," portraying the colonial regime as "a totalitarian and fascist political machine that wrung out the lifeblood and economic vitality of the Korean people, who were powerless victims" (Palmer 2013, 7–8).[8]

There have been variants on this argument. At something of an extreme is the "ethnocidal" argument, well articulated by Kim Kyu Hyun (2005, 103–104): Japanese colonizers sought to eradicate Korean identity altogether, absorbing it into the ontological category of the Japanese imperial subject. K. Itoi (2005) goes even further, asserting that in the eradication of Korean identity some 80 percent of the historic shrines, palaces, and historic monuments of Korea were destroyed—indeed an erasure; however, no sources are offered for this claim. A more moderate claim of destruction, though from the same historiographical perspective, is Lee Man-hoon (1995). As Peter Duus (2003, 128) has observed, until recently most English-language histories of Korea have seen Japanese colonial rule as a rupture or erasure of the "natural" trajectory of the Korean nation—an erasure creating a blank space in the national narrative whereby Korea's history was no longer the possession of Koreans. There is also an economic variant of the argument: that capitalism in Korea predates Japanese colonization and is discernible in "sprouts" burgeoning during the Chosun dynasty that would have flowered even without forced colonial modernization.

In *Offspring of Empire*, Carter Eckert acknowledges that some manufacturing and a market economy were certainly emerging in pre-colonial Korea; however, he rejects the nationalist argument that these sprouts were nipped by colonial exploitation (Eckert 2014). Cha Myung Soo (2010) argues in a similar vein. Eckert's work, when first published in 1991, led to criticism from Korean scholars for its questioning of the then-dominant nationalist paradigm and of its attendant "sprouts theory." That paradigm still thrives, moreover:

> The South Korean government provides financial support to museums, public monuments, and research centres, such as the Truth Commission on Forced Mobilization under Japanese Imperialism . . . and Independence Hall of Korea . . . , to propagate this paradigm [highlighting compulsory labour, the comfort women, and other issues related to the exploitation of Koreans] to the Korean public.

> The perception created by forced mobilization studies is that all Korean men, women, and children, with the exception of a handful of collaborators, suffered during the war. (Palmer 2013, 8)

In his brief review of Korean historiography, Brandon Palmer sees the nationalist paradigm fracturing: whereas "old" history has stressed successive dynasties, great kings, military adventures, and similar events, the nationalist view has more recently drawn on a revisionist history from the perspective of the common people (*minjung*) that highlights the exploitation of the common people.

Colonial modernity, precolonial modernity

The nationalist paradigm has been challenged in recent decades by Korean and Western scholars who advocate a *colonial modernity* theory. This would see Japan's colonization of Korea, including its draconian wartime mobilization, as crucial to the modernization of the peninsula. The task for scholarly endeavor is to explore the ways that Koreans encountered modernity within Japanese colonialism. Among scholars of "colonial modernism," Palmer (2013, 10) cites Yun Haedong in particular as "one of the best scholars in this field," especially in his *Another Reckoning of Modern Times* (2006, in Korean) and *A Rediscovery of History before and since Liberation* (2006, in Korean).[9] Issues of colonial modernity are also dealt with in particular by a number of authors in Shin Gi-Wook and Robinson (2001): it is broadly argued that the proper topic for scholarly debate is the *complexity* of relations among colonialism, modernity, and nationalism. It is through such a framework that Chung Chonghwa (2012) views a vibrant colonial-era cinema in Korea from 1923 to the early 1930s, focusing on the cooperation or collaboration between Japanese and Korean filmmakers. Korean and Japanese filmmakers are seen to have been in competition and negotiation with each other within a complex film sphere launched with Japanese capital and technology.

The colonial modernity theory is itself challenged, however. Colonial modernity would posit that Japanese colonialism was decisive in shaping the modern notion of Korean nationalism, whereby the introduction of a national system of schooling, transportation, and communication, variously mediated through print capitalism, enabled Koreans to imagine themselves as members of a Korean nation, albeit against the colonial intent of their becoming loyal imperial subjects (Lee Hong Yung 2013, 6). The contrary view, which might be seen as a theory of precolonial modernity—perhaps Korean modernity—would assert that Koreans had already developed a sense of national identity by the time of the Japanese intrusion, albeit not yet equivalent with modern ideas of nationalism. Lee cites John B. Duncan to the effect that the Korean Peninsula had "an extraordinarily long experience of unified political rule," from the seventh to the twentieth century. Duncan insists that "not only the traditional elites, but the nonelite social strata had developed a national identity despite their wholehearted subscription to 'cardinal Confucian social values in the second half of the dynasty'" (Duncan, n.d., in Lee Hong Yung 2013, 7). Andre Schmid concurs with the Duncan argument, rejecting the colonial modernity notion. While not denying the modern element of Korean nationalism, he also stresses the sense of *pre*modern nationalism in Korean history.[10] A "subjective awareness" of "a sense of space that transcended any single dynasty," from at least the seventh century, meant that early nationalist writers did not need to imagine from scratch the nation as a spatial entity (Schmid 2002, 18–19).

Lee Ki-baik's magisterial history was first published in 1961, in the era of democratic hope sandwiched between dictatorships; this, too, was mostly within a nationalist framework, albeit modified in later editions and also in Eckert et al. (1990), which built on Lee's work and which listed him as a coauthor.[11] Lee Ki-baik's monumental work raises the difficult issue of "voice"—the sound or tone of the writing.[12] Lee (1924–2004) had as his academic advisor Yi Byeongdo (1896–1989), who had been a member of the Japanese-era Korean History Compilation Committee and is associated with the Japanese colonial view of history. Correspondingly, Lee's work is also often criticized as an extension of Japanese colonial policy. Yet, in contrast with its genealogy, its voice is unrelentingly anti-Japanese, and its final chapters are preoccupied with the evils of Japanese annexation and exploitation, leaving the reader to wonder about the bias of its narrative.[13]

Carter Eckert et al. in large measure base their *Korea Old and New: A History* (1990) on Lee Ki-baik (1984). Reflecting their source, the account of precolonial Korea again echoes Korean History Compilation Committee perspectives, while the anti-Japanese voice dominates the account of the colonial era. Yet, seemingly contradictorily, Eckert's *Offspring of Empire* ([1991] 2014) reads as a far more nuanced analysis of the Japanese era, approaching a colonial modernity perspective. Yet here too Eckert's questioning of "sprouts theory" has led to criticism of his work as continuing the historiography of the colonialist Korean history committee.

Alternative in both perspective and voice is Hwang Kyung Moon's *A History of Korea* (2010), as well as Bruce Cumings' *Korea's Place in the Sun: A Modern History* ([1997] 2005). Cumings' work, like Lee Ki-baik's, is monumental in scale and impressive in its scholarship;

however, it also presents problems. Its voice might be judged to be more evenhanded and its writing more engaging, at times journalistic; however, its interpretation is also revisionist and politically charged—it is not Japan that is to be reproached but America. In his two-volume *The Origins of the Korean War* (1981 and 1990), Cumings describes that event as a civil war and US policy for post-1945 Korea as the progenitor;[14] in *North Korea: Another Country* (2004), that state's belligerence and unpredictability are sheeted home to America's unrelenting destruction of Korea in the Korean War. Both the voice and content of Cumings' works reflect his political commitment.

Especially influential in the critique of the nationalist historiography have been studies laying bare the collaborationist role of the Korean colonial elite. The impact of such studies has been in two, often opposing, directions. First, in making clear that Koreans were complicit in colonial-era suppression and exploitation, they have both redirected and reinforced the nationalist paradigm, albeit in condemnation of the collaborators. Second, and later, hitherto-forbidden Marxist and radical-populist perspectives called into question the structural conditions in which collaboration had emerged, effectively undermining shrill and self-righteous pronouncements-from-afar of both collaborators and outraged nationalists.[15] Especially interesting in this unmasking has been Moon Yumi's *Populist Collaborators* (2013), on the 1904–1910 Ilchinhoe (Advance in Unity Society).

Modernity

Modernization describes a process; modernity describes a condition. While the idea of colonial modernity has achieved some recent salience in the debates, it is not unproblematic, as the discussion of Lee Hong Yung, Duncan, and Schmid has made clear. So, what do we mean by "modernity"? The idea of modernity first surfaced in eighteenth-century Western Europe, and was associated with the industrial revolution in England, the social revolution in France, and rationalist Enlightenment thought. Though originating in the West, with its spread to other regions it has assumed different forms, also revealing that there are different paths to modernity, Soviet/Chinese Communist and German/Japanese fascist modernities clearly being among them (Moore 1993).[16] Likewise, East Asian scholars have posited an "East Asian modernism" distinct from other manifestations. These "alternative" paths, however, can scarcely be understood outside the context of the trajectory of Western modernity. The East Asian manifestation, as Tu Weiming (1994) has observed, has similarly been largely a response to the challenge of the modern West.

Korean thought and life in the early colonial period would therefore seem to have been moving in the interstices of three rival ideas of modernity. First, the images and practices of Western modernity would be present as background, as it were, though it came aggressively to the fore with American and European support for the Japanese colonial enterprise. Second, Japan's modernity—always in some reaction to the West—came with the colonization and modernization of its perceived geopolitical sphere as its legitimating agenda. Then, third, there were both the memory and the reality of an emerging, precolonial Korean modernity—perhaps a protomodernity, though this too is contested in both colonial and modern historiography.

An especially challenging thought is presented by Everett Taylor Atkins (2010). Here the focus is not on the Koreans but the Japanese and the phenomenon of their fascination with Koreana—Korean architecture, folk theater and songs, dance, shamanism, communal values, and the wider culture. Koreana, Atkins argues, provided the Japanese with a poignant vision of their own migration paths through the peninsula and thereby of their "primitive selves"—indeed, it yielded an uncertainty regarding their own, Japanese modernity. The reader is reminded that the act of gazing and being gazed at fundamentally transforms both the observed and the observer. Both Japan and Korea and their respective cultures were transformed, even enriched—albeit traumatically—by their mutual encounters.[17]

It is interesting to see Atkins' work alongside that of Jun Uchida. In *Brokers of Empire: Japanese Settler Colonialism in Korea, 1876–1945,* Uchida (2011a) upends the conventional focus on the relationship and tension between the colonial state and Korean society by adding the obscured history of the Japanese settler community and not taking for granted its subservience to the Government-General. Elsewhere, Uchida (2011b) explores the role of affect and sentiment in shaping cross-cultural encounters in late colonial Korea as seen through the eyes of Japanese men and women who grew up in Seoul. A level of complexity is added that is elsewhere mostly ignored—simplistically stated, the underlying tension was not two-way but three-way.[18]

The Atkins and Uchida arguments offer a perspective from which to view Seoul as a space of mutual engagement with the clashes of modernity. As both Koreans and Japanese negotiated their way through these interstices between incompatible modernities in their everyday colonial lives as well as in scholarly thought, we might identify these constantly evolving negotiations as the reality of colonial modernity and the proper subject of present investigation—in the present book through contemplating the spaces of the present city.[19]

The dictatorship and historiography

Memory, asserted Maurice Halbwachs (1992), is socially produced. Rarely has it been more strenuously yet restrictively produced than in Korea's long era of dictatorship. However, ideas of history were far from constant and unchanging in the colonial period, and so too were they in the postcolonial era of renewed repression and resistance. The strident nationalism of the era, in which Japan was demonized and the "true" Korea legitimized against the counterclaim of the North, albeit crosscut by a further, American counternarrative. Korea's dilemma was in its dependence on an increasingly railed-against United States and its simultaneous emulation of the Japanese post-1945 development model. Any balanced history writing was close to impossible.[20]

The nationalist historiography of the dictatorship era tended especially to focus on the origins of the Korean resurgence—the "Miracle on the Han." The miracle would be traced mostly to Korean entrepreneurial genius and to enlightened state guidance, yet here again the story is contested: as Kim Hyung-A (2004) observes, development studies since the late 1970s have tended to interpret the economics of the Korean case in terms of either a market-oriented neoliberal approach or, alternatively, a statist approach in which the state's role was the key to the politics behind the "economic miracle." The dictatorship collapsed in 1987 and finally ended in 1992 with the departure of the last military president. There is thus some significance in the 1991 publication date of Carter Eckert's *Offspring of Empire*. Eckert's work effectively undermined the simplistically nationalist position that colonialism had interrupted the evolution of Korean development, at worst erasing an emerging economy. Eckert argues that a balanced view of the colonial period must take into consideration the Japanese contributions to the construction of infrastructure upon which the postcolonial Korean economic expansion could ride, with investments in schools, public health systems, railways, and hydroelectric projects.

Moreover, *Offspring of Empire* has been seen as highlighting the unquestioned assumption underlying both the colonial project and the postcolonial "Miracle on the Han," namely the goodness of growth and of the modernizing project itself (Kim Hyung-A and Sorenson 2011, 4).[21] This questioning of history's implicit extolling of growth had been common in the West in the 1960s, in both popular culture and scholarly discourse; we can note Barrington Moore's warning, from 1966, against the imagined goodness of modernizing progress: "It is well to recollect that there is no evidence that the mass of the population anywhere has wanted an industrial society, and plenty of evidence that they did not. At bottom all forms of industrialization so far have been revolutions from above, the work of a ruthless minority" (Moore 1993, 506).

The task set for Lee Jin-kyung's *Service Economies* is to demystify the "Miracle on the Han"—in her analysis it is no miracle at all but a logical outcome of war and market being intrinsic extensions of each other in US global expansionism, all riding on "the proletarianization of sexuality and race" (Lee Jin-kyung 2010, 1–3). She specifically invokes Paul Virilio's notions of "dromology" (mobilization; the movement of laboring bodies as resources) and continuity between the "production of destruction" and the production of wealth to account for the trajectory onto which postcolonial Seoul was launched (Virilio 1986). The convergence of these forms is seen to underlie the Park Chung-hee fervor for developmentalism (Lee Jin-kyung 2010, 24).

Although the nationalist paradigm has continued to receive official support from successive Korean governments—there is still the overriding agenda of national legitimation vis-à-vis the counterclaims of the North—nevertheless, other narratives emerge. Questioning industrialization and the social and cultural price that Koreans have paid for it, the moral basis of the "miracle" comes into question as well. As observed by diverse authors in *South Korean Social Movements*, edited by Shin Gi-Wook and Paul Chang (2011), issues of civil society become salient, as do questions of the form and nature of society itself.

Part 2

SITES, MEMORY, IDENTITY

From these considerations of the uncertainties of history, we return to Nora's distinction between history and memory, now to focus on the latter. Pierre Nora's magisterial seven-volume collaborative project, *Les lieux de mémoire* (Realms of Memory), endeavored to define, variously, the French Republic, the French nation, and, finally, France as an idea. Significantly, the third part (comprising volumes 5 through 7) was titled *Les France*—plural, not singular. The project assembled 132 articles to explore the construction of the French past. The concern was to conceptualize the relationship between history and memory.

Realms of memory

Lieux de mémoire—"realms of memory," although *lieux* may also be translated as "sites"—will cover the range of places, both physical and intellectual, wherein the memories of "a nation" might be constructed, contained, and contested. They are not necessarily "sites" in the geographical sense, as they can also include the flag, anthems, celebrations and festivals, a name, an event, and literary monuments. Nora attempts a definition: "[A] lieu de mémoire is any significant entity, whether material or non-material in nature, which by dint of human will or the work of time has become a symbolic element of the memorial heritage of any community" (Nora 1996, xvii). Nora's project built on the work of Halbwachs (1992) on the social framing of memory; Nora looked at "how social institutions and contexts made possible certain memories, encouraging certain recollections while discouraging others" (Legg 2005, 481–482). Central to Nora's argument is the idea of sites of memory (heritage?) as compensation for a profound loss. In the modern age most people no longer live in *milieux de mémoire,* environments of memory, so, Nora argues, "*Lieux de memoire* exist because there are no longer any *milieux de memoire,* settings in which memory is a real part of everyday experience" (Nora 1996, 1).

Nora defines the project as

> a history in multiple voices . . . less interested in causes than in effects; less interested in actions remembered or even commemorated than in the traces left by those actions and in the interaction of those commemorations; less interested in events themselves than in the construction of events over time, in the disappearance and reemergence of their significations; less interested in "what actually happened" than in its perpetual re-use and misuse, its influence on successive presents; less interested in traditions than in the way in which traditions are constituted and passed on. (Nora 1996 1:xxiv; also in Hue-Tam Ho Tai 2001)

Maurice Halbwachs (1992) has argued that memory is socially produced: social institutions and contexts make possible certain memories, encouraging certain recollections while discouraging others. There is Ernest Renan's aphoristic observation on compelled forgetting in the "necessary" construction of "the Nation":[22] "[T]he essence of a nation is that all the individuals have many things in common and also that all [must already] have forgotten a great many things. All French citizens are obliged to have forgotten the Saint Bartholomew [massacre], the massacres of the Midi of the thirteenth century" (Renan 1947–1961, 892). In the case of Korea there have been multiple obligated forgettings as selectively presented historiographies have prevailed.

Environments of memory

Lieux de mémoire exist as compensation for a profound loss. As Stephen Legg summarizes, "[T]hese sites are now necessary because most people no longer live in milieux de mémoire [environments of memory]. Nora claimed that, with the rise of modernism and its attendant traits of globalisation, mediatisation, democratisation, and massification, modern media is substituted for collective memory. What we have now is not lived memory, but reconstructed history. To compensate for this lack, sites of memory have arisen" (Legg 2005, 483–484).

It is this distinction between *lieux de mémoire* and *milieux de mémoire* that is most interesting to the present argument. The distinction can be relaxed somewhat from what seems to have been Nora's intention. There are locales where some continuity with the past is assured even though modern media and technologies intrude and new urban development has transformed the environment that people can vaguely remember from the past, whether their own past or that of others. Typically there will be sites and artifacts (*lieux de mémoire*) from a diversity of pasts that can indicate the continuum of history. In contrast, there are locales without this suggestion of continuity—new housing estates, for example, where the antiquity of the culture rests indeed on the display of the flag, a memorial, replicas of heritage streetlamps, and such. Seoul mostly tends to fall into this second category. The destructions of the twentieth century were so intense that there are now only isolated relics and museum pieces from a Korean antiquity with very little to indicate evolution from then to now.[23]

That said, Seoul presents two prevailing space morphologies that could well define the megacity (figure 1.1). The first is the ordered world of the housing estates—vast realms of identical high-rise housing blocks of the modern, tiger economy. The second is the disordered, typically labyrinthine expanse of poorly constructed two- and three-story, small-scale, multiple-use blocks from the decades of struggle that followed the 1953 stalling of the Korean War but which, nevertheless, suggested some link to an older, disordered world and its history. Both are to be categorized as boxlands, one of order and relative affluence (albeit too often merely pretended, a theme for chapter 5), the other of disorder, small scale, frequently dilapidation and remnants of an earlier age of struggle and poverty and, arguably, environments where memories can still survive, albeit from little more than a generation or so. In the context of the city's transformations, it will be suggested that this latter, labyrinthine world of alleys, boxes, and small-scale enterprise might present as *milieux de mémoire*.

FIGURE 1.1 Two morphologies, 2012: the eight-lane road is Highway 1; *left,* a Chamwon-dong (Gangnam) housing estate, one of many; *right,* an older Seoul, a land of little boxes on which the housing estates depend for their services, markets, and entertainment. Note the bucolic woodland trail between high-rises and highway. Source: Google maps, modified by the author.

Against the regimented towers and the smaller-scale boxlands, it is palaces and the names of ancient dynasties that will be used to conjure up the nation's antiquity and to construct a national memory—as well as, it must be added, modern media and popular culture, the theme of chapter 5.

Part 3

SEOUL

The task of following chapters is to "make sense" of the sites and spaces of Seoul—to understand, interpret, read the city. The Nora distinction between *lieux de mémoire* and *milieux de mémoire* is salient here. Consideration of the former will draw attention to the monuments—to Admiral Yi, King Sejong, the palaces (including the reconstructions in both physical- and cyberspace), and the surviving shrines and relics, but also to the emblematic, contradiction-ridden survivals from the Japanese construction of the city. The reading will involve diverse languages—Korean and Japanese, but also body language (what a statue's pose might convey) and, especially, architectural language.[24] Official architecture, as well as that of corporations and institutions, always carries messages, variously explicit and subliminal, sometimes intended and sometimes unintended. A first question must therefore relate to the trajectory of Korean architecture.

Lieux de mémoire and architecture

An excellent general survey of Seoul architecture is *Seoul Architecture and Urbanism* (Korean Institute of Architects 2000), by some thirteen academic authors and published by the Seoul Metropolitan Government. There are also various books illustrating Chosun-era palaces, fortifications, shrines, and other survivals under the rubric *World Heritage in Korea,* and published by the Samsung Foundation of Culture and UNESCO. Other sources on the Chosun monuments include Choi Jong-deok (2006) on Changdeokgung Palace and Hoon Shin Young (2008) on the dynasty's palaces generally. On the architecture of more recent decades, the most useful sources are the architectural journals. None of these sources, however, provides a consistent, theoretically coherent interpretation of the architecture of Seoul and of Korea more broadly, in the sense of interpretation or reading: To what events does the architecture attach? What are the contested histories that might rage around it? What memories might it trigger?

In following chapters, the architecture and spaces of the city will be interrogated in the context of the historiographical debates of the present age—the nationalism paradigm (indeed, rival nationalisms), the precolonial modernism theory, colonial modernism, and their variants. Kal Hong's *Aesthetic Constructions of Korean Nationalism* (2011), as its title signals, looks at a diversity of Seoul sites and monuments and how they have been used by various regimes—colonial, dictatorial, and democratic—to support the construction of the idea of nation appropriate to the intention of that regime at that time. It is a transference of classical history—great dynasties, great leaders, great events—to the reading of the present city. The spaces of everyday life are not addressed.

Quite different is Todd Henry's *Assimilating Seoul* (2014). Its focus is on the city's public spaces in the colonial period as "contact zones," showing how ordinary residents negotiated pressures to become loyal, industrious, and hygienic imperial subjects. In revealing the intersections of Korean and Japanese histories in the spaces and architectural expressions of the city, Henry challenges both Korean and Japanese-colonial nationalisms, thereby providing a frame through which to observe the Namsan Shinto Shrine and the two colonial expositions on the cleared grounds of Gyeongbokgung Palace, as well as neighborhood-scale programs for better hygiene.

There is another architecture, however, that would draw attention to a colonial modernity view of history. Modern architecture came to precolonial Chosun in part through missionaries and their church and institution building, and, more interestingly, through a few modern buildings designed by Japanese architects in a Japanese hybrid styling.[25] This styling reached something of a Korean flowering in the first decades of the colonial era—the architectural referencing was all Japanese, with effectively no allusions to Korean themes. Seoul would be signaled as a city of the empire and its architecture would need to be read through a colonial-modernity lens.

It will be argued in chapter 3 that the key figure in the officially sanctioned, emblematic architecture of the dictatorship era was architect Kim Swoo Geun, effectively the state architect at that time and charged with setting the characteristics of a new, modern, Korean architecture. Kim, however, had received his architectural education and early experience in Japan, and early buildings for the Park Chung-hee regime carried obvious references to the prevailing concrete monumentalism of Japan's more celebrated architects. As late as 1999, when the emblematic Jongno (Samsung) Tower was completed, though designed by a Uruguayan-US architect, the complaints from Korean architects were to the effect that "it is just another Japanese building."[26] One could argue that colonial modernity persists, at least in the signification of the city, even to the beginning of the twenty-first century.

Standing most dramatically against the shadow of colonial modernity is nationalist modernity's most dramatic intervention into modern

Seoul. On 15 August 1995, the fiftieth anniversary of the end of World War II and thereby of the Japanese colonial era, a grand ceremony was held to commence the destruction of the Japanese Government-General Building. Then in the 2000s Gyeongbokgung Palace, that greatest monument of Chosun Korea, was rebuilt—more correctly, a vast modern building complex was constructed as a replica of the ancient palace.

Authenticity and nostalgia

The simulacrum of the new-ancient Gyeongbokgung raises issues of authenticity and nostalgia. Are we witnessing, in the present, some nostalgia for an imagined, precolonial past and the abandonment of ideas of authenticity? It is a question that will run through the chapters that follow, particularly chapter 5, where dreamed pasts permeate modern Korean media. One is left to speculate if identity is being sought not in a remembered past but in a dreamed one, founded on a sense of loss and nostalgia. Legg (2005) quotes Susan Steward (1984, 23) on the nature of the nostalgic: "The nostalgic dreams of a moment before knowledge and self-consciousness that itself lives only in the self-consciousness of the nostalgic narrative. Nostalgia is the repetition that mourns the inauthenticity of all repetition and denies repetition's capacity to form identity."

Nostalgia is almost the dialectic opposite of authenticity. It signals a temporal distancing or disconnection and can be seen as a surface over the loss of older understandings (authenticity) and of memory. One can usefully note Lionel Trilling's advice that "authenticity," a term central to the deliberations of the existentialist philosophers, is best not totally defined; however, Trilling does use such a simple understanding as "to stay true to oneself" (Trilling 1972; also Taylor 1991). A broader understanding of authenticity would refer to the attempt to live one's life according to the needs of one's inner being, rather than the demands of society or one's early conditioning. The conscious self is seen as coming to terms with being in a material world and with encountering external forces and influences that are very different from itself; authenticity is one way in which the self acts and changes in response to these pressures (Kaufmann 1975). Nostalgia, however, is an escape from this demand.

One element of the Korean Wave, that modern explosion of a new Korean culture, has been an abandonment of oneself to imagined pasts and imagined ideas of "family" and "family values." This is scarcely nostalgic; it is simply entertainment. Or is there far more to it than that? A subject for chapter 5.

Milieux de mémoire and a Seoul vernacular

There is a still celebrated vernacular architecture and urbanism of the past in the *hanok* or traditional houses of Korea—sited for climate, using natural materials, with thatch or tile roofs, and the heated *ondol* floor system—and, in urban areas, the narrow and labyrinthine alleyways in which the houses would be found.[27] In a fine review of the "urban" *hanok*—where the emphasis is plainly on "urban"—Jung Inha (2013, 29–35) sees this as a form of housing that first appeared in the 1920s as the primary type of urban housing in Korea, especially in large cities. The urban *hanok* were a translation of older housing forms by new housing companies based on small artisan groups adapting to the new conditions of rapid urbanization, housing shortage, and increasing density.[28] Smaller allotments and the commercial pressures to make a profit led these new companies to develop a dwelling form in which the previously multiple courtyards would be aggregated into a single, internal courtyard. While Japanese settler housing mostly followed Japanese models, the urban *hanok* predominated in Korean areas, continuing as the model for the Seoul housing companies into the 1960s.

The *hanok* have mostly gone, a legacy of war, however, the "empty space" of the courtyard will be a recurring theme in later architecture, and the unplanned alleys persist—the right-side boxland morphology of figure 1.1 being a case in point. The boxlands of the post-1953 struggle and the unmanaged boom that followed are to be seen as a new but mostly unstudied vernacular, uncontrolled, operating in an unregulated, informal economy, presumably the product of house-building companies that were descendants of those of the earlier decades. Valérie Gelézeau (1997) has written briefly on life in these neighborhoods, although it is represented in an architecture that, unlike the urban *hanok,* remains mostly untheorized but is clearly to be seen as another, later vernacular.

Jordan Sand (2013) has looked at similar vernaculars in Tokyo, Seoul's unacknowledged (denied?) alter ego—Tokyo was obliterated through US firebombing in 1945, Seoul in 1951–1953; both were rebuilt, mostly badly and chaotically, in the few years thereafter. Yet in both cases that rebuilding was according to old practices and old conceptions of neighborhood space, as well as to each city's cultural and political traits. Sand describes the outcome: "Every city has its own vernacular: a language of form, space, and sensation shaped by the local history of habitation. Newcomers encounter a city's vernacular in a torrent of signals demanding interpretation. Occupants, by contrast, apprehend the city's vernacular intuitively, navigating it without needing to bring it to consciousness. The landscape of the vernacular city is a fabric continually being woven" (Sand 2013, 2–3). Sand describes lands of small lots, local street grids but no uniform overall street plan, construction in wood (more brick and concrete in Seoul), low-rise buildings, dense shopkeeping, and petty manufacturing neighborhoods. All this is also to be found in Seoul—witness the right side of figure 1.1. There is constant change in these areas, as small buildings are modified, added to, demolished, replaced, and adapted to new uses; typically, a building will acquire a small prayer room, be designated a church (while retaining its previous uses), and thereby acquire a conical spire topped by a red, illuminated cross.

A task for chapter 4 is to seek some understanding of the production and present lives of these areas—how they fit in to a culture in which the regimented towers also find a place.

Part 4

SEOUL AND NEW MEDIA

In the seminal *Imagined Communities,* Benedict Anderson grappled with the question of how, in modern times, polities variously centered around dynasts of varying (and typically shifting) degrees of power and prestige metamorphosed into "nations." The nation, for Anderson, is essentially abstract and socially constructed—it is "imagined." As he defines it, "[I]t is an imagined political community—and imagined as both internally limited and sovereign" (Anderson 1991, 6). It is internally limited in that it is to be defined by boundaries, in contrast with ancient definitions in terms of centers of power where "borders were porous and indistinct, and sovereignties faded imperceptibly into one another" (19); it is sovereign in itself, in contrast to previous notions of the personal sovereignty of some dynast at the center of power. So, how has this metamorphosis occurred? How has this imagining come about?

The applicability of Anderson's ideas to Korea would be questionable—as noted above, a Korean nationalist historiography would insist that an understanding of a Korean nation had spanned a millennium and more, preceding any of the "nations" on which Anderson's work rests (Duncan, n.d., in Lee Hong Yung 2013, 6; Schmid 2002).[29] Yet Anderson's key argument is persuasive, that people can work and struggle for a particular form of nation only if that form can first be imagined: "What, in a positive sense, made the new communities imaginable was a half-fortuitous, but explosive, interaction between a system of production and productive relations (capitalism), a technology of communications (print), and the fatality of human linguistic diversity" (Anderson 1991, 42–43).[30] These conditions might have been met for the emergence of Japan as a modern nation, and they would presumably have needed to be counteracted (by Japan) if Korea was not to become such a nation—a question for the historiography debates and for chapter 2. What is especially interesting is the applicability of these ideas to the continually emerging and reforming Korean nation (nation, not the Republic) of the present. While the economic miracle of the 1960s and 1970s made Korea "great" and met the requirements of Anderson's first condition, the irony was that it was based on a Japanese model and dependent on favored access to the US market—that is, it rested on economic neocolonialism. Yet, for all that, the Anderson condition was fulfilled, albeit somewhat bitterly and in need of further "imagining away."

It is the second condition, media of communication, that presents the real difference in the Korean case. Not only did the post-1953 (post–Korean War) reimagining of Korea occur in the new age of constantly evolving and transforming electronic modes of communication (television, computers, the Internet, the mobile phone, the blog, and social networking); it also arose in a society that seized the vanguard role in the development of such technologies and their potential for use.

The media and their attendant smothering, saturating advertising transform both public and private realms. "[A]dvertising in its new dimension invades everything, as public space (the street, monument, market, scene) disappears. . . . It is the same for private space. In a subtle way, this loss of public space occurs simultaneously with the loss of private space. The one is no longer a spectacle, the other no longer a secret" (Baudrillard 1985, 129–130). Perhaps the ultimate expression of retreat from the exposure of both public and private space is the Korean *bang* (literally "room," "song box"), the enclosing cubicle to which the assailed individual can retreat for electronic games, karaoke, the Internet, video—the offerings proliferate with the genius of human invention and entrepreneurial wizardry. It is a theme for chapter 4.

Private space is transformed by television—the endless soapies that mimic domestic life, to be mimicked in turn by everyday life (the global reach and transforming effect of the Korean Wave and the generation of a new historiography to see Korea as countercolonizer, as it will be argued following). Population simulates the media, which, in turn, hypersimulate the population until there is no original but only a world of simulacra—everything a copy. So everyday life implodes into the hyperreality of the spectacle, a world without depth or meaning.

New media and the city

Jean Baudrillard's has been a notable voice in speculating on these issues of the media revolution and its transformation of urban space. While many would dismiss his pronouncements as hyperbole, they have value in focusing the mind on where urban space might be heading in a new media age. In the 1970s Baudrillard argued that, in the age of "consumer capitalism," domination is no longer effected through capital (as means of production and as commodities produced) but increasingly through appearances and images. We no longer consume products but signs—of television, of advertising. The material objects of consumption have value for us precisely as signs—of identity, of status, of culture, of achievement and so on (Baudrillard 1972). In Korea in the present, some four decades later, it is a world that is called into question in the parodied "Gangnam Style," an issue for chapter 5.

Baudrillard's later writings emphasized consumption in terms of signs. In the discourse of consumption, Baudrillard asserts, "there is an anti-discourse: the exalted discourse of abundance is everywhere duplicated by a critique of consumer society—even to the point where advertising often intentionally parodies advertising" (Lechte 1994, 234–235). The critique of consumer society is close to the revisionist view of Korean nationalist historiography consequent on Eckert's 1991 undermining of it (Eckert 2014). The extent to which the disordered profusions of Korean advertising—to be confronted in following chapters—are to be seen as intentional or, alternatively, as unconsciously herdlike (in either case an assemblage) is contentious.[31] It is Baudrillard's argument that the task of domination in consumer capitalism shifts to the signifier (the sign) rather than the signified (the thing or idea or commodity represented by the sign) and thereby to the media—either through a decoupling from meaning (the world is reduced to spectacle, unreadable, structures of domination thus rendered opaque) or through the arbitrary assignment of meaning to signifiers (most notably in the transformation of products, although Baudrillard also adds that, in the transformation of relations of production, class is communicated away). So is this the Korea of the Park Chung-hee dictatorship and the violent "disappearance" of class? Or is it to be seen as the reemergence and reinterpretation of Confucian discipline—order?

Given the increasingly necessary dependence of capitalism on endlessly expanding consumption, these transformations have had to become ever more frenetic: assignment and then devaluation of *exchange* values to trigger yet a new round of consumption, dependent on ever more frequent assignment and devaluation of *sign* values—*meanings*.[32] Social integration thus rests increasingly on communication—sign value, therefore ideology and the sphere of culture—rather than on simple consumption.[33] We will see, in following chapters, the wild riot of such communication in the "back streets" of modern Seoul—also in the frenetic Christian witness of Seoul's religious proliferation.

Baudrillard's boldest assertion is that the code supplants the sign, that the era of the code supersedes the era of the sign (Baudrillard 1993). The code, here, is easily understood: it is the binary code of computer technology, the DNA code in biology, the digital code in information technology. Does the biblical text in Korean Christianity also become a code—phrases to be endlessly broken down and paraded, the ubiquitous banner carrier, the quiet distributor of printed snatches of text, the screaming proselytizer in the subway carriage?

The extreme position of the Baudrillard argument is far from universally accepted—originality and creativity still reign supreme—and it might be judged not especially helpful in the present instance. However, it does succeed in drawing attention to the phenomenon of *production according to a code*—to reproduction—and to its salience in presently emerging Seoul. Those reproduced antique monuments (the reconstructed Gyeongbokgung Palace being the paradigm case) are now likewise reproductions according to the rules of a code—an assembly of copybook Chosun elements and emblems. They follow modern rules derived from ancient images. The seemingly endless parades of identical residential towers would also seem to support Baudrillard's argument: they, too, are built to a code with no distinction between original and copy. Only the number painted on the top of each tower distinguishes it from its neighbors.

Baudrillard's somewhat hyperbolic utterances on the city in "the era of late capitalism"—"reality" as a depthless screen, surface brilliance, and indifference but across nothing, the end of both public and private realms, the beginning of the age of simulacra—might say something about the city in the present metamorphosis of the age. For now, they will be seen more as a question whose exploration it is the task of the narrative to follow.

CHAPTER 2

ERASURE AND REINVENTION

Korea to 1945

The present chapter is to ponder a two-part question. Korean historiography overwhelmingly depicts the Japanese era darkly, as the death of "old Korea," perhaps even of Korean identity itself. So, the first part of the question: to what extent should we see death (eclipse, distortion, erasure) as historiographical vis-à-vis actual? Stated more bluntly, is the erasure of old Korea merely a product of more modern, nationalist historians, politicians, and ideologues, or did it actually happen and how much? The second part of the question is this: to what extent was erasure, variously historiographic and actual, really part of interweaving, mutually opposed, yet thereby mutually invigorating understandings of modernity, and therefore also *enabling*? Gayatri Chakravorty Spivak (1996, 19) writes of colonization as providing an "enabling violence" or "enabling violation" that can free or enrich the discourse of culture and indeed of nation. To what extent is the Japanese era to be seen as containing seeds for the much later outbursts of new creativity in more recent times—the economic "Miracle of the Han," the new avant-garde, the K-wave? (Chapter 3 will need to take this question further, to ask how the further tragedies of the Korean War and the long military dictatorship were also destructive of the past yet also enabling of later creativity.)

The question can be posed more bluntly. There are continual charges that colonization erased Korean culture; there was certainly erasure written on the fabric of the city of Seoul. There is also a more recent historiography (chapter 1) that would assert that colonization also brought enrichment (multiplicity, otherness) to the urban culture of Seoul, again written upon the city. So, in understanding Seoul there is a terrible tension, almost a dialectic, between erasure and enrichment. How are conflicting historiographies to be negotiated and the city thereby to be read?

The present chapter will be in four parts. The first will take the form of a selective history to the beginning of the Japanese era, with the second then extending the account to the end of that era. Both parts are to trace the political and social trajectory of Korea but also the evolution of the extraordinary diversity of ideologies, ideas, and cultural resources with which Koreans were later to confront the post-1945 world and which persist, even further enriched, into the present. Although reading as a form of history, the focus is on the geography and spaces of the city. Part 3 of the chapter deals more explicitly with the question raised above: in what ways might the Japanese intervention be seen as eroding—even erasing—old culture and identity and in what ways might it have been enabling of a new Korean modernity? Part 4 then deals with that further question of the extent to which erasure was actual and to what extent a product of modern Korean historiography—has the outrage been enhanced in some distorted national remembering? In that sense, part 4 returns to themes of chapter 1.

A note on method: to repeat from the preface, this and following chapters are based on an interweaving of themes and ideas—historiography, architecture, urban form, literature, film, religion, television, and popular culture. The purpose is to invoke reflection on challenging juxtapositions, throwing accepted ideas and their supposed underlying wisdom into doubt, thereby to see the city and its story anew.

Part 1

SEOUL AND KOREA BEFORE COLONIZATION

Ancient Korea is essential to any engagement with present Korea, and thereby Seoul, in three senses. First, it presents contested origins to legitimize North versus South, and Korea versus Japan, into the present day. Second, it provides the wish images in which modern Seoul's past would be imagined and its present identity would be socially constructed, both physically and in cyberspace.[1] Third, the old kingdoms were theaters of beliefs and ideologies, variously competing and overlapping, contested and hybridizing, contradictory yet coinciding, that still run through the culture of the present. They account in large part for the extraordinary intellectual vigor of the South and much of the vibrancy of Seoul.

Korea in antiquity was in some sense a peripheral kingdom, on the edge of a Sino-centric world. With its proximity to China, it came to share the latter's Daoist and Confucian traditions; in the second century BCE it had adopted the Chinese writing system, and in the fourth century CE, its Buddhism. Like the Japanese, Vietnamese, Tibetans, and diverse Central Asian peoples in the orbit of ancient China, the Koreans regarded China as the apex of human civilization and were seemingly happy to adapt desirable Chinese ways of doing things (Clark 2000, 4). Subsequently, the Korean language was codified and given an alphabetical structure in the fifteenth century, in part to differentiate the Koreans from the Chinese in the perennial search for clarity of identity through language (see chapter 1, in relation to the Benedict Anderson argument). In ancient times Korea was a fulcrum for the transfer of continental culture to Japan, while also being periodically caught up in raiding parties and the resulting skirmishes with its island neighbors.

The foundational legend has the proto-Korean Gojoseon (ancient Joseon, Chōsen, or Chosun) kingdom founded in 2333 BCE by Dangun (Tan'gun), the Posterity of Heaven. Its capital may have been in Liaoning (in present-day China) but around 400 BCE moved to Pyongyang. In 108 BCE a Han Chinese invasion ended Gojoseon, and a succession of small states ensued until the emergence of the three kingdoms of Baekje, Koguryo, and Silla. The mountain-ringed valley of the Han River had been chosen for the capital of the southwestern Baekje (Paekche) kingdom around 18 BCE. While the Baekje capital was somewhat mobile, shifting between sites, all of these were within the region that would now be called Greater Seoul—Wiryeseong (present day Hanam), north and south of the Han River, and Bukhan in northwest Seoul (present-day Goyang). In present-day Seoul's Pungnap-dong there is Pungnap-toseong, a flat earthen wall at the edge of the Han River, oval-shaped and with a circumference of some 3.5 kilometers. Based on research during the Japanese occupation, it is speculated that this structure was an element of Hanam Wiryeseong, the first capital of Baekje. A further, outlying fortress of the supposed Hanam Wiryeseong is Monchon-toseong, with its surviving earthen ramparts on the Olympic Park site. In the fourth century the somewhat putative kingdom of Baekje became a more full-fledged kingdom, acquiring Chinese culture and technology through contact with the Chinese southern dynasties; in turn, Japanese culture, art and language were strongly influenced by the kingdom of Baekje.

The relationship between Korea (specifically Baekje) and Japan is contested. At the extreme there is the view of Korea as the onetime ruler of Japan and "the fount of all Japanese civilization" (Farris 1994, 24–25). Against that is the more modest claim that Baekje art "became the basis for the art of the [Japanese] Asuka period (about 552–644)" (Hatada 1969, 20); furthermore, Bruce Cumings (2005, 34) cites recent evidence, "weighed dispassionately," that Japan obtained metals, metal technologies, military technology, and strategy from Korea.[2] Cumings also notes speculations on Korean origins of Japan's imperial house (33), suggesting that such speculations may account for Japanese reluctance to permit the archaeological opening of imperial tombs— what might they find? The embarrassment (for Japan) continued: as recently as the late 1500s and early 1600s, massive numbers of Korean potters were forcibly abducted to Japan to engineer the birth of the Japanese Imari porcelain tradition. The contested relationship might be seen as underlying, in part, a determination on the part of many Japanese in the twentieth century to suppress Korea and all memory of it. Yet there is also Everett Taylor Atkins' (2010) counterobservation of the extent of Japanese commitment to Koreana and a view of Korea as what Japan may have lost in its headlong rush to modernity.

Three kingdoms vied for dominance in the Korean Peninsula and adjoining Manchuria in ancient times. Baekje was centered on the southwest of the peninsula, and Koguryo was in the north, branching far into Manchuria and what is now Pacific Russia; between these two was Silla.[3] In the 660s Silla effected a unification of the peninsula, also becoming strongly allied with Tang China;[4] in the ninth century Silla in turn collapsed to yield a multiplicity of states. Then, in 918, the Goryeo (Koryo, Korea) state was founded and the Han valley, locale of the erstwhile Baekje capital, continued as locale for the new capital, at Gaeseong or Songdo (now Kaesong in North Korea but on the border with South Korea and effectively within the broader Seoul region).[5] In 1392 the Yi (or Chosun, Joseon, "Morning Calm") dynasty replaced Goryeo through a largely bloodless coup. The choice of name represented a claim for both antiquity and authenticity, casting back to that imagined birth of the Korean nation in the third millennium BC when king Dangun had founded Old Chosun. With the new dynasty in 1392, Goryeo (Korea) would cease; the nation would proclaim return to its (Chosun) origins.

The post-1945 partitioning of the peninsula also partitioned its historiography. Both North and South would claim Old (and new) Chosun; the North would title the country Chosun, the South would take the more recent (1890s) Han'guk. From the Three Kingdoms period, the North conferred national legitimacy on Koguryo, with its legendary center in the sacred mountain Paektu, which also thereby became central to the founding myth of the Kim dynasty—Kim Jong-Il, we are told, was born there.[6] The South, contrarily, claims Korea's true descent to be through Silla, with its capital at Kyongju or Gyeongju (north of Busan). The presidents of South Korea from 1961 to 1996, both those elected and the dictators, came from this region; the first president, Syngman Rhee, had his legitimizing ideology located in Silla.[7] It is Baekje that is omitted from these rival claims of origin—and, more vehemently, from Japanese claims.[8]

In August 1394 Taejo, founding monarch of the Yi (Chosun) dynasty, established Hanyang (the present Seoul) on the same site as two previous dynastic capitals but as an entirely new foundation. Ryu Jeh-hong (2004, 17) argues that Taejo, having established his dynasty by coup, needed to "denaturalize" (destroy) Gaeseong, the previous "naturalized" capital of the Goryeo dynasty, and then to invoke the already "naturalized" *pungsu*, the Korean geomancy, bringing its principles to determine both the location and geometry of the new capital. Lee Sang-hae (2000, 15) has outlined two principles of Hanyang's (Seoul's) planning. One lay in the doctrine derivable from *pungsu*, seen as an "image-text":

> The name Hanyang is itself a reflection of its [*pungsu*] principles. In the theory of negative-positive (*yin-yang* in Chinese), yang denotes the sun filled southern slope of a mountain overlooking its river to the south.[9] Hanyang then means a site situated south of the North (pronounced "puk" in Korean) Mountain (pronounced "ak" in Korean), or Pukak [Pugak], and north of the Han River. In terms of geomantic configuration, the city occupied a valley encircled by a range of mountains: Pukak as the Principal Mountain; Namsan the Southern Mountain; Naksan the "Left Blue Dragon"; Inwangsan the "Right White Tiger."[10]

The second principle flowed from the metaphysics of neo-Confucianism, whereby "the city was an instrument for implementing the ritual institutions, and the first order of its plan was the proper placement of guardian shrines of the state" (Lee Sang-hae 2000, 15).

The first decision facing the Chosun, in the context of this new orthodoxy, was the siting of the main royal palace, Gyeongbokgung Palace, in the north of the city but under the protecting south slope of Pugak, the North Mountain, which, however, was not visible from the palace due to an intervening mountain slope, but was majestically visible from the great north-south axis of Taepyeongno (now Sejongno, figure 2.1). The city thereby gained the effect of legitimizing

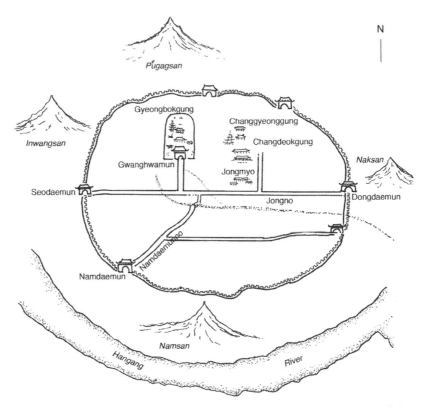

FIGURE 2.1 The idealized city of 1394: four geomantic mountains, three main and three subsidiary gates, a discontinuous, bent axis (regularized in the Japanese era and renamed Sejongno in the present time), and palaces beneath the most sacred of the mountains, facing south. Source: based on Lee Ki-Suk (1979, 79–82); Kim Won (1981, 3–10); King (2008a); and Gelézeau (2014, 167).

Taejo's coup by naturalizing his palace. Jongmyo (Chongmyo), the royal ancestral temple, was to the east of the palace, and the shrine to the guardian spirits of land and crops to the west. The kingdom's main administrative functions were located along the north-south Taepyeongno, which stretched from Gwanghwamun, the ceremonial gate to the palace, to Hwangtoyeon, an open plaza (Lee Sang-hae 2000, 14; Gelézeau 1997). Hanyang thereby became a "natural" city—nature and its spirits reigned (Ryu Jeh-hong 2004, 17).

The main gates to the city were to the east and the west, and, consequently, the main roads ran east-west. About six hundred meters south of Gwanghwamun, Taepyeongno was crossed by Jongno, the most important of these east-west roads, "the street of the bell" whose ringing would signify the opening and closing of the city gates, and the street of shops to serve the royal court and thereby the commercial and business street of the old city, a commercial preeminence that persists to the present day.[11] North of Jongno were the residences of the aristocracy, to the south the plebeian districts.

While the north-south, east-west grid characterized the principal avenues of Hanyang, it did not have the same rigorous geometry that one would encounter in the Chinese cities, most notably in the Tang dynasty capital, Chang-an. The discontinuous Taepyeongno is one aberration; a stream running southeast from Kwanghwamun yielded the line of the diagonal Insadonggil; within its somewhat irregular grid squares, minor streets and lanes follow no discernible plan. The contrast between the processional avenues and the labyrinthine alleys behind them would appear to reflect an ancient tension between the display of power and the concealment of private space, a tension also evident in the Chinese metropolises—witness the tension between the gridded avenues of Beijing and the hidden *hutongs* (laneways) within the grid squares. (The ancient tension translates, in modern Seoul, into that between the grand corporate boulevards and the ordered arrays of seemingly identical apartment blocks, on the one hand, and a more chaotic, labyrinthine, disordered space of the "back streets," alleys, and "real life" on the other. It is the dichotomy of morphologies introduced in chapter 1, figure 1.1.)

Ideologies (1)

Throughout the Chosun era there was a continuing struggle between Buddhist belief and ritual, and Confucianism. The Chinese-style, Confucian civil service examinations were first held in Korea in 958. Confucians had long looked down on Buddhism as an intrusion distracting the masses from the hard work of building a society based on justice and propriety, where humanity and science would be the guide rather than superstition, the spirits, and the gods. Confucianists were especially offended by the seeming indolence of monks, as well as their celibacy and hence their disrespect of parents in refusing to beget children and thereby continue family lines.

In the United Silla period (668–918), Korean Buddhism had thrived, even while adjusting to Confucian norms, and the Silla capital of Kyongju was reported to have been dense with temples. The Goryeo kingdom (918–1392) likewise celebrated its adherence to Mahayana Buddhism while simultaneously basing its examination and administrative system on Confucian principles.[12] The founders of the Chosun dynasty in 1392, however, attacked Buddhism and other folk religions as corruptions that served only to mislead the common people. The temples in towns and cities were demolished, and the founders ordered that no temples were to be built within the new capital of Hanyang (Seoul). Only temples in the mountains could remain standing (Clark 2000, 41). (The absence of temples in the present Seoul urban landscape, especially when seen against the forest of churches, is extraordinary.)

Neo-Confucianism had arisen in China in the Tang dynasty (618–904), reaching something of a zenith with Confucian scholars of the Song dynasty (960–1279). Zhou Dunyi (1017–1073) is seen as its first true pioneer. Neo-Confucianism developed both as a renaissance of traditional Confucian ideas and as reaction to the more metaphysical ideas of religious Buddhism and Daoism. Neo-Confucianism was a social and ethical philosophy that would bring a more syncretist and tolerant approach to Confucianism, more open to Buddhist and Daoist teachings—though not without resistance—and more academic and "scientific." While borrowing metaphysical ideas from Daoism, neo-Confucianism emphasized humanism and rationalism in the belief that the universe could be understood through human reason—the task was to create a harmonious relationship between the individual and the universe. Reason would supplant (Buddhist, Daoist) meditation.[13]

Neo-Confucianism was introduced to Korea by An Hyang (1243–1306) in the Goryeo dynasty, at a time when Buddhism was the dominant religion.[14] It gained both influence and followers, mostly from an anti-aristocratic middle class that became the vanguard in overthrowing the old dynasty and setting up the Chosun. Neo-Confucianism became the state ideology of the new dynasty; Buddhism was seen as poisonous to neo-Confucian order and accordingly was restricted and persecuted. Although the early Chosun reformers might have been Buddhist in their private lives, they agreed that the organized Buddhist religion had to be suppressed, its monasteries and lands confiscated, and their members returned to "useful" occupations. Remaining Buddhist clergy would be banished to mountain-dwelling monasteries and Korea would be a neo-Confucian state (Clark 2000, 9; also Duncan 1996).

The founding Chosun monarch Taejo had given priority to the establishment of institutions of Confucian learning.[15] The fourth monarch, King Sejong the Great (r. 1418–1450), brought together Confucian humanism and progressive administration in what almost amounted to a welfare state. Arguably his greatest cultural achievement was the creation of the Korean alphabet, *han-gul*. Sejong's reign is commonly seen as premodern Korea's golden age: Koreans had invented movable metal type printing around 1234—two centuries before Gutenberg (in the 1450s)—perfecting the method in 1403. Then, in 1420, Sejong set technicians to the task of mechanizing the process: "We are prepared to print any book there is and all men will have the means to study" (Cumings 2005, 65, quoting Gale 1972, 233).

There were similar advances in mathematics, the physical sciences, and technology that were comparable with China and certainly far ahead of the West and Japan.

Although Buddhism was restricted, Sejong returned to a private Buddhist devotion toward the end of his reign. There was always the Buddhist fightback, however, and King Sejo (r. 1455–1468) significantly strengthened the Buddhist practices, in part to reinforce monarchical power by suppressing the *yangban* ("two branches") class of office-holding aristocrats and the Confucian institutions. His successor, Songjong (r. 1469–1494), ninth king of the Chosun dynasty, worked to restore Confucian rule and reinforce the scholarly class.[16] The anti-Sejo literati had used the institution of the royal lecture (haranguing the king) in an attempt to abolish Buddhist ritual and other anomalies from the life of the court.[17] Land-tenure issues— hence those of social class—were always at the core of the struggles. Although tensions were always there, this was the peak of the resurgent neo-Confucian school.

Another basis of Confucian-Buddhist conflict related to the forms of society that each would imagine. Deeply embedded in Buddhism is the idea of human equality; enlightenment is open to all. Gong Fuzi (Master Gong, Confucius, 551–479 BCE), on the other hand, had taught that people are *not* created equal, nor do they become equal during their lives; some are stronger, some weaker; some will labor with their hands, others with their minds; what matters, rather, is the principle of mutual duties and obligations. A society's most moral people should be its leaders, where moral knowledge is best acquired through the study of philosophy, history, and literature. Thus the soundest investment is in education; the pathway to honor and authority—to being truly respected and followed by others—is via success in the Confucian examination system. To the Confucian mind, the Buddhist focus on meditation and otherworldliness presented as indolence at one level, as unscientific superstition at another, and the property and wealth of the temples would be put to better use if invested in the education of the people.

The Confucian system subsequently disintegrated—went underground—in the face of Western encounters and Japanese oppression, only to reemerge in the present age. John Duncan (2000) refers to "the plasticity of Confucianism" throughout the nineteenth and twentieth centuries. Korea's two most prominent neo-Confucian scholars were Yi Hwang (1501–1570) and Yi I (1536–1584); they are today commemorated on Korea's one-thousand- and five-thousand-won banknotes, respectively. Major thoroughfares in modern Seoul are named for them.

Boyé Lafayette De Mente suggests that, for older Koreans in the present day, the most important word in the Korean language might be *aboji* ("father")—indeed, Korea's traditional culture might be described as a father culture because of the central role that fathers played in the social structure and in day-to-day living for over five centuries (De Mente 2012, 1). The place of women, by contrast, was always circumscribed (Seth 2002; Kim Youngmin and Pettid 2011). As something of a corollary to the neo-Confucian system, man and wife were to be placed in different realms of duty and obligation. Whereas women in the Goryeo period could enjoy a small measure of freedom—widows, for example, could remarry—the Chosun wife would find herself spatially confined, bereft of property, nameless, and effectively a gift to her husband's family and household; she had no rights of inheritance. Her best hope—usually realized—was to rule the inner sanctum of that household (Ko et al. 2003; Jung Ji-Young 2011). Ancestors were to be venerated, with ancestor "worship" being arguably Korea's most important tradition, albeit inauspiciously instituted with a new law in 1390. Also to be venerated were teachers, "the greatest Men in the Kingdom" (Ledyard 1971, 123, 218–219).

During the Goryeo era the wealthy ruling class had been referred to as the *yangban* ("two branches") class, indicating the two types of official, civil and military, although it was in Chosun that the system reached its full power.[18] Entry to the *yangban* required either having passed the merit examination or having been appointed as a favor by the king or a high official as "merit subjects." There was always tension between the examination passers and the merit subjects in their struggles for power and royal support. The enormous power of the *yangban* and their bitter and often violent divisions progressively undermined the Chosun kings and reflected their corresponding weakness. It was in the *yangban* class that women were most constricted: marriage was a union arranged between two surnames and could not be changed within a lifetime. Husbands could kill adulterous wives; concubinage, on the other hand, was to be tolerated (Haboush 2003).[19]

There were exceptions to this repression, however. While neo-Confucian ideologues attempted the eradication of Buddhism, the common people retained attachment to Buddhist practices and their comfort, but also to folk religions, shamanism, geomancy, and fortune-telling. Though condemned by both Confucians and the modern world, these thrived then and still persist today, constituting a "second tradition" in conflict with elite culture. In this second tradition, women typically found pathways for their artistic expression; they could escape the constricting virtues: the shamans, for instance, were typically female.

The sudden shift in the status of Korean women at the end of the twentieth century, to be observed in chapter 5 below, must be seen as extraordinary against such a historical background.[20]

In 1592 the Japanese warlord Toyotomi Hideyoshi invaded both Ming and Chosun realms in the Imjin War (Hawley 2005).[21] Though ultimately defeated in a second invasion in 1597–1598 (principally by the Korean admiral Yi Sun-sin), the Hideyoshi invasions destroyed government records, cultural artifacts, archives, and historical documents. There was land devastation, population loss, and loss of artisans and technicians. As the land registers were destroyed, the basic class relationships were overturned; the class structure began to crumble.

Postwar uncertainty was complicated by the collapse of Ming China and the rise of the Manchu Qing and was spurred by the rise of revolutionary ideas. The *yangban* elite shunned Sejong's *han-gul* alphabet as too easy, instead adhering to the idea that Chinese characters were beyond the ability of the lower classes and hence constituted a barrier to protect their own privileged positions. Slowly, however, use of the "too easy" *han-gul* began to permeate to the otherwise bypassed royal and *yangban* women (and even down into the non-*yangban* strata), who began to produce a literature of diaries, memoirs, and stories. The theme of the novel *Hong Kil-tong chon,* by Ho Kyun (1569–1618), was that all people are born equal and that, if provoked, the lower classes together with the peasant class could become a powerful force in the struggle for social justice (Lee Ki-baik 1984, 244). There was also the *Chunhyangga* (Song of Chunhyang), one of the five *p'ansori* (ancient song dramas) surviving today; it is about a woman of chaste reputation but also about resistance to the aristocracy (Eckert et al. 1990, 175, 190; Clark 2000, 72–74).[22] It continues to be immensely popular and has been made into over a dozen films, as well as the more recently popular Korean drama series *Delightful Girl Choon-Hyang* of 2005, part of the Korean Wave output.[23] Such ideas gave encouragement to the people and further undermined the prestige of *yangban* (gentry) society.

Even among the *yangban,* however, there were impulses to reform. A central theme of neo-Confucianism had been truth through a better understanding of reality—"the investigation of things" (Clark 2000, 15). A group of *yangban* accordingly set up their own school of thought called *silhak* ("practical learning") in response to the increasingly metaphysical nature of neo-Confucianism, its arid scholasticism, and its disconnect from the rapid agricultural, industrial, and political changes in Korea from the late seventeenth to the early nineteenth centuries. Especially significant to the movement was the novelist and philosopher Bak (Park) Ji-won (1737–1805) (Park Ji-won 2011).

Silhak scholar Yi Su-gwang (1563–1628) traveled to China and returned with the new Western learning then spreading in Beijing, also initiating a tradition of interest in Korean history (Eckert et al. 1990, 168). Western scientific ideas—mathematics, astronomy, study of the natural world—had been introduced into China by Jesuit missionaries, and these in turn came to infect *silhak*. Jesuit philosophy and theological exegesis were also adopted, and some went so far as to establish their own branch of Catholicism in Seoul, as the beginning of Korean Christianity.

A consequence of the Hideyoshi invasions of the 1590s had been reinforcement of Korean ideas of the Japanese as barbarians, pirates, and cultural inferiors (Haboush 2016). Another had been a strengthening of Korean seclusion—a "contemptuous exclusiveness," the nineteenth-century American intruders called it (Drake 1984, 105). Yet neighborly relations with the Japanese continued as Korean officials would be dispatched periodically to Edo; Busan in particular long facilitated the minimal official trade between Korea and Japan and, in the nineteenth century, developed into an almost extraterritorial base for Japanese commercial, agricultural, and then military ambitions (Kyung Moon Hwang 2010, 145).

While the Korean king acknowledged Chinese suzerainty and tributary obligations to the Chinese emperor, practically this amounted to very little: China's policy was effectively one of "benign neglect," leaving Korea with substantive autonomy as a nation. Japan, however, was perceived by the Koreans as yet another state in the Sinic thrall. By the nineteenth century, Korean policy was mostly one of "no treaties, no trade, no Catholics, no West, and no Japan" (Cumings 2005, 91, 100). There were bloody pogroms against native Catholics in 1801, 1839, and 1846 (Eckert et al. 1990, 183–184). By gunboat diplomacy, Japan established unequal treaties with China in 1871 and with Korea in 1876, albeit written within the norms of diplomatic language of the time. The barriers had been breached by the erstwhile cultural inferiors.

Ideology and the end of the Chosun age

In the nineteenth century, amid conditions of peasant revolt and virtual civil war, Ch'oe Che-u (1824–1864) formulated the ideology of Donghak, or "Eastern Learning," to stand against "Western Learning" (Catholicism), though the doctrine also incorporated elements of Catholicism (Lee Ki-baik 1984, 258). Donghak was to rescue the farmers from prevalent poverty and unrest and to secure political and social stability. In a trance Ch'oe Che-u had experienced a revelation compelling him to spread a message of spiritual enlightenment throughout Korea.[24] He envisioned a new world order based on human equality, a theme later formalized in the doctrine of *innaecheon* ("humans are Heaven"); in the new religion of Cheondogyo (Religion of the Heavenly Way), the orthodox form of Donghak, this became the central tenet of the religion's theology, persisting into the present. Cheondogyo arose in 1860 as a mixture of elements of Confucianism, Buddhism, indigenous Songyo (teachings of the ancient Silla kingdom's *hwarang*, or "flower of youth" class),[25] native Korean beliefs in spirits and mountain deities, and modern ideas of class struggle that one might now consider Marxist, together with nationalistic and anti-foreigner (anti-Western, anti-Japanese) sentiment; it also proclaimed a strong millenarian message, to the alarm of establishment circles (Eckert et al. 1990, 187). It underlay the abortive Donghak Revolution of 1894, which was seized, many decades later, as an ideological fore-bear by both North and South Korea (Bell 2004; Beirne 1999; Hong Suhn-kyoung 1968).

Ch'oe Che-u's ideas rapidly gained acceptance, and he set his doc-trines to music so that farmers could understand them more readily. There were satirical mask dances and village magic performances. His teachings were systematized and compiled as a message of salvation, incorporating the syncretized elements from Confucianism, Bud-dhism, and Songyo referred to above, together with modern humanist ideas. Exclusionism from foreign influences was another characteristic of his religion, which incorporated an early form of Korean national-ism and rejection of alien thought. The early Donghak slogan is reveal-ing: "Drive out the Japanese dwarfs and the Western barbarians, and praise righteousness" (Hatada 1969, 100).[26]

Although the Chosun government executed Ch'oe Che-u in 1864 on charges of treason, his movement thrived and poverty-stricken farmers gathered under his standard. There were large-scale Donghak demonstrations in 1892; in 1893 Donghak believers went to Hanyang (Seoul) and demonstrated in front of the royal palace. The uprisings increased to effectively become a revolution. The Donghak Revolution occurred when Korea was on the verge of radical transformations that were in part precipitated by that revolution. Society was stagnating under a rigid Confucian social hierarchy whereby peasants were over-taxed and generally oppressed by corrupt government officials and the *yangban* class—the Donghak Revolution would have ended the taxa-tion of the peasantry and crushed the *yangban*. External forces, includ-ing Western encroachment, the impending collapse of Qing China, and the aggressive rise of Japan, were causing considerable alarm in Korea (Bell 2004). In 1875 there was a Japanese provocation—the so-called Unyo Incident—followed by gunboat diplomacy in 1876 to force a treaty and the entry of a Japanese legation in 1880 (Eckert et al. 1990, 200–201).

Among many of the intelligentsia there was an emerging pro-Japan push, albeit enmeshed with elements of Korean nationalism.[27] Following a military mutiny in 1882, a small and rather clandestine group formed, variously referred to as the Progressive or Independence Party, wanting to emulate Japan's Meiji Restoration and hoping for Japanese support. Finding reform blocked by conservatives centered on the family of Queen Min, on 4 December 1884 they initiated a violent coup in Hanyang (Seoul). A false report of an uprising of Chinese troops based in the Chinese legation was conveyed to King Kojong, who was evacuated to Gyeongun Palace (today's Deoksugung Palace) and then urged to seek protection from the garrison of the nearby Japanese legation. The Chinese troops moved into action, the coup was defeated, and key Progressives fled with the retreating Japanese guards to asylum in Japan. Among those fleeing was Seo Jae-pil (Philip Jaisohn, 1864–1951), who then traveled to America, where he studied medicine and became the first Korean to receive US citizenship (Lee Ki-baik [1961] 1984, 275–279).

Following their intervention, the Chinese tightened their hold on Korea's government, though it was increasingly countered by mounting Russian presence and influence.[28] From their refuge in Japan, Progressives continued in vain to call for reform (Kim Okkyun 2000, 256–258), while Korea descended into increasing chaos.

In 1894 Chon Pong-jun (1854–1895) assumed Donghak leadership, heading a popular revolt against the district authorities of Gobu County in Jeolla-do Province (around the present city of Gwangju); when peaceful demonstration proved ineffective, the farmers turned to violence and full-scale rebellion, which spread throughout the province. Again the immediate cause was the corruption of local officials, crushing taxation, and opposition to the *yangban* aristocracy, but also strong anti-Japanese sentiment. Alarmed at the support engendered by the uprisings, the royal court asked for Chinese intervention (Oliver 1993; Weems 1964). This, however, was a fatal move: Japan responded by invading in force, first driving out their Chinese rivals and occupying Hanyang, then turning to the Donghak, who were ultimately crushed. Chon Pong-jun was captured and beheaded, and Donghak troops and farmers were massacred by the Japanese. The Japanese demanded that the Korean government order Chinese troops to leave, as the Japanese officials announced their intention to maintain their presence in Korea to help sort out the country's domestic mess. The Japanese military based itself south of the city at Yongsan, between Namsan and the river. On 23 July 1894 the Japanese occupied the royal palace and imposed "protection" on King Kojong. Two days later, the Sino-Japanese War of 1894–1895 erupted, with total victory going to the Japanese. On 8 October 1895, Queen Min was assassinated in Gyeongbokgung Palace, allegedly by Japanese "ruffians" at the behest of the Japanese minister. With the aid of Russian sailors, Kojong escaped to the Russian legation in February 1896, from where he succeeded in recovering some of his power, returning to Gyeongun Palace in February 1897. Caught in the middle between rising popular nationalism at home, China's decay, and Japan's expansionist modernization on its periphery, Chosun Korea clambered for survival, some assurance of independence, and the semblance of international equality, on 12 October 1897 declaring itself to be the Great Han (Daehan) Empire and its erstwhile king to be the Emperor Gwangmu—just like China and, more to the point, Japan.

Gwangmu (Kojong) ruled from Gyeongun (Deoksugung) Palace rather than the vastly grander and only recently reconstructed Gyeongbokgung.[29] The extent of the latter made it difficult to defend in the increasing turmoil, as demonstrated in the assassination there of Queen Min; the Deoksugung, on the other hand, had a small periphery and was thereby more secure. Additionally, the Deoksugung had proximity to the Russian legation and thereby to its defending garrison—it was also no coincidence that Japanese advisors were now being replaced by Russians. The Deoksugung was also interesting for its architecture, for this was a hybrid assemblage like no other. Initially, like other royal palaces, it had comprised halls and other elements in traditional architectural forms, many dating from the 1592 war against the Japanese, and correctly oriented to the south. Subsequently the complex was reoriented to the east, against all tradition, with a new main Junghwajeon throne hall (from 1902) and the eastern gate becoming the Daehanmun imperial gate. In 1906 many of its elements were then reconstructed. The reorientation has the effect, intended or otherwise, of signaling a break from the Korean/Chinese orthodoxy. Equally radical was the insertion of a second, Western-style palace as the new imperial residence, including the imposing Neoclassical Seokjojeon, designed for Kojong by British architect John Harding in 1900 but not completed until 1910. Though Kojong was deposed in 1907, he continued to reside here until his death in 1919, and both he and the palace thereby became emblematic of the Daehan Empire's claim for global (Western) connection but also of its lost independence.[30]

The spirit of independence was also expressed in 1896 with the founding of the Independence Club, principally by Seo Jae-pil, now returned from America; it mostly comprised veterans from the 1884 abortive coup (like Seo) and middle-ranking government officers. It was established to implement two symbolic projects, first the erection of Independence Gate to replace Yeongeunmun Gate (Welcoming Gate for Obligation, sometimes translated as Welcome to Beneficent Envoy of Suzerains), which was a symbol of unequal diplomatic relations between Korea and Qing China and of Korea's tributary status. The Yeongeunmun had been built around 1407 in the Ming era, just outside Donuimun (Loyalty Gate), the great west gate to the city, for the ceremonial reception of the Chinese emperor's ambassador; it was demolished in 1896 following the Japan-China Treaty of Shimonseki to symbolize the end of tribute. The second project was to transform the adjoining Mohwa-gwan (Hall of Cherishing China) into an Independence Hall and Independence Park (Eckert et al. 1990, 232–233).

A month after the declaration of the great empire, on 20 November 1897, the new nationalism was duly celebrated with the ceremonial inauguration of Dongnimmun (Independence Gate). Again architecture took on a symbolizing function. Whereas the Yeongeunmun had been in a Ming Chinese form, its replacement, Independence Gate, is in a modernist hybrid styling—its designer was Korean-American Seo Jae-pil, an independence activist, medical doctor, and founder of Korea's first newspaper in *han-gul*.[31] Despite Seo's American experience, the styling presents paradoxically (to this observer) as akin to Japanese modernism of the time, though its avowed model was Paris' Arc de Triomphe. Symbolically, the two supporting pillars of the old gate were left intact in front of the new one—its erasure and that of Chinese suzerainty would continue to be represented.

In 1905 Korea came to enjoy Japanese protection (more like Japan); then on 29 August 1910, it received the ultimate privilege of annexation, to become de jure part of Japan. Korea ceased to exist as a politically independent state.

Part 2

COLONIZATION

The post-1868 Meiji (Enlightened Rule) government in Japan found itself confronting three interlinked dilemmas. First, how was Japan to enrich and strengthen itself? From the 1880s onward an argument developed for "dissociation from Asia" (*datsu-a ron*) whereby Japan would distance itself from Asian countries to join the ranks of the Western imperialists. In this matter, Naoki Sakai (2000, 792) invokes the concept of *negativity,* "without which the reflectivity necessary for self-consciousness cannot be achieved."[32] Negativity might be implied in the notion of otherness, alterity, difference; it is certainly implied in *defeat.* Naoki Sakai cites the wartime historiography of Masao Maruyama, which asserted that the moment of negativity could be detected in Japanese thought in the seventeenth and eighteenth centuries, whereas the Chinese never succeeded in giving rise to their own negativity. Implicit here, in the justifying argument of Japanese political superiority over China, was the old thesis of "flight from Asia, entry into Europe"—Japan should be capable of modernizing itself while (the rest of) Asia must wait for the West's initiative (Maruyama 1974). Yoshimi Takeuchi ([1947] 1993), an ardent sinologist, argued the opposite; the point to be made here is that the material interests of Meiji Japan sought ideological justification in a historiography that was always already contested. To achieve this self-modernization and thereby join "the West," the Japanese would need to acquire colonies in Asia, expanding from their islands to the Asian mainland. The foothold for this was seen to be the Korean Peninsula.

Second, the turn from feudalism to capitalism brought the need to secure commodity markets, then to secure export markets for Japan's products; for these, colonies would be essential, especially with the Western powers entering an era of strident imperialism in the 1880s.

Third, Japan faced a need for food security following a population boom, with a related need for resettlement space. Many Japanese migrated to Hokkaido and other parts of the Japanese archipelago, as well as to the Americas and Australia. However, Korea and especially Manchuria were increasingly seen as the logical areas for colonization (Park Chan Seung 2010, 83–86).[33]

There are other arguments presented to throw light on the colonization of Korea. If Manchuria was viewed as the more logical sphere for Japanese expansion, then the colonization of Korea is seen in some part as a strategic attempt to keep other potential colonizers out (Russia, Britain?). Also running through Japanese legitimizing ideology was a thread of enlightenment, seeking to end Chosun corruption and decay and bring about a better-educated, more hygienic, and more industrious Korean population.[34] Additionally, colonization was rationalized as Japan "returning" to an ancient origin. There were also some less noble arguments: after the Meiji Restoration and the end of the samurai age, invasions would provide an outlet for the energies of disestablished samurai; colonization, in turn, would provide opportunities to spread Japan's "imperial glory" (Eckert et al. 1990, 198).

The Japanese annexation of Korea was a gradual process. In April 1904, during the Russo-Japanese War, the Japanese Imperial Army under General Kuroki Tamemoto effected a landing near Incheon, then moved on to occupy Seoul. The war concluded on 5 September 1905, ending Russian influence in Korea and Manchuria; on 17 November 1905 the Eulsa Treaty with Japan was arbitrarily imposed on Korea, with American support, establishing a Japanese protectorate.[35] British acknowledgment soon followed.[36] When Kojong mounted a diplomatic effort to reestablish sovereignty in 1907, he was forced to abdicate in favor of his son. A two-tier system of administration developed in Korea: on one hand was the royal government of the Daehan Empire; on the other was the Japanese Residency-General, or what Lee Ki-baik (1984, 308) terms "government by advisers." While responsibility might still lie with the royal departments, the Residency-General was always influential. After the 1907 deposition of Kojong, all authority passed to the Residency-General.

General Terauchi Masatake, as the third resident-general to Korea, executed the Japan-Korea Annexation Treaty in August 1910, thereby becoming the first Japanese governor-general. The first decade of the formal colonial period was the "military rule" era (Kyung Moon Hwang 2010, 162). In the cities, and especially in Seoul, there was effectively a police state as the Japanese struggled to stabilize their colony, although the consequence was to transform gathering discontent into an ensuing explosion, on 1 March 1919—the March First Movement.

Pro-Japan sentiment had persisted after the failed 1884 coup, manifesting in aspects of what Lee Ki-baik calls the "forces of enlightenment" (elsewhere the Patriotic Enlightenment Movement),[37] and especially ambivalently in the 1904–1910 Ilchinhoe (Advance in Unity Society), which ardently embraced Japan's discourse of "civilizing Korea" and saw colonization as an opportunity to advance its own populist agenda. Both the Japanese colonizers and the Korean elites disliked the Ilchinhoe for its aggressive activism, which sought to control local tax administration and reverse the existing power relations between the people and government officials. Ultimately, the Ilchinhoe members faced visceral moral condemnation from their fellow Koreans when their language and actions resulted in nothing but the emergence of the Japanese colonial empire in Korea (Moon Yumi 2013). There were also strong anti-Japan movements: as Brandon Palmer (2013) observes, Koreans' long-standing animosity toward Japan culminated in active Korean resistance to colonial rule, of which the two main instances were the "righteous armies" and the March First Movement. From 1907 to 1912, small bands of righteous armies fought against colonial rule, with some 17,600 Korean fighters and civilians allegedly killed in the process of their suppression. The March First Independence Movement of 1919 was a peaceful peninsula-wide protest with nearly a million participants and a signal event in recent Korean history.

Ideologies (2)

The 1 March 1919 event needs to be seen in the context of continuing ideological evolution in Korea. Japan's annexation of Korea came as an overlay across an intricate web of ideologies and beliefs. While neo-Confucianism had collapsed in the onslaught of (Japanese) modernization, its ideals of self-discipline, order, respect, appropriate behavior, and national dignity simmered beneath any surface of subservience. The Confucian insistence on the material, on science and "the real," continued in tension with the Buddhist preoccupation with the immateriality of the phenomenal universe. Jesuit-infused Christian modernism and openness to Western science, philosophy, and theological exegesis had interlaced with both Confucian and Buddhist orthodoxies to yield, in turn, the still-persisting (in the twenty-first century) Donghak ideology.

Despite its virtual annihilation in 1894 at the hands of the Japanese, Donghak could stand as a powerful symbol of Korean resistance; furthermore, it was distinguished as an indigenous, democratic, nationalistic, and modern political philosophy. The argument has been that, whereas China eventually had to turn to an imported, Western ideology for its modernization (Communism), Korea could claim to have found a guiding ideology in its own traditions and powers of invention (Kang Wi Jo 1968, 48). Cheondogyo, the religious formulation of Donghak, had failed to be similarly crushed by the Japanese, becoming instead the vehicle for the historical enhancement of the Donghak myth of resistance. Kirsten Bell (2004) cites Kim Yong Choon (1978, vii): "What is Korean thought? Answering this question might involve several traditions such as Buddhism, Confucianism, Shamanism, Christianity and Ch'ongdogyo [Cheondogyo]. However, Ch'ongdogyo alone is the major indigenous tradition developed in Korea, while Buddhism, Confucianism, and Christianity are of foreign origin, and Shamanism is relatively common in many parts of the world."

Cheondogyo certainly had its nationalistic element and provided motivating ideology for the 1 March 1919 Korean Declaration of Independence and the consequent March First Movement against the Japanese. Of the thirty-three signatories to the declaration, fifteen were Cheondogyo; however, it should be noted, sixteen were Protestant (Kyung Moon Hwang 2010, 171). Nevertheless, other elements of Cheondogyo developed into the Ilchinhoe referred to above, which openly supported the annexation of Korea and from which it subsequently benefitted.

Nor was there any political consensus among the Christians. While there was nationalist sentiment, most entered a form of social contract with the authorities to refrain from political activities in order to avoid persecution. A degree of cooperation with the state persisted until the outbreak of war in 1937 when the issue of Shinto worship came to the fore, and then the 1942 expulsion of American missionaries.[38] Even here, however, there was no social consensus: among Catholics, for whom shrine worship was common, the respect for Shinto shrines was less problematic.

This fragmentation of ideologies, both Cheondogyo and Christian, characterized positions toward the Japanese colonial authorities, as well as toward pathways to modernity. It characterized the March First Movement and then persisted into the diversity of positions that underlay the post-1945 maelstrom. The role of Christianity here cannot be exaggerated: the mission stations—churches, schools, hospitals, and missionary residences—expressed a Western civilization that created a sense of awe and mystery among Koreans, who were experiencing modern amenities for the first time. Missionary compounds provided a window on the Western world that was not distorted by any refraction through Japanese colonization or ideology. The demand for education was overwhelming; consequently some 800 schools accommodating approximately 41,000 students were founded by the missionaries, with many independence fighters among the alumni. The Christian population reached 315,000 in the mid-1930s, and around 500,000 by 1945; although their numbers were much smaller at the time of the 1919 uprising, the glimpse presented of a Western modernity was a powerful motivation.[39]

The March First Movement

The end of World War I and the breakup of empires had encouraged expectations of Korean independence. Erstwhile Emperor Kojong died in January 1919, with rumors of poisoning, and independence rallies against Japanese invaders occurred nationwide on 1 March, to be suppressed by force as a result of which some seven thousand people were killed by Japanese soldiers and police. In the aftermath of the 1919 suppression, on 13 April 1919 the Provisional Government of the Republic of Korea was formed in Shanghai, with Syngman Rhee (1875–1965) as president. This did not achieve recognition by world powers, although a form of recognition was given by the nationalist government of China. The Provisional Government coordinated armed resistance against the Japanese Imperial Army during the 1920s and 1930s, including the significant Battle of Qingshanli in October 1920, in eastern Manchuria. The Korea Independent Army lured a larger Japanese force into battle, inflicting them with a major defeat and forcing a Japanese withdrawal from the area. The Battle of Qingshanli is considered a great victory for Korean guerrilla tactics.

In the aftermath of the 1919 uprising and events in Manchuria, the Japanese came to realize that they were on "the wrong side of history" —their form of repressive colonization had found itself in the wrong century. Always concerned with appearing "modern," this realization was the beginning of their "cultural" policy, and there was a relaxing of Japanese control. In the 1920s the colonial government was headed by a more humane governor-general, Admiral Viscount Saito Makoto (1858–1936), who permitted Koreans to assemble, speak, and publish their own newspapers and magazines; he improved education and allowed Koreans to join religious and even political organizations (Clark 2000, 17). In 1907 the Japanese had passed the Newspaper Law, effectively preventing the publication of local papers. Only the Korean-language *Taehan Maeil Sinbo* continued publication because it was run by a foreigner, E. T. Bethell. Hence for the first decade of colonial rule there were no Korean-owned newspapers, although books and several dozen Korean-owned magazines were published (Robinson 1988). In 1920 these laws were relaxed, and two of the three major Korean daily newspapers, *Dong-A Ilbo* and *Chosun Ilbo,* were established in 1920. In 1932 a double standard applying to Korean vis-à-vis Japanese publication was removed. However, the Japanese government still seized newspapers without warning, with over a thousand such seizures recorded between 1920 and 1939. By 1940, with the Pacific War increasing, Japan again shut down all Korean-language newspapers. In the 1920s, however, the cultural nationalist movement was wide-ranging; certainly there was censorship, but there was also a vibrant liberal and even Marxist literary and artistic movement, well into the late 1930s (Robinson 1988).[40]

Many Koreans still advocated armed insurrection as the only path to independence; others, however, saw their task as the advancement of the culture and the reinforcing of identity to yield, ultimately, a future generation as the basis on which to build a new Korea. There were two moderate-nationalist movements that focused on a more gradual approach to national resurgence. The first was the National University Movement established in 1922 and led by the Society for the Establishment of a National University, as an outcome of intelligentsia concerns—there had been a long and proud tradition of elite education in Korea, though it was now deeply threatened.[41] Colonial schools had a strong emphasis on Japanese language acquisition, cultural values, and Japanized Korean history; there were few opportunities for college education in Korea, so most college students ended up in Japan. A national fund-raising campaign was launched. Within six months, however, infighting among cliques, typical of the era, undid the project. The Japanese authorities announced the establishment of an imperial university for Seoul, the Keijo Imperial University (1924–1946), with new buildings scheduled for 1926 (Eckert et al. 1990, 290–291).

One factor in the collapse of the national university project was the withdrawal of support by the more radical student groups, including the All Korean Youth League. Student radicalism was strong, and paradoxically reinforced from Japan: Korean students traveling to Japan may have become somewhat assimilated into Japanese ways and thought, yet that was often into Japanese radical, left-wing thought, as Japan was also in some social turmoil at that time. Socialist thinking at the student level was in a mismatch with the second moderate-nationalist movement, the movement for incremental independence: worsening economic conditions, Government-General economic reforms, and general concern regarding economic dependency led to the Korean Production Movement of 1923–1924. Korean businessmen had been lobbying for subsidies and concessions so that they could compete on equal footing with Japanese enterprises; however, now the strategy shifted to mobilize national sentiment to support Korean industry and products. The effect of such a shift in consumer behavior would be the accumulation of Korean capital to compete with Japanese capital (Eckert et al. 1990, 291–293).

Repression

In April 1926 Sunjong, the last Chosun monarch, died. Apparently genuine sorrow combined with hostility toward Japan to produce an outpouring of both grief and anger. Mindful of how the death of Kojong had led to the March First Movement, the colonial police moved to suppress the threatened mass demonstrations, which, however, proceeded in a variety of forms. Student radicalization increased, spreading through the country and culminating in the Gwangju Incident of 1929, in which fighting erupted between Korean and Japanese students, the police blamed the Koreans, and there were mass arrests, followed by further escalations. By early 1930 demonstrations had spread across the country (Lee Ki-baik 1984, 364). The Gwangju Incident led to tightening military rule in 1931. Then with the outbreak of the Sino-Japanese War in 1937 and World War II, Japan attempted the total Japanization of Korea, although the effort was always more frustrated than effective. The Japanese governor-general from 1936 to 1942, General Jiro Minami (1874–1955), ordered cultural assimilation of Korea's twenty-three to twenty-five million people: Korean culture became illegal; worship at Japanese Shinto shrines was made compulsory; and use of the Korean language was progressively banned, as was the study of Korean literature and culture, to be replaced with that of Japan; while the school curriculum was changed to outlaw teaching in the Korean language and to abolish the teaching of history. Koreans were pressured to adopt Japanese names. Korean cultural artifacts were destroyed or taken to Japan. From 1939 onward, education would be aggressively redirected to the task of converting Koreans into useful, Japanese-speaking imperial citizens.

Assimilation efforts became extreme, with total mobilization in 1943; Koreans would be educated as "new Japanese" (Palmer 2007). Lee Ki-baik has described the last, frenetic attempt at assimilation:

> The leading figures in the Korean Language Society were arrested in October 1942, on charge of fomenting a nationalist movement, and as a result of the severe torture to which they were subjected by the Japanese police, Yi Yun-jae and some others among the Korean linguists died in prison. Novelists, poets and other creative writers were forced to produce their works in Japanese, and in the end it was even required that Japanese be exclusively used in the schools and in Korean homes. Not only the study of the Korean language but also of Korean history was considered dangerous. (1984, 353)

Many Koreans were transported to Japan to work in mines and factories as Japanese workers were drafted into the military; women were also put to work, mostly in factories, although increasing numbers were sent with Japan's military as cooks, laundresses, and coerced prostitutes—the "comfort women."[42]

Using Japanese and Korean sources, Brandon Palmer (2013, 3) estimates that from 1937 to 1945 Japanese colonial authorities recruited at least 360,000 Koreans to serve in the military as soldiers or civilian employees, and a further million as industrial laborers within Korea. By the end of World War II, between four and seven million Koreans had been mobilized throughout Japan's wartime empire.[43] Resistance to mobilization manifested within Korea, even more so outside the country. The Shanghai-based Provisional Government formed the Korean Liberation Army in 1940, bringing together many of the Korean resistance groups in exile. On 9 December 1941 the government declared war on Japan and Germany, and the Liberation Army participated in Allied action in China and Southeast Asia. An assault on imperial Japanese forces within Korea was planned; however, with the 1945 Japanese surrender, this goal was never achieved. At war's end, there were vast armies of Koreans who had fought on both sides.

The mobilization era and the question of assimilation

Where assimilation had always underlain colonialist ideology, with various threads running through Government-General policy, mobilization brought it to new levels of enforcement and extremism that seemed to go back to an earlier colonizing experience. Mark Caprio argues that Japan's earlier history of colonial rule, notably of Ainu and Ryukyuan peoples, had tended more toward obliterating those cultures than incorporating those peoples as equal Japanese citizens. With their annexation of Taiwan in 1895, the Japanese moved more toward European models, such as England and France, in developing policies for assimilation.[44] England's assimilation of the Scots and the Welsh is cited. Caprio suggests that there was indeed a potential for Korean assimilation but that very few initiatives were taken to implement the policies. Instead, the Japanese maintained separate communities in Korea with two separate and unequal schooling systems, and very little intermarriage or effort to hide their disdain for Koreans as inferior (Caprio 2009).[45]

Takashi Fujitani (2011) makes the provocative comparison of Korean soldiers recruited or drafted into the Japanese Imperial Army with Japanese Americans similarly recruited into the US military. In the last years of the Pacific War, as Naoki Sakai (2000, 805) observes, referencing Edwin O. Reischauer, Japan and the United States engaged in the ideological war for the hearts and minds of multiethnic Asia.[46] Both, accordingly, were compelled to adopt explicitly antiracist strategies in contradiction to popular perceptions of their histories. The dilemma for Japan was that it needed to project antiracism at precisely the moment when it had to forcibly recruit the Koreans into the effort of total warfare.

In their attempt to disavow racism even as they reproduced it, Japan and America moved closer together (Fujitani 2011). Sakai adds that after 1945, as the United States assumed responsibility for Japan's colonies, Japan was relieved of the burden of decolonization. Korea, on the other hand, was left with the abiding bitterness of experiences of resistance versus collaboration, with its attendant uncertainties of identity.

Part 3

ERASURE OR RADICAL BREAK?

While the concern here is with the effects of the Japanese colonization both at the time of and subsequent to the 1945 liberation, there is always the question: to what extent are we observing the effects of colonization, and to what extent those of modernization? Certainly late Chosun was caught up in that maelstrom of modernity that marked the turn to the twentieth century. Furthermore, in some ways the 1910 declaration of formal colonization was tokenistic, as Japanization had been a gradual process of the preceding decades. The following discussion of modernity-colonization's effects, observing the blurred boundary between Chosun and colony, will be thematic rather than chronological; its purpose is to explore how these effects are to be read off the space and fabric of modern Seoul.

Migration and land

In the late nineteenth century Japanese merchants had settled in Korean towns and cities seeking economic opportunity so that by 1910 Korea was reputed already to have Japan's largest overseas community. Japanese settlers were interested in acquiring agricultural land even before Japanese landownership was legalized in 1906. Terauchi Masatake, as governor-general, advanced settlement through land reform, which was initially popular with the wider Korean population.[47] Hwang Insang observes that colonial economic exploitation and control was symbolized in the Land Survey and the Company Law, with the former serving as the foundation of Japan's colonial rule and the structural basis for economic exploitation of the colonial economy.[48] A new Land Survey Bureau conducted cadastral surveys that established ownership on the basis of documentary evidence (deeds, titles, etc.); ownership was denied to those unable to provide such written proof, and these turned out to be mostly aristocratic and absentee landlords who could only quote traditional rights. Considerable private lands thereby fell into the hands of the Government-General. Additionally, under the Forest Law of August 1911, all government mountain forests came under the Government-General; a Forest Survey Ordinance in 1918 further extended forest areas to Government-General ownership.

As land was increasingly acquired by Japanese individuals and corporations, many Korean erstwhile landowners, together with agricultural workers, became tenant farmers; as often happens in Japan itself, they were forced to pay over half their crop as rent. Then, additionally, they had to pay tax. Landowners were mostly Japanese or Japanese collaborators, while tenants were all Korean. Cumings (1981) reports that in 1942 there were 2,173 Korean and 1,317 Japanese owning more than fifty *chongbo* (approximately 123 acres); the largest of those, holding 500 acres or more, comprised 116 Koreans and 184 Japanese. It is not possible to determine how many of those Korean landowners were enjoying the benefits of collaboration with the government.

By the 1930s the growth of the urban economy and the migration of farmers to the cities had weakened the power of the landlords. With the onset of the wartime economy, realizing that landlordism impeded increased agricultural productivity, the government brought the rural sector under the wartime command economy through a Central Agricultural Association in which membership was obligatory.

At the cataclysmic end of colonization in 1945, some 750,000 Japanese resided in Korea, contrasting with the 20,000 to 30,000 French nationals in Vietnam. Whereas most French in Vietnam were engaged in colonial administration, only 40 percent of the Japanese in Korea were in colonial administration, while the rest were civilians. Japan's aggressive migration policy, however, had Japanese mostly settling in the Korean cities and seizing power in the Korean economy. They lived in their own quarters separate from Koreans and enjoyed a privileged status in education and health services.[49]

Economy

Cyhn Jin (2002) is among scholars who have argued that Japanese rule worsened economic conditions in Korea; Atul Kohli (2004), on the other hand, concludes that the economic development model instituted by the Japanese was crucial in Korean economic development and was maintained by the Koreans post-1945. The latter is a view also supported by Jones (1984) and by Savada and Shaw (1990), who argue that Japan's economic development brought little benefit to Koreans although its aftermath was more positive, a point to be taken up following.

While the core interest remained colonial, namely to exploit Korea's resources, in the 1920s new efficiencies and structural reforms were brought to this enterprise. Furthermore, restrictions on native enterprise were eased, thereby stimulating the emergence of many Korean family-based companies that would later evolve into the giant conglomerates that eventually came to dominate the Korean economy, such as Samsung and LG, a story to be reprised in chapter 3. Kyung Moon Hwang (2010, 165) especially draws attention to the family-owned Kyongsong Textile Company, which eventually branched out into other industries and regions, with factories in Manchuria and elsewhere. Especially influential has been Carter Eckert's account of the same company (chapter 1). Eckert's book had concentrated on a single, remarkably successful Korean family, the Kims of Koch'ang County. The brothers Kim Songsu and Kim Yonsu had profited from a Japanese opening of the rice market between 1876 and 1919, allowing them to accumulate capital, with which the family established the Kyongsong Spinning and Weaving Company, or Kyongbang, in 1919 for the production of yarn and cloth. From 1919 to 1945 Kyongsong grew substantially, a success that Eckert attributes in part to Japanese colonial control, as well as to government subsidies and loans and to Japanese-enabled access to raw materials (cotton from China), machinery and expertise (from Japan), and markets (initially China, later the Japanese military for uniforms). He further notes that Kyongsong provided support to the Japanese ideology of Naisen Ittai ("Japan and Korea as one"), reflecting only a weak commitment to Korean nationalism generally on the part of the Korean bourgeoisie. The group continued to prosper after 1945 and into the present.

In this era Korea acquired an industrial capitalist class whose interests were in harmony with Japanese imperial goals and that accordingly enjoyed colonialist support. Correspondingly there also arose an industrial proletariat, albeit minute alongside the larger, agricultural population; however, this was a very low-wage proletariat, without legal or political protection. By the 1920s there was also a developing proletarian sensibility within the (Marxist) intelligentsia movement of New Tendency literature (Kimberley Chung 2014).

Industrialization and the burgeoning of Korean enterprises brought a reordering of the social structure, not least through a dramatic rise in social mobility. Especially dramatic were changes in the status of women: increasing numbers moved into education and far more into factory employment. With the advent of the "new woman" or "modern girl," new opportunities arose for new enterprises to produce the commodities and publications that a proto-bourgeoisie could be encouraged to demand. The publications, in turn, provided the media for women's voices to now be heard. Increasing numbers of Koreans traveled to Japan for education, returning to Korea awakened by the liberty and "style" of a culturally advanced middle class that would then be emulated, albeit in the cities rather than the countryside, and then mostly in Seoul.

Henry H. Em begins *The Great Enterprise: Sovereignty and Histo-riography in Modern Korea* with a reference to an essay of September 1932 in *Tongkwang* by Kim Ki-rim, announcing 1930s modernity as the era of short hair and calling on "Miss Korea" to cut her hair—the essay had argued that modernity would not be identified by "sport, speed, sex," but by short hair, and "women of status venturing outside in daytime unconstrained by marriage and motherhood. Indeed by the 1930s one could have seen in colonial Korea baseball games, beauty pageants, exhibitions, display windows fronting the new department stores, street cars, street lights, and cafés that enabled crowd watching" (Em, 2013, 1). Being modern was not easy. Some Korean women con-formed to the dictates of colonial modernity; others, however, took deliberate pains to distinguish between what was "modern" (Western) and thereby legitimate and what was "Japanese," hence illegitimate. Yoo (2008) suggests that what made the experience of these women unique was the dual confrontation with modernity and with Japan as a colonial power.

Diverse aspects of economic change related to new infrastructure. There was massive investment by the colonial government in com-munications and transportation infrastructure, schools and technical training centers, hospitals and other health initiatives—all, certainly, catering to the Japanese migrant population to assist the colonization process yet also improving the welfare of many Koreans. This might be seen as merely a continuation of innovatory programs under the old Daehan Empire whereby Seoul had acquired railways, trams, electric-ity, hospitals, industrialized mining, and other hallmarks of a modern city, except that these had been implemented when Korea was already coming under the Japanese sway.[50] Furthermore, it was the accelera-tion and scaling up of these that distinguished the colonial era.

The experience of rapid industrialization and modern infrastruc-ture under the Japanese, in both Korea and Manchuria, is seen to have had long-lasting effects. Cha Myung Soo (2010) has argued that "the South Korean developmental state, as symbolized by Park Chung-hee, a former officer of the Japanese Imperial Army serving in wartime Manchuria, was closely modeled upon the colonial system of gov-ernment. In short, South Korea grew on the shoulders of the colonial achievement, rather than emerging out of the ashes left by the Korean War, as is sometimes asserted." We return to this theme in chapter 3.

Education

The long lineage of the Korean educational tradition has already been referred to—Lee Ki-baik (1984, 119, 130) can allude to the struggles in the Goryeo (Koryo) age between the National University (founded in 992, in Gaeseong) and the more prestigious twelve private academies. The tradition had then been enriched over the centuries through Buddhist and Confucian insertions.[51] The colonial imposition thus came on top of something very ancient, albeit privilege-focused, but also quintessentially Korean. The Japanese in Korea produced a public education system modeled after the Japanese school system, with elementary, middle schools, and high schools culminating in Keijo Imperial University (1924–1946) in Seoul. The university was closed by the US military on 22 August 1946 and subsequently merged with nine other colleges to form Seoul National University. As in Japan, education was seen primarily as an instrument of "the formation of the Imperial Citizen." The public curriculum for most of the period was taught by Korean teachers in a hybrid system focused on assimilating Koreans into the Japanese Empire as well as emphasizing Korean cultural education. Integration of Korean students in Japanese-language schools and Japanese students in Korean-language schools was discouraged but nevertheless increased over time. Korean history and language would be taught alongside Japanese history and language until the early 1940s.

In 1921 there were government efforts to strengthen Korean media and literature throughout Korea but also in Japan. There were incentives for ethnic Japanese to learn Korean, although this may have been as much to garner Japanese cultural acceptance as to foster cooperation between Koreans and Japanese. Japanese policy moved more aggressively toward cultural assimilation in 1938 (Naisen Ittai, "Japan and Korea as one"), with reform advocated to strengthen the war effort. By 1943 all Korean language courses had been phased out.

Although the Japanese education system may have been detrimental to Korean cultural identity, its introduction of universal public education was instrumental in the improvement of Korean human capital: near the end of Japanese rule, elementary school attendance was around 38 percent. The system produced hundreds of thousands of educated Koreans who later became "the core of the postwar political and economic elite" (Duus et al. 1996, 336). Against that assessment is the reality that adult literacy was around 22 percent in 1945; in 1970, by contrast, it had reached 87.6 percent.

Park Chan Seung (2010) argues that colonial Korea developed as a dualistic society. The main lines of differentiation were between an upper class, mostly Japanese but also comprising small numbers of Koreans, and a great majority of Koreans with a relatively few Japanese. In other words, the divide became multilayered, as much economic as ethnic.

Transgressions, erasures, architecture

While debate persists among historians about the benefits or disbene-
fits of land reform, educational development, and economic modernization, one finds few mentions of the colonial government's actions to
conserve elements of Korean culture. Instead the emphasis is on Japanese acts of destruction of Korean heritage and identity. Some of this
conservation effort was to attract tourism, yet there were also real
attempts to promote aspects of Korean culture; Korean studies were a
significant focus in Japanese scholarship, and there were committed
Koreaphiles even among the Japanese administrators. The remnant
royal family was especially used in the conservation of traditional
Korean culture and was allocated a colonial government budget for
that purpose; cultural organizations were similarly funded.

Nevertheless it is the erasures and cultural distortions of the colonial society that have especially preoccupied postcolonial commen-
tators and popular media. K. Itoi (2005) asserts that the Japanese
destroyed an estimated 80 percent of the historic shrines, palaces,
and cultural monuments of Korea; however, no sources are given for
this somewhat arbitrary and seemingly exaggerated claim.[52] Certainly
there was heavy-handedness; there was also pillaging, with tens of
thousands of cultural artifacts removed to Japan.

On what had been the grand Gyeongbokgung Palace forecourt the
Japanese built their own multistory, domed, administrative headquarters, the Government-General Building, oriented to the north-south
axis of Taepyeongno (Taihei Boulevard in the Japanese era) but at an
angle to the remnants of the palace. Gyeongbokgung Palace had been
destroyed in 1592 during the (Japanese) Hideyoshi invasion, whereupon
the royal family and the court moved to the second or Changdeokgung
Palace, which, with the third or Changgyeonggung Palace and the
Jongmyo ancestral shrine constituted a vast integrated realm termed
the "East Palace" complex (Korean Institute of Architects 2000, 56–63).
The main Gyeongbokgung Palace had been rebuilt in 1867, and stood
until its destruction ("deformation") again along with much of the city
following the Japanese infiltration and then annexation in 1910. It had
been mostly abandoned in the late nineteenth century with Kojong's
removal to Deoksugung Palace and, while its destruction by the colonial government had the effect of erasing the centrality of the monarchy, many of the removed buildings were demolished and reerected at
Changdeokgung Palace with the agreement of the royal family.

Kal Hong (2011, 16–31) and Todd Henry (2014, 92–129) have
recounted the story of the 1915 Korean Industrial Exposition, constructed in the Gyeongbokgung Palace precinct, in part to extol the

benefits of colonization and in part to open up the previously "forbidden" palace to the wider public, and thereby to erode the mystery and authority of the Chosun dynasty.[53] The visitor entering through the ceremonial Kwanghwamun Gate would abruptly confront the monumental Ilhogwan (First Exhibition Hall) in a "Renaissance plus Secession style" immediately in front of the main throne hall, blocking the view to what had been the symbolic landmark of the Chosun dynasty. Then, for the 1929 Korean Exposition, the old palace buildings had been effectively cleared from the site; the exhibition complex was behind the recently completed Government-General Building, and the main axis of the exposition had accordingly been turned from south-to-north to east-to-west (Kal Hong 2011, 32–43). Visitors would enter from the east, through the now relocated Kwanghwamun Gate, which had been moved from its previous axial position, effectively to provide an unimpeded view to the Government-General Building. Whereas the earlier exposition dated from the more militaristic first decade of colonization, that of 1929 was in the more liberal era of the 1920s; accordingly, Kal reports, the latter celebrated progress under the Japanese guidance but also images of "Korean local culture," "Korean atmosphere" and "Korean uniqueness."[54] However, it was a Koreanness achieved by some fake "ancient" buildings, ironically replacing the real palace buildings demolished to make way for them.

In any consideration of the Government-General Building, one needs to take a step back. In 1912 there had been a city ward improvement plan that clearly indicated the colonial government's early ideas for their transformation of the city: the colonial headquarters building would be located between the Gyeongbokgung and Changdeokgung Palaces, from which axial and diagonal boulevards would radiate to the south, southeast, and southwest, with the rest of the city also organized on Beaux Arts principles. By the time of the 1919 city ward improvement plan, the decision had been made to place the Government-General headquarters (completed in 1926) in front of Gyeongbokgung Palace; likewise the radiating boulevards would also now focus on that site. Subsequently Beaux Arts planning ideas were abandoned and the principal streets of the historical city accepted, although they were to be straightened and widened (Jung Inha 2013, 10–11). So Beaux Arts ideas displayed in the 1929 Korean Exposition expressed a goal already under threat.[55]

The Government-General Building was designed by German architect George de Lalande. After his death in 1914, planning was taken over by Ichiro Nomura, architect of the equally grand Japanese Government-General Building in Taiwan. The building was ceremoniously dedicated on the auspiciously selected date of 1 October 1926.

Its neo-Renaissance and Art Deco hybrid styling was that favored for the greatest symbols of empire, set initially in the seminal Tokyo Station of 1898–1914, of which more below.[56]

Todd Henry notes a critique of the Government-General Building as "an instance of geomantic rape" (Kim Song-nyae 2000, in Henry 2014, 266n49). Henry begins his account of Keijo (Seoul) with reference to the Government-General's other "most auspicious" intrusion into the spiritual landscape of the city: "In the fall of 1925, after nearly fifteen years of planning and over five years of construction, the Government-General, the colonial state that had ruled over Korea since its annexation by Japan in 1910, unveiled an imposing Shinto shrine atop Namsan. . . . Namsan was quickly becoming the geographic centre of a growing metropolis known in Japanese as Keijo (Kyongsong [Keongseong]; present-day Seoul), the empire's showcase city on the peninsula" (Henry 2014, 1). With the completion of the Government-General Building in the old Gyeongbokgung Palace grounds and the construction of the grandiose Taep'yongno (Taihei Boulevard), now extended south from Jongno, Korea Shrine and the Government-General monument could be read as the two anchoring poles of both city and colony—the spiritual and the political.[57] The Taihei axis further connected with the (Japanese) City Hall as civic focus, then, turning southwest around Namdaemun, most auspicious of the old city's gateways, it continued to the new (Japanese) Seoul Station as symbol of (Japanese) modernity. More on this anon, especially its geomantic violence.

Choson Jingu (Korea Shrine) was in the *shinmei-zukuri* style of Ise Jingu, the holiest of all Shinto shrines, which honored two deities: Amaterasu, the mythical ancestress of the Japanese state, and Emperor Meiji, Japan's first modern monarch. The shrine thereby symbolized an unbroken imperial line. Henry goes on to quote a mystified Japanese proponent of Shinto who noted that Japanese would approach the shrine with reverence and prayerfully, whereas Koreans would do so merely with curiosity, just "looking around," and asks, "What is the cause of this? Will Korea Shrine end up being a shrine only for the Japanese?"[58] The focus of Henry's book is on the spaces of colonial Seoul as "contact zones," revealing the intersections of Korean and Japanese lives in the city, and thereby of their histories. The ambiguities of these intersections were represented in the architecture of colonialism.

New architecture

The incremental Japanese intrusion had been economic as well as military and ideological. The Korean government initiated a very active reform movement in 1894–1995 with Japanese tolerance, including a program of state capitalism and the initiation of a modern banking system.[59] Japan's increasing financial influence and the inflow of Japanese capital was met with efforts from the Chosun government to assimilate modern banking. The Daehan Cheon-il Bank was established in 1899 with the support of King Kojong, in the hope of protecting Korea's national capital assets against the growing influence of the Japanese banks over Korea's finances. The bank's head office, the Gwangtonggwan on Namdaemunno, was designed by the Architectural Bureau of the Takjibu, the Ministry of Finance of the Daehan Empire, as one of the few Western-style buildings of Korea in that era.

A fire badly damaged the Gwangtonggwan in February 1914, and the building's detail was much altered when it was restored and reopened in 1915—in the Japanese era. It had been built mostly of red brick and granite, in a Neoclassical style, and on a symmetrical plan. Originally it had had Ionic pilasters, but after the fire the Ionic capitals were replaced by a hybrid Baroque–Art Nouveau form as the building took on the eclectic styling favored by the Japanese (figure 2.2). The restyling may have served a quite specific purpose: by making what was by then the Joseon Sangup Bank neo-Baroque, it was identified with the grander Bank of Chosun designed in 1907 for the Japanese Dai-Ichi Bank and completed in 1912 as the central bank for Korea during the Japanese colonization.[60] As was common in the Japanese colonial empire, it was in an eclectic, hybidized style, although with strong references to the French Renaissance. Seoul was to be architecturally Japanese, to signal the new identity of its institutions (figure 2.3).

Another notable building of the last years of old Korea is the Daehan Hospital, one of Seoul's most beautiful buildings. It was built in 1907 to house three merging medical centers, on a hilltop outer garden of Changgyeonggung Palace, with the Takjibu Architectural Bureau again responsible. The architect, however, was a Japanese employed by the Takjibu, and the building's styling, not surprisingly, was typically Japanese-imperial neo-Baroque from the outset. The very large building of the former National Industry Institute of 1908 was also from the Takjibu and designed by a Japanese architect, this time in a German-Renaissance style and built entirely of wood. Though formally established by the Agriculture, Industry, and Trade Ministry of the Daehan Empire, it was more an initiative of the Residency-General and reflected Japanese policy. It was Korea's highest institute of industrial education, with six departments, again reflecting Japanese policy: architecture, civil engineering, applied chemistry, metallurgy, dyeing, and ceramics. These hospital and institute buildings, and subsequently

FIGURE 2.2 Gwangtonggwan, 1909, restyled in the Japanese manner after the fire of 1915.

Keijo Imperial University, are gathered together in the Daehangno area of the East Palace complex.

In the last years of Chosun there were also significant religious buildings in Western revivalist styles. The Chungdong First Methodist Church from 1897 is now Korea's oldest existing Protestant church. It and the nearby Pai Chai Hak Dang, Korea's first modern intermediate school from 1885, were both founded by American missionaries and are in decidedly American styles. They are in the old legation quarter of Jeong-dong around Deoksugung Palace.[61] Arguably the finest building from that genre of Western religious buildings is the Gothic Revival, Catholic Myeong-dong Cathedral. Completed in 1898, it was designed by French missionary priests, most notably Eugene Coste, but built by Chinese bricklayers using local red and black brick and with vaulted ceilings. The consequence is a curiously hybrid building: despite the French medieval styling, the smooth and precise brick surfaces are distinctively Chinese. The Myeong-dong Cathedral played a significant role in the 1980s dictatorship era as a refuge for demonstrators; it continues to serves as a locale for protesters for various causes (Clark 2007, 182).

Using the same fine brickwork and also in a Gothic Revival style from the same designer as Myeong-dong Cathedral is Yakhyeon Church, founded in 1892 and the oldest Catholic church in Korea (the

FIGURE 2.3 The Japanese colonial style in Seoul: the Japanese Bank of Chosun Building, completed 1912, later the head office of the Bank of Korea (architect Tatsuno Kingo).

last bloody pogrom against Catholics had been as recent as 1866);[62] close by is Seosomun Park. Seosomun Gate area is located outside Seomun Gate, which served as an execution ground for the Chosun persecutions of Catholics, where forty-four Catholic Korean martyrs are buried.[63]

The Romanesque-style Anglican Cathedral is from 1926, though it was completed only in 1996. It was designed by English architect Arthur Stansfield Dixon. There are also Anglican and Catholic cathedrals in Incheon (from 1891 and 1897, respectively), again in imported Western styles. These and many other churches mark both the increasing Christian penetration into late Chosun and Japanese Korea, and the increasing presence of other architectural traditions.

Altogether more purposely hybrid is the Cheondogyo Central Temple, dating from 1921. Cheondogyo had produced many independence activists, including a large number of the leaders of the March First (1919) uprising, as noted above. The temple building, coming fast on the suppression of that movement and designed by Japanese architect Nakamura Yosihei, suggests something of the subsequent conciliatory policy of the Japanese. Its architecture would be classified as an eclectic amalgam of Art Deco and Art Nouveau, and decidedly internationalist.[64]

It is the railway system that most directly explains the architectural colonization. For Japan, the railway was central to both the imagining and the functioning of their empire, providing its connecting armature.

In Korea, a new era began in 1899 with the opening of the Kyeongin railway linking Seoul and Incheon, the forerunner of the present subway Line 1; Yongsan Station opened in 1900 and then Namdaemun Station. Yongsan Station was reconstructed in 1906 and was what the Japanese believed to be one of the finest architectural works in Korea. It was destroyed in the Korean War. Then in 1925 the Japanese built Seoul Station, replacing the earlier Namdaemun Station, in the same style as that of Tokyo—the new technologies of communication were to be the symbol of both the unity and the modernity of the empire (Coaldrake 1996, 227–230). The material effect of the railway system was to open Korea to regional and, ultimately, more global trade.

Tokyo Station had been designed by Tatsuno Kingo as the preeminent Meiji emblem of Westernization. It faced Imperial Palace along a nine-hundred-meter avenue and, in turn, connected via rail and ferry to Pusan (Busan) Station in Korea, also designed by Tatsuno. That station then connected by rail to Seoul Station, in the same eclectic style and designed by Tsukamoto Yasushi of Tokyo Imperial University; it, in turn, lies at the southern end of the Taepyeongno (Taihei Boulevard) north-south axis that was extended southward in the Japanese modernization of the city's street network, and thereby linked to the Government-General Building at the northern end of the newly opened axis. As the governor-general faced the emperor via the new technologies of communication, the integrity of the empire was symbolized in the emblems of Westernization. In Seoul, Tatsuno Kingo is best represented by the old Chosun Bank Building of 1912, referred to above.

Seoul Station met yet another agenda. It and its accompanying rail links were built so that the Japanese could use the Seoul-Uiju and Seoul-Wonsan lines in their projected invasion of China.[65] In the late 1990s Seoul Station defied photography: a highway access ramp cut diagonally across its façade, as if to "strike it out." It presented the ultimate symbol of Korean erasure of the Japanese memory. In the 2000s the ramp was removed, the forecourt redeveloped according to prevailing urban design principles, and the station restored (figure 2.4). It now functions as a fine exhibition space (of which more in chapter 3).

Both Seoul Station and the Government-General Building were central to the way the Japanese would represent their colonial capital. The size of the latter was exceptional, exceeding anything of the British in India or the Dutch in the Indies. Its significance, however, lay in far more than its style and its size. The cardinal principles of Korean architecture, as articulated by the modern nation's most respected architect, Kim Swoo Geun (1931–1986), are (1) harmony with the natural setting, (2) love of simplicity and plainness, (3) moderate and elegant

FIGURE 2.4 Seoul Station, completed 1925 (architect Tsukamoto Yasushi).

line (especially at the roof), and (4) human scale.[66] The Government-General Building transgressed all four of these principles. As Lee Man-hoon (1995) notes, some forty-eight structures within the palace complex were demolished:[67] "Among reasons for the Japanese to build the colonial government building in front of Kyŏngbokkung [*sic*] was a theory that they wanted to crush the national spirit of the Korean people by interfering with the geomantic layout of the Chosŏn [*sic*] capital, which was centered around the palace. By blocking powerful natural forces which emanate from the palace site located between Mts Pugaksan and Namsan, the Japanese hoped to make Korea their eternal servant" (1995, 80).

The past was to be disregarded, its memory thereby reduced to the insignificant. Worse, the plan form of the Government-General Building—a double square—matched the (Chinese) character (*il*) that is the first part of the word "Japan" (Ilbon, Nippon) (Jane Song n.d., 45).[68] However, when this was combined with those characters described by Pugaksan and the (Japanese built) Keongseong (Capital City) City Hall, the effect was to signify Great Japan.[69] The city itself would proclaim the new nationality. A new geomancy would prevail: by removing the previous Kwanghwamun Gate—eternal separation of hidden, mysterious, royal power from a baser world—and by linking Government-General, city government, and railway, the newly constructed north-south avenue "made the imperial power visible in the urban space" (Kal Hong 2011, 48). One returns to Kim Song-nyae's (2000) condemnation of the Government-General Building as "an instance of geomantic rape." There was yet further violence: the Japanese cut a second major east-west road (Yulgongno), roughly parallel to Jongno and across the front of their Government-General Building (and thereby across any memory of the old palace), and—final outrage—cutting through the East Palace complex.[70] However, it was even more brutal than a simple cut, for surviving members of the royal family still resided in the East Palace, and the effect of the bisection was to isolate the royal family in Changgyeonggung Palace, now to the north of the intruding road, from their ancestors in the Jongmyo Shrine to the south. The effect of the strategy was to reverse auspicious emblems of the Korean geomantic system, violating the symbolic landscape and destroying its power (Choi Chungmoo 1997a). As Ryu Jeh-hong (2004, 19), citing Choi Chungmoo (2002), summarizes the strategy, "The Japanese colonial regime made reverse use of several Korean cultural symbols of the geomantic system, destroying auspicious sites where influences on good fortune converged, thereby violating the sexual topography." Todd Henry (2014, 29) refers to a "re-spatialising" of Keijo (Hanyang, Seoul), in part to desacralize the Korean royal house; the royal residence would be relocated while the previous palaces would be opened as public parks, the old sense of mystery and the sacred thereby transgressed. An unanswered question is to what extent these violations were real and intended, real but unintended, or constructed in later memory to be propagated as motivation to anti-Japanese sentiment. The answer will shift with the historiography of the moment. It suffices to observe the hyperbole that characterizes, seemingly universally, Koreans' responses to the reordering of the city's symbolic landscape.

Modernizing Japanese Seoul

While Japan's annexation of Korea was with the alleged "consent" of the Korean emperor and his government,[71] there was suppression of diverse Korean institutions and cultural expressions. It was always an ambivalent suppression, however: the Chosun dynasty had for five hundred years suppressed Buddhism in favor of their own strict Confucianism; as noted above, Buddhism had retreated to the rural communities ("Mountain Buddhism"), and monks were forbidden entry to the city. In 1895 the Japanese effected an end to the policy, and Buddhism became free—but Japanized. Japanese officials and businessmen coming to Korea brought their own forms of Buddhism with them. Although Mahayana Buddhism had originally traveled to Japan via Korea, in the sixth century CE, within Japan it had diversified into a variety of sects able to accommodate the relative diversity of Japanese culture—some sects even permitted monks to marry and have families, and the Japanese encouraged the Koreans to follow suit. The consequence was bitter division between the Chogye order, which maintained celibacy, and the T'aego order, whose priests married. Korean Buddhism was also affected by a Western missionary emphasis on a rationalist paradigm in religious discourse and then, following the anti-Japanese March First Movement, it became increasingly nationalistic—Japanized and nationalist (Cho Sungtaek 2005).

By the 1930s the Japanese were using architecture to signify the empire as modernizing and globalizing, as it had previously been mobilized to signify unity and integration. An early example of this more austere, modernist style was presented in the 1926 Dong-A Ilbo press building (figure 2.5), as well as in the 1931 Main Hall of Keijo Imperial University designed by Park Gil-ryong, one of Korea's first modern architects (Park had also been the architect for the iconic Hwasin Department Store on Jongno).[72] A further example of the modernist style is the grand Art Deco building on Taepyeongno from 1935, built by the Japanese as the "center for citizens," later the National Assembly hall, then subsequently the Seoul City Assembly Building, albeit more "internationalist" than Japanese (figure 2.6). Equally "international" was the 1938 Seoul office of Mitsui and Company.[73]

Seoul planning

Kang Sukhi (b. 1934) writes of "the pre-modern customs that maintained the traditional style of living" that he recalls from his childhood in Seoul of the 1930s, the formative years for a later, innovative avant-garde.[74] Ordinary life went on. Some elements in Korean society resisted the Japanese infiltration, others collaborated, but most simply adjusted to the new realities.

FIGURE 2.5 The Dong-A Ilbo, completed 1926, the oldest press building in Korea—popularly claimed as an example of early Korean modernism.

FIGURE 2.6 The Citizens' Center, completed 1935, subsequently the National Assembly, now the Seoul City Assembly.

"Pre-modern customs" may have survived in Japanese Seoul, as Kang perceived; however, the survival was in the face of an agenda of modernization at the hands of the colonial government, although, as outlined above in relation to land reform, education, hospitals, economy, public institutions, and their architecture, it was a modernization that was already in motion in the 1890s and 1900s. The first manifestation of modern city planning came in 1897 with the construction of Tapgol (Pagoda) Park as a response to Western ideals of creating parks for the health and moral improvement of citizens, albeit the elite citizens in this case. Many common citizens had their homes razed in the process of its land clearance.[75] Even before the first railway, linking Seoul and Incheon, the first electric tramway opened on 1 May 1899: the first tram departed Jongno for Cheongnyangni to the east of Dongdaemun Gate on 17 May, amid great pomp and celebration.[76] There were nine carriages of which one was reserved for King Kojong, who used it to visit the tomb of his wife Queen Min, recently murdered by Japanese-sponsored assassins. The tram drivers and conductors were Japanese, until, on 26 May, a traffic accident involving a tram led to an anti-Japanese riot, a subsequent standoff, the departure of the Japanese drivers, and hence closure of the system until American tram drivers could be imported several months later.

The tramway was initiated by two American businessmen, Henry Collbran and Harry Bostwick.[77] In return for the right to establish a tram service in the city, they were required to install electric lighting in downtown Seoul.[78] In 1909 Collbran was forced to sell his company to the Japanese, who by then had established a virtual stranglehold on the Korean economy. The Japanese were equally as committed to tramways as to railways, although the rationales were different, and the network continued to grow. In 1910 Seoul had 37 tramcars, and by 1935 there were 154.

Hon-machi (Ch'ungmuro in the present Myeong-dong area) had been the historic center of the Japanese settler community, with Yongsan rapidly developing further south as Seoul's boomtown and new home to the Japanese military, the railway, and a growing settler population.[79] Where the settler region of the city, the "southern village," received government investment in infrastructure and urban improvement, the "northern village" of the Koreans languished. Although the division was stark—indeed a "divided topography"—Henry (2014, 236n26) cites Namiki Naoto (1997) to the effect that there were increasing instances of ethnic mixing in both villages during the colonial period, suggesting that the division calls for a decidedly nuanced reading.[80]

The railway and the Japanese town of Yongsan marked the real breakout of Seoul from its old walled confines. In 1914 the first formal expansion of the city boundaries occurred and the city walls began to lose both their symbolic and their functional significance. Tramways were developed from Gyeongbokgung Palace, now the site of the colonial administration, along the north-south axis of Taepyeongno, past the City Hall, farther along the axis that the Japanese had now extended through the old city, through Namdaemun (South Gate), past the new Seoul Station, and finally to Yongsan and a new road along the Han River, which was bridged in 1917, to connect Yongsan to the burgeoning commercial area of Mapo (Henry 2014, 34).

The bridge and road from Yongsan led to Yeouido, an island in the Han River and locale for the Japanese aerodrome, and ultimately to the industrial center of Incheon. The old internal road structure of the city that had endured for five centuries was suddenly replaced with that of a modern city: the main thoroughfares were widened and new roads built in a program termed "the ordering of streets," which was effectively code for establishing economic, social, and military control over the city (Gelézeau 1997, 74).[81]

Between 1910 and 1926, the New Keongseong (Seoul) Program and Project for the Modification of the Districts brought changes partly linked to the imposition of road widening and straightening. The first urban planning ordinance had been promulgated in 1914 and, in a second expansion of the city boundaries, Yeongdeungpo (Yeouido) was the first area south of the Han to become officially part of Seoul (Korean Institute of Architects 2000, 22). A 1926 city plan proposed expansion of the historic city eastward and westward, to accommodate the influx of poor Koreans from the countryside; however, as the Japanese population was expanding southward to the booming Yongsan, the effect of the plan would be to reinforce ethnic segregation, thereby making it easier to favor the latter in the provision of urban services.[82] The plan would also strengthen the connection between Seoul (via Yongsan) and Incheon, to the commercial benefit of the Japanese community. A further plan was published in 1928, notable for its advocacy of "land readjustment"; neither plan received significant government support.[83] Another plan was proposed in 1930, and there followed a Town Planning Act in 1934.[84] A program of residential, commercial, and industrial zoning was introduced, dividing the city into functional areas according to prevailing wisdom adopted from the West. Land readjustment was again introduced, and historic districts were to be razed; however, the only readjustments seem to have been in the suburbs.

Meanwhile Jung-gu, the old center of Chosun Seoul, continued as the commercial center of the expanding city; within Jung-gu, Jongno became the center of political control under the Japanese but also a focus of what little Korean entrepreneurial activity survived. Yongsan was the military zone while the city's expansion was mostly to the south, beyond Yongsan.

Survival

There is another side to the coin of Japan and its late-colonial Korean "assimilation" and suppression. It is expressed in a tribute from Korean composer Kang Sukhi to his friend, fellow composer and foundational video artist Paik Nam June, whom we shall meet in chapter 5 (Kang Sukhi 2007). Kang sets out to depict the Seoul of the 1930s, the era of both his and Paik's childhood—they were born in 1934 and 1932, respectively.

Despite the Japanese imposition of Shinto and emperor worship, Korean traditional culture persisted, based in the continuing fusing of Buddhism (albeit simultaneously indigenous and Japanized), Confucianism, and shamanism. In Kang's memory, it was in shamanism that everyday customs were most firmly grounded. Scenes from previous centuries seemed to persist:

> Seoul in the 1930s preserved the premodern customs that maintained the traditional style of living. Although tramcars were running along the streets in the city center, there were boats from the

West Sea carrying smelly pickled shrimps in Mapo. Women dressed in white, with their hair in chignons, could be seen washing clothes in Cheonggyecheon stream, which flowed through the centre of Seoul; well-dressed women with their faces hidden under long hoods; chimney-sweepers passing through narrow alleys striking gongs; men clad in white overcoats and gat, the traditional cylindrical hat, with long beards and outstretched smoking pipes between their lips; . . . the procession of funeral biers heading from Jongno. . . . Dozens of strips of funeral odes flapping from the bier procession. (Kang Sukhi 2007)

Kang describes the tramway and Dongdaemun Market, "where every kind of foodstuff was available and drapers were selling silk fabric by the roadside." He recalls the tallest building on Jongno, Hwasin Department Store, a six-story building with Seoul's only elevator and escalator. Hwasin Department Store of 1937 was designed by "the first Korean architect," Park Gil-yong, backed by one of the few Korean entrepreneurs, Park Heung Shik (Korean Institute of Architects 2000, 72).[85] Kang also remembered old palaces and shrines; however, there was also the Japanese Government-General Building: "Jungangcheong stood in front of the old palace blocking its view, so passers-by sometimes cursed it, saying, 'Damn Japanese, blocking the view of our palace, where our king used to rule the country, with their colonial government building'" (Kang Sukhi 2007). There were also school excursions on a boat across the Han River to its still-rural opposite bank for picnics: "[T]hey took a boat across the river and had a wonderful time." There was oppression, insurrection, but also a measure of cultural survival, of everyday life and fun. Suppression was never complete; indeed it could, in a later age, have had the countereffect of nurturing nostalgia and the (re)imagining of a never-lost identity. Lee Hoon, writing in 1936, could observe that Seoul was also quiet, indeed somnolent, a backwater, at a standstill. It lacked the vigor and bustle of a Western trading city or of Shanghai or Tokyo. It was merely an administrative center (Lee Hoon K. 1936, 195, in Cumings 2005, 162). Also rich in reminiscences of late colonial Seoul are the accounts from some fifty elderly Koreans in Hildi Kang's (2005) *Under the Black Umbrella: Voices from Colonial Korea, 1910–1945.* Most people, Hildi Kang says, have read or heard only the horror stories, which, though true, tell only a fragment of the truth of colonial life. There is also a truth that is more ambiguous and more human, of the small-scale realities of life in colonial Korea.[86] Park Wan-suh, who was born in 1931 in a small village near Kaesong, in her autobiographical novel *Who Ate Up All the Shinga?* (2009) recounts a childhood in which the whole world was Korea and everyone in it was Korean. Yet slowly, in her remote world, the tendrils of a darker nature began to insinuate themselves—there were Japanese, an iron-grip suppression, and war. Her account describes the hardships of everyday life.[87]

In a similar vein, Kyung Moon Hwang (2010, 179–182) has noted that cultural production in the late colonial era also focused on this life of the everyday.[88] The first outpouring of "new literature" was in the 1930s, from novelists who had often graduated from newspaper reporting, and their writings, correspondingly, were mostly of "ordinary life," whether mundane or tragic. Furthermore, these were ordinary lives in the interstices of tradition (memories, often a sense of nostalgia, loss) and a new modernity. So there was Ch'ae Man-Sik, whose masterpiece was the novel *Peace Under Heaven* and whose short stories critiqued the disrupting whirlwind of modernization on everyday life, as well as the extraordinary impact of new education and its dislocation of lives (Ch'ae Man-Sik 1993; also Kim Chong-un and Fulton 1998). Pak Tae-won wrote *A Day in the Life of Novelist Kubo,* serialized in 1934, as a plotless, Joycean meander through the streets and places of Seoul—the coffeehouses, restaurants, and theaters of the 1930s, as well as the grandest of new modernist symbols, the department stores.[89] The splendid Seoul Station is seen as a place of people waiting, together yet isolated, lonely individuals (Walsh 2011; Hanscom 2013).[90] The Korean Artists Proletarian Federation (KAPF), founded in 1925, rallied authors to the struggles of everyday life but also to the themes of class consciousness and Marxist critique (Kimberly Chung 2014).[91] Typical here was Yi Kiyong, whose novel *Hometown* was serialized in the *Chosun Ilbo* newspaper in 1933 to 1934. Yi focused on villagers and their struggles to adjust to the exploitative social relationships of early capitalism. Again the theme was everyday life in the face of modernization rather than colonization. Kyung Moon Hwang (2010, 181) sees Yi's novel as emerging from a melodramatic imagination; we will observe in chapter 5 that the transit from a melodramatic to an ironic imagination marks the rise of Hallyu, the Korean Wave, in the 2000s.

There were other everyday lives lived in Korea whose imagination and sense of identity would have been very different from those depicted in the Korean literature of the time. Jun Uchida (2011a) refers to the thousands of Japanese civilians, merchants, traders, prostitutes, journalists, teachers, and adventurers who left for a new life on the Korean Peninsula. Though forming one of the largest colonial communities in the twentieth century, these settlers and their empire-building activities have all but vanished from the public memory of Japan's presence in Korea. They were "interstitial"—their leaders played multiple roles, between the settler community and the Government-General, between Japanese colonizer and Korean colonized, between colony and metropole. Their stories were swept away in the Japan phobia that followed 15 August 1945.

Part 4

THE PROBLEM OF HISTORIOGRAPHY

We return to the question of disputed historiography introduced in chapter 1. While old memories and practices survived, there was also a real speeding up of the embrace of modernity, and a loss of old culture and its heritage. The extreme anti-Japanese sentiment that erupted post-1945, and that in many aspects persists into the present, is ample proof of a sense of destruction of national identity and its *lieux de mémoire,* sites of memory. To what extent, however, was this extinction real (having actually happened), perceptual (residing more in the constructed memories of Koreans, perhaps as a product of propaganda), or historiographical (existing in the contested depictions of events and the recountings of memories)? Then, to the extent to which it might have been real, how much was it intended, and how much more contingent on other agendas?

"Real" erasure

The modern chronicles of the Japanese intrusion into Korea, of the compelled "agreements" of 1904 and 1907 and then the formal annexation of 1910, mostly agree in their portrayal of imperialist aggression and, thereby, the attempted extinction—or at least assimilation— of the actuality of a Korean nation. Similarly there is reasonable consistency in accounts of the 1910s as a decade of suppression and insensitivity—the media suppression and the heavy-handed treatment of the palaces serving as instances. The 1920s and early 1930s are not so easily judged; the disruptions would seem more those of modernity's onslaught, albeit speeded up by the "enabling violation" (Spivak 1996) of colonialism. Here there was still a sense of some continuity with the incipient modernity of late Chosun. With the 1937 mobilization and then the 1942 enforced assimilation, erasure must be seen as increasingly intended.

The 1910 annexation had presented a dilemma for the Japanese, as the Koreans were now "inside" the vastly expanded, "greater" Japan, yet it was not an unfamiliar dilemma. The Japanese Empire was in its Meiji form an assimilating state, in policy if not consistently in practice: local cultures such as the Okinawans, the Ainu (of Hokkaido and Sakhalin), and the Taiwanese were tolerated.[92] Even Kyushu can be seen as a major variant of the system. The Japanese administrative system was correspondingly very decentralized. The assimilation of the Koreans therefore could appear to the Japanese as relatively unproblematic.

Benedict Anderson's (1991, 149–150) comment on racism throws some light on the dilemma: "The dreams of racism actually have their origin in ideologies of *class,* rather than in those of nation: above all in claims to divinity among rulers and to 'blue' or 'white' blood and 'breeding' among aristocracies. . . . on the whole, racism and anti-semitism [anti-Koreanism] manifest themselves, not across national boundaries, but within them. In other words, they justify not so much foreign wars as domestic repression and domination." Then again, "nationalism thinks in terms of historical destinies, while racism dreams of eternal contaminations, transmitted from the origins of time through an endless sequence of loathsome copulations: outside history" (149). Troubling to the Japanese memory, however, was the ancient role of Korea as transmitter of continental Chinese culture to the islands of Japan.[93] The intermediary, erstwhile cultural colonizer, copulator, was to be erased—a task for Japanese historiography.

In 1925 the Korean History Compilation Committee was established, administered by the governor-general of Korea and engaged in collecting Korean historical materials and compiling a history of Korea. Ancient Korean history was distorted to validate Japanese colonization: Korea's onetime rule over Manchuria was written out, and the northern part of the peninsula was portrayed as an erstwhile colony of China, while the southern peninsula is claimed to have been a colony of Japan under the hypothetical Mimana. Archaeological excavations were carried out and artifacts were preserved; where the evidence failed to support Japanese ideas, the evidence was simply moved to enable it to do so.

Mimana is a name used in a ninth-century Japanese text, *Nihongi,* and likely refers to one of the Korean states of the Gaya confederacy (first to fifth centuries). Mimana's existence, location, and Japaneseness are disputed in East Asian historiography, especially between Korean and Japanese historians. One possibility is that Mimana refers to the Korean Baekje state that had relations with Japan.[94]

Chung Yong-Hwa has commented on the Japanese ideological self-justification for their imperialism in Korea. Since 1885 a Japanese version of Orientalism had been stressing the uniqueness of Japan from "the Orient" (Korea, China, and so on). Korea and China were seen as "un-scientific" and still filled with Chinese "servility" and Korean "wretchedness." "Japan invented and emphasized Korea's national diseases. Japan generalized Korea's traditional culture as the *yangban*ism of class discrimination, dependence, and *sadaejuui* (doctrine of 'serving the great') and denounced it as the etiological cause of their restrictions. Claiming that they would cure such diseases and lead Korea into civilization, Japan justified their imperialism" (Chung Yong-Hwa 2006, 129).[95] Japan sent anthropologists to Korea to photograph traditional villages as evidence of Korea's "backwardness" and need for modernization (Atkins 2010). Chung concludes, however, that Korean people subsequently produced their own sense of Orientalism ("auto-Orientalism"), falling into "the trap of 'philosophy of enlightenment'" (2006, 130).

Naoki Sakai (2000) identifies what is arguably the most devastating incidence of Japan's erasure of Korea, namely its postwar ideology and historiography. The US occupation administration intentionally allowed the Japanese to maintain their sense of cultural and historical continuity, thereby helping to nurture the desire of the Japanese to narrate their own self-serving story/history; war crimes would be mentioned, but not crimes against humanity nor those of colonialism. Leo Ching (2001) sees the "miracle" of postwar Japan as essentially an almost immediate turn from complete external orientation to complete internal orientation and subjectivity, all made possible by the US appropriation of Japan's colonies and Japan's immediate alliance with the United States in the Cold War. Japan never had to go through the harsh but important process of decolonization. Japanese nationalists, Sakai argues, are incapable of confronting the complicity between their nationalism and US hegemony; furthermore, "[a]s long as the Japanese were allowed to secure the sense of national cohesion in their cultural tradition and the organic unity of their culture, they would never be able to engage in serious negotiation with people in East and Southeast Asia who were directly victimized by or related to the victims of Japanese imperial nationalism. They may well be generous and forgiving to individual Japanese nationals but would never forget the past deeds of Japanese imperial nationalism. 'They may forgive but never forget'" (Sakai 2000, 810). The effect of its mandated forgetting is that Japan was spared the crisis of decolonization and postcolonialism—no shame, no guilt. It is the "Japanese War Responsibility Amnesia" (801), to which must be added the *post hoc* nonexistence of colonialism.[96]

There is a counterargument. In *Primitive Selves: Koreana in the Japanese Colonial Gaze, 1910–1945,* Everett Taylor Atkins challenges the prevailing view that imperial Japan demonstrated contempt for Koreans through suppression of Korean culture. Instead he sees a past and present fascination with Korean culture; moreover, he argues that Japanese preoccupation with Koreana provided the empire with a poignant vision of its own past, albeit imagined, now lost. The gaze at Korea was through the lens of myth: their ancestors had migrated through Korea, and here they might find their "primitive selves." They seemed to see in the Koreans a communal living and social solidarity that allowed Japanese to grieve for their own former selves and the values they had lost in their headlong drive for modernity. As Atkins observes, "[C]olonial access to Korea gave Japanese an opportunity to meditate intensively on their own historical and modern identity. The themes of loss and nostalgic longing for a purer cultural self are central to Japanese experiences of modernity" (Atkins 2010, 3).[97] As Dusinberre (2013) comments, the originality of the Atkins argument is that it juxtaposes the historiography of the Japanese Empire with that key theme in the domestic historiography of twentieth-century Japan, namely popular nostalgia for a purer cultural identity—empire and the "epistemology of loss."

In turn, Atkins suggests, specific objects of the Japanese gaze—folk theater, dance, shamanism, material culture—became emblems of Korean postcolonial national identity. Atkins reminds us that "following accepted anthropological wisdom of recent decades, . . . the acts of gazing and being gazed at fundamentally transformed both the observer and the observed" (Atkins 2010, 1–5).[98]

Korean historiographical erasure

The paragraphs above refer to Japanese distortions of history. What, then, of Korean distortions? The fury in the immediate post-Japanese period was fanned by the independence ideologues returning from abroad, determined to suppress any internal and arguably more moderate voices and suborning the fury to legitimize their own grabs for power. There was virtually a contest of rival, ideologically driven expressions of outrage—who could be the most anti-Japanese? This is a story for chapter 3; the present point, however, is that the sense of outrage has survived in Korean writing and popular attitudes into the present. Nevertheless it is useful to observe that since around 2000 the voices have somewhat moderated, as a comparative reading of the journals can suggest—observe, for instance, the pages of *Korea Journal*.

More recent writing is now turning both to the "normal times" and "normal lives" of the 1920s and early 1930s, but also to Korean participation in a darker history. Japanese atrocities did not go unassisted. C. Sarah Soh (2008) recounts the stories of the so-called comfort women, mostly Korean women forced into prostitution by the Japanese army. They have usually been labeled "victims of war," a simplistic and convenient view that makes it easy to pin the blame on the policies of imperial Japan and relegate the events to a sad past. Soh, however, reveals that the forces of Japanese colonialism and Korean patriarchy were both complicit in the enslavement—women were cast into sexual slavery after fleeing abuse at home, others were press-ganged into prostitution with the help of Korean procurers. Finally, an array of factors, from South Korean nationalist ideology and policies to the ideologically delimited aims of the international women's human rights movement, have contributed to the incomplete but persisting view of the tragedy. Bruce Cumings (2005, 179) comments, "Japan fractured the Korean national psyche, pitting Korean against Korean with consequences that continue down to our time." This can be seen as the ultimate tragedy, albeit with Korean complicity.[99]

There is a recent footnote to the tragedy. In 2010 Korea marked the centenary of Japan's annexation; the anniversary was not similarly marked in Japan.[100] On 14 December 2011, there was installed a life-size bronze statue of a girl in traditional Korean dress, seated on a chair, hands on lap, gaze fixed on the Japanese Embassy across a narrow street in downtown Seoul. The statue, named the Peace Monument and financed by citizens' donations, was installed to mark the thousandth weekly protest at the embassy by women, now in their eighties and nineties, who are survivors of the wartime sexual slavery. Japan's chief cabinet secretary described the incident as "extremely regrettable" and announced that Japan would request the monument's removal. The Korean government response was that they had no intention of ordering its removal. The erasure would be erased, truth restored (figure 2.7).

A final reprise from Pierre Nora's argument on *lieux de mémoire*:

Memory fastens upon sites, whereas history fastens upon events. (Nora 1996, 18)

FIGURE 2.7 The Peace Monument at the Japanese Embassy, installed 2011. Seoul is a city of protest like no other: protests against the Japanese, protests against the Americans, protests against the heritage of the dictatorship, protests by one political party against another; most often, however, the protesters are Christian—for Jesus.

The Peace Monument, a site, is clearly meant to ensure that the memory survives, regardless of attempts to revisit the history.[101]

Afterword

There is some irony in the Provisional Government of the Republic of Korea locating itself in 1920s Shanghai, arguably capitalism's greatest carnival of corruption, "a Heaven on top of a Hell," with its opium and prostitution ("The Singsong Girls of Shanghai"),[102] and, from 1928 on, focus of General Chiang Kai-shek's nationalist (Kuomintang) Chinese regime located in Nanking (Nanjing) near Shanghai. Shanghai was also the birthplace of the Chinese Communist Party (in 1921). Syngman Rhee's putative government-in-exile would evolve in a political environment of intrigue, corruption, and anti-Communist violence.

Bruce Cumings (2005, 158) notes that outcast classes around 1900, in Korea as in China, turned to Christianity for its ideal of equality before God. By the 1920s, however, they were increasingly likely to turn to science, democracy, and socialism. Reformers such as Park Chung-hee and Kim Il-sung could find nothing in their own, Korean past—"They ran rushing to a future, the past of which [scholarship for its own sake, the erasures] they could not escape" (158).

Kim Il-sung (1912–1994), of a Presbyterian Christian background, had joined the Chinese Communist Party in 1931; he also joined various anti-Japanese guerrilla groups in northern China and, in 1935, became a member of the Northeast Anti-Japanese United Army, a guerrilla group under the Chinese Communist Party. Also in 1935 Kim took the name Kim Il-sung, meaning "Becoming the Sun." By the end of 1940, pursued by the Japanese, he escaped across the Amur River into the Soviet Union; he became a major in the Soviet Red Army and served in it until the end of World War II. With the Red Army's unexpectedly easy entry into Pyongyang on 15 August 1945, Stalin realized that he needed someone to head a puppet regime; Lavrentiy Beria recommended Kim ahead of several more qualified candidates, mostly because he had no ties to the indigenous (and thereby uncontrollable) Communist movement; indeed, he allegedly could not even speak Korean. In September 1945, the Soviets installed Kim as head of the Provisional People's Committee. Arguably Kim's greatest accomplishment was his establishment of a professional army, the Korean People's Army, aligned with the Communists.[103]

The significance of this story is that Kim Il-sung and Syngman Rhee and their respective regimes had emerged from the two opposed ideologies of the maelstrom of 1930s and 1940s China. It was the making of modern Korea's tragedy.

There were always, however, other persisting ideologies. Although Cheondogyo lost its religious adherents in the postwar (postcolonial) period, its power of national motivation persists. Kirsten Bell (2004) found, in the late 1990s, that contemporary Koreans would confess to little knowledge of it and that the Office of Religious Affairs estimated its surviving membership at only 26,000. Its ideology, however, continues to infuse the contemporary *minjung* culture movement (chapter 3); it is also claimed as the ideological foundation for North Korean Communism, while the Cheondogyo Cheongudang (Cheondogyo Young Friends Party) is one of the three major political parties in North Korea.

Present Korea can be seen as "saturated with ideas and ideologies" (Clark 2000, 59). In the South it is a maelstrom of Buddhist spiritualism and egalitarianism, Catholic and Protestant Christianity, and their various commitments to scientific rationality and the goodness of work—all modulated by Confucian restraint, self-discipline, and respect for order and hierarchy; then there is the persisting memory of Cheondogyo, the *minjung* theology and movement, and the proliferating new religions; and always there are the reassuring practices of shamanism. Otherwise competing ideologies intersect, overlay, and strike new ideas off each other. The North, on the other hand, has only the glory of Kimilsungism, the cult of the Great Leader; the rest is beneath the surface, unexpressed.

CHAPTER 3

RE-IMAG(IN)ING THE NATION

Seoul and Park Chung-hee

As with the previous chapter, this one will be in four parts. The first continues the historical sketch of chapter 2, to consider the disasters of the immediate post-1945 period and the Korean War of 1950 to 1953, and then the immense and altogether different impact of the Park Chung-hee dictatorship, the continuing military dictatorship of Chun Doo-hwan, and the subsequent explosion of democratic fervor. To be confronted is the dilemma that modern Seoul is to be seen in large measure as the monument to the repressive dictator Park Chung-hee. Part 2 examines the impact of these events in relation to the urban space of Seoul—in large measure Seoul is still "the city according to Park." Part 3 addresses the reimagining and reinvention of the city—the cultural production of the present megalopolis. Part 4 turns to the question of Seoul and Christianity, surely the most extraordinary present manifestation of that maelstrom of ideologies that characterized Korea's fraught confrontation with modernity and colonization, addressed in the previous chapter.

I use the term *re*invention here, as in the book's title, rather than simply invention. Reinvention can have multiple implications, and so it does here. There is a positive sense of reflection, reform, renovation—flexibility and openness are suggested. There is a darker meaning ("reinventing the wheel"), of coming late—Japan following America, Korea following Japan. We look for this diversity in the stories of post-1945 Seoul.

Part 1

PARK CHUNG-HEE

"The difference between the inventions of 'official nationalism' and those of other types is usually that between lies and myths" (Anderson 1991, 161n10). Benedict Anderson's aphoristic footnote contrasts "popular nationalism," typically arising in local intelligentsias from the conjunction of modern communication, capitalism, and indigenous language, with "official nationalism," which (threatened) hegemonic groups throw up in defense against such popular movements. Korean popular nationalism, festering throughout the Japanese era, found itself confronted by two radically opposed official nationalisms after 1945. Both were founded in lies, yet equally both sought to appropriate the myths, both popular and esoteric, introduced in chapter 2.

The end of the Japanese colonial period in 1945 saw the partitioning of Korea and an increasingly hysterical confrontation of rival nationalisms—North versus South, as each claimed Korean authenticity. Though it inherited the capital, the South rapidly collapsed into delegitimizing compromise and corruption: while both nationalists and Communists had promised retribution against Koreans who had collaborated with the Japanese, the 1945–1948 US military government reemployed them. In large measure the colonial institutions continued; the military government based itself in the Japanese Government-General Building, renamed Jungang-cheong (Central Hall), though the American occupiers called it The Capitol. (It was, after all, at the end of an axis and had a dome.) The Americans also occupied, conveniently and somewhat seamlessly, the Japanese military zone of Yongsan.

There was one significant, symbolic erasure on the fabric of the city to mark the break, however. In October 1945 the Seoul Shinto Shrine, Choson Jingu, was destroyed. Subsequently, in 1970 during the Park Chung-hee era, the "Patriot Ahn Jung-geun Memorial Hall" was built on the site of the removed shrine, to honor Ahn Jung-geun, the assassin of Ito Hirobumi, the first Japanese resident-general—he had also been the first prime minister of Japan. No stronger expression of anti-Japanese sentiment could surely be imagined.[1]

In 1948 the United States installed the regime of the aged and corrupt Syngman Rhee (1875–1965, president 1948–1960) and the Jungang-cheong continued its role as the center of government.[2] On 25 June 1950 South Korea was invaded by forces of the North; Seoul was abandoned by Syngman Rhee on 27 June; it was rapidly overrun and changed hands four times between the Chinese-backed North and the United Nations–backed South. As the North Korean forces withdrew in September 1950, they torched the Jungang-cheong along with much else of the city. The city was finally retaken by UN forces on 14 March 1951 and the (South) Korean government returned to Seoul on the symbolic date of 15 August 1953.[3]

Juergen Kleiner (2001) has observed that the first phase of the Korean War almost saw a Korean reunification, albeit under the erstwhile Chinese Communist Party apparatchik and anti-Japanese guerrilla Kim Il-sung. In its second phase, however, the UN–United States counterattack and the subsequent Chinese and Russian intervention and then stalemate hardened the division beyond all chance of reconciliation and left (South) Korea in a state of perpetual uncertainty. It also left both North and South in a state of economic annihilation, cultural obliteration, and the scramble for some new sense of identity. The annihilation was far more than merely physical and economic, as it was crosscut by forces of class, ideology, religion, and material interests, to leave conditions that would disable the compromises and reconciliations that might permit even a modicum of later tolerance.[4] The North, however, emerged out of all this the stronger in terms of infrastructure, economy, and living conditions; the South had been virtually destroyed (Kyung Moon Hwang 2010, 220).[5]

We briefly return to *Who Ate Up All the Shinga,* Park Wan-suh's autobiographical novel of 2009 introduced in chapter 2, with its account, part harrowing, part nostalgic, of a childhood in Japanese-occupied Seoul. More terrifying are her experiences in a post–Korean War Seoul: she and her surviving family members are accused of Red sympathies, even collaboration, and must take flight in a destroyed world. Park readily acknowledges her dependence on the often-unreliable medium of memory, finding herself "forced to fill in the interstices of erased recollections with the mortar of imagination" (Park Wan-suh 2009, xii). There are counter-memories, however: Stephen Chung (2014b, 103–104) cites an iconic photograph from 1956, "Early Summer, Midopa" by Im Ung-sik, displaying high fashion and the good life (for some) in early postwar Seoul.[6] The surface glamour described by Chung highlights nothing more than the Americanization and terrible division of the time.

The repression, corruption, and vote rigging of the Rhee government reached a climax in the 15 March 1960 presidential elections; protests by students and citizens broke out in the leftist-leaning city of Masan in the southern Gyeongsang region and soon spread nationwide. On 19 April students rallied in Seoul in what would be called the

April Revolution. The Jungang-cheong again became a target, now as symbol of the hated Rhee government, and was again severely damaged, not to be restored to its former Japanese glory until 1962 (it was later refurbished and opened as the national museum from 1986 to 1995). The short-lived Second Republic replaced that of Rhee but faced both political and economic instability. For a year (April 1960 to May 1961), civil society thrived. As Bruce Cumings (2007, 22–23) notes of Seoul, "At this time South Korea had more college students per capita than England, more newspaper readers per capita than almost any country in the world, and a concentration of administrative, commercial, industrial and educational energies in one great capital city—much like Paris. A very lively salon society animated the capital, publishers brought out thorough rewritings of modern Korean history, and students began to imagine themselves the vanguard of unification with the North."

In an environment of social unrest and political turmoil, in part a manifestation of the rise of civil society and its demands, Major General Park Chung-hee led a coup on 16 May 1961, the "5.16 coup d'état," and thus commenced the Third Republic. In 1972 a new Yusin (Restoration) Constitution gave Park effective control over the parliament, the possibility of permanent presidency, and the Fourth Republic.[7]

Forgetting

Ahn Byung-ook (2002, 9) has raised the issue of "settling the past" in modern Korean historiography, "bringing out the truth," dealing with the atrocities. In 1945 there had been something of a social consensus to settle the ignominious past of Japanese colonial rule; this, however, was "interrupted and delayed under the historical conditions of the three-year US military government in South Korea."[8]

Park had served in the Japanese colonialist army and effectively continued the colonial regime; the Japanese and the Americans were tolerated, and the atrocities and collaborations of the Japanese era officially forgotten. A 1965 treaty normalized relations with Japan, enabling Park to attract Japanese investment in infrastructure and heavy industry and thereby to emulate the model of industrialization that he had witnessed during his colonial military experience in Japanese-colonized Manchukuo (Manchuria) in the 1930s. Government-corporate cooperation to expand exports was also on a Japanese model, in turn leading to the giant Korean financial conglomerates, the *chaebols,* again emulating the Japanese and to be discussed following. The Japanese colonizing state had amply demonstrated the "bureaucratic-authoritarian" path to industrialization that both North and South Korea had learned well. The post-1965 diplomatic and economic embrace of the Japanese was widely unpopular, and vivid memories of the colonization persisted, despite official forgetting.[9] To legitimize the forgetting, a new memory had to be invented: in his speeches of the 1960s, Park increasingly attributed the colonization to an Anglo-Japanese alliance, then to "the British Empire."[10]

Park Chung-hee and the miracle

Park, that "quintessential example of colonial legacy," had maintained close contact with Japan, and his values were oriented accordingly (Ahn Byung-ook 2002, 9). Like Kim Il-sung, he had come of age in Manchuria in the depths of depression, war, and disorienting change (Lee Chong-sik 2012).[11] There he witnessed young military officers organize politics and young Japanese technocrats build new industries. The "Korean economic miracle" occurred on his watch and was explicitly based on what he had observed from the Japanese and continued to observe in Japan's dramatic postwar recovery. However, the model was more the Manchurian model of military-based, forced-pace development than Meiji or post-1945 Japanese.[12] The major issue facing Park in the early 1960s was the grinding poverty of the population and the need for economic policies to overcome this poverty.[13] With effectively no private savings pool or capital reserves, Park nationalized the banks in 1961 (in part echoing the Japanese after 1910) and merged the agricultural cooperative movement with the agricultural bank; the government also took direct control over all institutional credit. The regime had been beneficiary of the preceding Rhee regime's decision to use massive American foreign aid during the 1950s to build an infrastructure of nationwide primary and secondary schools, modern roads, and a modern communications network.[14] So the task for Park was, in part, one of mobilizing a young, motivated, educated workforce.

Central to Park's policy was the first Five-Year Economic Development Plan, to start in 1962, the first such overall development plan for Korea.[15] This and the following five-year plans would be the responsibility of the Economic Planning Board (1961–1994), a "super ministry" in charge of both planning and budgeting. The first plan consisted of initial steps toward the building of a self-sufficient industrial structure that would be neither consumption-oriented nor over-dependent on oil. Six clear priority areas were set: (1) development of the energy industries, such as coal production, electric power, and wider electrification; (2) expansion of agricultural production aimed at increasing farm income, with a focus on fertilizer production, and correction of structural imbalance in the national economy; (3) development of basic industries and economic infrastructure; (4) maximum utilization of idle resources, increased employment, and improved conservation and utilization of land; (5) improvement in the balance of payments through export promotion; and (6) promotion of science and technology.[16] In its implementation, there was a promotion of the textiles sector. Lee Ki-baik (1984, 383) displays data from 1962 demonstrating textiles as the absolutely dominant sector of the formal economy at that time. The vast garment district of Dongdaemun Market remains its most tangible heritage in the present Seoul landscape (chapter 4).

The Japanese-style "developmental state" was the model, with a capable bureaucracy and a gung-ho private sector productively bedded together, wages kept low (by brutality when necessary), and with the peculiar Korean form of the financial-industrial conglomerate, the *chaebol (jaebeol)*, based on the Japanese *zaibatsu* (a giant family trust, presiding over a conglomerate or group, "family values" exploded to the level of the absurd), as its primary engine (Woo Jung-en 1991; Kim Hyuk-Rae 1998). So Hyundai, Samsung, Daewoo, and Hanbo tended to follow the pattern of Mitsubishi and Mitsui, albeit on diverse trajectories.[17]

Samsung

Nothing illustrates the place of the *chaebol* in Korean society and on the urban landscape as graphically as the story of Samsung (Hemmert 2012, 31–37).[18] In 1938, Lee Byung-chul (1910–1987), from a large landowning family in Uiryeong County, came to Daegu City and founded Samsung Sanghoe, a small trading company, eventually with forty employees, dealing in groceries produced in and around the cities as well as in its own noodles. The company prospered, and in 1947 Lee moved his head office to Seoul. With the Korean War he was forced to abandon Seoul and started a sugar refinery, Cheil Jedang, in Busan. After the war, in 1954, Lee founded Cheil Mojik, building the country's largest woolen mill in Chimsan-dong, Daegu.

In 1948, Hyosung Group founder Cho Hong-jai had invested, with Samsung Group founder Lee, in a new company, Samsung Mulsan Gongsa (Samsung Trading Corporation). This grew to become the present Samsung C&T Corporation. Cho and Lee eventually separated, and Samsung split into Samsung and Hyosung groups.

Samsung diversified into many areas, and Lee sought to establish Samsung as an industrial leader in a vast range of enterprises, moving into businesses such as insurance, securities, and retail; the basis was industrialization and the idea of large domestic conglomerates, protected from competition and assisted financially. In the late 1960s, Samsung Group entered electronics, with its manufacturing facilities in Suwon; its first product was a black-and-white television set. In 1980, Samsung acquired Hanguk Jeonja Tongsin, based in Gumi, birthplace of Park Chung-hee. It thereby entered the telecommunications hardware industry, starting with switchboards, then telephone and fax systems, becoming, crucially, the center of Samsung's mobile phone manufacturing. These came together as Samsung Electronics Company in the 1980s.[19]

Lee died in 1987, and Samsung separated into four business groups: the remaining Samsung Group, as well as Shinsegae Group (discount stores, department stores), CJ Group (food, chemicals, entertainment, logistics), and Hansol Group (paper, telecom). Today these separated groups are independent and not part of or connected to the Samsung Group.

In the 1980s Samsung Electronics had begun to invest heavily in research and development, which was crucial in pushing Samsung to the forefront in the global electronics industry. Also in that decade, the group initiated plants in Portugal (1982), New York (1984), Tokyo (1985), England (1987), and later and most notably, Austin, Texas (1996). Its construction division built one of the two Petronas Towers in Kuala Lumpur as well as the iconic Taipei 101 in Taiwan and Burj Khalifa in United Arab Emirates. Its aerospace division manufactures aircraft engines and gas turbines. In 1996 Samsung acquired the foundation of the prestigious Sungkyunkwan University, founded in 1398, though tracing its origins back to the year 992 (National University, referred to in chapter 2).

In the 1990s, Samsung became the world's largest producer of memory chips and of liquid crystal display screens; in 2012 it became the largest mobile phone maker. The group comprises some eighty companies. Samsung produces around a fifth of Korea's total exports; if a nation-state, in 2006 it would have been the world's thirty-fifth-largest economy.

So, how is Samsung to be seen within Korea itself? "Calling Samsung South Korea's biggest, most profitable and most globally recognized brand barely explains the intense and often mixed emotions the name evokes among South Koreans. In Samsung, they see the clearest example of the good and bad things that have resulted from their country's transformation from a war-torn agrarian society into a global technology powerhouse" (Choe Sang-hun 2012). Rancor runs high in Korea against Samsung and other family-controlled conglomerates, which are often accused of corruption, manipulation, and the stifling of smaller, entrepreneurial companies—hence of stifling real innovation. Starting in the late 1990s and Korea's entanglement in the Asian economic crisis, there has been a long-running and increasingly active campaign by civil society groups to force the breakup of *chaebol* groups. The specific targets of this campaign have indeed been Samsung, but also SK Telecom, Daewoo, LG, and Hyundae (Kim Sunhyuk 2007, 64). Daewoo, once the second-largest *chaebol,* was in fact dismantled by the Korean government in 1999. We return to the story of Samsung in chapter 5.

Economic reinvention

There was a further Japanese connection underlying "the miracle." In 1965 Park Chung-hee had taken the unpopular step of normalizing relations with Japan, for which the latter paid a reparations package of US$800 million in grants and cheap loans. Park plowed the compensation into modernizing the economy and infrastructure, including some $118 million into building an integrated steel mill, as the foundational plant of Posco, now the world's third-largest steelmaker.[20] Other *chaebol* also benefitted, leaving very little to compensate conscript wartime laborers, estimated by Seoul to have numbered 780,000. Indeed, it was not until 1975 that Seoul passed a law to compensate them; the government's offer of 300,000 won (about US$255) was seen as virtually an insult; only 8,500 applied. Instead, the anger directed toward Tokyo became similarly directed toward Seoul and the benefitted *chaebol,* fanning the popular anti-*chaebol* sentiment of the present.

The curtailment of labor rights—also thereby supporting the *chaebol*—and the suppression of political liberties produced a stable, disciplined, low-wage, secured profit environment, all assisted by access to US and broader global markets in the context of Cold War competition (South Korea as bulwark against both China and North Korea). There was a further source of assistance to the Park agenda deriving from the surviving Korean culture: the long Confucian tradition seems to have left a respect for order, hierarchies, and self-discipline. Furthermore, in what was a military dictatorship, there was the common realization that only the economic sphere was readily open to creative people.

The Second Five-Year Economic Development Plan (1967–1971) stressed modernizing the industrial structure and the rapid development of import-substituting industries. The year 1967 marked the foundation of Guro Industrial Complex, Korea's first industrial complex of its modern rebirth, with a focus on textiles and the export-oriented garment industry.[21] This was also the time when Park was able to use Japanese "reparations" money to build the Posco integrated steel mill in Pohang, near his hometown. The Americans had denied Park's ambition in the 1960s; when the facility came online in 1973, it was the world's most efficient (Woo Jung-en 1991, 87–88).

The Third Plan (1972–1976), coinciding with Park's 1972 Yusin (Restoration), focused on building an export-oriented structure through heavy and chemical industries but also, apparently anticipating the future of Korea's place in the world, household electronics. It was popularly referred to as the Heavy Chemical Industrialization Plan (HCIP), also known as the "Big Push." Park's turn to chemicals was built on the experience, and in part the assets, of Japanese Noguchi Jun's Korea-based Nippon Chisso, the world's second-largest chemicals complex (Kim Hyung-A 2004, 165; Cumings 2005, 168; Kim Hyung-A and Sorenson 2011). Significantly, the industry developers sought to supply new industries with raw materials and capital goods and to reduce or even eliminate dependence on foreign capital. Equally significantly, new industries were to be established in the south of the peninsula, far from the border with North Korea, thus encouraging industrialization and development in the underdeveloped south—no doubt a strategy also geared to the management of social unrest in the southern region. To fund the HCIP, the government borrowed heavily from foreign countries (rather than as foreign direct investment) so that it could direct the investment itself. This direct borrowing subsequently left Korea vulnerable in the Asian financial crisis of 1997–1998.

The Third Five-Year Plan marked the great growth of the *chaebol*; Daewoo, for example, had been founded in 1967. Steel and other newly produced materials fed into a new shipbuilding industry, a Korean expansion in building construction domestically but also into America and other regions (Woo Jung-en 1991, 134–135).

The Fourth Five-Year Economic Development Plan (1977–1981) turned to industries designed to compete in the world's industrial export markets. There would be a focus on technology-intensive and skilled labor-intensive industries. An emphasis was placed on machinery and shipbuilding, also on iron and steel, petrochemicals, and nonferrous metals; however, there was also the portentous emphasis on electronics. This was the last five-year plan of the Park Chung-hee era—Park was assassinated in 1979. The Fifth Five-Year Economic and Social Development Plan (1982–1986) shifted the focus away from heavy and chemical industries to technology-intensive industries, most notably to electronics (televisions, video recorders, semiconductor products) and to information. It would take another decade for this shift to have its effect on Korea's assumption of world leadership—and, potentially, on the end of the world as we once knew it, a theme for chapters 5 and 6. The Sixth Five-Year Economic and Social Development Plan (1987–1991) continued the work of the fifth. By the time of the seventh plan (1992–1996), the shift was complete: the focus would be high-technology fields such as microelectronics, new materials, bioengineering, optics, and aerospace. High-technology facilities would go to seven provincial cities to better balance the geographic distribution of skills and industry across South Korea.

It is in the context of the massive shift of the Park Chung-hee era that Theresa Shim and John Daly have compiled essays to trace the growth of entrepreneurship in Korea. Central to the account is how political and cultural values during the Park dictatorship underpinned the discursive and sociopolitical practices both of the regime and of the founding families and "in-groups" of the new enterprises. Certainly the enabling role of the regime was central, but so were educational systems, cultural and "family" values, institutional capabilities and resources, and the talents of entrepreneurs at all levels of society. It is also argued that, while the Japanese *zaibatsu* may have been the model for the *chaebol,* the culture of entrepreneurship was more American in its derivation, especially in the early years of the dictatorship era (Shim and Daly 2010).

Some estimates indicate that, during the 1970s, Seoul had the world's most productive economy. Annual growth in industrial production was about 25 percent; there was a fivefold increase in gross national product between 1965 and 1978; in the mid-1970s, exports increased by an average 45 percent a year.[22]

A variation of the *chaebol* came with the corporate-restructuring companies, or CRCs, following the 1997 economic crisis. Whereas foreign investors provided much-needed liquidity to the Korean economy, public sentiment demanded that the hundreds of companies under bankruptcy protection and in urgent need of restructuring be fixed by Koreans. The government set up a regulatory framework to enable the CRCs, a Korean version of the private equity firm limited to investing in distressed companies alone. While divorced from the family basis of the *chaebol,* the CRC was similarly oriented to a "conglomerate" structure; likewise, it reflected a nationalistic ideology (Song K. 2003).

By the 2010s, enthusiasm for the *chaebol* was under question. On 29 March 2012, former prime minister Chung Un-chan resigned from a panel promoting "co-prosperity" for large and small companies, following apparent clashes with President Lee Myung-bak. His argument went as follows: "Family-controlled conglomerates here are ignoring economic justice and laws, while throwing even corporate philosophy into the dustbin." The context was a growing call for "economic democratization," whereby ultra-leftists were calling for dismembering thirty major *chaebol* into one thousand large, independent companies. "Chaebol reform is crucial for the entire economy, as the current closed, regressive practices within most conglomerates darken prospects by stifling creative entrepreneurship, especially among smaller businesses."[23] Former president Kim Dae-jung had vainly attempted *chaebol* reform via neoliberal means, only to strengthen their competitiveness. Increasingly the call has been for strong, almost revolutionary methods, against the embeddedness of *chaebol* cronies in the political party system.

The fostering of creative entrepreneurship—reinvention—is a recurring theme in political discourse as in anti-establishment rhetoric. We will see, following, its playing out in the space of the city—Cheonggyecheon vis-à-vis Gangnam, as one instance (chapter 4).

Park Chung-hee, nationalism, and culture

The 1960s and 1970s were dominated by the 1961–1979 Park military dictatorship and its ever-more-strident nationalism (against the North, the Japanese, and, increasingly, the Americans). Back in the Syngman Rhee era, American policy had been to restore Japan's economic strength as the real motor of Asian development; South Korea was to be mobilized in this enterprise, effectively as an adjunct to a resurgent Japanese economy. It was the same rationale that had underlain the early 1900s endorsement of Japan's colonization of Korea. Rhee had seen this as Japan's colonization of Korea revived. The Rhee agenda, seeming so preposterous in that time, was that Korea had to become a new Japan. Park would redeem the Rhee nationalist agenda and, indeed, lay the foundation for its fulfillment. Park Sang Mi (2010) has written on the shifting state-sponsored cultural policy in South Korea in the Park Chung-hee regime.

After Korea's normalization of diplomatic relations with Japan in 1965, Park adopted Japanese cultural programs as a model for expanding the regime's management of "Korean culture." Japanese strategies for managing cultural properties and "traditional values" were emulated in a paradoxical dynamic of nation-state building whereby the builders must copy other nation-states in order to create a "unique national culture." The difficulty for the Korean modernizers was that the nation they sought to emulate, Japan, was precisely that which had effectively suppressed and compromised earlier Korean national culture in the first place (Park Sang Mi 2010, 69).

The management of public sentiment was aided, however, by the vision of Japan's extraordinary economic and social recovery after the disaster of 1945—to emulate success would surely be glorious. The threat of North Korea could also be used by Park to mitigate mass demonstrations in March 1964 against his impending seeming capitulation to the Japanese: "To work to overcome one's sense of inferiority or antipathy toward Japan was to 'truly love' the South Korean nation because Koreans, as the argument went, would skillfully use Japanese assistance to strengthen South Korea and make it impervious to further outside influence [from Japan?]" (Park Sang Mi 2010, 72, citing President Park's speeches). For their part, the Japanese saw amity with South Korea as self-protection in the increasing psychological terror of the Cold War; it would also be an element in the work in progress of Japan's wished-for role as mediator between East and West and between developed and developing nations—as a "successful adapter of the world's diverse ideologies" (it was a role in which Korea, forty years later, would show every sign of supplanting its erstwhile model —a theme for chapter 5).

It is worth noting that, in seeking to emulate Japan's success, the Koreans would be following a unique—indeed, almost bizarre— model. T. J. Pempel (1998) has compared the Japanese political economy of the boom-time 1960s with that of the long, stagnant era beginning in the early 1990s, when the "bubble economy" collapsed and electoral politics changed. In the 1960s Japan was unlike any other Organization for Economic Co-operation and Development (OECD) country: a single conservative political party dominated Japan's electoral and governmental spheres in ways unmatched elsewhere; economic growth rates were typically double those of other OECD members; labor productivity was far higher; current account surpluses increased rapidly; savings rates remained consistently higher; and the country demonstrated a much greater ability to adjust to international economic crises—it was a dexterity that startled the wider industrialized world (Pempel 1998, 2). The 1948–1993 period saw Japan with the longest era of conservative electoral continuity and dominance of any modern industrialized democracy. Although the government seemed scandal ridden throughout the period, it also seemed self-correcting (5).[24] In many ways, Korea under Park could be seen to match this extraordinary model—except in the political sphere. Whereas Japan's long-lasting Liberal Democratic Party (LDP) government could claim legitimacy through electoral democracy, Park needed to seek it in other ways.

The Park regime initiated the First Five-Year Plan for the Revival of Culture and Arts from 1974 to 1978 (albeit twelve years after the First Five-Year Economic Development Plan). It took on three long-term goals: (1) promotion of national studies; (2) propagation of culture to the populace; and (3) introduction of Korean culture overseas. The slogan "Cultural Korea" was written in the exact same characters used in an earlier Japanese slogan. The program borrowed heavily from the wartime "Cultural Japan" project created out of Japan's competition with Western powers—Japan had even tried to subsume the remnant cultures of its colonies into the overarching framework of the "New East Asian Culture" of the great Japanese Empire. Witness, for example, the architectural stylistic imposition recounted in chapter 2—the cultural empowerment of the empire would be elucidated through the signification of its new, Japan-imposed monuments in Korea, Taiwan, and Manchuria.

Park Sang Mi (2010, 75) has observed that Korea's commitment of resources to its cultural programs in that era exceeded that of Japan and indeed of most developed countries. The explanation, it is suggested, is that the illegitimacy of the Park regime, based on a coup and subsequent repression, became dependent on its nationalist-cultural program to purchase a form of legitimacy via the currency of cultural capital: "The South Korean government consecrated national historical sites and figures [the *lieux de mémoire* of chapter 1]. The Korean alphabet designed in the mid-fifteenth century by King Sejong became the symbol of the national essence. King Sejong's name came to be widely used in state-launched projects or institutions. Furthermore, the South Korean state invested in repairing historical remains associated with earlier Japanese invasions" (74). In chapter 4 we will observe the continuing recruitment of King Sejong in the reinvention of Korea and the renaturalizing of Seoul—indeed, Seoul's sacred north-south axis of Taepyeongno was renamed for him.

Pseudotraditional architecture was invoked. "Ancient" Korean buildings were constructed with modular bays and upturned roofs (Ryu Jeh-hong 2004). The claim on antiquity, however, was purely visual, not aesthetic in the sense of expression of truthfulness in representation.[25] Ryu Jeh-hong refers to the postcolonial appropriation of the colonial: "The problem with these changes in land use and ownership lies in the reduction of traditional landscapes into foreign or hybrid landscapes without preserving the context of their grafting" (20–21).[26] Ryu's comment on the subsequent restoration of both Kwanghwamun Gate and Gyeongbokgung Palace presents the modern dilemma: "The traditional landscapes of palaces remain political landscapes that legitimate every Korean regime with their orthodoxy, while the naturalization of Japanese colonial hybrids haunt us like specters with their Western-style architectures with modern architectures around Gwanghwamun [sic] imposing a 'high living standard' of high-rise towers upon their viewers" (21).

There are similar ambiguities in toponyms. Ryu Je-hun (2012), in a study of naming in Bupyeong-gu, Incheon, has speculated on the survival of vernacular toponyms as substitutes for the Japanese names used during the colonial period. There have also been "resistant" vernacular toponyms, unchanged from Chosun times, as well as much modern renaming to supplant both Japanese and indigenous names. Since the 1940s, Korean pronunciations of some Japanese namings have provided alternatives to the official names. Ryu observes, however, that everyday conversation has, since the 1980s, dropped both indigenous and official names in favor of the names of apartment complexes.

In October 1972 Park declared a state of emergency, increasing the sense of an impending Communist threat and thereby allowing the state to tighten its grip on the national discourse and the media. Yet still the Park regime invoked the cultural program to win the voluntary support of the people. So the same month of October 1972 was designated the "Month of Culture," and on 20 October 1973, declared the "Day of Culture," Park proclaimed that a nation's fortune would be determined by its cultural power.[27] Park's "restoration constitution" echoed the same term used to refer to Japan's Meiji Restoration; his "Declaration for the Revival of Culture and Arts" was elaborated into the activities of the Yusin Chonguhoe (Friends of the Restoration), a new pro-Park political organization. Culture was seen as the spiritual power behind the nation's survival: Korea would be a "spiritual world power." The regime even adopted the term "spiritual mobilization" from the Japanese wartime state. Movies were censored (of which more in chapter 5) and there was a prohibition on "foreign-originating" forces such as "vulgar commercialism" (Park Sang Mi 2010, 77).

Also central to the Park Chung-hee cultural program was the Saemaul (New Community) movement, launched by Park on 22 April 1970 as an overarching set of local improvement programs to modernize the rural South Korean economy, which was still mired in poverty and backwardness while the cities were already palpably modernizing (Kim Hyung-A 2004, 133). It was based on ideas of Korean traditional communalism called *hyang-yak* and *doorae,* comprising rules for self-governance and cooperation. The first focus was on basic living conditions, with a subsequent concentration on infrastructure and community income. This again, however, was modeled on the Japanese, namely the postwar New Life movement. So, stated President Park, "The New Village [Community] movement is . . . a spiritual movement combining our traditional ethic of frugality and cooperation with the value of efficiency in a modern, industrial society [Japan?]" (quoted in Park Sang Mi 2010, 78). However, while the Japanese program had been essentially patriarchal in its ideology, emphasizing restrictive gender roles at home and in the workplace, the Korean initiatives were more focused on emancipatory roles for women and came closer to total mobilization.[28] It could be argued that this break from the Japanese model, toward an idea of the family based more on gender equality, set in train a cultural trajectory that, three decades later, enabled the role of a Korean cultural vanguard (chapter 5).

In the 1980s, however, rapid industrialization changed both the economic and the social environment, and the movement for gender equality lost momentum. The government later decentralized the movement; civil society was empowered to lead it and, since 1998, the focus has shifted to enhancing community voluntary services and international linkages to assist developing countries.[29]

Post-Park dictatorship and democracy

Park Chung-hee had been assassinated on 26 October 1979 by the head of his Central Intelligence Agency, to be succeeded via a coup on 12 December 1979 by another general, Chun Doo-hwan.[30] In March 1980 students and their professors returned to their universities from vacation, student unions formed, and there was wide agitation over the realization that military dictatorship would continue. This culminated in an anti–martial law demonstration at Seoul Station on 15 May. In retaliation, Chun Doo-hwan expanded martial law to the whole nation, closed universities, and further suppressed the press. The continuing strife now focused on the Jeollanam-do area in the southwest of the country, particularly in the provincial capital Gwangju, for a variety of geographical reasons: this had long been both the nation's granary and, additionally, a center for antiauthoritarian debate and action. It had also been neglected in the Park era in favor of his own native southeast Gyeongsang region.

On 18 May 1980, students gathered at the gates of Chonnam National University in Gwangju in defiance of its closure. Paratroopers opposed them and, from there, the demonstration escalated until, in the afternoon of 21 May, the army fired on a crowd in front of the provincial office and, in response, protesters raided armories and police stations to arm themselves, and gun battles began. The army was driven from the city. Gwangju was blockaded in the days up to 26 May. On 27 May, at about 4 a.m., troops from five divisions moved into the downtown area and defeated the civil militias. Estimates of casualties range from 170 to 2,000. The government considered the uprising as a rebellion instigated by opposition activist Kim Dae-jung, who was convicted and condemned to death; international outrage forced the government to reduce his punishment (Lewis 2002). Gwangju is seen as Korea's Tiananmen.[31]

The festering memory of the Gwangju massacre underpinned mounting opposition during the early 1980s. In the last days of the Park Chung-hee dictatorship in the 1970s, the idea had emerged for Korea to place a bid for the 1988 Summer Olympics. It was in part an attempt to emulate the 1964 Tokyo Olympics, which were seen as a "rite of passage" for a Japan seeking to emerge into a wider family of nations following the disaster of World War II. It was also an attempt by Korea to cloak a brutal dictatorship with some pretense of legitimacy—perhaps with the 1936 Berlin Olympics as an unintended model. After President Park's assassination in 1979, it was his successor, Chun Doo-hwan, who submitted Korea's bid in 1981.

Seoul was selected to host the 1988 Summer Olympics in a vote in the West German city of Baden-Baden on 30 September 1981, finishing ahead of the Japanese city of Nagoya. During the early 1980s, excitement over the impending games was infused with rhetoric of a "coming-out party" for Korea as a newly industrialized economy—a showcase to the world. The event was increasingly used as an impetus for improved relations with the Union of Soviet Socialist Republics, Eastern Europe, and the People's Republic of China. The threat of impending disaster loomed, however, with the 1984 Los Angeles Olympics, which were boycotted by the Eastern Bloc. This especially emboldened North Korea, which demanded to cohost the games—the de jure host, it should be remembered, was not the South Korean government but the city of Seoul. North Korea's demand was to host eleven of the twenty-three Olympic sports and for special opening and closing ceremonies. Meetings in Lausanne in January 1986 failed to resolve the dispute; North Korea and a few of its allies announced a boycott, and Seoul became the sole focus.

A final threat arose in 1987. The death of a Seoul National University student under police interrogation in January 1987 led to mass protests and a corresponding hardening of the Chun government, and then, in June, to massive antigovernment protests nationwide. The increasing political turmoil and violence jeopardized Seoul's hosting of the games; the International Olympic Committee surreptitiously explored the possibility of relocating the games, with Munich as a likely location. On 29 June 1987, Roh Tae-woo, the government's nominee to succeed Chun as president, succumbed to the demands for a transition to democracy and agreed to direct presidential election and the restoration of civil rights. In December elections for a new president were held; however, because the opposition could not agree on a unity candidate, Roh was directly elected virtually by default and served in the role of president during the 1988 games.[32] In 1992 elections, Kim Young-sam was elected president, the first civilian president in thirty years. Then, in 1997, Kim Dae-jung was elected.

Ahn Byung-ook (2002) sees the thirty-two years of military dictatorship as the most painful part of Korean history, marked by the killing of political enemies conveniently labeled "Communists," the suppression of the 19 April 1960 Democratization Movement that had, in effect, enabled Park's 1961 coup and the later suppression and massacre of the 1980 Gwangju People's Uprising (Lewis 2002; Shin and Hwang 2003). This last event cemented anti-American sentiment: alleged US complicity in the massacre convinced a new generation of young Koreans that the democratic movement had developed not with American support but in the face of daily American support for any dictator who could quell the democratic aspirations of the Korean people. The anti-American movement swelled, American cultural centers were torched (more than once in Gwangju), and students immolated themselves in protest of President Ronald Reagan's support for the military dictatorship.

Official reevaluation of the dictatorship, and the Gwangju massacre more specifically, began after restoration of direct presidential elections in 1987. In 1988 the massacre was officially renamed the Gwangju Democratization Movement; in 1995 a special law on the May 18 [1980] Democratization Movement enabled prosecution of those responsible for the 12 December 1979 coup d'état and the 1980 Gwangju massacre. President Chun Doo-hwan received a death sentence; President Roh Tae-woo was sentenced to life imprisonment. On 22 December 1997 they and all others convicted in relation to those events were pardoned by President Kim Young-sam (r. 1993–1998) on the insistence of incoming President Kim Dae-Jung (r. 1998–2003), the most eminent victim of Gwangju. In 2002, in the Kim Dae-Jung presidency, the Mangwol-dong cemetery where the Gwangju massacre victims were buried was declared a national cemetery. The spirits of the Gwangju uprising continue to haunt, however: in 2007 the May 18 Memorial Hall was completed; its displays, prepared by the Gwangju-based May 18 Memorial Foundation, overwhelm with their factual detail depicting the daily, almost hourly sequence of events of those days. The Memorial Hall seeks to counter decades of disinformation, to show how the brief moment of "liberated Gwangju" was not one of mayhem and violence (De Ceunster 2010, 28).[33] The cemetery and the hall are administered by the Ministry of Patriots and Veterans Affairs (MPVA), which also controls the National Cemetery in Seoul's Tongjak-dong, where the suppressors of

Gwangju are commemorated as national heroes. The MPVA organizes the annual May 18 commemoration in Gwangju, to be confronted by opposed ceremonies and protests from the Gwangju families' organizations.

The reconstruction of the memory of Gwangju, albeit still contested, is a unique event in the modern history of Korea, which is, otherwise, overwhelmingly a history of erasures, of compelled forgetting. Here, however, one is to remember, painfully. Worse, Gwangju-style brutality continues, most notably in the present day against labor unions.[34]

The dilemma in any attempt to read present Seoul comes with the realization that, overwhelmingly, modern South Korea rests on the vision of the brutal dictator Park Chung-hee. In large measure, Seoul is Park's memorial. Where, however, are the countermemorials that deconstruct the brutality and antidemocracy, thereby to release the unique brilliance of the Park vision? In one sense, in remembering only one aspect of the complex genius of Park Chung-hee, the outsider turns away from his greatest monument—modern Korea, the "Miracle on the Han"—in disillusionment and cynicism. Park holds an ambiguous position in present Korean historiography. There is the comment in Eckert et al. (1990, 377–378) that antipathy toward Park in later sentiment and historiography has been tempered by the far greater loathing of Chun. Park's family was respected, even revered, whereas Chun's was seen as corrupt; Park's coup had been relatively bloodless, Chun was tainted with Gwangju; Park had delivered economic growth, which, by 1980, was being taken for granted so that people now sought greater freedom and equity, which Chun forcefully resisted. Park and his wife received prominent burials in the National Cemetery, while his daughter, who had dutifully taken her mother's place by Park's side after her mother's assassination, was subsequently democratically elected president; Chun received a death sentence (De Ceunster 2010, 24).[35]

Uk Heo and Terence Roehrig (2010) have argued how democratization has affected all aspects of South Korean society. For instance, democratization allowed for a more frequent alternation of political elites, from conservative to liberal and back to conservative, mostly manifested in wavering between rampant developmentalism and ideas of a decidedly neoliberal welfare state. These alternating elites would also initiate different policies for dealing with North Korea and would hold different views on Korea's role in its alliance with the United States. Ideological divides in Korea thereby became more stark and the political process more combative, including on the streets of the cities. Politics, in Korea, remain explosive (Armstrong 2007, 5).

Part 2

PARK AND THE CITY

The following will interrogate the present city, close to half a century after Park Chung-hee. Yet, in its representation it is still very much the expression of Park's vision and unable to be separated from his memory—even more so after the 2012 presidential election that brought Park Geun-hye to the presidency.

Park's nationalist project functioned at a variety of levels: the 1894 Donghak Rebellion was extolled as glorious precursor to his own state ideology of "nationalistic democracy," while the North similarly invoked that event as model for its own, Communist dictatorship.[36] Nationalistic democracy was in turn proclaimed as what distinguished Korea from alien (American?) models (Kim Kwang-Ok 1994, 201; also Park Chung-hee 1970, 107). Throughout all the turmoil of Park, Chun, Roh, and the eventual withering of the militarist state, the Jungang-cheong both sheltered and symbolized the government, first as the central government offices and subsequently, from 1986 on, as national museum.

The ancient city reimaged

In 1967, in the middle of Taepyeongno and facing south as if defending both the Japanese Jungang-cheong and Pugaksan, a statue of iconic national hero Admiral Yi Sun-sin (1545–1598) was constructed, allegedly representing Park Chung-hee as loyal soldier facing adversity (Ryu Jeh-hong 2004, 19). Significantly, Admiral Yi had been the hero principally responsible for repulsing the Japanese Hideyoshi invasions of 1592–1597. There had been an earlier statue of Admiral Yi, ordered by Syngman Rhee in the Korean War crisis and unveiled in 1952 in the Chinhae naval port in southeast Korea. Chinhae was associated both with Yi's battles and with the Asia-Pacific anti-Communist alliance. At that time Yi's image served as an instance of anti-Japanism, but in that instance it also served to speak against perceived threats of North Korean Communism (Kal Hong 2011, 58).[37]

The nationalist project was also given architectural expression, as new monuments of the state received incongruous, neotraditional, curved tile-roof forms to evoke the old palaces—though invariably on undistinguished modernist boxes. Most notable is the presidential palace, Cheong Wa Dae, on the lower mountain slope behind the memory of the vanished Gyeongbokgung and overlooking the central government's administration in the Japanese Jungang-cheong.

The location of Cheong Wa Dae was the site of an ancient royal villa. In 1939 Japan had built an official residence there for its governor-general, later dismantled during Kim Young-sam's presidency, in 1993. In 1948, President Syngman Rhee used one of the few old buildings there as his office and residence. Similarly, Presidents Park Chung-hee, Choi Kya-ha, and Chun Doo-hwan used it as an office and residence. In the 1980s, while President Roh Tae-woo was in office, a new complex including an office building, official residence, and press center, called Chunchugwan, was built, to be opened in April 1991. Its orientation was auspiciously though surely unintentionally toward the US Embassy at the intersection of Taepyeongno and the transgressive, Japanese, east-west Yulgongno. Its complex of ceremonial buildings received curved, tradition-evoking blue tile roofs.

Geomancers have long considered the area of Cheong Wa Dae, or the Blue House, as highly auspicious. An inscription on a stone wall, decreeing it to be "The Most Blessed Place on Earth," was found behind the official presidential residence during the construction of a new building in 1990. It is set, auspiciously like the Gyeongbokgung, between the sacred Pugaksan, its two flanking mountains of Naksan (the Left Blue Dragon) and Inwangsan (Right White Tiger), and the protective Namsan to the south. In front flowed the Cheonggycheon Stream and, beyond, the Han River.

Kwanghwamun, the ancient great South Gate to the palace complex and the focus of the north-south axis, was subsequently rebuilt across the front of the Japanese administrative headquarters and on the original orientation—hence at an angle to the Japanese building. Photographs from the 1970s show the incongruity of the monumental neo-Renaissance and Art Deco hybrid pile intersected by the lower but vaster-scale gateway, in its effect an eloquent expression of the unresolved tensions in the imagining of Seoul in the twentieth century. Then, amid much controversy as to whether the unconscionable past is to be remembered or forgotten, the Jungang-cheong itself was demolished, with ceremony and celebration, on 15 August 1995, the fiftieth anniversary of the Japanese surrender—"Dismantling the former colonial government building to restore the national spirit," declared Lee Man-hoon (1995, 79). Controversy over the demolition persists.[38] The Jungang-cheong carried traces of many histories and the debates brought into focus contested questions of national identity and colonial legacy. The advocates of removal argued that the building not only blocked the people's view to the (already demolished) royal palace but additionally disrupted the flow of *pungsu,* the cosmic energy of Korean geomancy; its siting by the Japanese was, indeed, seen as having been intended to disrupt that flow. The counterarguments stressed that the building was an embodiment of twentieth-century Korean history and needed to be preserved for future generations. Elements of the building were eventually preserved at the outdoor amphitheater of the also controversial, nationalistic Independence Hall of Korea.[39] The amphitheater is in the form of a reverse tumulus, an open graveyard, displaying the afterlife of the colonizer, its dead body dissected (Kal Hong 2011, 101).

There was, however, some bitter irony in the dismantling of the Jungang-cheong, for only two months earlier the Sampung Department Store, in the new "downtown" of Gangnam, had dismantled of its own accord during the late afternoon shopping hours. Ryu Jeh-hong (2004, 12) quotes Choi Chungmoo (1997a): "The two simultaneous destructions in 1995 present an inherent paradox in the Korean postcolonial condition: the dismantlement of the former Capitol Building . . . as the symbol of colonial order, and the collapse of a department store building, which problematized the capitalist order that had been believed to overcome the former, the colonial order."

The Sampung Department Store collapse, on 29 June 1995, was the largest peacetime disaster in Korea's history. Five hundred and one people died, and 937 were injured. Originally designed as a four-story office building, it was changed to a department store during construction, with a number of support columns cut away to allow for escalators. It was completed in late 1989 and opened to the public in July 1990. Subsequently a fifth story was added, and then heavy air-conditioning units were installed on the roof, all exceeding planned design loads. By April 1995 cracks were appearing in the structure; on 29 June these widened dramatically and there was vibration through the structure but no warnings were issued to patrons; at 5:50 p.m. it collapsed. Subsequent investigations laid blame on corruption involving the building's owners and regulators and on faulty construction. The Sampung scandal, together with the earlier collapse of the Seongsu Bridge over the Han River in 1994, focused attention on the alleged greed, poor construction standards, and corruption that had plagued Korean construction during the boom of the 1960s, 1970s, and 1980s.

It was in this context that the decidedly well-constructed Jungang-cheong was demolished in 1995–1996. The lost empire would be reclaimed, and there were tentative steps to re-create the destroyed Gyeongbokgung Palace—the forty-eight demolished structures would each be rebuilt. So now the curving south-to-north axis of Taepyeongno and Admiral Yi Sun-sin would focus, successively, on (1) the gateway, (2) the memory of the Japanese headquarters, (3) the emerging image (simulacrum) of the long-vanished Gyeongbokgung royal palace, (4) the blue, neotraditional forms of the presidential palace on the mountainside (the Blue House), (5) the intervening mountain

itself, and then (6) the much higher Pugak behind that. Each symbolically twists the axis, to deny the significance of the others, and with the
US Embassy ultimately at the fulcrum (figures 3.1 and 3.2). In more
recent times the US Embassy has been the most visibly guarded of
Seoul's monuments—a fortress of concrete and steel, and emblematic
of the animosity that grew in the decades of the American support for
the Park dictatorship (Kim Jinwung 2001, 172).

There is yet a further subversion of meanings in the expansion of the
city to the south. The Japanese had stationed their military in Yongsan
(Dragon Mountain), the area between the city's southwest gate and the
Han River, outside the walled city and historically the entry to the city
for trade, visiting legations, and invaders. The further physical expansion of Seoul was overwhelmingly to the south, across the Han River.
The effect of this was that Namsan, the Southern Mountain, was now to
the north of the greater part of the city, while the geomantic, protective
Pugaksan was largely invisible (Chung Sae Wook 1997; Jung Inha 1997).
When Namsan acquired the Seoul (telecommunications) Tower, Seoul
could be seen as now coming under the spiritual protection of the new
cosmology of communications technology and the cyberworld.

In the 2000s that part of Taepyeongno north from Jongno to
Kwanghuamun Gate was redesigned and redeveloped to commemo-
rate King Sejong and his era as a Korean golden age. The main road-
way, now renamed Sejongno, became a pedestrian plaza and the
monumental statue of Admiral Yi was joined by one of King Sejong,
symbolically standing guard over the US Embassy alongside (itself
otherwise heavily guarded by a large police presence) (figure 3.3).

Undoubtedly the most sustained effort in reclaiming (reimagining) antiquity has been the rebuilding of the main Gyeongbokgung Palace. As a reconstruction it is impressive: it demonstrates the
endeavor to reestablish "the national spirit" and further to obliterate
the Japanese legacy. By 1945, the only buildings of any distinction in
Seoul were Japanese, or else Chosun of Japanese design or provision;
there was the surviving East Palace complex, but it was still occupied
by members of the erstwhile royal family and not accessible. All the
main palaces—Gyeongbokgung, Changgyeonggung, Deoksugung—
are now splendidly displayed, each with its contingent of Chosun-uni-
formed guards constantly performing drills to the delight of armies of
excursioning schoolchildren.

The Gyeongbokgung reconstruction, despite efforts at artificial
aging, remains unconvincing: it is all too consistent, a reproduction to
a code (in the Baudrillardian sense of chapter 1) in which any distinction between original and reproduction is to vanish and with every
element exhibiting the same (fake) age. It is an immensely popular

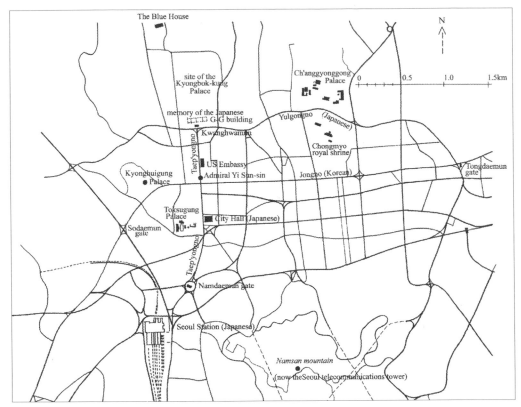

FIGURE 3.1 The city center after 15 August 1995: as the city has expanded to the south, the "south" (now cyber-world) mountain becomes the new "north" (protecting) mountain. Source: King (2008a).

FIGURE 3.2 Taepyeongno, the view north: *left,* Admiral Yi Sun-sin (Park Chung-hee) and (discreetly behind the trees) the central government offices; *center,* Pugaksan, the Blue House (hidden behind the ghost of the Jungang-cheong), the Japanese Jungang-cheong (erased!), and Kwanghuamun (restored); *right,* the US Embassy. Source: King (2008a).

FIGURE 3.3 Taepyeongno (Sejongno) in 2012: Admiral Yi is joined by King Sejong; beyond, *from left to right*, the Blue House on the mountain slope, Pugaksan, the restored Kwanghua-mun, the restored Gyeongbokgung Palace. On the right is the US Embassy.

and undoubtedly educational stage set. Its completion is scheduled for 2030 (figure 3.4).

On the evening of 10 February 2008, people throughout South Korea, in horror, watched an emergency televised news report with images of Seoul's iconic Namdaemun, the great South Gate, officially Sungnyemun, engulfed in flames.[40] The "Gate of Exalted Ceremonies," it had been constructed in 1398 in the early Chosun dynasty and had stood as an official symbol of Korean cultural heritage ever since its 1962 designation as the number one national treasure.[41] In a sense, the reality of the great ceremonial axis—of the city itself—had ended. Investigators later determined that a seventy-year-old Korean man had deliberately set it ablaze: perhaps this was some emblematic moment of national disillusion. It had survived both Japanese geomantic distortion and wartime obliteration, yet this catastrophe set the mind of the mass media back to the Japanese: how was it that the Japanese protection of their own cultural heritage had not been learned by the Koreans? What had gone wrong in the Korean case (Park Sang Mi 2010)?

New capitol

The ambivalence is completed with Yeouido Island in the Han River to the south of the old city and location of the Japanese-era "international" airport. There had also been a runway at Gimpo built by the

FIGURE 3.4 The reconstructed Gyeongbokgung Palace, 1989–2030.

Japanese forces in 1939–1942; this played a major role in the Korean War. In 1958 Gimpo was designated as Seoul's international airport, replacing Yeouido. Gimpo, in turn, was replaced by Incheon International Airport in 2001, thereby to be relegated to the status of Seoul's second airport.

In 1975 the National Assembly Building—a democracy monument for the dictator Park Chung-hee, but actually a styleless recollection of the old, domed, Japanese headquarters—was placed at the end of its own, new axis on Yeouido Island. Such, however, may not have been the original idea: there had been an architectural competition for the National Assembly Building, to be located in the Namsan (South Mountain) area. The allegedly winning entry was based on the cardinal principles articulated by Kim Swoo Geun, its designer, and previously outlined in chapter 2 in critically assessing the Jungang-cheong. It would have comprised a group of human-scale pavilions somewhat consistent with those principles, though strictly modernist in styling. The competition was subsequently canceled following the 16 May 1961 military upheaval, the site shifted to "virgin" Yeouido, and the design task assigned to a committee.[42] Kim Swoo Geun had also been responsible for a subsequently abandoned 1960s master plan for Yeouido Island (Korean Institute of Architects 2000, 196).

The National Assembly, however, is merely the epitome of an aesthetic of blank boxes: Seoul is a city of blank space—space without

FIGURE 3.5 The National Assembly Building, completed 1975, photographed in 2012. While the building in its provision, its confrontingly monumental presentation, and restricted access, may not be democratic, its park would certainly claim to be so.

purposive architectural signification. There are ancient survivals, also ancient reproductions, and blank modernist boxes, with very little "in between" that can indicate a continuum of history. The very few "in-between" monuments are principally associated with the Japanese modernization (chapter 2).[43] Public access to the National Assembly Building is for the most part restricted; token displays of democracy are instead relegated to its surrounding gardens, a popular picnic venue (figure 3.5).

Yeouido Island additionally became a venue of boxlike corporate towers. The 63 Building, officially 63 City, is a skyscraper of 249 meters that, when completed in 1985, was the tallest building outside North America and Korea's tallest building until 2003.

In summary, the modern Korean state presents as an amalgam of "modern European administration and Japanese appropriation of both Korean and Japanese conventions" (Choi Chungmoo 2002, 111). As Kim Won Bae (1999, 20) summarizes the dictatorship,

[C]ities were used as production platforms in the early years of economic development. Cities were thus growth machines until the late 1970s when the developmental state was for all purposes autonomous. They gradually transformed into a jungle without a king in the 1980s. The major function of the growth machine was the production of goods, while the main interest in the jungle was territorial expansion—land speculation. Furthermore, the growth machine was the subject of the creator's [Park's?] order, whereas the jungle was not so easy to systematically control.[44]

Kim Won Bae is here referring to Langer's idea of four images of organized diversity applicable to an understanding of Korean cities: bazaar, jungle, organism, and machine (Langer 1984, 20). In the context of this model, however, it might be realistic to claim that both machine and jungle persist in the present. It will be argued below that the "jungle" is best understood as an expression of the logic of "assemblage."

The growth of Seoul

While Seoul's population in 1945 has been estimated at around 900,000 (370,000 in the late 1930s), its effective evacuation and destruction in the Korean War had left it as a depopulated ruin by 1953. The economic devastation meant that it had no chance to cope with the influx of refugees at the end of the war; the city became a poorly built, overcrowded slum, and, as there were neither the administrative nor the financial resources to reorganize property boundaries surviving from the feudal era, it became a city of poor construction, unplanned, on inappropriate land allocations. By 1960 its estimated population was 2,400,000. The population continued to explode in the 1960s at some 6.5 percent growth per year, now fueled by the Korean "economic miracle"; the miracle, however, did not enable more considered urban planning, development control, or better standards of building. By 1970 the estimated population was 5,530,000, then 8,370,000 by 1980, and 11,000,000 by 1991 (Lee Ki-Suk 1979; also Seoul Statistical Yearbooks). By 2011, the Seoul National Capital Area, which included the contiguous Incheon metropolis, had a population of over twenty-five million.

There had been a tentative metropolitan plan in 1962, but the rate of population growth and uncontrolled building simply overwhelmed it. Congestion and its consequential opposite, sprawl, became the city's most contentious problems. Arguably the first comprehensive planning effort came in 1966, with the Basic Urban Planning for Seoul; there was a land use plan, and a transportation network was introduced. Greatly influenced by Sir Patrick Abercrombie's 1944 Greater London Plan, the city would be broken up into small, self-contained, and well-planned communities within larger designated areas of the city. These communities would be organized into a "concentric city," defined by three concentric circles around the historic core: there would be a daily zone defined by a ring road at roughly five kilometers distance, a weekly zone at approximately fifteen kilometers, and then a monthly zone at forty-five kilometers.[45] A series of ten-year plans ensued; however, the infrastructure changes that they called for had to be implemented by expropriating land and clearing and demolishing housing. A 1969 plan, still weak on implementation strategies, provided a framework for the city's expansion, which, in the main, was eventually followed.

Following Langer above, a dialectic of machine-versus-jungle suggests a framework in which to consider the 1969 plan for Seoul's expansion (Jung Inha 1997). This was a combination of English "New Town" thinking and Scandinavian "Finger Plan" ideas; most significantly, it was the expression of the Park Chung-hee vision for the city. The order of a finger plan, structured on an armature of new roads and subway trains, would overlay and hopefully bring some sense of order to the chaos of disordered, proliferating expanses of slums, squatter settlements, and unplanned sprawl (figure 3.6).

The plan provided a context for the Yeouido Island redevelopment (the new "capitol") and for a "new town" south of the river, on a southwest "finger" (Guro, Seoul's first modern industrial complex, under the 1967–1971 First Five-Year Economic Development Plan). The further extension of that finger would incorporate the separate city of Incheon into a vastly expanded, integrated urban complex (Jung Inha 2013, 54). A south finger would acknowledge the reality of the city's expansion to the area south of Namsan, the Southern Mountain, and between Namsan and the river; it then crosses the river toward the southeast to the extensive Gangnam-gu District, which was to include the riverside facilities for the 1988 Olympic Games at Jamsil. Gangnam would, in the 1990s, evolve into Korea's Silicon Valley, though to be locally and incongruously named "Teheran Valley"—a discussion for chapter 4.

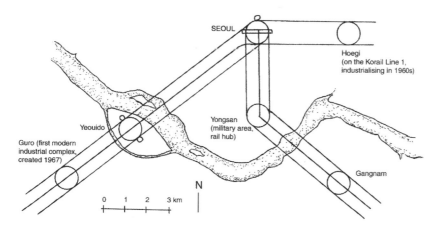

FIGURE 3.6 The 1969 "finger" plan for Seoul's growth. Source: author, based on Jung Inha 1997; 2013, 53–54).

A third finger was to the east from the old city toward Naksan, the Eastern Mountain, incorporating Hoegi, which was already industrializing in the 1960s.

It is not surprising that there was no planned expansion to the north, as had been intimated in the 1966 plan, for that would be toward the Demilitarized Zone (DMZ) and the eternal threat to Seoul's existence. Growth to the north did subsequently occur, however, most notably along the Korail Line 1 to Dongducheon, also to the northwest and, much closer to the DMZ, to Paju.

In 1971 the city formed a National Land Development Plan that strongly influenced future residential land use but also resulted in increased development in Seoul's inner core. This latter, however, had a negative impact on urban sprawl, as less available land in the inner city led to leapfrog development and increased sprawl. Then, in 1974, a further plan implemented the idea of multiple cores to accommodate the sprawl of commercial and financial services that might otherwise have gone to the old inner city, effectively translating the 1969 "finger" plan into an implementable program.

In the Japanese era, planning had followed the idea of a single-core city—initially the area within the old walled city south of Jongno, extending into the new Yongsan beyond Seoul Station to the south. The area north of Jongno had been described as "the native village." Yongsan was in part eclipsed when the bridging of the Han River opened Yeouido Island to development. The 1969 plan nominated three centers: the historic city center, including Seoul City Wall area, to be fostered as an international cultural center; Yeongdeungpo and Yeouido as an international financial center; and the emerging district of Gangnam as an international business center.[46] A series of further master plans worked for the most part within the 1969 thinking: the first was established in 1990, with 2000 as its target year; a second in 1997 set 2011 as target; and a third in 2006 set 2020.[47] The 2020 Seoul Master Plan (of 2006) was then revised with that for 2030: in addition to the three main centers there would be seven regional centers and twelve local centers.[48]

The regional centers beyond the three cores in turn were seen to provide links to further cities in the greater Seoul region, specifically to Incheon (to the west), Suwon (to the south), Sungnam (to the southeast), Namyanglu (to the east, though somewhat more tentatively than the others), then Dongducheon (to the north), and Paju (to the northwest, bordering the Demilitarized Zone). Thus the "finger thinking" of the 1969 plan was expanded to define a vastly expanded metropolitan region, where the fingers were described as "city axes for interface among centers and mutual development with nearby cities."[49]

Significantly, the vastly expanded metropolis would, however, return to the geomantic order of the Choson dynasty city: the four sacred mountains of the walled city would be replicated in four outer mountains: Bukhansan in the north (against Pugaksan), Guanaksan in the south (against Namsan), Yongma in the east (against Naksan), and Deokyang in the west (against Inwangsan)—Gangnam thereby under the protection of a new "Right White Tiger" (chapter 2). Thus the sacred landscape of the city was also extended.

Transportation

The need for an effective transportation and land use plan was especially emphasized in the 1969 plan. The planning of the 1960s had called for a rapid transit system in the hope of relieving road congestion. Significantly, it was in the 1960s that the old Seoul tramway system came to its end. The defeat of the Japanese and then the Korean War, when Seoul changed hands four times, had virtually destroyed the tramway system: in 1951 the Gyeongseong Electric Company, which operated the trams, had 111 cars but, on any given day, less than half these would be able to leave the depot. As American cities were closing down their streetcar services in favor of the automobile, there were secondhand cars available: in 1952, 20 were imported from Nashville; subsequently in the 1950s the system acquired secondhand cars from Atlanta (20) and Los Angeles (15); by 1964 there were 16 routes operating with 223 cars over 76 kilometers of track. Some 350,000 people were using the trams each day. There was also the Kyongsong Tramway, established around 1933 from a terminal at Seoul's East Gate opposite the city tramway company's car barns, operating two suburban streetcar lines over 14.4 kilometers of track into the east and southeast semirural suburbs.

By the mid-1960s the tram system was in economic crisis, despite the scale of its operation. The local government would not allow the operators to increase fares, even though it was an era of rampant inflation—the policy of affordability was leading to huge losses. The equipment was wearing out, and the rail tracks had not been renewed in decades; the entire system needed rebuilding, but a then-poor city could not afford such an investment. However, the defining factor was the rise of the automobile: cars were rare (a mere 16,624 registered in 1965 in a city of some three million), yet these were the conveyances of the elite who found themselves constantly inconvenienced by stopping-and-starting trams. Trams were going out of fashion worldwide, and it is likely that this intellectual fashion played an even larger role than economics. The Seoul tramway system began to be

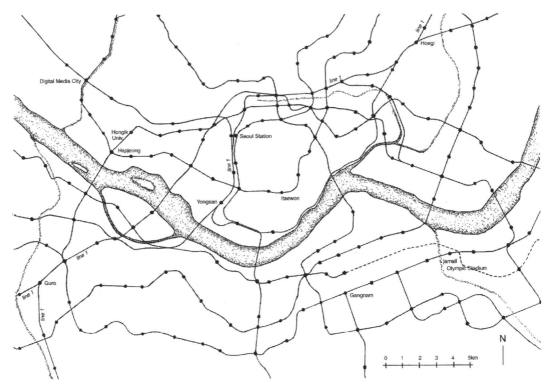

FIGURE 3.7 The rapid transit system, 2012. Only the inner-city subway system is indicated here. The system is constantly expanding, and this depiction, like any other, will have only temporary validity. Source: author, based on 2014 subway maps.

dismantled in 1966 and ended in November 1968. There had been similar though more limited systems in Busan (opened in October 1915) and Pyongyang (opened in May 1923 to replace an earlier horse-drawn tramway). Busan's system ended in May 1968, and Pyongyang's during the 1950–1953 Korean War, although it has more recently been reestablished.[50]

The development of the Seoul subway rapid transit system was initiated in the 1970s and continues today, with new lines constantly coming into service. Korail (Korea Railroad Corporation, the national railroad operator) began operating Line 1 in 1974; Lines 2, 3, and 4 followed in the late 1970s and 1980s. Though focusing on the old walled city area, the extensions were mostly into areas that were still partly rural. Seoul Metropolitan Rapid Transit Corporation was formed in 1994 to operate Lines 5 through 8; Seoul Metro Line 9 Corporation was formed in 2009 to operate Line 9. There is additionally an Incheon metro that connects with one of the branches of Line 1 and another five Korail lines. This yields a total of twenty-two lines, including the Incheon and Korail sectors, over a length of 755 kilometers. Seoul Tourist Association guides in the early 1990s could direct one toward

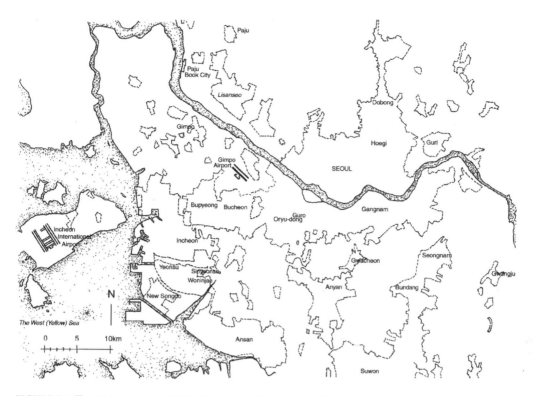

FIGURE 3.8 The city's expansion, 2014, where the built-up area is indicated within the broken lines—the rest is mostly inaccessible, either mountains or estuarine mudflats. Source: author, based on Google map.

four networks: Korail's Line 1 and Lines 2, 3, and 4; by 2001 there were eight lines. In 2012, reference could be made to twenty-two lines; another seven lines or extensions were under construction, and a further eight systems were in the planning stages. There are also several light rail transit systems in production.[51] Seoul now has the world's largest subway network, while its public transportation infrastructure is the world's densest (figure 3.7).[52] Together with new highways, this system has enabled a massive spread of the metropolis into its erstwhile rural countryside, albeit still as a very high-density and mostly high-rise city. While "finger" planning still rules and facilitates the planning and operation of metro lines, the fingers have proliferated, as observed above (figure 3.8).

The most current urban plan (in 2016) is the Seoul General Plan 2030, developed through the Seoul Development Institute, founded in 1992.[53] A special focus, now, is on the preservation and maintenance of cultural heritage sites and buildings, as well as the development of cultural resources, in part to foster tourism in the city. Planning, like the nation more broadly, shifts from a focus on development toward one on consumption.

Rebuilding the city

There was a population explosion in the postwar "poor years" of the 1960s and 1970s, following the economic development plans of the 1960s under the motivational banner "the modernization of our fatherland." This population increase had been poorly housed, however, in part in dense apartment blocks, but mostly in informal settlements in hilly districts and on riverbeds (Ryu Jeh-hong 2004, citing Jang Gyu-sik 2003, 82–85). The consequence was a city characterized by unplanned interstitial development, sprawl, and slum conditions.

To address these conditions, two types of collective residential renewal were subsequently adopted. The first was a public residential redevelopment program known as Jae-Gae-Bal (JGB), which clears areas of residential squatters and substandard housing and then builds high-rise apartment complexes. JGB was originally conceived as a squatter renewal program in the early 1970s but subsequently evolved into redevelopment measures for substandard housing more generally. The second form of residential renewal is private sector and more recent, called Jae-Gun-Chuk (JGC), which means "house rebuilding." This is based on the voluntary formation of a property owners' association to proceed with a joint development project, usually to replace existing apartments with new apartments. It may cover either a single building or a designated Apartment District (Kim Kwan-Joong n.d., 2).

There is an irony here. A 1928 city plan, in the Japanese era, had proposed "land readjustment" to resolve the chaos of the colonial city. Land would be amalgamated, "civilized" grid planning imposed, and the land reallocated according to planners' rationale of that age. The plan collapsed, and the backwardness of Korean culture was blamed.[54] A half-century later, the strategy reemerges as JGB—Korean culture, it would seem, is not immutable (Henry 2014, 52–53).[55]

JGB was boosted in the early 1980s following introduction of a partnership development method known as Hapdong renewal. This is based on a contractual arrangement between the property owners' association (providing the land) and the development company (executing the project from land clearance to apartment construction). In return, each previous property owner gets a new apartment while the development company secures a return by selling the extra units that they build. That return, needless to say, depends on very high density to enable an abundance of extra units, as well as on the demand that accompanied Seoul's chronic housing shortage (Kim Kwan-Joong 1998).

Because much of the postwar squatting was on the unplanned hilly slopes adjacent to the downtown area, JGB sites are similarly concentrated in those areas, in districts such as Sungbuk-gu, Sungdong-gu, and Mapo-gu. By 2000, Kim Kwan-Joong could report that some 107 projects had been completed, accounting for 102,430 apartments, with another 62 projects underway and 26 due to commence.

The JGC program, by contrast, is reserved for apartment buildings that were built at least twenty years previously and deemed to be under the minimum structural safety standards. Thus especially targeted have been the four- to five-story walk-up flats from the 1970s, comprising units mostly of less than sixty square meters, with poor facilities and heating systems, in a poor state of maintenance, and with low income occupants. The small-scale "general" JGC program began in 1990, applying to individual sites usually with less than 300 units per site; by 2000, some 308 projects had been completed, with 76,557 units, another 413 projects under way, and 278 ready to commence.

The larger-scale Apartment District JGC program would address the redevelopment of far more extensive areas. The Apartment District is an overlay zoning district, devised for planned residential development in the 1970s, mostly as five-story walk-up apartment complexes. Beginning around 2000, the JGC program would, in its first stage, clear more than 50,000 housing units in 1,180 buildings in forty-three sites on some 960 acres. The existing plot ratio of 0.93 would treble to the 2.75 allowed by the city's Apartment District Master Plan, to yield an estimated 62,700 units—an increase of 12,700 new units (Kim Kwan-Joong n.d., 5). Kim adds, however, that some 60 percent of the apartment owners are estimated to be absentee, speculative owners, indicating that the same proportion of Apartment District occupants are renters.

Mention should be made of two other programs that account for the conversion of Seoul to a high-density, high-rise metropolis. The first is mixed-use housing termed MXD (Ju-Sang-Bok-Hap, literally "housing-commercial combination") that utilizes the high plot ratio of commercial zoning to develop high-density apartment towers. The second is public housing, also producing high-rise apartment blocks.

Both the JGB and JGC programs have the effect of transforming affordable, small rental units for lower-income people into housing for Seoul's burgeoning middle class. The shift to high-rise apartments also signaled the waning of the tradition of multifamily living in detached houses (Clark 2000, 138). Multifamily living may persist, but it is migrating to apartments in high-rise blocks. A number of factors would seem to have underlain this epochal shift. One would have been the "poor years" prior to the 1980s that yielded a dwelling stock that would inevitably need to be replaced to meet the demands of a suddenly more affluent age. A further, more underlying cause, albeit less explicable, has been the increasing popularity (or is it more acceptance?) of apartment living. Interestingly, Valérie Gelézeau suggests that Park's early experience of Japan's Manchukuo experiment led him to equate the traditional with the countryside and the countryside with the backward—so not only should people move off the land but they should also change the way they lived. The new blocks would be a potent symbol of Park's idea of modernity (Gelézeau 2003). However, she suggests, the inspiration for the new estates was Japanese, despite their Western-style bathrooms and kitchens and despite the Western appellation *nyu t'aun* (new town) attached to the Chamsil first megaproject. The design of the new complexes as well as the layout of the housing units was very different from Koreans' previous experiences, and much adaptation in lifestyles was called for.[56] From her extensive study of the estates and their occupants, Gelézeau concludes that the apartment blocks are admired for their comfort and security, but that there is social isolation and lack of contact with neighbors, in sharp contrast with traditional lifestyles—people reported missing the friendly greetings of the old communities that they might remember from the past or now occasionally visit.[57]

There was another factor behind Park's espousal of high-rise apartment estates: these would provide a market and incentive for the new construction *chaebol,* preeminently Hyundai. Gelézeau reported that apartments built in the 1970s and early 1980s, typically five-story walk-ups, were in part meant as temporary, low-cost housing: her interviews with building companies revealed that they knew they were to build only for thirty years, when the *chaebol* builders would then move in to replace them. Many of the apartments that she had focused on, such as the complexes in Mapo-gu, had already undergone several reconstructions within a span of thirty years.

The incentive to construct also related to the housing price inflation in an era of severe shortage that would ensure a high economic return to owners, thereby triggering a rush to speculative investment. While Seoul's housing prices were somewhat stabilized by aggressive supply, especially in the 1990s, investment in apartments was still seen as a lucrative option. By 2007, however, housing prices were more often moving downward; by 2009 Seoul was reported to have one of the lowest gross rental yields in the world; by 2011 of all countries recorded it was tied for the lowest with Taipei.[58]

While the city has been socially transformed by these various strategies, so too has its physical appearance. As JGB sites are mostly located in the old hillside residential communities, they are visible against the mountain backdrops, block scenic views, and dominate their surroundings. JGC projects, in turn, occur in the middle of low-rise communities throughout the city: as "stand-alone" apartment blocks, they are in sharp, interrupting contrast with their fine-grained neighboring areas—the older areas become a city of staccato, visual disruptions. Old, labyrinthine, tightly interwoven street patterns are broken. There is also social disruption: "Walled and gated, the new apartment complexes foster the sense of enclaves and of indifference to the adjacent neighborhood" (Kim Kwan-Joong n.d., 12). The 1980s saw a vast surge in construction of high-rises in Seoul, continuing into the subsequent decades. These were often on Western-style grid layouts, in marked contrast with the more informal, even chaotic patterns of Korean tradition.

The 2005 Korea Census indicated that 53.0 percent of the population lived in condominium blocks labeled as "apartments," 31.9 percent in detached houses, and 13.5 percent in townhouse or duplex-type houses (Seo 2008). With a total population of 24.5 million at that time, the Seoul National Capital Area was the world's second-largest metropolitan area. The rural population is more likely to be in detached houses; the urban population is overwhelmingly in apartments though, not solely high-rise—much of Seoul and other Korean cities remain the boxland of smaller and usually older flat blocks. It is the "two morphologies city" observed in figure 1.1 of chapter 1. Homeowners and two-year-based residents are prevalent—in the main it is a relatively stable apartment-dwelling population.

Exterior space, interior space

Expansion of this high-rise city from around the mid-1960s was, in large measure, via increasingly large estates of mostly identical apartment blocks and, also increasingly, in "new towns" following the planning of the 1970s. Standards of space and amenity in the early decades were Spartan; however, with rising national affluence and the move of the *chaebol* into housing estate development, Seoul became arguably the closest approximation to the world that Le Corbusier imagined in his 1922 Ville contemporaine, designed to house three million people, with its Beaux Arts formality, antibourgeois aesthetic, futurist dedication to new technology, socialist program, and English garden landscape (*Le Corbusier et Pierre Jeanneret* 1935; King 1996, 51–52)—all this despite its allegedly Japanese derivation via the vision of Park.

Most of the Corbusian elements are in place in the Seoul sprawl except for the English garden;[59] and the program is more corporate-capitalist than socialist.

Any socialist lineage of the city's imagery, however, is counteracted by the advertisements that adorn its vertical surfaces. The ubiquitous advertising boards and LCD panels can also be read in the context of the space use of modern Seoul: exterior, public space is less the setting for civic life than the signage-adorned realm that one passes through in transit from one interior to another. Public space rarely invites the pause or lingering rest that one expects in European or even, occasionally, North American cities. Accordingly, architectural design is more likely to be focused on interior than exterior space. The blandness of Seoul exterior (urban) space becomes explicable.

That said, outdoor leisure is certainly enjoyed by more mobile Seoulites, most typically in the mountainside forests, and in visits to ancient temples, ancestral homes, and beach or mountain resorts. There are also the remnant mountain monasteries, relics of the Chosun banishment of Buddhism to the mountains and forests: their still-surviving monastic life is, every weekend, invaded and compromised by "fun."[60] The transportation constraints of areas beyond the city limit the fun, however (Clark 2000, 153).

More recently, Seoul has become a city of public parks, often along riverbanks and streams. The 1960s planning for Seoul made very little provision for green space. The 1971 planning had provided for a greenbelt, albeit four decades after the peak of the European greenbelt movement and having the unplanned effect of reserving land that in later decades would be developed for housing. The 1988 Olympics had forced a cleanup of the city, and this included rehabilitation of the city's few parks and the creation of a few more. The Seoul Master Plan 1990, however, advanced this small achievement: parks and green space were provided for, scenic areas were to be maintained, and construction was restricted on the surrounding mountains and hills. What may to a Western eye appear to be the incongruities of Korean public and private space will be reprised in chapter 4. It suffices for now to observe that Seoul seems to present a hypercapitalist public image of an advertisement-adorned, capitalist-corrupted Corbusian utopia, while the spaces of the everyday become visible only to the walker who might stray, beyond the daunting realm of corporate towers and multitowered housing estates, into a "back-street" world of disorder, entertainment, and small-scale creativity and invention. It is worth noting, however, that the traditional house has always been closed to the passing eye (Clark 2000, 93–96; Jung Inha 2013, 29–35). We search for these spaces of the everyday in chapter 4.

Part 3

RE-IMAG(IN)ING THE CITY

Throughout the 1980s there were attempts to present a new, motivating vision of an urban world worthy of "the modernization of our fatherland." While the vision of international emergence, political legitimacy for a dictatorship, and showcasing a new economic power might have been the message to be communicated through the glorious events of the 1988 Olympics, the medium of the communication had to be the fabric of the city itself. This posed a challenge in the 1980s: the city presented as hurriedly and poorly built, chaotic and massively overcrowded. The image-building project required the slums to be either removed or screened. People living in slum areas would be expelled, in many cases by paid thugs, leading to organized resistance by strongly politicized students (much emboldened by the 1980 student uprisings), clergymen, and local residents.

It is worth observing that the 1980s image building was never completed. Slums persist, both in the surviving poor housing from the early migrations into the city and from the crammed apartment blocks of the 1970s and following decades. The regimented apartment estates of the twenty-first century are frequently constructed over land cleared of the villages and rural-immigrant settlements of previous decades. A well-hidden example is the Guryong slum, almost alongside Gangnam; it developed as a shantytown in 1988, created by residents who had been pushed out of their inner-city slums by the government to "clean up" Seoul for the Olympics. Ironically, the Olympic Stadium complex has also now, in the 2010s, been recolonized with shanties in the screening bushland intended to enhance its presentation and on remnant earthworks (presumed survivals from Wiryeoseong, the Baekje capital founded 18 BCE). Areas of poverty and poor housing abound in older industrial areas such as Guro-gu.[61]

Attempts at urban beautification, albeit by violence, continue. On 12 August 2011 *yongyeok* (people hired by government to destroy illegal houses or the shops of poor tenants) invaded an urban poor community in Jaegeon in the Gangnam District. Much of the settlement had burned to the ground in an accidental fire on 12 June 2011, whereupon the community began rebuilding their houses, to be confronted by some one hundred *yongyeok* at 4:30 a.m. who had been sent in to destroy the rebuilding effort. Video of the mayhem and destruction went viral.[62] Slums can be found in most districts of Seoul, typically hidden behind concrete or metal walls and frequently under threat.[63]

A counterstory from Busan relates to the shantytown of Gamcheon, which has been transformed into an arts neighborhood.[64]

Proliferating Seoul

The expansion of urban Korea has gone far beyond the capital city envisioned in the 1960s. Despite an explicit decentralization policy articulated in the early 1960s, Seoul's immediate region now holds close to five times the population of that time; since 1989 new towns have been established beyond the old borders of the metropolis. Examples include Bundang in the southeast, which has had its own subway line since 1994, and Ilsan on Line 3 in the northwest, which is now a center for television production, as well as home to Kintex, the Korean International Exhibition Center. Korea is highly urbanized: around 80 percent of the national population is living in urban areas. Most of these people are located in the Seoul-Busan corridor, which contains, besides Seoul (10.42 million), five of the six largest cities in Korea: Incheon (2.63 million), Suwon (1.19 million), (Daejeon (1.44 million), Daegu (2.51 million), and Busan (3.64 million).[65]

Since 2004 the Korea Train eXpress (KTX) high-speed train system has been in service in the corridor, reducing travel time between Seoul and Busan (the northernmost and southernmost cities in the corridor, respectively) to two hours and forty minutes. The massive suburbanization of the peripheries of the corridor's constituent cities has blurred old distinctions between urban and rural. The loss of the rural also implies the loss of the city as a centralized social entity. Thus, by the action of the high-speed train linking once-distinctive cities, Seoul becomes a new form of networked metropolis, simultaneously decentralized in its population and workplaces, multicentered functionally, and highly centralized in its political control and in symbolic capital.

New architecture

In the colonial period—with the exception of some measures at historical conservation[66]—there had been a concerted attempt to dispatch traditional Korean architecture to the past and to replace it with Japanese architecture. Korean architecture schools were closed, and Korean architects were required to train in Japan and upon their return encouraged to design exclusively according to Japanese models and styles. Whereas it might have been expected that Western influences on Japanese architects at the time would have been transferred to Korea, this did not happen. In Korea, over a period of some thirty-five years, there were almost no influences from Art Nouveau, Art Deco,

Bauhaus Modern, or 1930s–1940s Moderne except very mediately through Japanese essays in "modernity" (and traces of Art Deco in their civic monuments, as in the case of Japanese-trained Korean architect Park Gil-yong, noted in chapter 2). Western architectural ideas came to Korea only indirectly through the post-1945 presence of the Americans in the country and the opening of American architecture schools to Korean students.

Korean architects were constrained to small-scale domestic buildings, the repair of damaged missionary churches (well funded from overseas donations), patchwork construction on damaged infrastructure, and boxlike hospitals and schools—all simply constructed under military supervision. Although Seoul had escaped the worst of World War II destruction, it came close to annihilation in the Korean War, with the consequence that Korean architecture by Koreans became even more limited to patchwork and small-scale, boxlike constructions to meet urgent needs, limited budgets, and inadequate materials.

The effect of the boom decades of the Park dictatorship was merely to continue this styleless, unreflective rush to build. The new American-trained architects brought back little more than a preoccupation with skyscrapers and proceeded to serve the new demands from the *chaebol* for mass company housing for their workers with extensive estates of bland, uniform blocks of cheap apartments. While these might have been the models dominating the architectural discourse of the 1960s and 1970s and conforming to the essentializing architectural ideals of Mies van der Rohe, Le Corbusier, and their acolytes, nothing could be more divorced from traditional ideas of Korean housing (figure 3.9).

While the 1980s and 1990s were an era of poorly planned, poorly designed, and precipitously constructed dross in Korea's "Asian Tiger" rush (Kim Won Bae's "jungle"), there were also endeavors to find characteristics of a "Korean modern" architecture. Central to this quest was a small group of young architects beginning their careers in the Park Chung-hee era and including, notably, Kim Chung-up (Kim Joong-eop) and Kim Swoo Geun, the latter referred to above in relation to the aborted National Assembly Building competition and the Yeouido Island master plan. Kim Chung-up (1922–1988) continues to be revered as an architect-poet of nature and something of a hermit.[67] Upon his return to Korea in 1955, he focused on exploring the formal systems of traditional Korean architecture so that he could define their essential characteristics and express them in new and uncompromisingly modern forms. His French embassy in Seoul continues to intrigue with its reminiscences of Pulguksa structures; it would

FIGURE 3.9 Rows of apartment buildings, Banpo-dong, Seocho-gu Gangnam, 2012.

commonly be seen as his masterpiece (Jung Inha 2013, 85). However, it is the story of Kim Swoo Geun that throws a particular light on the search for an identity.

Kim Swoo Geun and the quest for identity

Kim Swoo Geun (1931–1986) had entered Seoul National University in 1950, to major in architecture. The Korean War ended that endeavor, and Kim moved to the Tokyo National University of Fine Arts and Music, eventually graduating in 1960 with a master's degree from Tokyo University. During his study there he had been interned in Hirada Matsuda's architectural firm. He won the Korean National Assembly Building competition in 1959, and in 1960 returned to Korea. In 1961 he founded his own architectural firm, which in time metamorphosed into the SPACE Group; also in 1961 he began to teach at the architecture department of Hongik University (of which more anon). He designed some two hundred projects within and beyond Korea.[68]

In 1962 Kim was appointed head of the building committee for the Asian People's Anti-Communist League Center—it is now identified as Freedom Center and has sunk to the status of a wedding hall. Park Chung-hee's coup d'état had occurred only a year previously, and the young military regime, negotiating with Taiwan, Japan, and the United States, became host to the symbolic center for international anti-Communism. The new regime, decreeing itself to be "revolutionary," approved the monumentalism of the center's sculptural concrete and the perceived internationalism of its architectural language as appropriately symbolic of international anti-Communism.[69] Its obvious references were to Le Corbusier's Parliament Building in Chandigarh and to Japanese concrete monumentalism of the period.[70] Adjoining the Asian People's Anti-Communist League Center, on the slopes of Namsan, was the Tower Hotel, also by Kim. This was an international-modernist high-rise building in Seoul's Jung-gu District, from 1969; it is a fine piece of 1960s International Style design, and could be located anywhere. It was also Korea's tallest building at that time: its seventeen floors represented South Korea and its sixteen allies in the Korean War, at a time when Korean people tended to be terrified of anything taller than a couple of floors.

Also from that period was the Sewoon (Se-un) Mega Complex (figure 3.10). In 1944, to prepare for the expected bombing raids from Allied forces, the Japanese began to clear a fifty-meter-wide and 1.2-kilometer-long corridor in central Seoul as a firebreak. At the northern end of this strip was Jongmyo Royal Shrine (in the Korean War period slated for demolition for a projected parliament building). After the end of World War II, this long strip came to be occupied by squatters, refugees, and brothels, an embarrassment to administrators anxious to change the image of a city that, by 1953, was mostly a bombed ruin. Sewoon Mega Complex, from 1967, was to be part of the first redevelopment project of modern Seoul. Four rectangular

FIGURE 3.10 Model of Kim Swoo Geun's Sewoon Mega Complex: dichotomous typologies that prefigure the Seoul of the present. Source: Seoul Station exhibition panel, April 2012.

blocks of mixed-use facilities, linked by pedestrian bridges and decks, traversed the four main east-west roads of Seoul. With rooftop parks and playgrounds, schools, theaters, and efficiently planned residential units, this would be a city within a city, a symbol of a modern Seoul. The complex assembled a plethora of small shops and textiles companies, a focus of labor productivity but also labor radicalism. Its derivation from the ideas of Le Corbusier, this time from the residential *unités d'habitation,* is clear; more significantly, the Mega Complex is to be seen as prefiguring Seoul as a world of vast, planned, soul-less highrise estates—that is, as prefiguring the present Seoul. The Sewoon Complex planning was linked to the "modernization" of the city that also included the Samil Expressway (1967–1971) over the top of the ancient Chongyecheon Stream and the Samil Building (of 1970) at the entrance to the expressway.

Present plans are for all four buildings of Sewoon Mega Complex to be demolished in order to connect Jongmyo with Namsan via parkland. The locality comes full circle, to approach its 1944 (Japanese) state as open space.

Kim's master plan for Yeouido Island has been referred to above. As part of the "Supreme" Master Plan thinking of the 1970s to develop Seoul into a multicentered metropolis, the island in the Han River would transform into the "Manhattan of Korea." The plan comprised linear megastructures extending along an axis linking the National Assembly District and a new City Hall District. Here the obvious reference is to Kenzo Tange's 1960 plan for Tokyo Bay, with its intention to transform the fundamental structure of that city. Elevated decks would cross the boundaries of private property; technology integrated with enlightened capital would overcome existing checkerboard subdivisions. In order to implement principles of sunlight, as well as green and open space, the plan demanded large amounts of both public and private capital, speedily invested and concentrated. Kim's utopian plan, like that for a National Assembly, was abandoned. Instead, Yeouido, now a central commerce and banking district of Seoul, was developed along a traditional grid plan. Kim never made another city plan.

Kim also designed many houses in the 1960s, although they are rarely considered defining projects of his early period. Unlike the career path of other great architects, who begin to define their first architectural principles with houses, then move on to larger institutional projects, Kim began his career as the virtual state architect of Korea. The houses do, however, demonstrate a commitment to 1960s International Style ideals: references here were mostly to Frank Lloyd Wright (rather than Le Corbusier), notably to his emblematic Fallingwater—the monumentalism of the institutional projects was missing.

The turning point in Kim Swoo Geun's career was the Buyeo Museum, the national museum for the ancient Baekje kingdom, the claimed origin of Park's envisioned Korea. Following the unpopular reparation settlement and normalization of relations between Korea and the still-hated Japan in 1965, the Park regime began to push toward a conservative, nationalist cultural policy. In an atmosphere of extreme anti-Japanese sentiment, Kim's design for the gate to the Buyeo Museum was accused of being a torii, the entrance gate to a Japanese Shinto shrine—reminiscent of the hated Korea Shrine, Choson Jingu. The charges struck at the most basic instincts of both accusers and accused: both building and architect were put on trial-by-media for false identity. A panel from an exhibition of Kim Swoo Geun's work quotes him "defending his design from attacks that it looked Japanese" (1967): "The architectural style of Buyeo Museum is neither that of Baekje nor that of a Japanese Shrine. It is the style of I, Kim Swoo Geun."[71]

The museum has long since been replaced. There is now both history and legend claiming that, through a process of penitence and self-discipline, Kim Swoo Geun broke away from his earlier sculptural monumentalism, commencing a new period of work that would define his identity and, indeed, that of modern Korean architecture. Disillusioned by his experience with the Buyeo Museum and the Korean Engineering Consulting Corporation with which he had been associated, he turned inward to his own practice within the SPACE Group and toward "smaller things," which he now believed to be the carriers of genuine culture.

The 1970s are generally seen as marking a second period in Kim's work, with the 1971 SPACE Group Building in the Jongno District of central Seoul as a turning point, in which he began to seek a new modern yet characteristically Korean space. Traditional dark gray brick would be used, and a variety of scales and textures would be played with; there was a focus on voids over solids, reminiscent of the urban *hanok*; also interesting was Kim's ornamental approach here—somewhat unusual in more formal, elitist Korean architecture, though certainly characteristic of the decorated forms of the streets and markets. The turn was toward fragmentation and smaller elements. Another exhibition panel quotes Yoon Seung Joong on "the design approach of Kim Swoo Geun of the 1970s" (1986) "Architecture is dividing. . . . Dividing means that there is no initial system or space, but that on a site, a form is given, which is divided to satisfy the system."[72] It was this idea that underlay the winning entry to the National Assembly competition, referred to above, as grouped, human-scale pavilions.

FIGURE 3.11 Model of Kim Swoo Geun's Cheongju National Museum. Source:Seoul Station exhibition panel, April 2012.

A fine example of Kim's work from this period is the Arko Art Center and Arko Arts Theater from 1977. It presents as a form of gateway or passage rather than a building—again, a void. The Arko Art Center home page expresses the building's intent as being to display "the meaning and context of the site and the city. The architecture consists of two buildings linked together, and the first floor which links the two buildings connects and allows communication between Marronnier Park in front and Naksan in the rear."[73] The Arko complex can also be seen as carrying forward the idea of the bridged block from the Sewoon Mega Complex.

In the 1970s, Korea's Ministry of Culture planned a series of national museums in the provinces. Continuing the conservative policies of the 1960s (Park) era, there was a strict directive that all of its museums were to be designed with traditional tiled roofs; it was a directive that created a style that dominated the architectural landscape for public cultural institutions. Kim Swoo Geun was appointed architect for the Cheongju National Museum and set about defining a design that would adopt traditional forms into a modern architectural configuration. Sited on a mountain slope, the museum brought together spatial approaches that Kim had explored in a number of schools of Seoul National University, together with the parallel wall systems from the SPACE Group Building. The intricate system of parallel walls and roof systems referencing traditional forms defined a composition reminiscent of traditional hillside villages—and of Tange's Tokyo Bay proposal. The building was completed in 1987 (figure 3.11).

The 1970–1971 entry for the Plateau Beaubourg (Centre Pompidou, Paris) competition took Kim's experiments with scale to their limits. He began with five-by-five-meter boxes, massing them together in different configurations, eventually settling on a repetitive pattern of parallel walls centered around a courtyard—again the centrality of the void (the *hanok*). Movable partitions would bring flexibility to the exhibition space, while the planned variations in form and space could allow happenings that transcend intentions—"happening" and "coincidence" were key terms in the more global intellectual discourse of that time. In effect, the design was a multiplication of the SPACE Group Building and stands as the diametric opposite of the winning competition entry by Renzo Piano and Richard Rogers.

No similar attempt at an architecture-by-assemblage characterized Kim's design for Seoul's Olympic Main Stadium. In 1973 Kim Swoo Geun was commissioned to provide a master plan for a sports complex in the newly planned southeastern region of Seoul (his Tokyo University master's thesis, on case studies for Olympic facilities, had been under Eika Takayama, who had been involved in master planning for the Tokyo Olympics).[74] The Seoul facilities were to accommodate the Asian Games and National Sports Festival, at that time the largest sports event in Korea. The architecture of the main stadium was based on massive, sculptural concrete piers, like hands, "holding" the seating areas and defining its exterior; in 1981, when Seoul was selected as host for the 1988 Olympics, steel cantilevers ranging from thirty to forty meters were added to the hands to form an elegant yet monumental curved roof. While the size of the Jamsil Olympic Stadium provided no opportunity for Kim to demonstrate his commitment to complexes of small-scale elements, it could display another of his principles, namely "moderate and elegant line, especially at the roof"; it might also be seen as a further exercise in his aesthetic of parallel walls. The curve of the building's profile was claimed to reflect the curves of a Chosun dynasty porcelain vase (figure 3.12).

FIGURE 3.12 Model of Kim Swoo Geun's Olympic Main Stadium. Source: Seoul Station exhibition panel, April 2012.

The 1979 Yangdeok Catholic Church in Masan, South Gyeong-sang Province, marks the beginning of a third period of Kim's work, which would combine the textural, spatial, and scale interests of the 1970s with the more formal bravado and monumentalism of the 1960s. While the early sketches reveal the parallel walls as the starting point of the design, these are bent to define a sculptural space; ornamental brick and post-and-lintel elements create a powerful architectural presence. This was followed by the 1980 Kyung Dong Presbyterian Church, near Dongdaemun Gate in Seoul, arguably the masterpiece of this late period. As with the Masan church, there is an array of finely designed spaces to accommodate the multiple community programs that associate with religious institutions in Korea, here packed into a tight and differentiated section on a very restricted site. A ring of parallel-walled monoliths, inward leaning, created a rooftop chapel open to the sky (subsequently, sadly, roofed). The building seems reminiscent of something very monumental and very ancient—perhaps the defensive walls of old Korean capitals.

During the 1980s the SPACE Group designed a number of large commercial projects, reflecting the growth of the corporate private sector in Korea, even as it continued to suffer under the military regime. Rarely, however, did these display Kim's consistent hand. In 1983 the group designed the United States Embassy Building on Sejongno in central Seoul, attributed to Kim (indicated in figure 3.1 and visible to the right in figure 3.3). However, it is a relatively undistinguished office block and more representative of the group's corporate practice than the ideas of the group's originator.

Also significant was Kim's role in publishing the monthly *SPACE* in 1966, the first general art journal in Korea, to record and distribute Korean culture. He also established the SPACE Gallery in 1972 and the SPACE Love theater group. The architect Min Hyun-sik has seen Kim as obsessed with the question of how to effectively convey and adapt Korean tradition into contemporary architecture.[75] He is also seen as significant in crossing diverse genres, as a seminal cultural activist, and as an educator successful in mentoring a range of subsequently prominent architects.

While the move from Kim's monumentalist preoccupations of his 1960s "first" period to the more disintegrative concerns of the 1970s "second" period might be seen as some ideological shift, it is more useful to see that both positions coexisted in some state of dialectical tension throughout the 1970s and 1980s. There is an alternating between relatively conventional modernist and highly idiosyncratic, ideology-infused works. Kim's argument on disintegration of space is an interesting counterpoint to that of urban space as an assemblage.

While the brilliant intrusions of disorder into Seoul space (Namdae-mun Market, and the "back streets" of virtually every Seoul district) might be seen as disintegrative of some imagined order, yet they are also to be seen as manifesting assemblage logic (to be considered in chapter 4). Kim's disintegration is the exact opposite of this—it is always the logic of the willful designer.

The story of Kim Swoo Geun is also to be seen as reflecting the search for a Korean identity in an age in which antecedents have been blurred at best, erased at worst, in a long era of linked intrusion and erosion. The search, however, has not been without its contradictions and consequent ambiguities. Kim's early experience had been in Japan, significantly at the moment when a group of brilliant young Japanese architects were energetically searching for an architecture that could express their own national resurgence. The turn to monumental concrete forms, as well as to the parallel walls idiom, have been seen above as mirroring the thinking of Kenzo Tange (1913–2005); the monumentalism and the distinctive articulation of structure also parallel Kunio Maekawa's work. In chapter 4 attention will turn to more recent Korean architecture, in which high-tech and free forms can be seen to reflect Korean explorations of digital technology's freeing of the architect's entrapment in the two dimensions of paper representation, yet here too Japanese forerunners can be spotted, notably Toyo Ito (b. 1941) and Itsuko Hasegawa (b. 1941).[76]

It is not to denigrate the real achievement of Kim Swoo Geun to observe that the sphere of Korean architecture seems still to intersect with that of Japan.

Part 4

THE CITY AND CHRISTIANITY

A further factor in the modernization of Korea and in the construction of the distinctive urban space of Seoul has been Christianity and its interaction with other ideological movements in Korean culture. In the seventeenth and eighteenth centuries there had been strong criticism from scholarly officials of Christian ideas as they had infiltrated into Korea from the Jesuit China Mission, especially through the writings of Matteo Ricci (1552–1610). Scholars of the *silhak* ("practical learning") school, thriving in the eighteenth century, believed in a social structure based on merit rather than birth; they were opposed by the mainstream academic establishment and accordingly saw the egalitarian values of Christianity as an ideological basis for their own beliefs. When the Catholic Church finally achieved a foothold in Korea in 1784, there was already a philosophical sympathy for its ideas among the educated elite and it could begin more as an indigenous than a missionary movement. The Catholic Church was also the first Korean organization formally to recognize the use of *han-gul*, the phonemic Korean alphabet first invented around 1446. Christian literature, including that for use in schools, mostly used the Korean language and the easily learned *han-gul* script instead of the official and elitist Chinese. In this way, too, Christianity could present as indigenous—perhaps more so than the Chosun court.[77]

Christianity in Korea was also aided by a certain parallelism with Korean traditions. So, shamanist Koreans had a monotheistic concept of a Creator-God and a foundational myth of three divine characters, thereby providing a framework for missionary explanation of the Christian Trinity. Even more powerful was the identification that many Christians forged with the cause of Korean nationalism during the Japanese colonial occupation. When Christians refused to participate in worship of the Japanese emperor, mandated in the 1930s, this resistance, albeit more theological than nationalistic, enabled Koreans more broadly to see Christianity as nonforeign—part of themselves as Koreans.[78] Furthermore, as observed earlier, the Christian mission stations, with their churches, schools, and hospitals, could present the shock of a Western modernity undistorted by colonial ideology.

Finally, Christianity's indigenous claim was in part expressed through *minjung* ("common people") theology. Lee Namhee (2007) has explored the rise and role of *minjung*, recounting how a group of activists mostly from university campuses—the *undongkwon* (student activists)—dealt with the challenges of an oppressive government, the contradictions of capitalism, and the memory of their own "failed history." They set their task as the reimagining of that history and of their identity and as the reshaping of Korea's future. The *undongkwon* determined to emphasize the *minjung* as the proper subject of their attention and as the "motor of history." In that sense, the *minjung* movement harkened back to the motivating ideas of the Donghak uprising and its 1894 revolution but also to its Cheondogyo theology; there were also antecedents in the Confucian *silhak* social reform movement, of the late Chosun era, which had developed to counter the uncritical, metaphysical, asocial preoccupations of neo-Confucianism. Its turn to the "common people" caused *minjung* to cast more than a mere glance to the North Korean anticapitalist ideology—indeed, Lee notes that in the mid-1980s the movement tended to divide into two camps, one pro–North Korea and the other more orthodox Marxist-Leninist (Lee Namhee 2007).[79]

Minjung theology, somewhat akin to the Catholic liberation theology then prevalent in Latin American states, arose in the 1970s to provide the more explicit ideological underpinnings of the movement. It came about as the more political aspects of the Christian Gospels wove through the ideas and principles of Marxism-Leninism and the memories of Cheondogyo and *silhak*. Though based on the "image of god" idea in Genesis, *minjung* theology also incorporated the traditional Korean idea of *han,* which suggests a sense of inconsolable pain and absolute helplessness. *Minjung* theology would depict the ordinary Korean people as the rightful masters of their own destiny. One manifestation of *minjung* theology in the last years of the Park dictatorship was the rise of Christian social missions with campaigns to advance the interests of farmers and the industrial proletariat, effectively assuming the role usually claimed by trade union movements. It is instructive to note that both Presidents Kim Young-sam (a Presbyterian) and Kim Dae-jung (a Catholic), long opponents of military governments in Korea and often imprisoned for their efforts, subscribed to *minjung* theology. Kim Dae-jung, in particular, is seen as one of the great leaders of the cause.

Lee Namhee (2011) has argued that, in the 1990s, progressive discourse moved from *minjung* (people) to *simin* (citizen), linking this shift to the end of dictatorship as a new context for reform, to the collapse of political Marxism in Eastern Europe, and a corresponding defensive rigidity creeping into *minjung,* and the perception (in the 1990s) of the failure of the social ferment of the 1960s.

Protestant proliferation

One of the panels in the 2012 retrospective exhibition of Kim Swoo Geun's work, at Seoul Station in 2012 and discussed earlier, refers to Korea as "a country with the largest and most aggressive Christian congregations in the world."[80] While Catholicism had long predated the advent of Protestantism in Korea, it was the latter that most significantly transformed the urban culture (and the cityscape). By 2003 some 53.9 percent of Koreans aged fifty-nine and over reported having a religion; of these, Buddhists were 47.0 percent, and Catholics 13.7 percent, but Protestants 36.8 percent (Jang Sukman 2004). In younger cohorts, Protestantism would have been even stronger. Protestantism was especially professed among the educated, professionals, middle-class, and the urban; it tends to be pro-American (despite the urban focus of anti-Americanism) and exclusivist (and hence intolerant). Seoul is in the main Protestant, the rural areas Buddhist. The post–Korean War surge is clear from the growth in Protestantism membership (from 500,198 recorded for South Korea in 1950 to 8,760,336 in 1995). However, it is the fragmentation and proliferation revealed in the explosion in numbers of churches that is astonishing— from 3,114 in 1950 to 58,046 in 1996. In 1996 there were 168 Protestant denominations in Korea (Lee Won Gue 1999, 237–238).[81]

Presbyterianism has been especially disintegrative, with its fragmentation variously economic, theological, and politically ideological. A congregation will "separate" to keep its property and revenues to itself; the separation will often be justified on grounds of theological nicety or political commitment. A significant divide had occurred in the 1970s between the liberal "Christian Presbyterians" (Kijang, or Kidokkyo Changnohoe) and the more conservative, mainstream "Jesus Presbyterians" (Clark 2007, 180). The Kijang Presbyterians arose out of a long liberal tradition of social activism and anti-Japanese resistance, with regional origins in northeastern Korea (notably Pyongyang) and the ethnic Korean area of Manchuria. In the 1970s their antidictatorship stand in the South was widely seen as muddle-headed and a persistence of leftist thinking. Their leader was the Reverend Kim Chejun, their center the Han'guk Theological Seminary in Suwon, and there was in part an embrace of the *minjung* theology (Hong Young-gi 2010). The legacy of the Protestant fragmentation is ubiquitous in the space of Seoul, ranging from the often confrontational proselytizing on subway trains and stations, streets, and seemingly constant rallies[82] to the evangelizing pamphlets, religious tracts, posters, and billboards to the bewildering forests of conical spires, with their red-illuminated crosses on otherwise nondescript, boxlike buildings, most commonly also adorned with a pastiche of advertising boards mixing religious text, local enterprises and services, esoteric logos, and global brands.

Certainly there are reactions to the Korean frenetic turn to religion. While anti-Christian sentiment is scarcely unique to Korea, Lee Jin Gu (2004) has examined the use of the Internet to express this opposition: the Internet sites in particular assail religious exclusiveness, God-centrism (as distinct from a focus on a social program), and religious toadyism.

Jang Sukman (1999, 188) makes the point that Protestantism saw itself as American, whereas Catholicism was seen as French;[83] and Protestantism could argue superiority over Confucianism and Buddhism, as being "not really religious." The point can be linked to the ongoing "Asian values" debate, which, in the Korean context, is largely about Confucianism—making Confucianism compatible with present-day democratic ideas and "modernity" (see various papers in this debate in *Korea Journal,* 41, nos. 2 and 3 of 2001). Protestantism, it seems, has been able to present itself as more compatible with Confucianism.

It is also possible, however, that Protestantism could simply occupy a vacuum that came with the collapse of the "indigenous" but also hybridized Cheondogyo.

Gapyeong and the Unification Church

A unique twist on both the *chaebol* and Korean Christianity is represented in the Unification Church, popularly though derogatorily referred to as "the Moonies." Mun Yong-myong was born in what is now North Korea in 1920, into a traditional rural family.[84] He attended a Confucian school, but around 1930 the family became fervent Presbyterians. Unification Church members believe that Jesus appeared to Mun on 17 April 1935, asking him to complete the work unfinished after the crucifixion. Mun accepted the commission, changing his name to Mun Son-myong—Sun Myung Moon. In 1946 he was imprisoned by the Communist authorities in North Korea, to be released by the advancing US forces during the Korean War.

Moon formally founded his church on 1 May 1954, calling it "The Holy Spirit Association for the Unification of World Christianity," alluding to the intention of the organization to be a unifying force for all Christian denominations. "Holy Spirit" in the original Korean would denote heavenly spirits rather than the Holy Spirit of Christianity; furthermore, "unification" also had obvious political implications. By the end of 1955 the church had thirty church centers in South Korea.

In 1958 missionaries were sent to Japan and, in 1959, to America. In the 1960s missionary work expanded into Europe, and in the 1970s into South America. The American expansion has been somewhat rocky: although President Richard Nixon expressed interest in the church in 1970 and then met with its leaders in 1972, Moon's subsequent actions defending Nixon were poorly regarded; critics increasingly criticized the church for its "brainwashing," and it became an increasing target of the anticult movement;[85] furthermore, it was caught up in the 1976 "Koreagate" scandal involving Korean politicians trying to buy influence in the US Congress. Moon also received backing from controversial Japanese billionaires and gangsters, and from Ryoichi Sasakawa, self-styled "world's richest fascist." In 1982 Moon was found guilty of tax evasion and served time in a US prison. To counter the mounting controversies, on 24 August 1992, the Reverend Moon proclaimed that he and his (second) wife are the "Messiah" and "True Parents" of all humanity. More recently, in 1997 the church became allied with Louis Farrakhan, leader of the Nation of Islam, an Afro-American Islamic organization.

The Unification Church has been a very profitable venture. It and its members own, operate, and subsidize enterprises involved in political, cultural, commercial, media, educational, and other activities. Its *chaebol*-like conglomerate, Tongil Group, was founded by Moon in 1963 to provide revenue to the church. Its initial focus was manufacturing, but in the 1970s and 1980s the church expanded into pharmaceuticals, tourism, and publishing; in 1989 Moon became the largest foreign investor in China; by 1998 the church was the thirty-fifth-largest of South Korean business groups, and currently it has four subsidiaries listed on the Korea Exchange. In December 1991 Moon traveled to Pyongyang and met with Kim Il-sung. Subsequently, starting in 1992, the church established business links with North Korea, eventually owning an automobile manufacturer, Pyeonghwa Motors, a hotel, and other property there; in 2007 the church founded a "World Peace Center" in Pyongyang.

The Unification Church's presence in Seoul has been as proselytizer, rally organizer, and aggrieved demonstrator—in 1975 Moon sponsored one of history's largest peace gatherings, of some 1.2 million people, on Yeouido Island. It has a megachurch in Seoul, while the church's main compound is in Gapyeong, some sixty kilometers northeast of Seoul.

Hybridization

The advance of Protestantism can be seen as another aspect of processes of hybridization that have also characterized belief systems more widely in the metamorphoses of Korean thought, reviewed in chapter 2. Another factor underlying Seoul's distinctive forms of hybridization, identified by Ryu Jeh-hong (2004, 15), is "a forced and exploitative hybridization of the global (new) on the local (old)." Certainly these collisions underlay the hybridization in Cheondogyo described in chapter 2 as in the later embrace and fragmentation of Protestantism. They are also omnipresent in the spaces of the city. Equally certainly, exploitative relations prevail. Yet Ryu's use of the term "forced" is problematic, and one searches for other explanations that could lie behind the merely descriptive "explanations" (a question to be reprised in chapter 6).

The effect of Korea's distinctive form of hybridization was a learned ability to negotiate traditional Confucian values and Western capitalistic (Protestant?) values in everyday encounters, especially in business and professional contexts. Theresa Shim Youn-ja and colleagues argue that this tension of conservative Confucian self-discipline with gung-ho Western-style, Protestant-ethic self-invention enabled the rise of particular forms of entrepreneurship and thereby, in part, the transformation of an agrarian, Confucian-based culture into the present global and technological powerhouse (Shim Youn-ja et al. 2008).

Daniel Tudor (2014, 24–33) writes of the *musok-in* (shaman) in the context of the history of shamanism, its practices, and its continuing role into the present. His chapter on shamanism comes before that on Buddhism. *Musok* is essentially practical: "Usually, a believer will turn to *musok* in order to produce some sort of benefit—good fortune or the removal of evil spirits—or to learn something about his or her destiny. Practitioners may follow a great many different gods and spirits. And the way these are followed depends on a number of factors, including the practitioner's personality and the region she comes from. . . . *Musok* is simply a 'belief in nature' . . . everything in nature—be it a person, an animal, a tree, or even a rock—has a spirit. *Musok* offers a way of communicating with those spirits, and possibly using them for some earthly benefit" (24–25). He goes on, "Unlike Japanese Shinto, another set of animist beliefs that became a vehicle for the state's ideology in Meiji Japan and has been somewhat standardized in its rituals, *Musok* remains disparate. Its countless gods are worshipped in ways depending on the individual character of the *musok-in* and of the teachers who initiated her" (31–32).

Shamanism, however, will also run through a Korean understanding of the world. Anthropologist Laurel Kendall argues that, underneath their space-age cityscapes, deeply wired lifestyles, avant-garde culture, and high fashion, Koreans maintain the vibrant shamanic traditions of their ancestors. Shamanism remains a vital force in Korean spiritual life; in particular, she argues, it assists Korean professionals in negotiating the anxieties of modern life (Kendall 2009). "Broadly speaking," she writes, "shamans are religious practitioners who engage the spirits on behalf of the community, either through encounters during soul flight or by invoking the spirits into the here and now of ritual space, conveying the immediacy of these experiences with their bodies and voices" (xx).

Shamans loomed vividly in the memories from the 1930s of composer Kang Sukhi (2007), cited earlier. He recalls numerous shaman houses behind Naksan (the mountain of the "Left Blue Dragon"), as well as at the base of Ingwansan and Yeongcheon, where shaman rites were constantly held (mountains are central symbols to such rites):

> Shaman houses were strewn with portraits and white flags. Typically, the interior of the house was decorated in garish colors, and there were long spears and straw-cutters. . . . Singing and dancing, shamans summoned the spirits of the deceased and revealed the secrets

of their lives or informed the family members what ailments or diseases they had died from . . . the shaman dances again; jumping up and down as if in an African Masai dance when they are possessed by spirits, and singing and moving right and left taking zigzag steps when trying to summon a spirit.

Kang sees much of Korean folk music as deriving from shamanism, as it is also the derivation for folk culture more widely. Though Confucianism had been sustained as Korea's state "religion" for six hundred years, shamanism always persisted at the base of the society.[86]

Shamans had traditionally ministered to the domestic crises of farmers through rituals that express the longings of the dead and the antics of greedy gods. They have been and remain in a particularly adversarial relationship with Korean Protestantism. For most of the twentieth century, shamans were reviled by both colonial and nationalist regimes as practitioners of antimodern superstition and, with the disappearance of village life, their demise would be predicted. On the contrary, however, shamans thrive in Seoul and other high-rise Korean cities; even among a new middle class and technologically sophisticated public there will be a rising clientele for shamanic intervention. Entrepreneurs whose dreams of wealth are matched by the omnipresent fears of ruin will seek to have the gods and ancestors articulate their anxieties through shamanic ritual; consumers' desires likewise are confronted by dilemmas about getting and spending, and communication with gods and ancestors will be sought to mediate the angst (Kendall 2009). Yet, for all that, shamanism remains an embarrassment to many educated Koreans (Clark 2000, 46).

The nature of the city itself redirects the mind to the sacred mountains and the power of their spirits. Kendall writes, "The rapid growth of the city of Seoul, both upwards and outwards, in the second half of the twentieth century produced an urbanscape where little seems permanent or even very old." Modernization and development, accounting in part for the new demands for shamanic ritual, have also affected the "production" of such ritual, causing "the peregrinations of some venerable old shrines, forced from their original locations by urban development, and the flowering of new commercial shrines on other mountain slopes. If urban development has reduced sacred terrain, cars and good highways have expanded the shamans' access to sacred sites within South Korea" (Kendall 2009, xxviii).

Kendall's achievement is to capture the tension between contemporary Korean life and the contemporary shaman's work, thereby to glimpse the role of traditional religion and reenchantment in a seemingly disenchanted age. The shamans are seen as nostalgically celebrated icons of a vanished rural world whose reality, however, persists. Such superstition and tradition occupy opposite sides of modernity's coin: the one by confuting, the other by obscuring, the vitality of shamanic practice.

The hybridity of Korean beliefs and worldviews may bestow the great strength of a diversity of spiritual resources with which to cope with the extraordinary stresses and instabilities of modernity; it is also possible, however, that as Western epistemes invade Korean ways of comprehending reality, Koreans will begin to perceive contradictions between these ("conflicting," "irreconcilable") beliefs and understandings in which there were previously no such contradictions. When Westerners refer to "Asian values," it may be that they are really referring to this idea of a principle of noncontradiction.

Democracy and the crisis of confidence

Despite the euphoria of the demolition of the Japanese Jungang-cheong commencing on 15 August 1995, the mid-1990s were a period of doubt and uncertainty. A train collision and ship sinking in 1993, then the Seongsu Bridge and Sampung Department Store collapses in 1994 and 1995, shook both public confidence and the civilian government. Former presidents Chun and Roh were indicted on charges linked to bribery, illegal funds, and, in the case of Chun, responsibility for the Gwangju massacre; in December 1996 they were sentenced to death and prison, respectively. The ultimate disgrace came in 1997 when Korea shared in the disaster of the Asian financial crisis and the government had to approach the International Monetary Fund (IMF) for relief funds. "Uncertainty and anxiety prevails our society today as we painfully awaken from a premature delusion of affluence" (Lee Kyong-hee 1997, 6).

The national disgrace of the 1997–1998 Asian financial crisis and consequent IMF bailout occurred as Lee Kyong-hee was finishing her book *World Heritage in Korea*. There was a bitter irony in writing of the glories of Korean heritage in the midst of seemingly accumulating crises of national confidence and with the memory of heritage's erasures.

Song Jesook (2006) has given two snapshots of the city's reaction to one consequence of the 1997 crisis, namely the rise in homelessness. Seoul Station Square, encountered above, became an emblematic space where new, "deserving" homeless people concentrated—homeless merely because of no-doubt temporary glitches in a virtuous, corporate-capitalist society. However, it had long been a locale of the long-term homeless—an "undeserving," indolent, charity-addicted underclass. The square thereby became a politically charged literary and physical topography and a location for protecting "normal" citizens from that longer-term, undeserving, and potentially violent class of homeless people. The second site of Song's study was a former textile factory renovated as a homeless shelter, which became an opportunity for promoting the image of a benevolent welfare state for protecting "deserving" homeless people—protected, indeed, from the undeserving. Song sees this new distinction as marking a transition from a developmental to a welfare state. However, as only short-term street-living people were deemed as "proper," this must still be seen as obeisance to the hegemony of capital and to traditions of Confucian hierarchy and order—to the minimal protection of the Marxian idea of the "reserve army of the unemployed." Song takes her argument further in her 2009 book, *South Koreans in the Debt Crisis*. There is indeed a shift in Korea to a welfare society; however, it is to an essentially neoliberal welfare society (Song Jesook 2009).[87]

The denizens of Seoul must face an even deeper cause of the national angst. The Demilitarized Zone (DMZ), the world's most heavily fortified frontier, is immediately to the north of the city, which is within artillery range of the Democratic People's Republic of (North) Korea. In a situation in which the two Koreas are still technically at war (the 1953 "resolution" to the Korean War was merely an armistice), Seoul exists in a constant state of annihilistic uncertainty. Concrete blocks straddle roads to the north to thwart Northern tanks, antisubmarine barriers block (but how effectively?) the Han River against infiltrating submarines and frogmen, subway stations and bridges are designed to impede the long-anticipated invasion from a nuclear-armed, ever-threatening, ever-unstable North (Jeffries 2010). Video monitors in the subway trains endlessly reprise civil defense lessons, there are constant civil defense exercises, the great depth of the subway stations reminds the commuters of the dual role of the subway as nuclear shelter, hotel rooms will contain survival equipment for the guests in case of attack, and the popular press is preoccupied with reports (allegations) of bizarre behavior from the "NK" (North Korea) leadership. Militarism also contributes to a sense of societal anxiety at what seems an even deeper level: while military regimes in the South have been abolished and a democratic system established since 1987, there are constant signs of the intertwining of military and civil society. There has long been a military response to industrial unrest; military service is obligatory for young men, which produces a collective biographical background.

The economy, the North, and the memory of a violent past (erasure, dictatorship) all conspire to underlie uncertainty.

CHAPTER 4

ERASURE AS HERITAGE

Reading Seoul

T his chapter is concerned with how present Seoul is experienced. Cities are not experienced as wholes, unless from space, perhaps fleetingly from the air, more comprehensively from a map. Rather, they are experienced as disaggregated places, always already fragmented, bits, moments, feelings, memories. A city is a collage, a collection, an assemblage.[1]

Whereas chapters 2 and 3 have focused on the social construction of Seoul and on the ideologies that have permeated that process, the present chapter seeks to understand the uses made of the city and how it is to be read—how the observer is to *make sense* of *what is seen*. Reading is concerned with images (*what is seen*) and with what those images might be revealing or else masking (ideas, meanings, ideologies—that is, with *making sense*).

The chapter is in four very unequal parts. The first is a brief discussion of how images and ideas intersect in urban space. It will introduce notions of dialectical image, montage as a technique, and collage as a result of that technique. Part 2 will occupy a greater part of the chapter and will view Seoul as a multiplicity of fragmented places, each distinct visually, functionally, and in its activities—something of a collage, a patchwork. All cities, to some extent, can be seen as fragmented into differentiated neighborhoods, each with its unique complexity of history, buildings and places, vibrancy, activities, and pathologies; in Seoul this fragmentation is augmented by the city's geography—the city is an aggregation of seemingly separate "towns," in the interstices between multiple dominating mountains and mostly in the lowlands of streams winding their way through those ranges of mountains.

It is a constantly disorienting city, made even more so by the metro subway lines that can take the traveler from one place where special mountains and landmark buildings are reassuringly visible, only then to deposit the traveler in another place—perhaps only two or three stations away—where there seem to be different mountains and the previous landmarks are hidden. Part 3 will therefore see the city as transits—as lines rather than places.

The city will therefore be walked through (also ridden through) as a collection of places and their experience—"grabs" from the spaces of an inconceivably vast city, randomly and without connecting narrative. While this might give an impression of how the city is seen and experienced and of how one might seek to make sense of its component spaces, there is still the question of what sort of city these elements assemble to form. Therefore part 4 of the chapter—also brief, like part 1—will move from the idea of collage to that of an assemblage. The idea of Seoul as assemblage will subsequently be taken further (in chapter 5) to ask a more demanding question: what sort of city is Seoul *becoming?*

Part 1

DIALECTICAL IMAGE, MONTAGE, COLLAGE

Urban space transmits messages—street signs, the name of a building, directions to other places. There is a second though more ambiguity-laden order of such communication, in the ways that buildings and places suggest their uses—this is a house, this an office block, school, park, apartment block, factory, highway, laneway. The ambiguity can arise from dissembling (this only looks like a holiday resort; it is actually a prison) or because uses have changed over time (old offices become loft housing, a house becomes an office or a clinic). Then there is a third communicative order: this may look like a house (it may *be* a house) but it was once the residence of a famous writer or the site of a gruesome murder; this entertainment zone hides a military encampment; these advertising boards screen informal or illegal enterprises behind them.

This third order of communication requires information other than that directly transmitted by the appearance of the building or place—the second order. That may come from a reading of its history, a plaque, or less directly from incongruous juxtapositions, a whispered story. Thus we come to that city of blank boxes encountered in the "impressions" of the preface that launched the present text and whose production was a topic of chapter 3 above. The blandness of Korean everyday space is ultimately misleading: while the erasures of history, the violent division of modern Korea, the compromises and accommodations of dictatorship, and the headlong rush of the "tiger economy" may all have underlain the production of the present city, the dilemmas and contradictions can be obscured in the blandness and the visual cacophony. At that third communicative order, there is thus some imperative to attempt a reading—to determine what might lie behind the phenomena of the present city.

The chapter accordingly turns from the grander spaces of the city (the palaces, gateways, axes of chapter 2, and the stories of their resurrection in chapter 3) to how one is to read the boxlike structures, the regimented order alternating with jumbled disorder of labyrinthine space, discordant images and signs, in the seemingly undistinguished, proliferating spaces of everyday Seoul. The method will be to present the city as a collage, a vast aggregation lacking the ordering of any author but where the aggregated components set up tensions, ambiguities, and contradiction that constantly call meanings into question.

"City as collage" could apply to most cities. Seoul presents as a patchwork of distinctive communities in rather unique ways, not least due to its topography, whereby its intervening mountains fragment it into seemingly separate towns, which are then reinforced by a high level of functional specialization (Oh Myung and Larson 2011, 1). Patterns of ethnic fragmentation are also unique: though South Korea is classified as a nonimmigration society, Seoul has been described as "a global city with ethnic villages" (Kim Eun Mee and Kang 2007, 64).[2]

Dialectical images, dialectical juxtapositions

Charles Baudelaire (1821–1867) famously redefined the phenomenal world: "All the visible universe is nothing but a shop of images and signs" (quoted in Benjamin 1982, 313). In the never-completed *Passagen-Werk* (Arcades Project), Walter Benjamin worked in the 1930s on ways of seeing—reading—the historical space of the streets and passages (arcades) of Paris in the nineteenth century.[3] The method was to be a juxtaposition of "dialectical images" ("I have nothing to say, only to show"), a vast collection of visual images, aphorisms, textgrabs, and ideas from a seeming infinity of sources, assembled into an elaborate filing system of some thirty-six "Konvoluts," or folders. This material, it seems, was eventually to be brought together as six provisional chapter divisions that would juxtapose a historical figure with a historical phenomenon. So there were to be "Fourier or the Arcades" (the too-early, anticipatory images of modern architecture), "Daguerre or the Dioramas" (the too-early anticipations of photography, film, and television), "Grandville or the World Expositions" (the too-early precursors of the commodity's slippage to pure image), "Louis-Philippe or the Interior" (the dust of the bourgeois era obscuring the traces of its own origins, even of revolution), "Baudelaire or the Streets of Paris" (the prefigurement of the loss of meaning—the desert of modernity), and "Haussman or the Barricades" (the dialectical tension between obliterating the past and actualizing its potential) (Benjamin 1978; Buck-Morss 1991, 51–53; King 1996, 186). The juxtapositions would "deconstruct"—demolish the myths and delusions—of each taken-for-granted phenomenon of the Paris of that time (as of the 1930s Paris of Benjamin's own time).

Benjamin's approach is savagely political. Space will be viewed as multivoiced cacophony, layered images, a "complicated tissue of events," to be deconstructed by the juxtapositions of images, both visual and textual, that are set up to refer to it. One might translate Benjamin's method from Paris to Seoul—"Park Chung-hee and the Jungang-cheong" (the Japanese reembrace, the *chaebol*, and the tiger economy), "Kim Swoo Geun and the National Assembly" (unmasking the imagining of the future city), "Paik Nam June and Television" (anticipating the Korean Wave and the city's modern translation to virtual reality, to be considered in chapter 5) . . . and perhaps others. More revealing, however, is to take the Benjamin method more directly to the scenes of the present city, to observe the too-frequently incoherent, perplexing juxtapositions and to ask: what contradictions in the society and culture itself might these contradictions in the city's imagery bring to reflection? What memories might be stirred?

Any application of the Benjamin approach in the case of Seoul needs caution. Because memories in Korea are contested, thereby fragmenting its historiography (the theme of chapter 1), an image (memory) from the past that is set against an observation of the present may lead to multiple, opposed unmaskings. The screaming Christian proselytizer in the subway carriage may be purposively ignored, but, if reflected upon, remembered antecedents and lineage will likely rush back to older ideological confrontations (chapter 2). The glance at a colonial edifice will summon conflicted histories and their distortions in memory; reflection on the regimented rows of apartment towers will be set against the reality of surviving old Seoul, the memory of "what good times have been lost" or of "what bad times we have left behind." Dialectical imagery is not predictable, but it does enrich the imagination and thereby the urge to creativity (chapter 5).

Benjamin's method can be illustrated through his assertion of *progress as fetish*. If the city seems ancient, it is because of the rapidity of technological change—innovation, new commodities, new ways of producing and marketing them, new forms of consumption. A second reading reveals that all of these "changes" are but shifts on the surface of the unchanging fetishization of change itself—"hellish repetition" (Buck-Morss 1991, 108). It is the city as a phantasmagoria, a world where fashion is the "measure of time"—Seoul, indeed, in the present age presents as the epitome of highest fashion—for, as Susan Buck-Morss writes, "fashions are the medicament that is to compensate for the fateful effects of forgetting, on a collective scale" (Buck-Morss 1991, 97–98). A near century of compelled forgetting in the case of Korea—though defiant memory always survives—leaves that only-ever-partial vacuum that can enable the fabulous outbursts of fashion that make for the new world of Korea—a story for the next chapter. "Monotony is nourished by the new," says Benjamin, to which Buck-Morss adds, "Hellishly repetitive time—eternal waiting punctuated by a "discontinuous" sequence of "interruptions"—constitute the particularly modern form of boredom" (1991, 104). Seoul, it seems, is newness itself.

Benjamin would pose two images of the space of the city: its "organic, naturalistic" growth unmasked as delusion, on the one hand, and modernity and its progress unmasked as Hell, on the other. Both, it seems, present as images of Seoul; both also, suggests Buck-Morss, "criticize a mythical assumption as to the nature of history . . . that rapid change is historical progress; the other is the conclusion that the modern is no progress" (Buck-Morss 1991, 108). These two conceptions of time and history are complementary; they are inescapable oppositions whose critique, we are told, must be directed to yield the "dialectical conception of historical time." Each image of the city, as "natural" history (evolution, the organically growing city) and as "mythic" history (the wonderful progress of the human race), is to erode the other. Only through space is time to be understood (King 1996, 192).

While this is only one part of the Benjamin critique, it is a useful one for present purposes. For Seoul, "natural" history is ambiguous—"nature" (ecological evolution) is still there, intact though possibly ignored; the idea of the "natural," organic evolution of the city and its life, however, is interrupted, destroyed, erased. "Mythic" history, by contrast, is intact and resplendent, progress is everywhere, fashion reigns; Benjamin's "progress as Hell," surely, could well be Seoul.

This, of course, is all grand scale and grand hyperbole. Ordinary lives go on in the ordinary spaces of an immense city. While Benjamin's critique (and Buck-Morss' critique of Benjamin) suggests a method for reading the spaces and signs of the city, how does this translate into a reading of the city of the everyday? The method of this chapter is to tour the spaces of the city, to observe the inconsistencies of a metropolis mostly of blank surfaces and undistinguished boxes, albeit then variously identified by numbers (on otherwise identical housing towers) or festooned in advertising boards—dialectical images and dialectical juxtapositions.

Part 2

SEOUL AS COLLAGE

This traverse of the city begins with "old" Seoul, still its symbolic center, then a sample of its distinctive neighborhoods, on to Gangnam as a new form of city, then, in part 3, a subway transit through the city—another dimension of its experiencing—to diverse attempts to "jumpstart" an even newer, seemingly artificial form of city. Places are selected for their political and ideological context or for their ability to throw light on the city's production, its underlying ideas, and their afterlife. Touristic Seoul is avoided unless, like the palaces, its sites illuminate that afterlife of the Chosun/Japanese collision or, like Gangnam, they are central to understanding the modern city's trajectory.[4]

Jongno: Front street, back street

The long, straight, east-west avenue of Jongno (Street of the Bell) is an appropriate place to begin a reading of Seoul space. It connects the north-south axis of Taepyeongno (Sejongno) to the ancient city's eastern Dongdaemun Gate and, as observed in chapter 2, was the street of shops that served the royal court in the Chosun era; its commercial and cultural preeminence persisted into the colonial period and in part to the present (figure 4.1). It also divided the town: north were the royal and aristocratic quarters in the Chosun age, south the plebeian; the order reversed in the Japanese era. At its intersection with Taepyeongno stands the Bigak Pavilion, built in 1902 to celebrate Emperor Gwangmu (erstwhile King Kojong), as well as the Bosingak Belfry, originally constructed in 1396 but destroyed and replaced many times. Its bell, which signified the time of day and also warned of disaster, gave the street its name. Also on Jongno is Tapgol Park and the Jongmyo Royal Shrine (chapter 2).

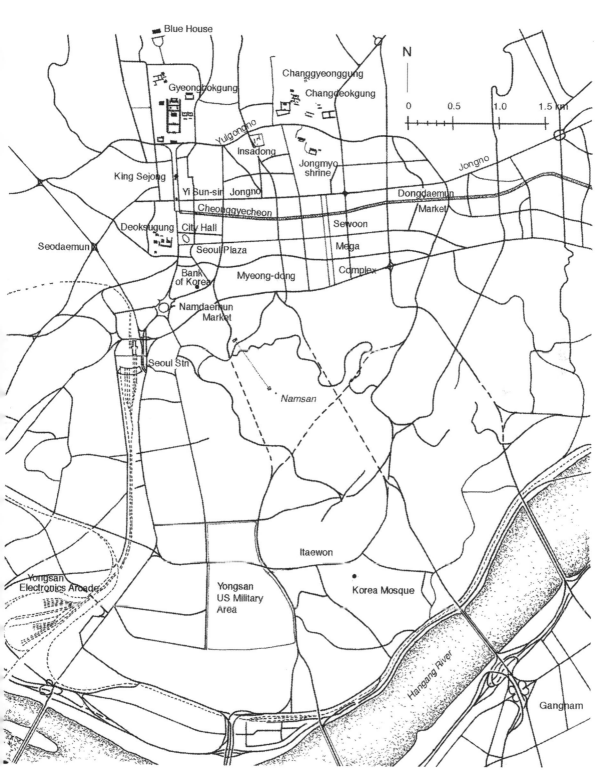

FIGURE 4.1 Old Seoul in the present era: the ancient Chosun City, Namsan Mountain, Yongsan (and Itaewon), and the Hangang River. Source: author, based on 2014 maps.

Tapgol (Pagoda) Park was once the site of Wongaksa Buddhist Temple, founded in 1465. It was laid out by Irish advisor John McLeavy Brown on the orders of King Kojong in 1897 as Seoul's first "public" garden, for the enjoyment of the aristocracy.[5] It was subsequently opened to a wider public in 1913, in the Japanese era. Tapgol Park was the starting point of the Samil, the March First Movement, 1919; here the Korean Proclamation of Independence was read.[6] As an emblematic place in Korean history, it is a popular locale for demonstration and protest. It was the terminal point for the Grand Peace March for Democracy on 24 June 1986 that led to President Chun Doo-hwan caving in to the demand for free elections.

While Jongno's economic centrality has in part been lost to other centers, most notably Yeouido and Teheranno (Gangnam), and in part to the general dispersal of economic activity across the greater metropolis, it still retains both economic and commercial significance and will commonly be referred to as Seoul's "main street" (Korean Institute of Architects 2000, 73). Many of Korea's largest bookshops are concentrated here; Dansungsa, the oldest cinema theater in Korea (established 1907), and a number of other important cinemas are on Jongno; office towers, shops, and restaurants line it; the ideosyncratic Jongno (Samsung) Tower, designed by Uruguayan but US-based architect Rafael Viñoly and completed in 1999, is symbolic of Jongno's continuing economic role;[7] it is on the site of the old, iconic Hwasin Department Store.[8] At the more informal end of the economic spectrum and at its eastern geographic end, there is the vast Dongdaemun Market and garment district.

The most revealing aspect of Jongno's spatial economy, and indeed of Seoul's more widely, emerges from a short stroll from the wide and emblematic Jongno into its parallel back streets. Jongno is some eight to ten traffic lanes wide, then add to that the generous sidewalks on either side. The "thickness" of the wall of fashionable blocks fronting the avenue varies—around its intersection with Tonhwamunno, for example, it is seventeen meters thick on the north side and twenty-nine meters on the south. Then, behind this decidedly imposing corporate and formal façade are the narrow back streets: that on the north side is generally six meters wide, that on the south, varying from only three to six meters. The Jongno back streets—bars, eateries, entertainment, small shops, services—present an urban landscape and economy surviving from an earlier era, though still thriving, serving the towers and corporations of the "front" street in what will be claimed, following, is an emerging urban vernacular. Front street and back street are to be seen as diametrically opposed urban worlds, yet they are clearly interdependent both economically and culturally.

There is yet another Jongno space, in sharpest contrast with both front and back street. Seoul's winter climate is very cold, and in some measure curtails street life; accordingly, much day-to-day commercial activity will go underground, to the subterranean shopping arcades that are mostly linked to various subway train stations. These range from the formal and organized arcades to groups of the more informal and opportunistic entrepreneurs selling assorted and often second-hand clothing, electronics, secondhand books, stationery, groceries, and assorted bric-a-brac. The Jongno underground arcade is especially extensive, regimented, and linked into the more corporate underground bookshops in the basements of larger buildings (figure 4.2).

Ultimately Jongno is to be seen as old, tired, passed-by. Life—for it is still there, and vibrant—is mostly in the narrow back streets. This world of dichotomous urban realms—front street vis-à-vis back street and then underground arcade, *chaebol*-corporate vis-à-vis the very small entrepreneur, the formal vis-à-vis the informal—characterizes the space of Seoul.[9] It is the point of the present chapter and, I argue, will dominate any reading of the space of Seoul; it is also the point expressed in the dichotomous urban realms represented in figure 1.1 of chapter 1.

Back street, boxland, box space

Back streets, behind the office towers of most districts, occasionally hidden behind the marshaled ranks of residential towers, with their fragmented space of small, boxlike buildings ranging from two to four or five stories, will be found in all but the newest and most antiseptic of districts. At the scale of everyday life, this boxland of Jongno, as elsewhere, increasingly becomes "box space" in modern Seoul. The "karaoke box," of mostly Japanese derivation and common in Japan and Hong Kong, more often called *KTV* in Taiwan and China and *videoke* in the Philippines, is *norae bang* in Korea—literally, "song box."[10] However, in Korea these are alleged to have emerged more from the games parlors than from the karaoke bars, often initially as small booths in corners of video-games rooms.[11] They first appeared in Busan (Pusan) at the beginning of 1990, as shops and technology came together to provide places where people could sing together accompanied by controllable music, up to the scale of a full orchestra. A typical establishment will have ten to twenty (or more) boxes as well as a main "karaoke bar" area in front; they might often sell refreshments, but many will not provide "beverages" and so are deemed suitable for families and children.

The *norae bang* went through a first crisis in 1992, and a second in 1994. Song Do-Young (1998, 100) writes, "Those crises were the

FIGURE 4.2 The complementary spaces of Jongno, 2012: (a) Jongno itself and the Samsung Tower (architect Rafael Viñoly), (b) back street, (c) underground arcade.

result of not only cultural dynamics but also . . . of technological development, of market & industrial environments, of control and regula-
tions, and . . . of differentiated daily life of residents." The keys to their
success, Song suggests, were new technology, the separation of singing
from drinking, and cheap slot machines operable even by children. In
2012 they could still be reported as the general way to enjoy Korean
popular music (K-pop).[12]

There are other *bang* (boxes) in the modern Korean space: there
are *PC bangs* (Internet cafés) as LAN gaming centers;[13] *DVD bangs*
or *video bangs* are establishments that have private rooms for couples
and friends to watch movies—they began to appear in the 1980s, the
motivation being mostly the seeking of privacy in a society in which
Koreans lived at home until marriage and there was a social stigma
surrounding public displays of affection. These rooms could often
transform into something less subtle in terms of what might transpire
there. There is also the *soju bang,* a pub,[14] and *manwhabang,* where
Koreans can go to read *manwha,* the Korean form of comics and print
cartoons. The term *manwha* is a cognate of the Chinese *manhua,* as is
the Japanese "manga."[15] There are also *jjimjil bang,* large public bath-
houses, usually gender-segregated but with unisex areas on other
floors; they are a popular weekend getaway for Korean families to
relax, soak, lounge, and sleep while the children play away on PCs. As
Song summarizes their role, "[The] urbanized environment of Korea
has been terribly lacking in time and space for cultural activities. That's
the effect of rapid growth oriented processes over the past 40 years . . .
pro-collective cultures which did not provide enough individual free
expression" (Song Do-Young 1998, 123).

The *bangs* are literally boxes. Floor space is typically divided into
the smallest cubicles that can still be used for their intended purpose;
bangs might occupy a single floor or multiple floors in a building.
Their roles relate to the typical crowding of Korean domestic space in
a period of changing values placed on privacy and escape. They especially boomed after the 1997 crisis, as the government helped create
the conditions for establishing small businesses. Kang Inkyu (2014)
sees the *bang* as signifying the metamorphosis of Korean culture to a
new, ever-emerging state of fragmenting cybercultures.

The *bangs* of Jongno back streets are mostly above small shops or
food outlets, and mostly labeled "PC" or "DVD."

Insadong: Labyrinth

Insadonggil can be seen, in one sense, as a back street to Jongno but
taken to an extreme (and without the *bangs*). In the early Chosun era,

there were two towns whose names ended in "In" and "Sa," divided by a stream that ran along what is now Insadong's main street, Insadong-gil. Its diagonal irregularity in an otherwise Zhouist (though partly Japanese-imposed) grid reflects old ecological processes and signifies an antiquity preceding the present city with its modernist imposed order. It became the area of subsidiary palaces, of which only the restored Unhyeongung Palace survives,[16] and a residential area for government officials in the Chosun era; it also housed Dohwaseo, the government-based royal painting institute of the dynasty. During the Japanese era, the wealthy Korean residents were forced to move and sell their possessions, whereupon Insadong became the locale for the trading of such antiques. In the Japanese era it was part of the "northern village" and a realm of Korean decay and poverty (Henry 2014, 9, 52–53). After the Korean War, the area became a center of the city's artistic and café life, evolving as a popular destination for foreign visitors during the 1960s and even more so during the 1988 Olympics. In the late 1990s there was a program of renovations and modernization, to further attract the tourists. This, however, provoked protests due to the consequent loss of its "historic character," leading to a halt in the officially endorsed renovations.

The promotional rhetoric on Insadonggil will commonly refer to it as a "traditional street for both locals and foreigners," the "culture of the past and the present," "unique," and representing "the cultural history of the nation" (Ch'oe Chun-sik et al. 2005). While it was once known as the biggest center for antiques and contemporary art trading in Korea, much of that activity has now relocated to areas near the newer "cultural hot spot" of Samcheong-dong north of Insadong, or to the luxury shopping locale of Cheongdam-dong in Gangnam, south Seoul. Accordingly, it is now commonly referred to as merely a "tourist spot" (Moon So-young 2009). Still, about one hundred art galleries are claimed to be clustered in the area as it reinvents itself, albeit now more as a tourist area. A consequence of the tourist focus is higher turnover of establishments and, increasingly, outlets for less expensive works by younger and "rising" artists. "Young people who felt that the threshold for art galleries was very high now feel free to enter our gallery after seeing small paintings through the show window," said Han Jin-sook, a curator at Gallery Topohaus. "Paintings are popular, especially as wedding gifts" (Moon So-young 2009). Gallery Topohaus' show window was in the form of a giant red heart surrounded by silver stars. The small-scale, almost grassroots rise of this new, decentralized production and marketing soon attracted the corporate sector, however: across the street from Gallery Topohaus arose Ssamziegil, a complex of small art galleries and handicraft shops opened in late

2004 by Ssamzie, a company manufacturing accessories and trading artwork.[17] Certainly Ssamziegil has helped Insadong to attract young people—as artists, as voyeurs, and as purchasers and thereby collectors. Yet, noted one manager, "[a]bout 70 to 80 percent [of customers here] are Japanese tourists" (Moon So-young 2009). Where Hongdae, to be discussed below, might be seen as a domain for cultural production (though more as a site where the putative cultural producers would "hang out"), Insadong is where they might seek to market their production.

Change—though in Benjamin's terms it is no change, just the delusion that the eternal present is always change—will continue to produce both the fantasy of culture and the consumer paradise. It will also reassure the young artist to continue in the delusion that their genius is real and recognized, until the reality of the commodity world slowly dawns. Fashion, the fetishization of novelty, seizes Insadonggil; the consequent inflated rents expel the creative and the champions of "alternative lifestyles"—to Hongdae, Samcheon-dong, and elsewhere. There may indeed be "no change," but there is certainly constant relocation, of which Insadonggil, like Jongno, is emblematic.

The reality of Insadong is that it is a collection of 1960s and 1970s small two- and three-story, boxlike buildings that have now been gentrified, often rebuilt, adapted, and commodified—it is heavy urban design applied to an indigenous muddle. The northern end is the fashionable, tourist stretch of the better-presented galleries and narrow radiating alleys with pseudo-ancient teahouses and fashionable shops (figures 4.3, 4.4, and 4.5). It goes downmarket as it goes south, toward Jongno, marketing Korean crafts, antiques, food, and music, to a more local clientele, hosting performers of indigenous music, religious practices, and local foods. The labyrinthine intricacy of ancient Seoul is retained as is the minute scale of its alleys, no doubt for its marketability; however, it is also part of a wider project of riding on the reconstructed memory of the Chosun age. Comparison of the area's present structure (figure 4.3) with the 1928 map of Insadong in Todd Henry (2014, 53), citing *Keijo toshi keikaku chosasho* (1928), reveals that only limited "improvements" have occurred since then. Tapgol Park has been enlarged and the southern end of Insadonggil reordered; however, the most significant change has been connecting previous culs-de-sac to provide east-west accessibility through the "village."

While the tiny establishments in Jongno's back streets are for the most part just boxes adorned with their advertising boards and other signage, on Insadonggil and in its alleys these are more often minimalist, understated, and self-consciously "modern." It is Seoul boxland taken to its limit.

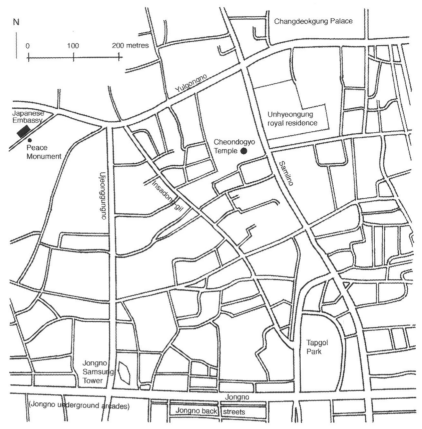

FIGURE 4.3 Insadong as labyrinth. While the colonial Japanese "modernized" the principal roads of the old city, the interiors of the blocks retained their premodern, Chosun, labyrinthine complexity. Source: author, based on 2014 maps.

FIGURE 4.4 Insadonggil, 2012: urban elegance and minimalist design.

FIGURE 4.5 Insadonggil boxspace, 2012: high elegance transforms Seoul boxland.

Namdaemun and Myeong-dong

South of Jongno and east of the ancient Namdaemun Gate, in the erstwhile plebeian district of precolonial Seoul and the upmarket commercial locale of Japanese Seoul, is Myeong-dong, recently Seoul's most "high-end" retailing district, though increasingly replaced in that role by Apgujeong-dong in Gangnam-gu, south of the river—this latter has Apgujeong Rodeo Street, homage to Beverley Hills. Then, between the gate and Myeong-dong is its obverse in the vast Namdaemun Market. The two zones, Namdaemun Market and Myeong-dong, constitute another labyrinthine district of narrow alleys that reflects its unplanned, unregulated, underclass genealogy (figure 4.6).

Namdaemun Market's history goes back to the beginning of the Chosun dynasty, when merchants established their businesses nearby, just outside the city wall. The present market dates from 1922 and is one of Seoul's two largest markets, the other being Dongdaemun Market at the eastern end of Jongno.[18] It comprises some ten thousand shops of all sizes, especially for clothing, agricultural products and other foodstuffs, everyday needs, and medical supplies. Namdaemun's commercial space is layered: its alleys are defined by formal buildings, many of them high-rises, with their ground-floor space used as shops and occasionally food outlets; there will be stairs to other levels; in front of the shops and often as extensions to them will be a layer of stalls, typically under retractable awnings, beneath which clothes and other wares typically hang from hooks and wires; in front of those again, though more often freestanding at intersections of the labyrinth, will be smaller, mobile stalls, often under multicolored umbrellas; a final layer are the food vendors operating from metal dishes on the ground.

FIGURE 4.6 Namdaemun Market as disordered space, 2012.

FIGURE 4.7 Namdaemun Market as diverse, intersecting economies, 2012.

There is all manner of merchandising; missing, however, are the vendors of pirated DVDs who characterize the street markets of Southeast Asian cities—the Internet and the DVD *bangs* have mostly replaced them (figure 4.7).

The chaos and disorder of the street surface is matched vertically on the façades of the enclosing buildings. Projecting from the buildings are layer upon layer of advertising boards for products, establishments, and services in a visual cacophony that would defy any disentanglement of messages. It is an adornment of façades that is repeated across the districts of the city.

Myeong-dong in the Chosun dynasty had been a residential area. In 1898 the Gothic-styled Catholic Cathedral was completed there (chapter 2) and, in the colonial period, the area became the Japanese colonists' primary commercial district. Much of its fine colonial architecture was destroyed in the Korean War. After rebuilding in the late 1950s, the area acquired the National Theater, bookshops, and teahouses, to become a center of Seoul's artistic life. In 1962 the junta generals put dampers on Seoul's raucous nightlife, at that time centered on Myeong-dong, in part to save electricity (Cumings 2005, 356). With the subsequent relocation of the National Theater, however, both art life and nightlife declined, and instead Myeong-dong began to acquire high-end shopping, thence to become Seoul's focus for high fashion.

Like Namdaemun Market, the adjoining Myeong-dong is a labyrinth and also displays the festoons of advertising boards projecting from building façades; however, they are better designed and more often associated with national and global names, and the more fragmented, smaller-scale buildings are interspersed with the department stores, office towers, and surviving colonial-era buildings—the Bank of Korea Building, for example (figure 4.8).

As corporations and, less often, state institutions seek "presence" with iconic buildings, these also come to distinguish the often dispersed districts in which they locate. The overdesigned Jongno (Samsung) Tower performs this function on present Jongno. Several towers distinguish Myeong-dong—the "split" Post Office Tower is one, the "bent" SK Tower is another.[19]

Cheonggyecheon

Unlike Myeong-dong or the immediate back streets of Jongno, Insadonggil presents as a display of purposive urban design. Although it follows an ancient streamline, there is no attempt to acknowledge that past in the design or signification of the space. The stream is missing. A far more interventionist and comprehensively designed project to transform the boxland of the city center is Cheonggyecheon, a 5.8-kilometer creek in downtown Seoul. Here also was an ancient stream, named Gaecheon (Open Stream), albeit artificial, constructed as part of a drainage system in the early Chosun era, thence to be regularly drained and refurbished throughout various reigns. It was renamed Cheonggyecheon in the Japanese colonial period and was

FIGURE 4.8 Myeong-dong, 2012. Like Namdaemun Market, Myeong-dong is labyrinthine but also upmarket; the indigenous muddle is interspersed with grand department stores and with monuments from the late Chosun and Japanese eras.

remembered from that era by composer Kang Sukhi (2007), cited earlier; he recalled it running parallel to the city's commercial Jongno, with women washing clothes in the stream, its life seemingly little changed from the old dynasty. It was also totally polluted, according to newspaper reports of the time (Henry 2014, 158–159). After the 1950–1953 Korean War, rural-to-urban migration turned Seoul into a slum city, and the banks of Cheonggyecheon acquired squatter settlements in flimsy makeshift houses. A twenty-year program of slum demolition and concrete covering of the old watercourse was crowned, in the

1967–1971 period, with the elevated, sixteen-meter-wide Samil highway over the top of it for its 5.8 kilometers. Together with the emblematic Samil Building, it served as a proudly displayed example of economic growth and urban modernization (Park Kil-Dong n.d., 10).[20]

In July 2003, Seoul's then mayor (and subsequent president) Lee Myung-bak resolved to remove the elevated Samil highway and restore the stream as part of a wider movement to reintroduce nature into what had become a "hard" urban concretescape. The project, with its underlying rhetoric and somewhat brutal manner of implementation, must be seen in the context of Lee's political ambitions and self-reconstruction. In *Cheonggyecheon Flows to the Future* (Lee Myung-bak 2005), published by Lee to coincide with the stream's (re)opening, we are told how he "endured developmentalism" (Park Chung-hee?) represented in the paved stream, how he had escaped from developmentalism, remaking himself as the man of "the future" to show the path to reembrace the nature of common people.

Accordingly there was rhetoric to promote a more eco-friendly urban design and, at the same time, to advance urban competitiveness with rival East Asian cities through amplified urban infrastructure (Lee Myung-bak 2006). Cheonggyecheon merchants demonstrated against the project in 2003, however, echoing antirestoration discourse raised by NGOs;[21] there were also protests and debate on the need for alternatives to high-rises and against unsystematic development, traffic problems, and the displacement of merchants.[22] The process was also widely criticized as being procedurally undemocratic and rushed, as the desires of the Seoul metropolitan government took precedence over all else (Cho Myungrae 2004; Ryu Jeh-hong 2004, 23).[23] The project continued, however, with the final cost of some 386 billion won (around US$281 million), and the stream finally opened to the public in September 2005.

While the attempted character of the restoration might be labeled "naturalistic," it is quite artificial. The stream had long run dry, and so the design called for 120,000 tons of water to be pumped in daily (Park Kil-Dong n.d., 13). Environmentalists, however, had previously called in vain for the restoration of the original upper reaches of the stream in order to use available and natural water flow in the watercourse.

The corridor's beginning, at the great north-south axis of Taepyeongno (Sejongno), is dramatically and elegantly signified in the immense *Spring* sculpture by Swedish American sculptor Claes Oldenburg; it plays on the notion of "spring"—rebirth, source of water, but also spring as a mechanism. It uses a conch shell as its generating springlike form, with a stone pseudo-rivulet running across the plaza to the artificial waterfall ("spring") that feeds the reconstructed stream

FIGURE 4.9 Cheonggyecheon: (a) *Spring* (sculptor Claes Oldenburg); (b) *Spring* and pond.

(figure 4.9). It is surely accidental that the sharply conical form of the sculpture also reflects the ubiquitous conical "spires" with illuminated red crosses atop all manner of shop blocks and other, small, boxlike buildings that house small churches throughout the Seoul region (and to be discussed further, below).

As completed, the restored stream begins at a fountain pool in the financial-government-royal district of Sejongno, below the stone rivulet that connects it to the symbolic *Spring,* then flows eastward along its old concreted channel; the rapids, rock pools, wetland swamps and marshes, ecological displays, walking paths, and climbing areas are simply additions, sitting atop the concrete channel that still lies beneath its surface (Stevens 2009). In the water, however, there are still some stones from the much older stream and its retaining banks, as well as traces of the vanished highway. On the high walls retaining the roads above on both sides, there are images and stories of past history; most dramatically, there is a vast tiled mural over several hundred meters long depicting the grand procession of King Sejong to Suwon. The stream changes along its length—stony and sculptural, then softened by limited planting, then more "naturalistic." The whole project is urban sculpture on a vast scale, in part as a vehicle for historical storytelling—reinvented memory, erasing the erasures of the past (figure 4.10).

FIGURE 4.10 Cheonggyechon as it passes through the Jongno financial district, 2012; *right,* the mural of King Sejong's procession to Suwon.

Both the economy and the architecture change along the length of the stream: corporate and "high-end" as it traverses the financial district near its beginning, then the less imposing boxland of smaller, mostly older buildings. Then, in its lower, eastern reaches, it enters the vast Dongdaemun Market area. This part of the present city is mostly from the 1960s and 1970s, built at a time when the stream was still extant, although the present market can be traced to Chosun era enactments of 1791 (Lee Ki-baik 1984, 230). Here, for around a kilometer, the stream is lined on both sides by long, standardized building rows from the 1970s, five to six stories to the north and five stories to the south, uncompromisingly modernist in style, dilapidated, seemingly underoccupied—almost abandoned—and now used as part of an extensive garment district. The more decrepit north side is a busy street market of continuous small stalls—a shoe zone, a pet-shop zone, and so on. It links to the extensive Dongdaemun Market district (figure 4.11). The southern side opposite the traditional Dongdaemun Market is the also linked Pyonghwa Market. Chun T'ae-il was a worker in one of the several hundred textile sweatshops there in the 1970s; he died on 13 November 1970 at the age of twenty-two when he set himself on fire to protest the failure of a petition for a Labor Standards Law—his slogan: "Workers too are human beings." On 30 September 2005, two days before the opening of the rehabilitated stream, a statue of Chun was unveiled at the Boduldari Bridge over the Cheonggyecheon in front of Pyonghwa Market (Kal Hong 2011, 118). Whereas these lines of buildings previously faced an elevated highway, they now face

FIGURE 4.11 Cheonggyecheon looking toward Dongdaemun Market and the garment district, 2012: identical five- and six-story blocks on both sides.

a very popular stream and its walkways. There are already signs of the gentrification that might be expected to follow the restoration of the stream: in 2012 the JW Marriott Hotel was constructed immediately facing Dongdaemun Gate. Also at the bridge across the stream at that point, platforms were under construction in April 2012 for a pop concert—a regular event—a younger generation being attracted into an old, albeit tired place, though briefly. More was to come.

In March 2014 the immense Dongdaemun Design Plaza was opened on the south side of Cheonggyecheon as the new centerpiece of the city's "fashion hub," designed by Iraqi-British architect Zaha Hadid and Korean studio Samoo, with its curving, elongated forms, and tautologically proclaimed as "neofuturistic" and "the world's largest asymmetrical free-formed building" (Ashin 2014). It also marks the corporate sector's spectacular takeover of what had been a district of informal, small-scale, and even chaotic invention and entrepreneurial vigor (Hwang Jin-Tae 2014), as well as a powerful response to the "Bilbao effect"—the shock of architect Frank Gehry's Bilbao

Guggenheim Museum of 1997—one for the ages, and a locale for the equally extraordinary exhibition in 2001 of the video art of Korean/universalist Paik Nam June, a topic for chapter 5. Also one for the ages.

In a critique of the effects of the Cheonggyecheon project, Ryu Jeh-hong (2004) has described three areas that it traverses, each locally renowned for small-scale, highly networked metal and molding industries, referring to "networks and processes of high-tech production based on multi-kind items and small quantities that colluded to constitute the system." The discussion leads to an interesting question that implies a broader critique of modern Korea's evolution: "This metalworking network producing multi-kind items and small quantities resembles a postmodern, or at least late modern, production system. How is it possible to form a postmodern system of production out of a pre-modern way of applying technology within a modernized space?" (24–25). The suggested answer is that, in the shambles of 1945, there were no means of production left behind in Japanese factories or flowing from American military bases except machinery parts. In the struggle for survival, small workshops arose to utilize this refuse in what was in effect a "premodern," informal, and folk subsistence economy and industry. When the Park-led shift to import-substituting manufacturing began, a premodern mode of industrial organization simply morphed into part of a postmodern, "flexible accumulation" mode in the sense argued by David Harvey—the collapse of the "consensus" of big corporations and big labor (the *chaebol?*) and its replacement with more "flexible" ways of organizing the creation and appropriation of wealth (Harvey 1989). In Harvey's understanding, vertical integration is broken down, processes are split up, their components are dispersed, and self-employed consultants and outworkers replace in-house experts. All this fluidity is, however, highly organized; there are strong coordinators in the form of the financial markets, and the key investment and management decisions are more centralized than ever before (King 1996, 116).

Ryu tells of the Sewoon Arcade area of Cheonggyecheon, discussed earlier in relation to architect Kim Swoo Geun. This has evolved into a network of technological know-how in computers, enabled by a diversified folk industry of deconstructing and reconstructing imported electronics, in a virtual explosion of innovation that would not be possible in a grand, mainline corporation. The disintegrated apparel industry in the Dongdaemun Market area of Cheonggyecheon has likewise increased the speed of imitation, design development, manufacturing, and marketing.

It is suggested that there were here two signal failures of the Seoul metropolitan government. The first was the failure to recognize both the vitality of the chaotic economies of the Cheonggyecheon corridor, ultimately built on the desperation of a post-1945 slum community. The second was to charge bulldozer-like into a world whose role, vitality, or vulnerability they saw fit to ignore. Yet it is likely that the national prosperity (the *chaebol,* the Five-Year Plans) ultimately rides on that world's flexibility, innovation, inventiveness, and transgressions. It represents another of the defining space types of Seoul.

Cheonggyecheon continues to evoke controversy. While one of its claimed effects has been to reduce the separation between the north and south of the old city, there was criticism that this would be achieved via intended gentrification of adjacent areas that house many shops and small businesses and, of course, those incubators of creativity suggested above. An emphasis on a hoped-for network of activities to be named the Cheonggyecheon Cultural Belt only deepened the sense of misgiving.[24] Then, in the face of the restoration of two ancient bridges over the stream in the name of a return to old culture—in effect simulacra in the sense argued by Baudrillard (chapter 1) and also represented in the re-created Gyeongbokgung Palace—there were attacks on the project's frequently articulated claims of a return to authenticity.

The criticism of Cheonggyecheon on the grounds of its inauthenticity is problematic: certainly there is no replication of wild nature nor of the "soft," fine-scale, intimate, designed nature of the traditional Chosun-era garden. Cheonggyecheon may, however, be seen as an urban-scale translation of older cultural practices of representing human responses to ecological reality—in this case to the ecology of an urban drain in a city district starved of green space. The adverse reactions might therefore be seen more as nostalgic yearning for specific, lost aspects of the culture—for the garden as a place of withdrawal and scholarly contemplation. The places of withdrawal in modern Korea are boxes rather than gardens and rarely for scholarly contemplation, as observed in relation to the *bangs* (unless, of course, the Internet is the new site of scholarly contemplation in a cyberage).

The question of authenticity is problematic in present Seoul, especially in light of the attempts to reconstruct the Chosun world and to obliterate that of the Japanese colonial age.

Dongdaemun and hybrid economy

The long Cheonggyecheon blocks and their adjoining Dongdaemun Market highlight the juxtapositions of Seoul space and their anomalies. There is Ryu Jeh-hong's (2004, 14) reference to the hybridity of Dongdaemun, drawing on Jan Nederveen Pieterse (1997), who in turn references Fredric Jameson and Ernst Bloch: "The uneven moment of social development, or 'the coexistence of realities from different moments of history' (Jameson 1994, 307) is no longer embarrassing: Pyeonghwa clothing stores in front of Migliore fashion centre in Dongdaemun [since 2014, in front of Cheonggyecheon Design Plaza], mom-and-pop stores alongside convenience stores, European restaurants next to Korean folk taverns, and traditional tea rooms next to coffee houses. This hybrid coexistence of different pasts is called 'the synchronism of the non-synchronous,' or the 'contemporaneity of the non-contemporaneous' (Bloch 1997)." Nederveen Pieterse (1997, 50) has drawn attention to the hybridizing effect of globalization (hybridization being a constant theme of the present account): "What globalization means in structural terms . . . is the *increase in the available modes of organization:* transnational, international, macro-regional, national, micro-regional, local." It is an effect that translates into modes of production: "The notion of articulation of modes of production may be viewed as a principle of hybridisation. . . . Counterposed to the idea of the dual economy split in traditional/modern and feudal/capitalist sectors, the articulation argument holds that what has been taking place is an interpenetration of modes of production" (50–51). The sheer speed of Korean development has precluded any neat transformation of one mode or era of production into another. Instead, we end up, in the urban landscape of Seoul, with radically disjunctive modes of economic organization coexisting, both reinforcing and undermining each other simultaneously—seemingly more so here than elsewhere.

Seoul's public markets in particular illustrate both the traditional/modern split and the "principle of hybridization" that brings these together. In Korea the public market does not appropriate a public square or a designated building; rather, it will occupy a street or group of streets, restricting or even ending vehicular movement. The markets are permanent, giving circulation space back to pedestrians and thereby, in a city of small and often-crowded apartments, providing a public space and local community focus—albeit also crowded (Gelézeau 1997, 77). The markets and the blank-walled laneways that they most typically appropriate are cultural survivals of ancient Hanyang; they also signify Korea as being linked to a Chinese spatial realm of communal lanes and walled, secluded houses. The markets thrive even in the newest areas of the metropolis; streets are seized in the absence of lanes and where the housing is high-rise apartment blocks. Yet the markets are now also of the twenty-first century; the more traditional stalls and their vendors interweave with outlets of the more formal (and "modern") economy.

Korea is distinguished by the sheer speed of its modernization, ergo of its globalization; when everything spins ever faster, there is no time for evolution and little time for reflection. The consequence is the sort of hybridization suggested by Nederveen Pieterse, in which the *chaebol* coexists with the wild disorder of the traditional market, Samsung with the proliferating stalls of Dongdaemun or Namdaemun, and the fragmented production of Cheonggyecheon with the global corporations lining Gangnam's Teheranno—indeed the coexistence of realities from radically different moments of history (Jameson 1994, albeit referring to Japan rather than Korea). The hybridization makes Korean space "different," enabling a larger-sized underground economy in Korea than in other OECD countries,[25] but thereby problematizing efforts to measure the "national" economy in the same way as others. Itaewon, Hongdae, and Insadonggil, but also both the grand and more minuscule markets, are manifestations of this intermingling of economies, of nationalistic exclusiveness but with global embrace, of order with disorder. An even more dramatic manifestation of proliferation and disorder, however, is represented in that forest of red plastic crosses that electrify the night skyline of Seoul.

In this context of ahistorical hybridization and coexistence of realities, Ryu Jeh-hong (2004) refers to the story of Seoul Plaza, another mayoral project of Lee Myung-bak. An open area is bounded on the west by the grand north-south axis of Taepyeongno, the Korean-traditional Deoksugung Palace, the Romanesque-Revival Anglican Cathedral, and the former National Assembly Building; on the north by the Japanese Art Deco City Hall; on the south by the American-Modernist Plaza Hotel. The modern history of Seoul seems to have been assembled here; it had also been a historic site of protest, notably for the 1919 anti-Japanese uprising and June 1987 democracy movement. In the early 2000s, a forty-year-old fountain was demolished, and the plaza's previous dominant role as a traffic intersection was ended and instead it was reopened in May 2004, grassed and with diverse art installations, ostensibly as a public open space and for "cultural displays." Ten days after the opening the public was forbidden to walk in the plaza, however: "Don't Walk, Just Look" was the instruction written next to the roped-off field—landscaping is only to provide spectacle (Ryu Jeh-hong 2004, 11). It has subsequently become a new location for anti-American protests—the (hybridizing, anti-colonial, neocolonial) story of Korea still playing out there (Kim Rahn 2008).

The hybridization and coexisting realities continue. In 2012 the old City Hall had been screened and hidden (for restoration). It would be overwhelmed by a very large, overdesigned, idiosyncratic new building. The old Japanese building is to be effectively embedded in—embraced by—the new, plastic-form, high-tech City Hall (Yoo Kerl, architect).

Boxlands 1: Itaewon

The spaces listed above are all within the old walled area of the Chosun city and evoke memories of that space and age. Itaewon, on the southern slopes of Namsan (South) Mountain, began its modern history later, as a residential area of the Japanese colonists in the early twentieth century. The Japanese departed in 1945, and the city was destroyed in the early 1950s. The city of the 1960s and 1970s rush was hurriedly, poorly built; it was also a city of transgressive insertions, none arguably more blatant than the American military area of Yongsan to the immediate south of the old walled city, which, in 1945, had simply and smoothly been taken over from the departing Japanese. Nearby but in the dreary, disordered boxland of the city itself it spawned Itaewon—"entertainment" places, bars, brothels, American music, and disorder. In the Cold War it could be seen as "the only alien space within Korea" (Kim Eun-shil 2004, 60); it was also a focus for resentment against the occupiers and their indigenous clients (the dictatorship). In more recent times it is seen more as one hybridized, ambiguously signed space among many. Itaewon can be observed in the context of Lee Jin-kyung's (2010) analysis of South Korean military labor in the Vietnam War, domestic female sex workers, Korean prostitution for US troops, and Asian migrant labor in Korea. Her argument, to reprise from chapter 1, is that the Korean "economic miracle" is to be demystified, to be seen at one level as a global and regional articulation of industrial, military, and sexual proletarianization, and, at another, as the transformation from a US neocolony to a "subempire." The "miracle" stood on a masking of the changing status of both Itaewon and Korea more broadly. The lesson of Itaewon is that it reveals the mask as just that—merely a mask, of advertising boards, surface glitter, and consumption. In a study of *kijich'on* (military camptown) prostitutes, Moon Hyung-Sun (1997, 1) comments that, since the Korean War, over one million Korean women have served as sex providers for the US military.[26]

In more recent times Itaewon has transformed into Seoul's center for international cuisine and cosmopolitan entertainment; it is still mostly visited by American military personnel stationed in the nearby Yongsan Garrison.[27] The main street, Itaewonno, runs for some 1.4 kilometers eastward from Itaewon Junction; off this branches a network of alleyways and arcades crammed with stores, restaurants, nightclubs, and bars. One of these alleys leads up to "Hooker Hill," resplendent with nightclubs and establishments of lesser repute and a favored haven for much of the military population of the nearby Yongsan US military base. Paradoxically, the prostitution market is in part Russian-supplied.[28] From the late 1990s on, Itaewon also gathered a moderately visible gay and lesbian community.

Itaewon is "ordinary space"—undistinguished boxlike buildings with advertising boards and neon signs. It is atypical in that the small-scale boxland is on the main road as well as on the lanes and back streets, although, even here, there are the "signature" corporate towers —most notably the elegantly designed Cheil Worldwide.[29] Whereas the back streets to Jongno (and of Teheranno, to be discussed below) are mutually defining, dialectic opposites of the front avenue, those of Itaewon are exaggerations—in some sense caricatures—of the main Itaewonno Road. The back street to the north has most of the finest and most fashionable bars and restaurants; that to the south is the notorious Hooker Hill. The back street behind the small bars and other establishments of Hooker Hill—a back-back street—is Muslim: the Seoul Central Mosque is here, discretely embedded behind a long building that has, among other things, PC *bangs* and Islamic coffee shops. The Seoul Central Mosque opened in 1976 and has been the target of a number of "incidents" and a consequent need for police protection. This back-back street has a proliferation of tiny enterprises: small shops, a few tailors, computer repairs, Indian halal cafés; they would be nearly the smallest to be seen in Seoul, no doubt reflecting the economically depressed status of the city's Muslim community.

In a discussion of Itaewon's mosque and small Muslim commercial community, Kim Eun Mee and Jean S. Kang (2007, 78–80) observe that the more numerous groups of its patrons are Indonesian and Bangladeshi. On the basis of Seoul Metropolitan Government

FIGURE 4.12 Itaewon space, 2012: Hannam-dong and cascading buildings appear as if constructed on top of each other. As Seoul is a landscape of mountainsides, it is also a landscape of seemingly precarious cascades.

data they find that both groups in the 2000s had small concentrations in the industrial southwest, mostly Geumcheon and Guro, with the Indonesians also in Seongdong and Seongbuk in the northeast. The mosque preceded the influx of the Muslim workers, and none of these localities would be seen to have much connection with Itaewon.

Itaewon possesses a visual drama in that it is built on very steep hill faces, with cascading buildings and spaces. It is quite unique in that most of its signage is in English (figure 4.12).

Only its nightclubs and the ladies of Hooker Hill hint at the compromises of Korean history—the American intrusion, the earlier rescue of the capitalist "progress" in the Korean War, the Japanese occupation preceding that of the Americans. If viewed in an earlier Cold War context, the Russian ladies of the nightclubs present as a wonderful anomaly—how many secrets transmitted across the pillow? In the present age, however, their presence seems to attest to no more (nor less) than the collapse of the Russian world and of one of the great myths of history (yet to be learnt by the Koreans of the North). Itaewon is fashionland in Benjamin's understanding, "progress as Hell," yet it is also a screen—albeit the paradox of a *revealing* screen—across the national humiliation (figure 4.13).

FIGURE 4.13 Itaewon space, 2012: Hannam-dong back street, an assemblage of high-end, finely designed, discordant boxes.

Yongsan (Itaewon) provides another, very different screen across the national humiliation: here is the immense War Memorial of Korea, originally conceived by the Roh Tae Woo government as an emblem of military glory to legitimize the military dictatorship that Roh had served and as a symbol of ethnocentric nationalism. Sheila Miyoshi Jager has noted the connection forged between "the military, manliness and nationalism," as well as the fact that the museum at the memorial virtually ignores the Japanese period—it is a blank, expunged from history (Jager 2003, 118, 129; Kal Hong 2011, 73).

Seoul is a metropolis of a multiplicity of distinctive neighborhoods, often very concentrated in what each is known for. The western side of Yongsan is sharply different from the eastern, Itaewon side; the west has the Yongsan electronics market, comprising some twenty buildings housing around five thousand stores selling computers and peripherals, stereos, appliances, electronic games and software, videos, CDs, and all things electronic. Stores range from the traditional retail to the noisily, aggressively entrepreneurial. The term *Yong pali*, "Yongsan salesperson," has been coined to describe ruthless, shameless sales behavior. Yongsan is thus a patchwork of concentrations—military base, Itaewon, Hooker Hill, Muslim focus, electronics mart—all effectively a reflection of Seoul itself as a multiplicity of interacting multiplicities, an assemblage, as will be argued following.

There is far more to Yongsan, however. In September 2010 plans were revealed for a new Yongsan Business Hub, to include an underground strip mall "six times larger" than anything else in the city, to house studios, galleries, and "concert stages for young artists."[30] The centrality of "young artists" in marketing everything Korean is a theme for the next chapter. There would additionally be three landmark buildings at the center of the district, a triangle of spikes allegedly inspired by an ancient crown, to be 100, 72, and 69 stories tall. The one-hundred-story "spike," designed by architect Renzo Piano, was proudly proclaimed as the world's most expensive building, to be built by Korea's Samsung Corporation, which also built the Burj Khalifa (162 stories in Dubai) and Taipei 101 (101 stories, in Taipei). Another "spike" would be the Yongsan Apartment, designed by the Dutch architects MVRDV: it would comprise twin towers, sixty and fifty-four stories (somewhat at odds with the elsewhere-proclaimed seventy-two stories), connected by "a pixelated cloud" of apartments, swimming pool, amenities, cafés, and a serene koi pond connecting the two towers. The "cloud" would be a ten-story bridge linking the buildings at their twenty-seventh floors. The response, however, has varied from the troubled to the outraged. "The 'pixelated clouds' evoked the clouds of debris that erupted from the iconic

World Trade Center towers after terrorist planes flew into them," charged New York's *Daily News*. MVRDV's response: it "regrets deeply any connotations The Cloud project evokes regarding 9/11. It was not our intention to create an image resembling the attacks nor did we see the resemblance during the design process."[31]

Yongsan Business Hub was initially proposed as a project of Korail (whose vast land holdings in Yongsan would thereby be greatly enhanced) and Samsung. The overall plan was designed by Daniel Libeskind, who, ironically, was the designer behind the rebuilding of the World Trade Center. Construction was scheduled for January 2013; however, by August 2010 the project's demise was already being predicted (Kim Tong-hyung 2010); by March 2013 its financial collapse was clear (Rosenberg 2013); a month later the project was abandoned.

Yongsan thereby presents three worlds in confrontation. First is the world of military domination—it was the center of the Japanese military colonial enterprise from as early as 1894, which seemed to pass seamlessly in 1945 to that of the American hegemony. The second is Itaewon. It was and continues to be the realm of American happiness—here are the places of escape, the nightclubs, entertainment "spots," and brothels, just beyond the gates of the US military realm. The third world of Yongsan is that of the global hyperspace—the electronics mart in which a new generation of Seoulites will seek the gadgetry to join a wider cyberworld. There is also a putative fourth world of Yongsan Business Hub, in which the ideas and the designers will no longer be simply "Korean" but, rather, "other," as an assembly of more global attempts at understanding and constructing what might constitute a "Korean world and space." There are different spaces, each standing against and contradicting the others: military space (with all its own contradictions), the hedonistic space of escape, the space of entrepreneurial vigor, and the space of capital and its regime of accumulation.

Boxlands 2: Hongdae

Another example of the ambiguity of Korean blank space is addressed in Lee Mu-Yong (2004): Hongdae, an abbreviation of Hongik Daehak-gyo (Hongik University), had been just another nondescript residential area in the 1950s but, in the 1970s, it metamorphosed into an art culture district following the establishment of Hongik University and its College of Fine Arts (figure 4.14).

Seoul is extraordinary in its proliferation of art districts and profusion of galleries and museums. One is tempted to identify Seoul as the Berlin of Asia; it reveals the power of destruction and erasure

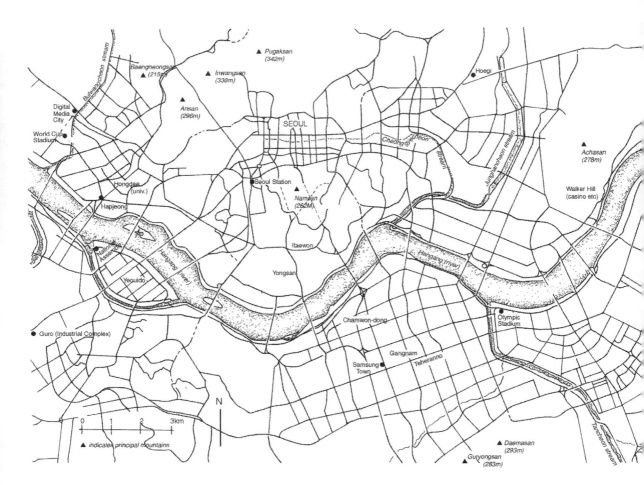

FIGURE 4.14 The wider city. Source: author, based on 2014–2015 maps.

that then seemingly enables the sudden release of creativity and the dream of representing both the idea of Korea itself and that other idea of Korea's place in a new, twenty-first-century world.[32] Claes Olden-burg's *Spring* at Cheonggyecheon may indeed provide a metaphor for Seoul and Korea (albeit from an American sculptor): the fantastic kinetic energy held within the spring by its suppression (1895 to 1945, to 1953, to 1987?), then the colossal drama of its sudden release (see figure 4.9). One looks at Seoul as the greatest manifestation of cultural resurrection. It is the theme of chapter 5 to follow but also of any read-ing of chaotic, even tawdry Hongdae—a wonderful place, like much else in what is simultaneously the ultimate Orwellian, Kafkaesque city of urban-design oppression, with all those seemingly identical gray-white towers. It is the greatest contradiction.

In the early 1990s a trendy café culture in pastiche (postmod-ern?) buildings inserted itself into Hongdae; it is now galleries and small theaters, art studios, handcraft furniture shops, art institutions, publishers, "culture spaces" and clubs, techno and trance. Many foreigners prefer Hongdae to Itaewon, given its relative lack of prostitutes and seediness.

The tiny shops that proliferate in the back streets and alleys are, in their "style," survivals from an earlier, harder age (even though many are from a more recent time). They are akin, in some sense, to the endless stalls and street markets and underground galleries. These small establishments proclaim their presence with signage, variously projecting signboards, decoration, and emblems. This, of course, is also the character of the establishments behind Jongno. The decoration in Hongdae becomes more inventive, however (this is, after all, a zone of art and performance), and there will be self-conscious design. Yet this is still to be seen as a "folk" vernacular. There are just a few instances, in Hongdae as in Insadong, where that self-conscious design will be expressed in an avant-garde architecture (figure 4.15).

Hongdae is an expression of the explosion of cultural production that accompanied the collapse of the era of dictatorship, albeit exploding as if from the vacuum of obliteration (the spring is released). The power of Hongdae may be in the exuberance that becomes possible

FIGURE 4.15 Hongdae, 2012: in both images indigenous muddle morphs into avant-garde.

in the lack of an artistic/cultural "establishment." Instead of a still-thriving, conservative, self-protective community of "old art," here it is nostalgia that is to be countered by the young students and a nascent avant-garde.

If authenticity—truth to oneself—is the dialectical opposite of nostalgia (chapter 1), then the confrontation with nostalgia might be seen as a condition of possibility for "authentic" creativity and reinvention.

Seoul, as observed above, is resplendent with "art districts," caught up in the shifts from freewheeling avant-gardism to commercialization and exploitation. Hongdae is only one of these "wild places" simultaneously in tension and collaboration with the ever-shifting and redefining art market. Yet it is still antinostalgic in its presentation (if not in the intentions of its entrepreneurs); thus it stands dramatically against the elitist, antiauthentic national enterprise of rebuilding the ancient palaces, gates, and grand monuments. It is as if in opposition to the "Chosun return," embodied in the reappearing palaces, that one can read Hongdae.

The national enterprise and the start-up nature of Hongdae come together, somewhat incompatibly, in the Seoul Art Space program of the Seoul Foundation for Arts and Culture (SFAC), established in 2004 by the Seoul Metropolitan Government. In 2015 there were fifteen Art Spaces listed, widely distributed across the space of the city.[33] The programs, facilities, and political agendas vary as widely as their locations. Thus Seoul Citizens Hall, in the basements of the new City Hall and like a symbolic rhizome under the older Japanese hall, is clearly a promotional instrument of the city government. Seoul Art Space Seogyo is an intrusion into the Hongdae area, its mission proclaimed as "the dream of being a hub of the art ecosystem in the Hongik University area"—to take it over? It exudes the discordant order of officialdom in the dishevelment of Hongdae.

Other Art Spaces would seem more creative in their intent. That at Geumcheon is proclaimed as being linked to the "urban regeneration" movement of Seoul city planning and as responding to the decline of the Guro complex (chapter 3); it was established in 2009 to provide an experimental art complex with residency programs, exhibitions, urban research projects, and an open studio—all accommodating both Korean and international artists. It occupies the buildings of an old printing factory.[34] Similarly, Seoul Art Space Sindang utilizes an old and bypassed underground shopping center from 1971; forty-two previous shop units have been converted into "creativity workshops" and exhibition halls. Yeonhui's Art Space is a small "village" for writers; Seoul Art Space Mullae has been fashioned from a strip of steel materials shops, with a theater and performance emphasis; Seongbuk has a focus on arts participation and health. There are also Art Spaces at Gwanak, Hongeun, Jamsil (dedicated to people with disabilities), and Namsan Arts Center (a theater), as well as Namsan Creative Center, Daehak-ro Creative Space, and Seoul Theater Center—all with an experimental theater focus.

It is instructive to see, in the mind's eye, the disciplined program of SFAC and the Seoul Art Spaces against the undisciplined disorder of Hongdae, and even more against the informal vigor of Cheonggye-cheon. And to ask: where is creativity most likely to be found?

Gangnam Chamwon-dong

Nothing could be further removed from the wild, unconstrained, exuberant disorder of Hongdae than the regimented discipline of the stiffly restrained ranks of identical apartment towers of Gangnam and a seeming infinity of other districts on the southern side of the Hangang River (figure 4.14). As Hongdae and the other areas contemplated above are in the north, this contrast might mistakenly be seen as a north-south distinction; we will see following, however, that the immense zones of identical residential towers are ubiquitous to Seoul. However, those of Gangnam, fronting as a vast wall onto the river and determining the river's character in its central reaches, are especially emblematic.[35]

One could take any of the hundreds of zones of multitowered housing for special discussion. For present purposes, a medium-sized estate in Gangnam's Chamwon-dong will be observed (figure 4.16; also seen in figure 1.1 from chapter 1). It abuts the Kyeongbu Expressway (Highway 1) and comprises forty-four residential towers, each some twenty-eight stories, together with its own schools (sizes of towers in Seoul vary: those of the estate immediately to the south are thirty-five stories). The soul-less, virtually identical, necessarily numbered towers have elaborate, overdesigned entrances, completely hidden car parking, a finely wooded landscape weaving through the blocks, woodland trails (albeit alongside an elevated highway whose scale is further visually augmented by ten-meter-high noise barriers) with exercise equipment liberally distributed along the trails. This is clearly an upmarket housing estate—"Gangnam style." It is also, however, the ultimate Corbusian, modernist landscape—one lives by numbers, in numbered towers in an idyllic woodland park, isolated.[36]

An underpass under the elevated highway leads to another, more varied urban landscape of both large and small, older apartment buildings, a very few separate houses, small shops, bars, and *bangs*—the necessary, complementary urban landscape that can supply what

FIGURE 4.16 (a) Housing estate, Chamwon-dong, Gangnam District . . . and (b) its obverse, on the opposite side of the Kyeongbu Expressway, 2012. These dichotomous worlds are within three minutes' walk.

the vast, regimented estate is planned to exclude. It is, in effect, the housing estate's back street; most estates, however, enjoy no such immediate back street. There is another, vaster, and far more vibrant zone of entertainment and escape little more than two kilometers to the south, in the Gangnam-Teheranno District, that serves, in various ways, much of the city.

Boxlands 3: Teheranno

It has been suggested above that the political economy of the Cheong-gyecheon Stream is to be seen in the context of a premodern, post-1945 subsistence economy of scavenging, recycling, and reinvention, morphing into a postmodern economy of disintegrated, flexible, small-scale, high-tech production and services on which the corporate economy of large-scale, globally connected activity ultimately rides. In such a view, new invention and creativity are always more likely to arise in the flexible world of Cheonggyecheon and similar zones of the old, disheveled city than in the corporate towers of the *chaebol*.

Cheonggyecheon's obverse is Teheranno (Tehran Street). Samneungno was a 3.5-kilometer stretch of Highway 90, in the Gangnam-gu District on the south side of the river; in the 1960s it ran through a relatively remote and underdeveloped area that was annexed into Seoul in 1963. Its name was changed to Teheranno to mark a 1976 visit from the mayor of Tehran (a street in Tehran was, reciprocally, supposed to be renamed after Seoul). In the following decades Gangnam-gu experienced phenomenal growth, with Teheranno becoming one of Korea's busiest streets, noted for the number of Internet-related companies operating there—Yahoo!, Korean rivals Daum and Naver, Samsung, Hynix, diverse Korean and international finance institutions, and major banks.

Teheranno is popularly called Teheran Valley and is the Silicon Valley of Korea, though more a steel-and-glass canyon than a valley. Except for the signage in Korean script, it could be any North American city center. It is believed that more than half of Korea's venture capital is invested there.[37]

There is a view that the impact of information and communication technologies (ICTs) on cities is essentially substitution, replacing the need for proximity and presence with telepresence (W. Mitchell 1999, 110).[38] Nigel Thrift (1997), however, sees this as myth, arguing instead that we need always to be aware of the ways that "culture, context and content mediate the contingent social constructions of ICTs, and their resulting effects" (Graham 2004, 98).[39] Some aspects of these effects will preoccupy chapter 5; other aspects are to be read from the (distanced) juxtaposition of Teheranno space and Cheonggyecheon space. Two lessons can be drawn from this relationship: the first is that neither Teheranno nor Cheonggyecheon is unique to Seoul; rather, both are different though inseparable aspects of a globally linked (hyper)-space of flexible corporate coordination and control (Teheranno) and an equally globally linked (and hyperspatial) realm of creativity and innovation (Cheonggyecheon).[40] The second lesson is that there are different genealogies and time scales involved in these radically different, interlinked realms. Within the context of Seoul, the most modern of metropolises, Cheonggyecheon and the space that it presents is "ancient," dating from the immediate post-1945 period of scraping for scrap materials and promising ideas; it evolves from pilfering, the junkyard, and local, small-scale invention. Teheranno space is new; its antecedents are the multinational corporation and the more home-grown, Japanese-modeled but ultimately indigenized *chaebol,* albeit often dating from colonial-collaborationist family enterprises from the Japanese era. There is a third lesson from Teheranno, relating to the fragmentation of Seoul space: that, however, will be deferred until later in this chapter.

While dialectical imagery might run through both Teherrano and Cheonggyecheon, it is their dialectical (though distanced) juxtaposition that is to be read as most clearly throwing "the miracle" into question—the Park-*chaebol* axis (and order) always inextricably linked with and dependent on the disordered, ultimately subversive "Miracle on the Cheonggyecheon."

Teheranno, a street and associated business district in Seocho-gu, is a glass-and-steel canyon, with ten to twelve lanes of traffic; it is both corporate "cool" (Samsung) and a display of earlier, less pretentious, and less architecturally sophisticated blocks. At the Gangnam subway station, and effectively the heart of Teheranno and of Gangnam as it is more widely understood, is Samsung Town (see figure 4.14). It is not a town but an office park and IT and electronics hub for the multinational Samsung corporation: Samsung Electronics, Samsung C&T, and Samsung Life Insurance have built three towers that are forty-four, thirty-four, and thirty-two stories, respectively. Samsung Town was designed by architects Kohn Pedersen Fox (KPF); it is "twinned," albeit symbolically, with Disneyland Paris and Sony World (Tokyo), which might suggest something of a fun park. It is, however, more corporate than fun (although the same cannot be said for its neighborhood, of which more following). The architecture of Samsung Town's towers is late modernist, beautifully elegant, internationalist high-tech. Immediately opposite, however, is the bizarre Gttower, designed by Dutch architecture firm Architecten Consort, a twisting, writhing, wavy steel-and-glass contortion that defies the corporate rationality of Samsung Town—its significance is that it demonstrates the free-form architecture that flows (seemingly literally) from the design processes that have been suddenly unleashed by the computer applications that Samsung (among others) seems to have bequeathed.[41] Gttower would seem to confront Samsung by highlighting the liberating power of the computer and Samsung's own failures of imagination in the realm of content—another issue for chapter 5 (figure 4.17).

This is also, incidentally, close by the site of the infamous 1995 Sampung Department Store collapse. The area houses the Korean Supreme Court and the Supreme Prosecutors' Office; nearby Seorae Maeul (Seorae Village) is home to much of Seoul's expat French community (Kim Eun Mee and Kang 2007, 82–84).[42]

The real surprise of Teheranno is immediately behind the corporate towers, especially in the back street on its south side—a muddled space of small buildings of two to six stories, with eateries, bars, *bangs*, and local shopping. It is every bit as vibrant as Teherrano, though differently and more frenetically so. This "landscape of entertainment"—widely exhibited in the ubiquitous back streets, also Itaewon, exuberantly in Hongdae, self-consciously in Insadong—can be seen as an urban vernacular. Like much vernacular, it responds to new tastes (desires, demands) and new technologies, especially those of consumption. So IT is inseparably part of it (figures 4.18 and 4.19). We return to Gangnam (style) anon.

FIGURE 4.17 (a) Samsung Town and, immediately opposite it, (b) Gttower, 2012.

FIGURE 4.18 (a) Teheranno, and (b) Teheranno back streets, 2012. Whereas Teheranno could be found anywhere, its back streets are distinctively Korean.

FIGURE 4.19 A Teheranno back street . . . almost the epitome of disaggregated, Seoul box-land, as well as of mountain-clinging Seoul, 2012.

Teherrano also replicates the underground malls ubiquitous in Seoul and described above in relation to Jongno, though here taken to a new extreme. COEX Mall is proclaimed to be Asia's largest underground shopping mall, with convention centers, exhibition halls, many malls, movie theaters, aquarium, a games area used for televising computer game tournaments, and stages for seasonal events and public performances by celebrities. With its corporate towers, the back streets and their entertainment zones, and then underground COEX, Gangnam presents interdependent realms characterizing Seoul more widely.

Part 3

SEOUL AS LINES

Seoul is places, locales, neighborhoods, as recounted above. It is also experienced as lines and transits, the highways snaking between districts and along the valleys, and the ever-proliferating network of the metro subway system, described in chapter 3. Seoul presents as a sprawling metropolis of dispersed and often-discontinuous towns strung along these highways and subway lines. Although now visually dominated by the multitowered estates of repetitive residential apartments, much of the city is from earlier decades and is characterized by unrepetitive small blocks on small allotments—the boxlands referred to above, frequently with small shops or other business premises at ground level, and two or more levels of very small flats above. Subsequent development has inserted newer high-rise towers into these older districts or else adjoining them on previously underdeveloped land; also, at subway interchange points, it has typically inserted corporate office towers and larger-scale commercial premises.

To the rider on the subway train who might randomly chance to the surface, Seoul does indeed present as a collage of seemingly disconnected, differentiated cities—the districts, towns, and neighborhoods often visually isolated from each other by the intervening mountains, referred to previously. Although any of these numerous lines could highlight this experience of the city as discontinuous and disorienting, the present account will turn to Line 1; it is the oldest and can especially relate to the pathways of the city's modern growth.

Line 1 and the Incheon corridor

Subway Line 1, following the older Korail commuter line from the Japanese era, began operating in 1974 (see figure 3.7). It runs from Dongducheon, indeed a dispersed town in a mountain valley to the north, through Seoul Station and on to the contiguous city of Incheon in the west. An extension to the south, completed in 2008, goes to Asan, a city of universities, spas, and hot springs, distant from the metropolis but increasingly a commuter city. Line 1 covers some ninety-five stations, and to traverse it is to observe the processes of the city's development.

Such a transit, northward, would begin at Seoul Station—a shambling, chaotic area of postwar rebuilding, a boxland hill town to the west and Namdaemun Market to the east, the Japanese station now the museum observed in chapter 3 and the new station a modernist display in glass and steel. The line passes under Jongno, Dongdaemun Gate and Market, and thence into the geological region of mountain and valley of the city's inner northeast. Here, at the intersection with the Jungang Line, is Hoegi Station: it is part of the broader expanse of the city and within the Dongdaemun-gu District (see figure 4.14). The area was developed mostly in the 1970s and 1980s and, accordingly, like Dongdaemun itself, the masses of older, smaller, two- to six-story blocks dominate. The multitower housing estates are few, small, and mostly the result of redevelopment of older neighborhoods under programs outlined in chapter 3.

Despite some proximity to inner Seoul, Hoegi reads as a separate, self-focused town. It has its own commercial precinct, its own

FIGURE 4.20 Hoegi, 2012: boxspace, churches, and wedding palaces.

proliferation of churches and universities (notably Hankuk University of Foreign Studies). It also presents, as a building type almost unique to Seoul, a splendid example of a wedding palace: it is a box, like most others, but adorned with fantasy domes, spires, and minarets. To stray for one moment from Hoegi, Seoul is a city of "districts," city-as-montage, and one of these is Ahyeon-dong Wedding Street, strategically adjoining the prestigious Ewha Women's University, concentrating wedding shops, galleries, and palaces, although wedding palaces are also distributed across the greater city. Equally as splendid as Hoegi's wedding hall are the churches, nondescript blocks like all others but distinguished by their attached, witch's-hat spires and indicative crosses, which are illuminated red at night (figure 4.20).

While Hoegi is clearly part of the more concentrated area of inner Seoul, from there Line 1 moves through the narrow valley of the Junghangcheon Stream, a tributary of the Han River—the Cheonggyecheon flows to it, near to Hoegi. One of the Line 1 stations in that narrow valley is Dobong. There are older, smaller flats and commercial premises around the Dobongsan subway station, as around Hoegi and other stations nearby, but then there are the massive, multitowered estates both interspersed in and surrounding this older development as newer development effectively overwhelms the older town.[43] At Dobongsan there is again the proliferation of churches: in one magnificent example, a vast, blue box is signified as a church only by its giant statues of Jesus and Mary.

As the line moves up the valley, the towns become newer, although their cores are always from an earlier time. At the end of the line is Dongducheon: while there has been a village there since at least the

Koguryo age (37 BCE to 668 CE), it is presently a small town from the 1970s that is now effectively overwhelmed by the outward expansion of the metropolis via the proliferating multitowered housing estates.[44]

Other aspects of the city's growth are manifested in the Line 1 corridor toward Incheon in the west. Whereas the corridor to the north traverses a mountain valley, this to the west is mostly across the alluvial lands and mudflats of the Hangang estuary, with mountains rising from it like islands. Also like islands are the numerous white multitower housing estates projecting from a sea of mostly brown, smaller, and older, but similarly dense, development scarcely distinguishable, in the distance, from the brown mud of the floodplain.

The line crosses Guro District, southwest of the old city. Guro Industrial Complex was Korea's first industrial complex of its modern resurgence, created in 1967 out of the Second Five-Year Economic Development Plan, with a focus on textiles, dressmaking, and other labor-intensive industries—all labeled as part of the "Miracle on the Han," with Guro being the "core" of the miracle (Kim Donyun 2015). In the 1960s and 1970s, Guro contributed 10 percent of national exports. It subsequently suffered decline but then rapidly changed from a manufacturing zone into a "futuristic" center for research and development and, since 2000, has developed into Korea's largest digital industrial complex. As elsewhere there are stands of identical high-rise housing blocks, as well as areas of older, low-rise mixed development from earlier decades.

Oryu-dong, some three kilometers farther along the Incheon corridor, is a neighborhood of the Guro District. Like other villages along the Seoul-to-Incheon line in the Japanese era, it has long been integrated into the metropolitan region. On the north side of the tracks it presents as a hillside community like many others in the broader region: it has apartment block complexes of various ages but also small, older blocks of flats, even some separate houses, small pockets of houses that predate the modern development era and that take roof-tile systems from a distant past. It is very complex spatially, in part due to the hillside location and in part to its development having been stretched over several decades. Very small-scale industry—effectively cottage industry—is interspersed with the housing and equally small-scale commerce. There are many churches, as well as a large Catholic college on the hillside; there is also a small private art gallery manifesting the virtually ubiquitous presence of new Seoul as congeries of art, its production, and inevitably its marketing (figure 4.21).

On the south side of the line are high-rise buildings from a previous decade, poorly finished and now poorly maintained in what is clearly a rundown area. There is also the Pyungkang Cheil Presbyterian

FIGURE 4.21 Oryu-dong churches, 2012. Churches are multiple in Oryu-dong, as elsewhere in Seoul. Look carefully: there are actually two churches in (a), and others behind the viewer in both (a) and (b).

Church and its associated Abraham Park Kenneth Vine museum of biblical artifacts.

Yeokgok, two kilometers beyond Oryu-dong, presents the imagery of a (noncentral) business district: office towers, high-rise apartment blocks, churches and their conical spires, and back streets and alleys. There is also one of Seoul's fifty-three Home Plus department stores.[45] Yeokgok (like many other noncentral business districts) provides an interesting contrast with high-corporate, high-fashion Gangnam and Teheranno: it is the contrast of a still-struggling underclass versus an ever-rising middle class, the unfashionable versus the fashionable, small-scale commerce and production versus the realm of corporate control, slowly dilapidating high-rises from the past versus the constantly reinventing architecture of internationalist elegance of Gangnam (figure 4.22).

Bupyeong is yet another (noncentral) business district in a long sequence along Line 1 (figure 4.23). It is also the interchange station with the Incheon Line 1 serving the city of Incheon and its environs: its northern arm from Bupyeong connects to the Incheon International Airport Line, its southern arm to the extraordinary New Songdo. Bupyeong has its ghosts: in April 2001 there was a brutal and illegal attack on unionists at a Daewoo plant, earning it the title "the second Gwangju" (Kwon Jong Bum 2011, 67–68).

FIGURE 4.22 Yeokgok, 2012: (a) undistinguished high-rise slabs (at the far end of the row is the Home Plus department store); and (b) two of Yeokgok's many churches.

FIGURE 4.23 Bupyeong shoe market, 2012: the surrounding architecture is again that of the undistinguished high-rises of the city's expansion along the armature of Line1 in the age of dictatorship and the "Miracle on the Han."

Incheon Line 1: Sinyeonsu to Woninjae

The southern line of the Incheon Subway Line 1 system runs southwest from Seonhak Station, under the broad avenue of Younsoo-2dong of Younsoo (Yeonsu) District, Incheon. Together with the subway and its next four stations, the avenue constitutes a long access corridor that connects (via other subway lines) to downtown Incheon and, far more remotely via Line 1, to downtown Seoul. Although the sense of order (regimentation) of this and other newer sectors of Seoul stands in dramatic contrast with the chaos of older areas, this is still a sprawling megalopolis that simply follows the flow of financial capital, always abetted by a capital-dominated planning system—the semblance of order is merely the consequence of the scale of its development. It is, indeed, the scale of the *chaebol* written on urban space. The convenience of its string of subway stations has seen the corridor here become prime residential space, especially on its northwest side, which, around the 1990s, became lined with a fine array of boxlike, mostly identical apartment blocks, as elsewhere distinguished from each other only by virtue of the large numbers painted on them.

The apartments' occupants hasten to assure the casual visitor or interviewer that this is *middle-class* real estate, that these are indeed upmarket blocks in an area of some prestige, and that the individual units are larger than those enjoyed by most of the city's denizens. In the late 1990s visitors to the Seoul region would commonly be taken to areas such as Sinyeonsu and Woninjae on this line, as examples of newer and more upmarket high-rise housing. By 2012 the estate had not aged well; furthermore, its standards were clearly below those of more recent estates such as those encountered in the Gangnam District, above; here car parking is at grade, whereas it is more often underground in the Gangnam estates. In Sinyeonsu-Woninjae there is a clear spatial hierarchy: the blocks near Woninjae Station are poorer, more run-down; there is a razor-wire fence between them and the slightly-better-presented estate to their immediate north.

Unlike inner Seoul or inner Incheon, with their disorder and wild displays of advertising boards and other signage, here the boxes are regimented, with only the name of a proprietorial *chaebol* occasionally displayed. There are interruptions to the discipline, however: periodically along the corridor, though discreetly hidden behind the screening blocks, there will be a small local shopping and community center—also a plain box, though smaller, discordant and riotously adorned with advertising boards as if to compensate for their banishment from the grand blocks. Inevitably, it seems, there will be a church somewhere or other in each such building, its spire and cross rising incongruously out of the boards and logos. As elsewhere, Christian witness is on aggressive display.

If the boards, crosses, and regimented blocks present as dialectic images in the sense of Buck-Morss' argument—throwing into question the dilemmas and contradictions of the society itself—here there is yet a further incongruity. On the southeast side of the avenue, near the Sinyeonsu subway station and opposite the procession of blocks, is another display of order and precision in the form of an immaculately reconstructed Chosun dynasty shrine complex.

Korea is not the only country that purchases or else reconstructs antiquity. The rebirth of Kwanghwamun Gate and Gyeongbokgung Palace are the most dramatic and politically charged cases, in this instance of full reconstruction. Woninjae presents a more modest case, in Woninjae Shrine on the southeastern side of the road and immediately facing one of the housing estates. Woninjae was constructed at the beginning of the nineteenth century to protect the tomb of and hold ancestral rites for Lee Huo Kyum, who was founder of the Incheon Lee family and was given the post of Lord of Sosung (the old name of Incheon) in the fifteenth year of King Hyunjong of Goryeo (Koryo) (1024). It was originally in Shinji Village but was relocated to make way for housing developments in 1994 and moved to its present site, which happily adjoins the founder's burial place.[46]

Woninjae Shrine is an elegant, understated assembly of traditional Confucian pavilions. Almost opposite it, embedded in the housing estate, is its dialectically opposed image: a disordered church, conical spire, and red cross. While small shop blocks adorned with a spire, a cross (illuminated red at night), and multiple advertising boards are ubiquitous in Seoul, this at Woninjae—one of several sprinkled through its estates—is especially poignant in highlighting the inseparability of Korean Protestantism and Korean capitalism (albeit at a very local scale). The shop block presents as a dialectical image in its own right, and in another sense in its proximity to the Confucian shrine. The mutually reinforcing effect of Confucian discipline and Protestant ethic in the formation of modern Korea has been alluded to in chapter 3; at Woninjae they come together as incongruous images (figure 4.24).

The Woninjae Shrine complex, like the reconstruction of Gyeongbokgung Palace, can certainly be seen as a reassertion of the cardinal principles of Korean architecture as articulated in the retrovision of Kim Swoo Geun. Its effect here is to point up the radical departure from such principles in the Corbusian-utopian world of the regimented blocks—as well as in the wild, undisciplined display of new (Protestant) religion in the churches-as-shops little more than one hundred meters distant. It is ironic that whereas the regimented blocks

FIGURE 4.24 (a) Woninjae Shrine and its dialectical opposite, (b) a festooned box (indeed, it is a church, albeit with additions), 2012; the high-rise slab blocks loom over both.

defy the Kim Swoo Geun precepts, the churched shop blocks can be seen to comply with at least some such rules: they are human-scale and harmonious with their (urban) environment. The shrine, on the other hand, is to be seen as representing the foundational source of such precepts; it is also surely to be seen as nostalgic—repetition as an act of mourning for the loss of the past.

Songdo

There is another space that, in the 1990s, would be juxtaposed with the regimentation of the subway line through Sinyeonsu and Woninjae, some three kilometers distant from it. The next subway station after Woninjae gives access to Songdo Resort, albeit now increasingly lost in new development, facing the West Sea and bordering Mount Cheong-nang to the northeast. The resort dates from the colonial era: the Japanese had opened the Suin Line in 1937 and decided to develop the Songdo coastline to make money from tourism; in 1939 the coastline was opened as a beach. After the Korean War the area was a US and British military camp. The military departed, and in 1963 the beach was reopened. Its hotels, food outlets, nightclubs, bars, and other entertainment adjoined a fun park (with a Ferris wheel, a few other rides, and a sledding slope) that opened in April 1964 to provide weekend escapes during the dour dictatorship.

It is the township on the landward side of the resort that is of interest. A somber element is the Incheon Landing Memorial Hall, opened in 1984 and overlooking the resort; it comprises a museum, monument, and lookout dedicated to those who died in the Incheon Landing of the Korean War. There are the flags of the sixteen nations that fought under the UN mandate, a memorial tower, and some relief carvings of soldiers and battle. The town is yet another landscape, mostly of architecturally undistinguished boxes. Not all of them, however, could be described as bland: they carry appliqué decorations evoking tawdry imaginings of "other places"—the classical world, an Alpine chalet, the fantasies of *The Arabian Nights*. While small incidences of fantasyland will be found in Insadong, Hongdae, and especially in the absurdist "wedding palaces" that occur in the forlorn business districts around so many subway stations, here they proliferated. The escapeland of the fun park has aged and now departed, suppressed by newer forms of family entertainment; the adjoining township has thrived, albeit to entertain entirely different groups—its bars and nightclubs and the barkers for available ladies reveal its role as an out-of-town Itaewon. The exuberance of architectural fantasyland is distinctive of Songdo; Itaewon is altogether more architecturally sober.

New Songdo

A far grander fantasyland is in the making, however. New Songdo is being developed on 1,500 acres (6.1 square kilometers) of reclaimed land in the Incheon harbor area, immediately to the south of the Songdo getaway township and some twelve kilometers south of central Incheon. It is part of an Incheon Free Economic Zone, a response to China's Special Economic Zones (SEZs). The rhetoric proclaims it as Songdo IBD (International Business District). Its designer is the New York office of the Kohn Pedersen Fox architectural practice, with Gale International and Korean steelmaker Posco E&C as the developer.[47] Its first phase opened in July 2009; by its completion date in 2015 it was planned to have 80,000 apartments, 4.6 million square meters of office space, and 930,000 square meters of retail. Its advertising blurb makes many claims: a sixty-eight-story Northeast Asia Trade Tower will stand as "Korea's tallest building" and "most advanced corporate center";[48] there will be the obligatory Incheon Arts Center, concert hall, opera house, and museum; a canal network inspired by Venice (after all, it is built on a saltwater marsh); a "Jack Nicklaus Golf Club Korea," with the usual appended luxury housing estate; top private "international" schools and an "international" hospital; and the Yongsei Songdo Global Academic Complex and the hoped-for campus of a major overseas research university.[49] Controversially, English is to be the lingua franca.

There has been some success in attracting splinter campuses of American universities, the first (in 2014) being State University of New York at Stony Brook, with courses in mathematics and science (Park Eun-jee 2013). This was joined by a unit of George Mason University from Fairfax, Virginia, with University of Utah also offering courses. A major research university, however, is still awaited.

The New Songdo master plan is clever and reflects the "postmodernist" design approach of Kohn Pedersen Fox, with intersecting diagonals enabling six zones to intersect to create the town's center: office, residential, and commercial zones can all face onto the generous one-hundred-acre Central Park. It is also very clever marketing, as one would expect from that designer (and on the earlier story of KPF, see Jencks 1987).[50]

The Cheonggyechong refashioning and New Songdo are both to be seen against the political program of Lee Myung-bak, who promoted the first as Seoul mayor (2002–2006, pitching for the presidency) and the latter as president (2008–2013). Lee had built his political career around rhetoric of green and low-carbon growth as Korea's avenue for a postindustrial future after sixty years of reliance on export-oriented growth (Lee Myung-bak 2005; 2006).

New Songdo suffered in the 2008 global financial crisis and there were scrambles for refinancing. Incheon's famously gung-ho mayor, Choi Ki-Sun, reinforced the state's backing for the project, emphasizing its "real quality." Yet there is always a doubt with such lifestyle theme parks: "'If you live in Manhattan, why would you want to live in a new town in Long Island or somewhere like that?' wonders Jongryn Mo, a professor at Seoul's Yonsei University."[51] New Songdo's rival may not be the Chinese SEZs but Seoul. Where are innovation, creativity, and cosmopolitan lifestyles to be found? The Teheranno-Cheonggyecheon dichotomy may be instructive, as one suspects that creativity arises in disorder more than in order, although, note that Teheranno is generating its own disorder in the vibrancy of its back streets.

New Songdo in 2012 presented an extraordinary scene: there are vast spaces, completely derelict, not a person in sight, and almost no vehicles. Some new trees, now stunted, had been planted in an otherwise bare landscape. It is desolate and disconcerting—one is alone, abandoned in an alien, surreal world. I arrived at New Songdo on 16 April 2012 through the very spectacular International Business District (IBD) subway station; I was the only passenger on the eight-carriage train. This would be the central business district for the new, emerging international economy. The names of other stations on the subway line reveal other aspects of the delusion: Campus Town, TechnoPark, BIT (Bio-Information Technology) Park, University of Incheon, Central Park, and then, at the end of the line, International Business District.

The reclaimed mudflats present as a vast expanse of weeds and desolation, with empty office towers and empty apartment towers rising forlornly from superbly engineered roads with no vehicles; pedestrian paths less well engineered and now breaking up as the reclaimed land subsides and the weeds intervene; and numerous office towers empty except for a small component of the proprietor's (Posco's) building—there is no sign of life in the distant high-rise housing districts (figure 4.25).[52]

Central Park could still prosper, as it is well designed; however, it is derelict and overgrown with weeds for the most part. There is a monument to the "Hello Kitty" marketing enterprise, now closed and abandoned.[53] It is all empty, and a sure sign that the lessons of 1997 have not been learned—overinvestment, capital idly tied up in unoccupied real estate, poor maintenance eroding the wished-for image. There is no visible provision for the disheveled, enlivening chaos of Seoul space—shops, stalls, street market, *bang,* entertainment. The only shopping in this grand new city are two coffee shops and a 7–Eleven convenience store.

FIGURE 4.25 The splendor of New Songdo, 2012: (a) a splendid residential district; (b) the grandeur of Central Park. It is an awe-inspiring experience to be the only person in an immense city.

The real question is: Would the visiting executive or conference-goer want to stay here or in Seoul or Gangnam or Hongdae? Would the innovators and creative thinkers live here or in Itaewon, Hongdae, Dongdaemun? It is the universal problem of start-up cities—they are competing with *real* urban space.

Completely missing is any evidence of an understanding of how Seoul urban space actually "works." There is no possibility for back streets with their small businesses (for family investments of time and effort, for petty entrepreneurs) or for local pastimes and entertainment.

The juxtaposition of the old, decrepit theme park of the Songdo Resort with the new, postmodernist lifestyle theme park of New Songdo—and they are within sight of each other—is cautionary. Theme parks age rapidly, and obsolescence very soon hits, as happened a decade and more ago with Songdo and seems already to be afflicting New Songdo. Organically evolved cities—inner Seoul as a paradigm case—seem somehow to regenerate, even after colonization, civil war, and dictatorship. It is the ultimate dilemma for planners designing the expansion (sprawl?) of their cities.

By 2015 New Songdo was still largely empty. Gale International was reported to be now walking away and in financial trouble as a result of it, though still managing aspects of the resort's residential component. New Songdo was by then in "real trouble."[54]

The Paju corridor

While the pages above have commented on aspects of the growth of the city through the medium of the generative Line 1 of the subway system, the northern bank of the river's estuary has necessarily been bypassed. The northern Paju corridor focuses on the city of Paju, "capital" of the DMZ (Demilitarized Zone) and just south of Panmunjom, an allegedly "grey, grim locale."[55] The present interest, however, is in Seoul's expansion into the corridor and, more specifically, the phenomenon of Paju Book City.

The Paju corridor might be traversed via the Gyeongui subway line or the expressway along the north shore of the Hangang River. Seoul is for the most part mountainous, although, once in the Paju corridor, as in that to Incheon, the landscape presents as clearly estuarine. The river is very wide and sluggish, and winds through an ancient estuary of mudflats and silt plains from which the mountains incongruously rise like islands from the flat, extensive plain. The corridor has long been agricultural and is still so: in the spring fields are prepared for sowing with last season's straw infusing the mud; then there is the annual cycle of summer growing and autumn cropping; and finally the expanses of plastic-covered hot houses for managing winter crops. The agricultural communities present as poor and poorly housed; many could be described as slums.

The corridor is also and more recently industrial, with factories and storage facilities interspersed with the farmland. By far the largest of these industrial-type facilities is Kintex, the Korea International Exhibition Center, from 2005, in the form of an airplane, with its swept-back, fifteen-story office tower as the tail fin.

The other intrusions, along the river in the south (Incheon) corridor and further back in the north (Paju) corridor, are the extensive estates of high-rise apartment towers. They present as discontinuous and dispersed (though certainly in the Incheon corridor they are not uniformly discontinuous). Seoul, indeed, presents as a dispersed metropolis—the mountains account for much of this, but it may also be a defensive planning strategy. There are the ubiquitous boxlike churches, with their conical spires and red crosses, usually on the lower, rounded hills of agricultural and industrial villages; on top of the higher mountains one will usually see a shrine—sometimes it will be mountain-Buddhist, sometimes shaman. The overall effect is of a disheveled landscape of incongruities and of the urbanization of the countryside.

Paju Book City

Another "new city" to Seoul (and indeed, like New Songdo, an element of its sprawl) is Paju Book City, some thirty kilometers northwest of the central city on what its proponents claimed would be an "urban wetland," adjacent to the Han River. It is a "national culture industrial complex" on a large site (some 396,000 square meters, in a 1.6-square-kilometer master plan), first proposed in 1989, as the country was emerging from its Dark Age of military repression, and commenced in 1998. Its claimed purpose was to assemble publishing companies, printers, paper manufacturers, and book publishers. It was initiated by publisher Yi Ki-Ung, who envisioned a city that might bring together the reconstruction of the culture, the rediscovery of the region's marsh ecology, and a new architecture for a rediscovered Korea. It presently comes under the aegis of the Ministry of Culture, Sports, and Tourism. Edwin Heathcote has described it as "[l]ike something imagined by Calvino or Borges, it conjures up a city of wisdom and surprise, of endless narratives, meaning, knowledge and languages. What it does not evoke is an industrial estate bounded by a motorway and the heavily guarded edge of the demilitarised zone. Yet somehow, South Korea's Paju Book City begins to reconcile these two extremes into one of the most unexpected and remarkable architectural endeavours" (Heathcote 2009). It is a fusion of industrial estate and office park. It is also an architectural zoo, of publishing houses each with its hopefully signature building. Most of these buildings, however, are either underoccupied or by 2012, and still in 2016, deserted. The overall impression is forlorn, ill-maintained, abandoned—a sunk investment. The city's broad landscape design was by London-based Architecture Research Unit (ARU) and dates from 1999. This is a unique example of a programmatic city, where everything revolves around "the book." The goal was to develop Korea's publishing industry by combining all the processes of publication: planning, editing, printing, logistics, and distribution.

Rhetoric around the project proclaims it to be a "City to Recover Lost Humanity"[56]—the implied recovery being both that of the memory of the ancient landscape (the marshes of the river estuary) and of the deeper human culture of Korea (loss, erasure). Again there is Edwin Heathcote's account:

> Publishing had gathered momentum and status after years of underground activity and censorship, and it re-emerged following the liberalisation of the regime in 1987 in an explosion of small, often family-run publishers. Their beautifully crafted books attempted to re-engage the nation with the history and culture that had been distorted, manipulated and lost over a period which included colonial rule from Japan, brutal civil war and military dictatorship. The project was also, at least in part, a reaction to the rapacious redevelopment of Seoul, the loss of the city's historic fabric and its rapid embrace of the culture of bigness and congestion (Heathcote 2009).

The city's Asia Publication Culture and Information Center claims to house book cafés, used bookstores, galleries, and restaurants; various exhibitions and fora are hosted; and there is a cultural center for children, with a performance hall, gallery, and book café (figure 4.26). The project is also intended to be something of a museum of contemporary architecture. There is the beautiful Mimesis Museum, housing a book publisher's private art collection, designed by architect Alvaro Siza, and based on flowing concrete forms around a central courtyard, allegedly inspired by a sketch of a cat—owing nothing, however, to any memory of the "lost humanity" of Korea. The finest buildings on the site, however, are those designed by ARU itself (with local partner Choi Jong Hoon). The first was founder Yi Ki-Ung's own Youl Hwa Dang publishing house. To the street it presents a dark, bland façade, and thereby a recollection of the traditional Korean courtyard house and its blank external walls—indeed, a box. Its internal courtyard, however, offers transparent membranes that might recall the paper walls of traditional *hanok*—the lost past held within the anonymous box of present Seoul? The second building was for the Positive Thinking Publishing House, designed as domestic-scale offices, in two units that enclose a small public plaza. These are of traditional dark-gray Korean brick set in a steel frame that evokes a Eurasian hybrid of Beijing (or Seoul?) courtyard houses and equally conservative Mies van der Rohe modernism.

Paju Book City might present as something of an architect's response to the assembled, decorated boxes of Insadonggil. What is missing, however, is the life and dynamism of Insadonggil and the organic chaos of its architectural production and constant reproduction. It is the difference between bottom-up production of both the built environment and of culture more widely (art, literature, books) and an imposed, top-down vision—as well as between informal urbanism and controlled urban design. Missing from Paju is the promise of enlivening chaos (informality as process) that might lead to the productive subversion of its "designed" disorder—which, of course, is in reality order. As Paju is designated as an industrial zone, building dwellings is difficult, yet some housing has been provided—very limited in extent but more spatially generous than what one normally finds in Seoul. There are stirrings of urban and commercial activity: a street market and some small shops, as well as a church on the hill behind the project and a small shrine on the mountain above.

FIGURE 4.26 The Asia Publication Culture and Information Center, 2012.

The architecture of Paju Book City is one of boxes, some very skillfully designed and detailed. However, they are internationalist in their styling and could be found anywhere. What is interesting is their presence here, in fringe Seoul: in this specific geographic and cultural context they can be seen as holding a mirror to the small-scale boxland of noncorporate, non-high-rise Seoul. Here the dialectical, mutually deconstructing imagery, in the Buck-Morss sense, may be stretched over some thirty kilometers, yet its power seems enhanced by that distance.[57] The urban design of Paju Book City has just such a deconstructive program: to reestablish the reality of the estuarine ecology—to bring wetlands back into the urban landscape, as well as to counter the culture of the city's modern development (figure 4.27).

FIGURE 4.27 Paju Book City as estuarine wetland and boxland, 2012.

Yi Ki-Ung has suggested that Paju Book City calls for a somewhat deeper reading than the merely architectural or ecological:

> Thirty-six years of Japanese colonial rule, followed by a chaotic liberation period, the Korean War fought between kin, and an indiscriminate influx of Western culture upon a Korean society made stagnant by authoritarian rule since the founding of the state until the 1980's in the economic order of the world's soaring industrialization: all these contributed to bringing intense psychological confusion and disorder to the people's sense of values. We have arrived at a stage today where life in urban to rural areas is extremely distorted.
>
> It is now time not merely to lament over the situation, but to find new alternative solutions. . . .
>
> Correcting the picture stained and distorted by history is not easy, but we expect this city [Paju Book City] to aid Korean society's expansion and reproduction by making a new milestone in Korea's desolate urban culture. Witness a new ideal in urban culture. It is our hope that such a specialized city will serve as a model in boosting Korea's general development of industrial structures.[58]

Here the wetlands imagery stands against both the back-turning development of modern Seoul and, perhaps more interestingly, the very sculptural "restoration" of the Cheonggyecheon rivulet of the old city. Note, however: both Cheonggyecheon and the Paju wetland are *designed,* and both raise the question of authenticity.

Paju Book City presents the same dilemma that confronts New Songdo. Would the creators of the new "cultural content" elect to live here? Arguably not. So, might it be the editors and subeditors who are to be relegated here? Editing, like writing, is a creative activity, and with online services, it is likely that the editors, like the authors, will elect to live elsewhere. So one is left to speculate that the obvious abandonment of Paju Book City simply reveals the logic of a wired world. Publishing, as distinct from printing, storing, and distribution, may ultimately be seen as a cottage industry, dispersed to editors' and copy editors' own homes.

There is one further, clearly intended dialectical image presented in Paju Book City. Adjoining the large, elegantly designed and emblematic Asia Publication Culture and Information Center is Seohojeongsa, a traditional Korean house that was originally an annex to the main house of Kim Dong-su in Ogong-ri, Jeongeup City. Built in 1834 and restored and moved to its present location in 2000, in 2001 the house was titled Seohojeongsa, meaning "cultivating the mind and having reedy creek in west": The notice board at Seohojeongsa on 18 April 2012 read, " 'Jeongeupsa' . . . is a traditional Korean popular song that was created in Baekje dynasty, and loved by people to Joseon dynasty through Goryeo dynasty. It says that a woman prays the Moon to shine brightly for her husband not to stumble in the dark. The Paju Bookcity [*sic*] chose it as their symbolic song, in the hope that the longstanding wisdom, integrity and trust brighten the publishers' way forward like the moon in their hearts." It is the same phenomenon of purchasing antiquity observed in the case of Woninjae Shrine—nostalgia is transformed into an urban design strategy.

Heyri Art Village

Something of a spin-off from Paju Book City is Heyri Art Village (also referred to as Heyri Art Valley). It was initially conceived, in 1997, as a "book village" linked to the larger project, but as it began materializing many artists joined and transformed it into a "cultural art village." With more than 370 artists claimed as its supporters (writers, artists, cineastes, architects, musicians), and with a collection of workrooms, museums, "art spaces," and galleries, it has become a significant focus for creative activity—perhaps giving the lie to the speculation immediately above. It has also assembled a collection of distinguished small-scale architecture that, for the most part, finely acknowledges its landscape. Kim Jun-sung, one of its principal architects, comments, "My vision of the project was to not merely focus on the expression of individual buildings but more so on organic ability to maintain the original setting" (Curley 2010). It is unlikely, however, that this "organic ability" can arise through formal design. Heyri's claimed attraction needs to be seen alongside Paju Book City's manifest lack of attraction; the claim, however, just may be justified: the (Confucian) scholar's retreat has long been a phenomenon of Korean culture, a place to which the Chosun artist or thinker would withdraw, either periodically or permanently, from a politically hostile urban realm. For some, Heyri may succeed in fulfilling that role—at least for a time. The brief retreat from Gangnam?

Against the ideal of the artist's retreat and Confucian-infused nostalgia, however, is another reality. The art village's restaurants, art shops, children's play areas, and other attractions manifest a canny commercial strategy on the part of Paju City and the village's entrepreneurs. Heyri Art Village is a theme park, skillfully marketed.[59]

The self-conscious creativity and tourist fun of Heyri Art Village presents perhaps the ultimate dialectic juxtaposition: only six kilometers away is the Demilitarized Zone, arguably the world's most heavily fortified border, to contain what is—equally arguably—the world's most repressive state (repressive against the freedom of creativity as historically understood and as Heyri Art Village would proclaim). The art village might well be seen as riding on the undoubted tourist attraction of the DMZ and its terror—questionably a retreat from Gangnam but also emotionally from the DMZ.

Yeongi-Sejong and new towns

There is one further case of projected escape from the maelstrom of Seoul and the thought of the North. In 2002, new President Roh Moo-hyan had planned to create a new South Korean capital on the site of the existing small town of Yeongi, which would be developed and renamed Sejong, for King Sejong the Great—the ultimate Chosun recall. The Korean Supreme Court, however, ruled a relocation of the national capital to be unconstitutional; accordingly, in 2004 the plan changed to the creation of an administrative center accommodating nine ministries and four national agencies and an envisioned population of around 500,000. The new "capital" opened on 2 July 2012, with thirty-six government agencies to be located there by 2015. The project has always been controversial, partly on grounds of its economic efficiency (Kang Hyun-kyung 2009, 2). The existing town has long been a significant educational hub, with university campuses (including a Hongik University campus); it is also, as a consequence, largely English-speaking. A further criticism has been that the agency relocations would result in separations of workers from their families remaining in Seoul (it is some ninety minutes from Seoul) and that Sejong City would accordingly experience a "toadstool" effect, with bars, nightclubs, *bang*, and worse mushrooming to provide entertainment for isolated workers. Sejong would become another Itaewon. The counterstrategy has been to promote Sejong as a hub of education, science, and business. Yet, again, how is it really to outweigh the attractions of Hongdae in Seoul itself—and of Itaewon or Gangnam, for that matter?

Mention must be made of five other projected "escapes." In the late 1980s the Korean government had initiated the "Two Million Home Construction Plan" to tackle a severe housing shortage and soaring house prices. Five new towns were planned to adjoin Seoul: Bundang, Ilsan, Pyeongchon, Sanbon, and Joongdong. By the mid-1990s the towns' residential areas had been mostly completed and the housing goal achieved; however, they remained largely dormitory suburbs to Seoul, with underdeveloped commercial and community services. Lee Chang-Moo and Ahn Kun-Hyuck (2005) could report, however, that by 2000 commercial dependency on Seoul had reduced though dependency for employment and for services continued.

It is interesting to observe that all five towns are at similar distances from inner Seoul (twenty to twenty-five kilometers), but that Bundang and Ilsan are much larger than the others. Bundang and Ilsan are also on undeveloped land more distant from established centers, while the other three are effectively expansions of existing built-up areas. Seemingly consequentially, the government's self-containment goal had been more successfully achieved in Bandang and Ilsan than in the other towns. Sejong, even larger and more isolated, may have a better chance. Witness, however, the travails of New Songdo.[60]

Fragments

There seems to be a (central, not-quite-central, or noncentral) business district at each of close to a thousand subway stations; there are multiple and proliferating centers for digital technology and production (Teheranno, Digital Media City, Guro Industrial Complex, New Songdo's wished-for TechnoPark, and BIT Park, . . .); art districts likewise multiply and proliferate (Insadong, Samcheong-dong, Hongdae, Cheongdam-dong, . . .); the *chaebols* similarly seem to be variously multicentered and uncentered (Samsung both everywhere yet nowhere); everywhere Seoul presents as a high-rise, "big" city characterized, nonetheless, by fragmentation and discontinuities.

In its fragmentation, Seoul might not be entirely unique, although it is difficult to think of any other city that, as a developed-world city, has taken such a form so late and so rapidly. Seoul illustrates the processes of developed-world fragmentation in fast motion. Rapidly increasing affluence, economic transformation (from third world to first world), and fragmentation have occurred simultaneously. All at high speed.

The account above has tended to present Seoul as a city of interior spaces. The space of everyday life might move from the confines of the boxlike apartment to the similar confinement of the office or workshop or factory, through the cavernous subway stations and the crowded, claustrophobic trains moving underneath the city. Almost emblematic of an interior city is its arrival and departure point: at Seoul Station, the Incheon Airport "Very Fast Train" arrives and departs from Basement 7. When one adds the underground shopping arcades and the new world of leisure in the microspaces of the *bang*, there is the image of a city of small spaces and underground lines of travel. One looks with difficulty for the interstitial spaces as venues of civic life.

This seeming caricature of the city might well hold for Seoul in winter. Seoul's is a difficult climate, very cold in winter and for most of the spring. While Korea's great invention of *ondol* (traditional under-floor heating) has been translated into the boxlike apartments, and there is heating, albeit less traditional, in other indoor spaces, exterior space can be forbidding.

For the rest of the year, however, exterior Seoul space explodes with life. The Western visitor will be disoriented by the extraordinary anomaly of the city's sophisticated, technologically bewitched denizens crowding the ubiquitous street markets. It borders on the incredible that the most modern of cities, global exemplar of what seems to lie ahead, could be a city of street markets, informal economy, street vendors, and disorder. For the chaos of its street markets—amplified by ever-present evangelizing street Christians and political protesters—Seoul rivals any city of Asia. The street markets and the disheveled back streets constitute one level of the city's real "living room."

With the outburst of spring, the parks and gardens arise as another level of the "living room." Winter sees Seoul as a gray, leafless place; spring brings the brilliance of cherry blossoms and then a lushly, verdant city; many of the parklands are new, the trees still immature, yet already this can present as one of the great, green cities.

The point of these observations is that Seoul emerges as a city of extraordinary contrast—the dialectic written on the fabric of the city. It is a multiplicity, confining interior spaces against a wildly exuberant exterior, civic realm, in the seeming absence of an intervening, interstitial, space of hybridity. There is, however, yet another space that is indeed interstitial: in cyberspace, interior and exterior hybridize—a theme for chapter 5.

Part 4

SEOUL AS ASSEMBLAGE AND THE PLACE OF MEMORY

The text above has described, at varying levels of detail, various fragments, bits, and pieces grabbed from the vast fabric that constitutes Seoul. How, though, are we to understand Seoul as something more than just the districts and transits that form the experience of the city? This is the question that preoccupies the remainder of the present chapter.

In his very thorough exploration of the Japanese understanding of the city and their would-be imposition of that thinking on to Seoul, Todd Henry (2014, 49, 52) sees all such thinking as captive to the organic idea of the city.

Gilles Deleuze rejected the *organic metaphor,* the superficial analogy between society and the human body, for explaining classes, groups, and human institutions—including, notably, the city and its spaces. The reasons for such rejection are well summarized in DeLanda (2006, 8–10). As an alternative approach to such explication, Deleuze has proposed *assemblages,* wholes characterized by *relations of exteriority.* So a city (Seoul) is to be seen as an assemblage of places, and places in turn as assemblages of streets, buildings, ideas, technologies (the hand phone, the Internet, the bicycle . . .), the watcher and the actor, the vendor, walls, gaps, interstices, a metro subway station, power, action, inaction, sounds, music, smells, memories, the rain—all have relations to other places, ideas, imaginings (Hongdae, an Itaewon back street, a Gangnam laneway). Such relations of exteriority imply that a component part of an assemblage can, in the mind's eye, detach from it and become part of a different assemblage, whether materially or affectively, where its interactions will be different (Deleuze and Guattari 1987; Deleuze and Parnet 2002); they also imply that the properties of component parts cannot explain the relations that constitute a whole—relations do not have as their causes the properties of the component parts between which they are established (Deleuze 1991, 98; DeLanda 2006, 11). An assemblage is marked by multiplicity, immanence, instability, by "becoming" rather than "being." Deleuze writes, "What is an assemblage? It is a multiplicity which is made up of heterogeneous terms and which establishes liaisons, relations between them, across ages, sexes and reigns—different natures. Thus the assemblage's only unity is that of a co-functioning: it is a symbiosis, a 'sympathy.' It is never filiations which are important, but alliances, alloys; these are not successions, lines of descent, but contagions, epidemics, the wind" (Deleuze and Parnet 2002, 69). The exclusion of lines of descent is to exclude organisms and species from the definition. It would similarly exclude the metaphor of the city as an organism. Assemblages, in this conception, are complex constellations of objects, bodies, expressions, qualities, and territories that come together for varying periods of time to ideally create new ways of functioning (Livesey 2010, 18).

AbdouMaliq Simone, in an exploration of the space of Jakarta, dwells on the inherent instability of an assemblage ("collection"): "As a collection, each component has to deal with the others, but they also have a life outside the collection, something that came before and that is ongoing. So when technology, people, things, and space operate as a collection, this process has various implications for the different networks in which each of these elements is individually situated. . . . Any collection of these things in one place inevitably has an impact on the places from which they were drawn. And they act back" (Simone 2010, 7–8). This is akin to Jacques Derrida's insistence on the notion of *grafting* to account for the nature of *montage* (and Derrida's "montage" can in some sense be equated with Simone's "collection" or Deleuze's "assemblage"). Gregory Ulmer (1985, 88) quotes Derrida at length to the effect that "no element can function as a sign without referring to another element which is not itself simply present" (Derrida 1981). So the interweaving of grafted elements in the montage results in each element "being constituted on the basis of the trace within it of the other elements in the chain or system." However, there is always more than one such chain for any sign and more than one level of meaning; indeed, insists Derrida, such meanings are "absolutely illimitable" (Derrida 1977, 185). Here memory cuts in, conditioned as always by the individual's understanding of a past that such memory would recall—history, the contestations of historiography. Thus we return to the themes of chapter 1. To graft will change the meanings of both the source and the montage: "Each grafted text continues to radiate back toward the site of its removal, transforming that too, as it affects the new territory" (Derrida 1981, 335). So, a question: how do the grafts that characterize the assemblages constituting Seoul radiate back, via distorted memory and contested history, to other sites (places, ideas, times)?

In *A Thousand Plateaus,* Deleuze and Guattari (1987, 88) suggest that an assemblage is to be understood in terms of two dimensions. On a first, horizontal dimension or axis are defined the various *roles* that an assemblage's components may play, from purely *material* at one extreme (a Cheonggyecheon rag-trade designer tied in to Dongdaemun Market) to purely *expressive* at the other (King Sejong alongside the US Embassy—Derrida's "sign"). These roles are not mutually exclusive, as a given element may perform both roles in varying degrees (Samsung City). The other dimension defines the processes in which these components variously become involved: these may either *stabilize* the assemblage by increasing its internal homogeneity or by stabilizing its boundaries, or *destabilize* it (DeLanda 2006, 12). Stated otherwise, "the assemblage has both *territorial sides,* which stabilize it, and *cutting edges of deterritorialization,* which carry it away"— the both stabilizing and eroding roles of a Gangnam back street, or the simultaneously symbiotic yet subversive relationship between Cheonggyecheon IT boffins and a Gangnam *chaebol* as an assemblage of convenience (Deleuze and Guattari 1987, 88).[61]

Urban assemblages are immensely complex, bringing together buildings, spatial relations, technologies, forms of power, and random and unpredictable actions.[62] Central to Deleuze's thought are multiplicities. The assemblage flies apart; as its components attach in other places and thereby form other assemblages—an architectural detail or a memory or a word sending the mind's eye elsewhere—so the identities of things and places will multiply, constantly unstable. Deterritorialization, becoming, constantly besieges (emancipates) the mind. The city's multiplicities of images and the dialectics of their contradictions, ambiguities, and discord bring back suppressed memories.[63]

Todd May (2005), on the idea of assemblage, suggests that immanence, duration, and affirmation of difference are concepts through which "the world becomes strange to us again." Assemblage thinking is part of the way in which *the city* becomes strange to us again, and its possibilities can be contemplated though never fully grasped.

It is here that the vitality and the constant "becoming" of Seoul are to be located. Cheonggyecheon; the bland buildings that line it; their diverse, low-rent occupants; the adjoining Dongdaemun Market—all can be seen as elements of an assemblage. There are relationships of interiority, yet those of exteriority seems to dominate: the computer boffin attaches to a wider realm of e-Korea (Samsung, the video games *bang*, other innovators and entrepreneurs—another immanent assemblage); the market vendor attaches to family, residential district, suppliers, and a shifting market demand; the mind contemplating Cheonggyecheon Stream will drift to the stories of King Sejong and his mural, to the stream's periodic pop concerts and performers, to the memories of its previous existences—other immanent assemblages.

The small Muslim street at the Itaewon mosque—effectively a back-back street to Itaewonno and encountered above—can illustrate the temporal character of assemblage. It is after the Friday prayers that the street most comes to life, a focus of community activity, attracting with both the mosque and its surrounding small shops. Then its participants will disperse to become elements of other assemblages—homes, workplaces, coffeehouses. Itaewon-dong also harbors "Nigerian Street," which will periodically gather the small Nigerian community; the neighboring Hannam-dong will bring together the Indian, German, and Italian communities; there are two China Towns, in Hyoja-dong and Yeonhui-dong, and a Japanese Town in Ichon-dong. Just north of the Hyehwa subway station, on Line 4, is a Catholic church at a traffic roundabout on Daehakno Road; on Sundays after the 11 a.m. Mass (in Tagalog), this small stretch of Daehakno becomes Hwehwa Filipino Street; there is a street market, with stalls and vendors of Filipino goods, exchanges of information; then, at 5 p.m. the market (and the assemblage) ends, relations of exteriority resume their power, and the Filipinos disperse. The street may remain, but it is now another place.[64]

It is as assemblage, unstable, always becoming, that Gangnam projects the constant immanence and the unpredictable and uncoordinated metamorphosis that underlies its dynamism and vitality. Likewise it is in the absence of such powerful, ever-changing relations of exteriority that Paju Book City's lack of any sign of vitality is to be located. Its purposeful isolation defies vitality. At a much vaster scale, New Songdo also attempts to divorce itself from the wild forming and transforming of assemblages and links—the proliferation of connections and liaisons—that distinguish Seoul.

This flying apart—immanence, becoming—explains the richness of Seoul space. It also explains the vastly greater richness of chaotic Seoul vis-à-vis "designed" New Songdo. Seoul is "from the bottom up," emerging from countless uncoordinated decisions over a century and more; New Songdo is the single great idea of a committee.

Assemblage thinking needs to be taken further. There is effectively a second emerging—perhaps already emerged though still always immanent—Seoul in cyberspace and increasingly global rather than local or national. As both manifestations of the city are to be seen as assemblages, they are also to be seen as breaking up and reassembling in new forms and constellations. This is the subject for the chapter to follow.

CHAPTER 5

NEW CULTURE
Seoul in the Korean Wave

The paucity of entertainment options in the 1970s is difficult to convey to contemporary South Korean youths, for whom a world without readily reproducible movies and music, and without cell phones, computer games, or leisure sports, is simply unimaginable.

— **John Lie,** *K-Pop*

In writing of the New Wave in Korean culture in the 2000s, Korean returnee John Lie describes a cultural amnesia—a loss of cultural memory and the erasure of a world of only a generation past. Yet this loss brings into existence new, almost bizarre ways to see Seoul and to imagine its future.

While the destructions of colonialism and war might lie beneath Seoul's post-1953 profusion of blank boxes and the subsequent and seemingly unending expansion and proliferation of the megalopolis, such conditions can be seen also to have resulted in an episteme—a way of constructing knowledge and understanding of the world—that enables the unprecedented cultural explosion of present Korea. It is the notion of "creative destruction," perhaps cultural succession, as an enabling condition for new invention. In the economic sphere this has most notably been articulated by Joseph Schumpeter (1950); in the cultural field, by Walter Benjamin, although it is ultimately to be traced variously to Karl Marx and Friedrich Nietzsche.[1]

The effect of the losses and distortions, together with the extraordinary acceleration of a superficial modernization, was to leave a void. The past has either slipped away, to be renounced, or to be imagined now in Disneyfied simulacra—the reconstructed palaces and their soldierly reenactments being the most dramatic manifestation, but also the purchased antiquity of Woninjae Shrine, the Seohojeongsa, and their ilk. This modernization, however, occurred at a singular junction in the transits of the age—in that cusp between an e-economy and age (the electronics boom on which the Korean economic miracle rode), and the emerging k-economy (where the drivers are no longer the *media* but the *contents* of those media). Although the period from about 1990 would seem most starkly to mark this metamorphosis, there were certainly earlier foreshadowings. The void is thus not to be filled but rather replaced by another space that is always already empty (cyberspace) and that constantly provokes the creation of contents. The world of remembered images is crosscut by another, of digital imagery and of cyberspace, also of the infinite possibilities that can explode to occupy that space.

The previous chapter was preoccupied with blankness, despite that infinity of advertisement boards and conical spires and crosses as an appliquéd montage—the eerily "modern" city of seemingly nondescript buildings and surfaces, as well as public spaces that could be found anywhere or nowhere (though often well and professionally designed in a conventional, academic "urban design" sense). The preoccupation that will emerge in the present chapter, however, is with contents. If Korean everyday life increasingly retreats into boxes—apartments in forests of high-rise concrete and glass, with the aged relegated to even meaner boxes, and leisure to the *bang*—what do Koreans listen to and watch in their reclusion? Equally significantly, what do other Koreans create as those new contents? The following is in four parts. The first addresses Seoul's preoccupation with media and the new contents evoked by media; the second moves on to the phenomenon of Hallyu, the Korean Wave that has risen from that preoccupation. Part 3 turns to the global reach of the Korean Wave and K-pop, as Seoul and Korea metamorphose into an unprecedentedly new form of global hyperspace: the city and urban space are redefined. The fourth and final part of the chapter reprises the discussion of Seoul as assemblage from chapter 4, to consider the implications of a new urban geography.

Part 1

MEDIA AND THEIR CONTENTS

The claim is constantly made that South Korea is "the most wired nation in the world"—also the most wire*less* (Oh Myung and Larson 2011).[2] By 2009, 95 percent of South Korean homes were connected to cheap, high-speed broadband Internet; its nearest rival was Singapore, with 88 percent.[3] Seoul was the first city to feature DMB (digital multimedia broadcasting), a digital mobile television technology, and WiBro (wireless broadband), a wireless high-speed mobile Internet service.[4] It has had a fast, high-penetration 100-megabits-per-second fiber-optic broadband network, to be upgraded to 1 gigabit per second by 2012. In June 2011 the Seoul city government announced that it would offer free Wi-Fi in outdoor spaces, providing residents and visitors with Internet access on every street corner. By the end of 2011 all buses, subway trains, and taxis would be equipped to offer wireless Internet to passengers; by 2015 the network would cover 10,430 parks, streets, and other public places.[5] An altogether new dimension is added to the realm of communication, in what can be seen as one of the most significant of all urban transformations—Seoul becomes a new sort of city.

The high concentration of people in tower blocks makes it easy to get fiber-optic cable to much of the population. High-speed broadband is cheaply and almost universally available; by 2007 nine out of ten residents had mobile phones, and Samsung and LG continue to pump out the gadgetry to a voracious local market. Seoul also pioneered "convergence": digital multimedia broadcasting was launched in South Korea in 2005. Other Asian cities—Singapore, Tokyo, and Hong Kong—are in pursuit. Singapore leads the challenge, especially on Internet access: in late 2006 the Singapore government said it would roll out free Wi-Fi broadband across the island and that by 2012 it would deliver wired broadband speed of up to 1 gigabit per second. That project continues. The rivalry between Korea and Singapore (and Hong Kong, Taiwan, the People's Republic of China . . .) is a theme to which we will return.

Korea is also claimed to have been the first to succeed in commercializing online games, in the mid-1990s (Yi In-hwa 2006). As Martin Fackler has observed, "[O]nline gaming is a professional sport, and social life for the young revolves around the 'PC *bang*,' dim Internet parlors that sit on practically every street corner." It is also alleged to be the first country to have to set up "boot camps" to treat Internet addiction among the young (Fackler 2007; also Song Do-Young 1998; Yi In-hwa 2006). Martin Fackler could report in 2007 that up to 30 percent of South Koreans under eighteen years old, or about 2.4 million people, are estimated to be at risk of Internet addiction; of these, about a quarter million probably show signs of actual addiction (Fackler 2007). To address the problem, a network of 140 Internet addiction counseling centers had been established by the government; treatment programs had been introduced at some one hundred hospitals; then, in 2007, the Internet Rescue Camp program was initiated, run on quasimilitary lines, part boot camp and part rehabilitation center. Korea is certainly not unique in having the problem of youth addiction to cyberspace; however, as it is in the vanguard of the problem, so is it apparently pioneering efforts to address it.

A more recent observation of online gaming—as industry, as social and cultural phenomenon, as economic transformation, and ultimately as "empire"—is Jin Dal Yong (2011; also 2010 and 2013). Korean government policies encouraged the development of online gaming both as a cutting-edge business and as a cultural touchstone. Games are broadcast on television, professional gamers are celebrities, and youth culture is increasingly identified with online gaming. As an industry, Jin recounts how Korean online gaming is increasingly global in its reach.

Songdo as "new ubiquitous city"

To observe the wired world raised to the next power, one can turn again to New Songdo, introduced in chapter 4 and finely spruiked in the wondrous rhetoric of Marthin De Beer, senior vice president of Cisco Systems, the information technology contractor for New Songdo:[6]

> If you've been to Songdo in Korea, it's amazing what is going on there. Every home will have a Telepresence unit built in like a dishwasher. And it's the developer that is putting those into new apartments as they get built out, because that is how education, health care and government services will be delivered right into the home. It will come to you. You don't have to go find it. And that is how they will reduce traffic congestion and pollution in the cities. . . .
>
> [Y]ou can literally sit back on the couch and see your friends and family in life-size, full high definition, right in your living room, and interact with them. It's not a small computer screen. You get a full view of everyone. (Dignam 2010)

De Beer made this statement in a June 2010 talk at a Bank of America/Merrill Lynch Technology Conference focused, of course, on video, telepresence, and networks. More interesting, however, was the talk's subtext: what are the social and psychological implications of reality's replacement with its virtual substitute? De Beer spoke of such "presencing" with one's banker, lawyer, accountant, tutor, "because now I can interview and hire a tutor that may be in a different city for my kids, and it's the best possible tutor I can find." However, he goes no further. The real effects on the individual, isolated in a world of virtual reality, are yet to be observed. Dignam's comment: Songdo may be able to show us the art of the possible.

Lest the transformative aspects of Songdo overexcite, it must be emphasized that, for Gale, Cisco, and its other proponents, this is an investment, and expected to harvest a rich return. The observation of (New) Songdo in chapter 4 casts some doubt on the richness of that return. So we can observe another, also rhetorical, assessment of the project:

> Cisco calls this Smart+Connected Communities initiative a poten-
> tial $30 billion opportunity, a number based not only on the reve-
> nues from installation of the basic infrastructure but also on selling
> the consumer-facing hardware as well as the services layered on top
> of that hardware. Picture a Cisco-built digital infrastructure wired
> to Cisco's TelePresence videoconferencing screens mounted in every
> home and office, with engineers listening, learning, and releasing
> new Cisco-branded bandwidth-hungry services in exchange for
> modest monthly fees. You've heard of software as a service? Well,
> Cisco intends to offer cities as a service, bundling urban neces-
> sities—water, power, traffic, telephony—into a single, Internet-
> enabled utility, taking a little extra off the top of every resident's bill.
> (Lindsay 2010)

The financial model, it seems, is akin to that of ancient rent farming. One must wonder, however, if Cisco picked the right farm, and whether Gangnam or elsewhere in Seoul might not have been a smarter target.

Media and the uncertainties of new invention

There may be a warning for enterprises like Cisco and projects like New Songdo in the uncertainties that accompany the endless prolifer-ation of new media. Although this chapter is more concerned with the contents than with the media conveying them, it is instructive to note the recent dilemmas facing the PC *bangs*.

Some think that the age of the *bang* may be passing. Yoon Ja-young (2012) cites a survey of Internet café owners (by the Korean Federa-tion of Small and Medium Business) showing 64.5 percent of them in deficit; one in three was barely breaking even, and only 1.8 per-cent saw a profit. Where there were an estimated 24,000 Internet cafés in Korea in the early 2000s, by 2012 the figure was around 15,000. The fall is attributed to the expansion of smart devices as well as to the provision of free Wi-Fi in coffee shops. Accordingly the Internet cafés are increasingly relying on online game players, although the games are also making the shift from desktop to mobile devices. Yoon cites a white paper on Games by the Korean Creative Content Agency:[7] while Internet cafés took 29 percent of sales in the 2009 games market, that fell to 19 percent in 2011 and was expected to be only 12 percent in 2013; in contrast, as smart devices become smarter, sales of mobile games were projected to have doubled between 2009 and 2013.

The uncertainties of new invention continue: the annual flood of new mobile devices, and of new games to be played on them, has continued to place old technologies and *bangs* under yet further pressure; so 2016 saw the release of the first commercially available virtual reality headsets, prefiguring the next wave of both consumer frenzy and youth distraction. Multiplayer games proliferate as evolving technologies enable ever-increasing connectivity between devices, thereby threatening the *bangs* and accordingly the spaces of the city.

From media to content

Nowhere have the transpositions of reality been more brilliantly manifested than in the extraordinary creativity of Korean electronic art. The National Museum of Contemporary Art, Korea at the base of Mount Cheonggyesan in suburban Gwacheon, as an example, is in the main a gallery of electronic art and imagery. It is set in a forest in low foothills of the main mountain range and was designed by architect Kim Tai Soo. Though thoroughly modern in its starkly geometric forms, there are apparent references to ancient Chosun-era monuments. The complex might be seen as a fine reflection of the quest for a modern Korean identity—and perhaps also as a counter to other expressions of that identity (Gyeongbokgung, Seohojeongsa, the reenactments of Chosun pageantry at the variously restored and reconstructed palaces).[8] It is in its electronic art contents that the real challenge to an understanding of Korea is to be found.

In 2001 the Guggenheim Museum in Bilbao, Spain, mounted a major exhibition of Korean art, again digital and diversely electronic, especially celebrating the seminal work of Korean composer and video artist Paik Nam June (1932–2006). From February to April 2000 Paik's work had similarly dominated the New York Guggenheim (Hanhardt 2000). Paik Nam June is widely considered "the father of video art" (Lee Yongwoo 2006; Kal Hong 2011, 85). The first phase of Paik's musical output began in 1947 with conventionally notated works and the Korean-flavored sounds of his youth. The seminal work of Paik grew out of the 1960s flowering of a Korean sense of impending freedom and its potential for a radical break. His first emblematic work was *TV Buddha,* a TV set and a statue of the Buddha are placed facing each other, as the Buddha contemplates his own image picked up by the video camera placed above the TV set (Lee Yongwoo 2006).[9] Both modern electronic technology and ancient Buddhist contemplation are set to deconstruct each other—Korea is itself deconstructed. There is something of a contradiction here, however: while Paik's work is widely seen as seminal to the direction of modern Korean culture, he spent much of his time from the 1950s on in Germany, the United States, and Japan, and was a founding member of the internationalist Fluxus Group, so that the idea of *Korean* cultural rebirth falls into the framework of emerging, internationalist, avant-gardist culture.

Paik's artistic debut was with a solo exhibition in Wiesbaden, Germany, in 1963, titled *Exposition of Music-Electronic Television.* Twelve television sets were scattered through the exhibition space and used to create unexpected effects in the images being received. Paik moved to New York in 1964 and began working with cellist Charlotte Moorman to combine video and performance. In their installation *TV Bra for Living Sculpture,* television sets were stacked in the shape of a cello; as Moorman bowed the television sets, there were images of her playing, collages of other cellists, and live images of the performance. Paik also incorporated television sets into a series of robots, sometimes built from bits and pieces of wire and metal, and later from vintage radio and television sets. He laid out a large garden in an exhibition space and planted dozens of television sets in it; he also hollowed out a television set and filled it with plants rooted in earth. To this he gave the title *TV Plant.* The implication seemed to be that, while technology itself was not necessarily of substantive relevance, it could be brought to some organic place in general culture by our contemplating the nexus (or its lack) between technology and nature (Hanhardt 2000; Hanhardt and Hakuta 2012). On New Year's Day 1984 Paik broadcast, via international satellite, "Good Morning, Mr. Orwell," which he had composed in Paris and New York, to negate the pessimism of George Orwell's (1903–1950) novel *1984,* which had warned of the oppressive power of television in a totalitarian state. The show was aired simultaneously in major urban centers, including Seoul (Kal Hong 2011, 140n1). There is no mention of it being aired in Pyongyang.

For the 1988 Olympic Games in Seoul, Paik built a tower from 1,003 monitors, titled *The More the Better;*[10] it now stands in the center of a spiral ramp in the National Museum of Contemporary Art, Korea. The "1,003" symbolizes October 3, Korea's National Foundation Day— the foundation of the ancient Gojoseon, the first Joseon or Chosun. The work is not merely at the center of the Museum of Contemporary

FIGURE 5.1 Paik Nam June, *The More the Better*, 1988. The assembled television sets are from an earlier age and technology—they are no longer manufactured and so cannot be replaced as they fail. The blank screens thereby measure the passing of their age and its technology so that *The More the Better* will in time become a ruin—a dead, electronic monument to a past time. Photographed 2012.

Art; the museum is effectively built around it. *The More the Better* is now a national monument (figure 5.1) (Kal Hong 2011, 85).

Paik was commonly called the founder of video art, philosopher of technology, composer, poet, information artist. Lee Yongwoo notes Paik's assertion that "the role of the artist was to anticipate the future.[11] He believed that when technology could be used like an artist's brush, technology would be humanized so that it could be applied for the true benefit of mankind [*sic*]" (2006, 39). While he certainly searched widely for Korean subject matter, it would be mistaken to find nationalism in this quest. Similarly, while it was scarcely coincidental that a Korean artist would be imbued with the excitement of video technology in Korea's decade of technological embrace in the 1960s, his significance (as both a Korean and a global artist) was in his turn to the potential content of this new technology—as well as in his turn to philosophical reflection on the relationships of power emerging in the new age.[12]

Aftermath to Paik Nam June

In Yongin at the southern extension of Seoul, on the Bundang subway line, sits the Nam June Paik Art Center. The idea of an institution dedicated to Paik was discussed with him starting 2001. In 2008 the center was opened to the public.[13] Accommodating exhibition halls, creative activity spaces, and archives, it is described as "a space of 'introspective anarchy of infinite light and life,' . . . a venue for the 'escape from enlightenment,' going beyond enlightenment." Paik, it is asserted, did not regard video and television as "a means for communicating messages, but as an explosion of time, instead creating a space for mandala-based televisuals, and for participation by the public where 'consilience' among heterogeneous fields can take place."[14]

There are younger followers in the tradition that Paik pioneered. Moon Kyungwon and Jeon Joonho project video installations in *News from Nowhere* (2012), retracing William Morris' 1890 novel that envisioned an agrarian society in which the divisions between art, life, and work were erased. Here, however, the erasure is to be of the borders between science, architecture, product design, engineering, philosophy, and religion in a postapocalyptic future—after the North-South apocalypse.[15]

The first generation of Korean modern artists represented by Paik Nam June was followed by a new generation of distinguished artists working in a variety of media. These include Chang Ree-seok, Chang Doo-kun, Paek Young-su, Chun Kyung Ja, Kim Tchang-Yeul, and Suh Se-ok. More recently, the Korean art world is represented by a group of painters and sculptors such as Chun Kwang Young, Park Seo-bo, Lee Jongsang, Song Soo-nam, Lee Doo-shik, Lee Wal-jong, Youn Myeungro, Lee Il, Kang Ik-joong, Lim Ok-sang, Kim Young-won, and Choi Jong-tae, all of whom have achieved international recognition.[16] Also notable for its urban focus, on North Korea rather than Seoul, is the photography of Back Seung Woo.[17] The diffusion both of media and of forms of expression might be linked to the example of Paik's "exit" from convention, but also to the explosion of art spaces and zones in the city recounted in chapter 4.

Korean official culture exhibits a wider embrace of the deconstructive power of digitally transmitted content. Sunday 15 April 2012 was the one-hundredth birthday of Kim Il-sung. From its permanent collection, the National Museum of Contemporary Art, Korea reprised a video art installation by William Kentridge (South African, b. 1955), *I am not me, the horse is not mine* (original 2008). The phrase was commonly a peasant's insolent reply in Czarist Russia to deny responsibility for actions; it has subsequently become a Russian proverb. The theme of the installation was based on Gogol's absurdist *The Nose*: television screens depict Constructivist cartoons, including a cartooned Stalin, with one screen displaying (in English) the text of the plenum of the Central Committee of 26 February 1937 that condemned Bukharin. The proclaimed purpose of the work is "to lay bare the institutional violence of Stalin's regime."[18] In Korea it is safe to assume that the conjunction of such a display with Kim Il-sung's centenary was not coincidental.

It is similarly not coincidental that Korea can be seen as enmeshed in the vanguard of the new cyberpolitics (Lee Eun-Jung 2004). In the context of increasing collusions between the political parties and the formal press (the Third Estate with an increasingly compromised Fourth Estate), there are inserted the ever-more-subversive Internet-based web journals—weblogs, or blogs—claiming the space of the Fifth Estate.[19] So the Korean OhMyNews online, an interactive news "paper," was founded in February 2000 and claims to have been the world's first "citizen journalism" outlet. Its motto is "Every Citizen is a Reporter," and in 2004 it was reported as having a readership of two million, and over 26,000 registered "citizen journalists." On some accounts it was credited with playing a key role in bringing President Roh Moo-hyun to office in the 2002 elections (*StarIn Tech*, Malaysia, 23 November 2004 1–3;[20] Yun Seongyi 2003; Oh Myung and Larson 2011, 156). Yun Seongyi (2006, 57) elsewhere reports that Roh's home page was logged on to by more than 300,000 "netizens" every day, and by 860,000 on the day of the election, quoting Britain's *Guardian* to the effect that "South Korea will stake a claim to be the most advanced online democracy on the planet with the inauguration of a president who styles himself as the first leader fully in tune with the Internet." While there are complaints that the Internet is unable to communicate the uplifting policies and messages of the Third Estate, that of course is precisely the point: its character is in its anarchic fragmentation and dissemination, and in its disorder. Its effect rather is "debunking, reinforcing, and cooling" (Yun Young Min 2003). Late modern politics, like late modern Protestantism (chapter 3), "flies apart."

Cinema

As "debunking" and "flying apart" characterize both modern Korean politics and the trajectory of Korean "high-culture" music and visual arts, so too popular culture—albeit sometimes unintentionally. All arise in the context of an enabling episteme of distortion of memory, reimagining of the past, naturalizing of material culture, and transposition of reality (a theme for chapter 6). Thus, indeed, can one view the extraordinary phenomenon of Hallyu, the "Korean Wave." Although the term refers to the popularity of South Korean popular culture that swept through East and Southeast Asia around mid-1999, its antecedents go back to the long evolution of the Korean cinema industry.[21]

There had been a brief Golden Era of Korean silent films in the years 1926–1930, sparked by the 1926 release and critical success of Na Woon-gyu's *Arirang*. Although the film did not have an explicitly political message (no nationalism, no Japanese bashing), the common use of a live narrator, or *byeonsa*, at the theater who could inject his own satire and criticism of the occupation, would give it a political subtext invisible to government censors. For all that, *Arirang* was seen by the police as a blatant attack against Japanese rule and accordingly banned (Eckert et al. 1990, 295).[22] More than seventy films were produced in this time, in a complex and evolving process of interaction between Japanese and Korean filmmakers, whereby "the latter played key roles in the formation of Korean cinema both despite and in conjunction with the heavy-handed influence of Japan's filmmakers, technology and capital" (Chung Chonghwa 2012, 138).[23] After 1930, however, the domestic film industry was virtually shut down due to censorship and mounting Japanese oppression; from 1938 on, all filmmaking in Korea was done by the Japanese; by 1942 the use of the Korean language in films was banned (Min Eungjun et al. 2003).

After 1945 there was a brief outburst of production with "freedom," understandably, as the guiding theme, although this abruptly ended with the 1950–1953 civil war.[24] The real rebirth began in 1955, enjoying support from the Syngman Rhee government, and then subsequently in 1960–1961, a year of unprecedented freedom in the period between the Rhee and Park administrations. With Park, heavy censorship and regulation returned—"family values" were to be encouraged, while any hint of pro-Communist messages or obscenity was to be purged. Despite the constriction, film production, film quality, and audiences increased throughout the 1960s to give Korea a strong cinematic culture; the 1970s, by contrast, marked a period of suppression and decline. "Political correctness" would rule cinema production. This decline was further hastened by "free" trade agreements with the United States that allowed an unrestricted Hollywood flood (Lee Hyangjin 2000; Kim Byeongcheol 2006).[25] Steven Chung (2014a) sees Shin Sang-ok (1926–2006) as arguably the most important Korean filmmaker of the postwar era, having directed or produced nearly two hundred films in a decidedly melodramatic genre. These included the highly regarded *A Flower in Hell* (1958) and *The House-maid and My Mother* (1961). However, by around 1972 his career was floundering in the wake of the dictatorship's censorship and the Hollywood flood, only to revive in spectacular fashion after 1978—we resume that story following.

Kathleen McHugh and Nancy Abelmann (2005) identify the 1955–1972 period as the "golden age" of South Korean films and the period of a "first renaissance" (of that earlier golden era of 1926–1930?).[26] The various papers that McHugh and Abelmann bring together focus on a number of intersecting themes: transnational connections (the debt to Hollywood but also to Italian Neorealism, French art, and even Mexican cinema), war and the plight of women (a strong emotional attachment to MGM's *Waterloo Bridge* of 1940), the dilemma of syncretization, and the indigenization of Christianity in Korea and its entanglement in the representation of women (McHugh and Abelmann 2005). These are themes that reemerged in the "second renaissance"—the "New Wave" Korean cinema—beginning in the 1990s.[27] This latter McHugh and Abelmann identify with tendencies toward both auteurism and melodrama, a critique that is also taken up by Moon Jae-cheol (2006). Where in Western cinema auteurism—the celebration of the author, the director, and originality—took the form of emphasizing film as art, in Korea the industry took such an idea as the operator for challenging the Korean film institution. The director and his or her film would challenge the institution and thereby its protecting, wider society. The strategy of the New Wave was to hybridize the two concepts of auteurism (the art-house cinema that engages the humanist vision of a single writer-director) and realism.[28] Hybridity is also emphasized by Kim Kyung Hyun (2011b, 186): "By fully embracing Hollywood, rather than rejecting it, their works display hybridity that equally engages national identity and global aesthetics, art and commercialism, conformity and subversion, and narrative coherence and stylistic flair."[29]

Moon Jae-cheol further argues that the New Wave's view of history was melodramatic: "These films reproduce the past through the lens of nostalgia, thereby emphasizing a sense of loss in the present. As Fredric Jameson said about postmodern film, there is evidence of a regression that cannot imagine a new history" (Moon Jae-cheol 2006, 44). A melodramatic imagination, following Peter Brooks (1976), would be one that seeks hidden moral values in a world in which values are being destroyed—"primal secrets or essential nature has been suppressed and awaits liberation" (Moon Jae-cheol 2006, 48; on the melodramatic in Korean cinema, see also Lee Young-il and Choe Young-chol 1998).[30] Moon goes on, however, to suggest that there was, by 2006, an emerging post–New Wave cinema in which the melodramatic was being supplanted by an ironic imagination and view of history. Irony builds on ambiguity of meaning—rather than look for hidden meaning in history, irony would point to the uncertainty of history by showing that positive truth is not possible.[31]

If Moon's observation has validity, then the suggestion would be that there can be detected, in the sensibilities of recent Korean cinema, some shift away from the preoccupation with nostalgia and loss in Korean society that has been a constant theme of chapters 3 and 4. The uneven shifts between nostalgia and irony preoccupy modern Korean literature embedded, as Stephen Epstein (1997) observes, in and reflective of historical context. One might reasonably question: is any such tendency to be observed in uses of the built environment to represent "the Korean condition"—in the neo-Modernist landscape of Cheonggyecheon or perhaps the siting and forms of the National Museum of Contemporary Art, in contrast to the nostalgic (melodramatic) reconstructions of palaces and palace guards? Where the historical reconstructions of Kwanghuamun and Gyeongbokgung Palace might be seen to express a melodramatic imagination, the reinvention of Cheonggyecheon is ironic. Irony also arises in the hyperspatial phantasmagoria—albeit accidental—of New Songdo? Are we likewise seeing a "new wave" urban design? We will return to this question.

The post-1997 explosion in Korean film production, as well as in both its domestic and international adulation, represents a breakthrough in artistic and marketing terms but is also, however, a phenomenon needing explanation. It might be seen, simplistically, as an issue of quality, as well as the sudden release of previously suppressed ideas and creativity. A partial explanation may also relate to a recurring theme of the Korean people's suffering as a result of their division and the longing for reunification. Arguably even more significant has been a hard, uncompromising "values" focus that marks New Wave Korean films. In writing on the "independent filmmakers," Park Young-a (2011) has drawn special attention to director Kim Dong-won (b. 1955), whose documentary *Sanggyedong Olympics* exposed the violence of the "eviction squads," local gang members hired to clear the slums in preparation for urban beautification for the 1988 Olympics. Deeply moved by the work of radical Catholic activists among the poor, Kim went on to direct a series of documentaries to unveil the condition of Seoul's shantytown residents. He went to live among his subjects but in his films avoided identification of individuals, instead relying mostly on long shots of groups of residents, to thereby depict the shantytown as "a community with a unified future and hope" (Nam Tae-je and Yi Jin-pil 2003, 35, cited in Park Young-a 2011, 193). Chris Berry (2003) has invoked the idea of a "socially engaged mode" in describing Kim's and related Koreans' work as the antithesis of a "commodity mode" of most Western documentary making, directed instead to the construction of a "counterpublic sphere." The avant-garde *Oasis* (2002) highlighted the plight of the handicapped and Koreans' inability to understand and accept them; *Oldboy* (2003) experimented with themes of psychological madness and sexual distortion; *Samaritan Girl* (2004) was about a teenage prostitute. *My Sassy Girl* (2001) was a romantic comedy, significantly based on a series of blog posts adopted into a fictional novel.[32] When released throughout East Asia, *My Sassy Girl* became a megablockbuster in Japan, China, Taiwan, and Hong Kong; it was also strongly received through Southeast Asia.[33]

If Shin Sang-ok is seen as Korea's "most important" film director of the late 1950s and 1960s, then the "best and most challenging" might be Kim Ki-young (1922–1998), known for his intensely psychosexual and melodramatic horror films, often focusing on the psychology of their female characters. The most revered of these was *The Housemaid*, released in 1960. It was a domestic thriller telling of a family's destruction through the introduction of a sexually predatory housemaid; it was lurid, expressionistic in contrast to the prevailing realism, set in an eerie house, and preoccupied with sexual obsessions, rats, and murder. *The Housemaid* was produced in that brief period of relative freedom following the end of the Syngman Rhee regime in 1960 and before the rise of Park Chung-hee in 1961 and new restrictions and censorship. To mark the film's fiftieth anniversary, director Im Sang-soo was invited to produce a remake of the original; the result, *The Housemaid* (2010), seeks to explore the change in Korean society over that time. Like the 1960 version, the 2010 film is melodramatic, even absurdist, an erotic thriller. In a 2010 interview, Im observed that, despite the obliteration of six decades of colonial oppression and the three years of civil war, there had emerged in the late 1950s a new middle class that, "while quite ordinary by Western standards," could afford to hire uneducated girls from the destitute countryside as housemaids. This had been the economic background to Kim's masterpiece. By 2010, however, only a limited class of the superrich could afford live-in housemaids in suddenly affluent Korea. The superrich, says Im, "are very separate from normal people, but they rule our society politically and economically from behind the scenes. I want to know who they really are, how they live, what they think. This film is part of my study of the superrich in Korea." It is a class that lives isolated, in a cultural vacuum—"they just copy the European traditional rich using new money. But, you know, when you copy someone else's life, inside there is only emptiness."[34] The 2010 film is far more than a remake; rather, the two versions are to be seen together, as dialectical images that expose one aspect of the evolution of the Korean class structure. Significantly, both deconstruct "family values," a constant preoccupation of the New Wave in Korea.

Bong Joon-ho's immensely successful *The Host* of 2006 presents a very different take on family values and domestic life, here interwoven with the blockbuster–monster–special effects genre: an unremarkable family is thrust into the extraordinary events of a human-consuming monster in Seoul's Han River.[35] The film becomes a commentary on the implications of America's military presence in Korea and of the complicity of the Korean political establishment. The monster, we are to assume from the film's cues, is linked to American biological experimentation and the aftermath is a tangle of official efforts at disinformation. Bong Joon-ho has rejected any charge of anti-Americanism, however: "In the broad sense, to compress it or simpl[if]y it as an anti-American film, I think that's not correct because there's always a history of political satire in the sci-fi genre. If you look in the broad sense, the American satire is just one part of it. There is also the satire against the Korean society and, even further, the whole system that doesn't protect the weak people. That's the greater flow of satire in this film, not that one part of anti-Americanism" (Bong Joon-ho, quoted in Blodrowski 2007). The seeming mirage of anti-Americanism won it the rare distinction, for a South Korean film, of official North Korean praise. The North Korean pleasure, however, may have derived from a lack of sophistication in reading the satire: the film is almost exclusively set along the banks of the Han River; the architecture is dark and futuristic; the river—the always feared, forever threatening pathway for that other monster of North Korean invasion—is constantly menacing. Or is there yet another reading of the river? Bong Joon-ho writes, "The Han River: The River has flown with us and around us.

A fearsome Creature makes a sudden appearance from the depths of this river, so familiar and comfortable for us Seoulites. The riverbanks are constantly plunged into a bloody chaos. The film begins at the precise moment, in which a space familiar and intimate to us, is suddenly transformed into the stage of an unthinkable disaster and tragedy."[36] Above all else, *The Host* may be seen as a commentary on the ambiguity of the Han River in the minds of Seoul people—"familiar and comfortable," as Bong insists, yet dark and threatening as he depicts it, defining the city yet also potentially the city's path of impending destruction.

Kim Kyung Hyun suggests an explicitly architectural reading of *The Host*. Bong is seen to be preoccupied with an evolving landscape "mauled by the hurried pace of industrialization and modernization." "Bong's depictions of landscape often show *nature beyond repair*. Countryside towns and farms are invaded . . . ; a wide-open vision of green forest is obstructed by rows of apartment buildings, which are ubiquitous in Korea . . . ; the Han River is inhabited by a monster and threatened by the sprawling cityscape . . . ; and a mountain is razed by miners and builders who extract rocks from it to make cement and other construction materials" (Kim Kyung Hyun 2011b, 190).[37]

Bong's films are seen as depicting "the global metropolis that is Seoul's parasitical dependence on nature and its destruction of ecological harmony. . . . [T]hese ruined landscapes are exploited as both the generic ingredients for his crime mystery, horror, and comedy, and the effective sites of new *virtual* realities" (Kim Kyung Hyun 2011b, 191).[38] *The Host* portrays a virtual city drained of its crowds. The dense masses of people who will occasionally occupy the riverbanks are absent. The absence, however, does not restore nature but instead places the viewer in a phantasmagoric state—a "perversion" of the landscape. Only when the city becomes virtual—reimagined as a barren, abandoned landscape—"does the presence of *flâneurs* (city strollers) and nomads become conspicuous" (compare this with my own flâneur-like stroll through the empty, abandoned streets of New Songdo, also drained of crowds, phantasmagoric, in chapter 4). Kim invokes ideas from Deleuze and Guattari (1987): vagabonds, whose "dwelling is subordinated to the journey" and here occupy "the striated spaces of sewers, tunnels and concrete holes," become crucial. In *The Host,* spaces of everyday urban life—convenience stores, corporate high-rises, gigantic parking garages, sewers—become what Deleuze and Guattari call the "operation of the line of flight," delineating a movement along which both deterritorialization and reterritorialization must occur. Such spaces in Seoul are constantly invoked as "lines of flight" (Kim Kyung Hyun 2011b, 196–197).

It is not difficult to find dark images of real (surreal?) Seoul that match the dark vision of *The Host*—the winter snow, the ice, and the mists ensure that. Observe figure 3.9 in chapter 3. A more sun-drenched, spring-blossomed image can be more suggestive: Digital Media City, some seven kilometers west of the old city, is yet one more of the futuristic "new cities" that inhabit some imagined, dreamed vision of a future Korea.[39] There are the majestic mountains and the small stream of the Bulwongcheon River that old villages would have lined and that the mean, brown-brick, 1960s and 1970s modernity would have supplanted. Then, behind this brown-brick, boxland Seoul and blocking out the majesty of the green mountains and the reminders of mountain temples and shamanic retreats are now the walls of Seoul's ubiquitous high-rise apartment towers. Older aerial photographs reveal the stream as a drainage line—anecdotally polluted with industrial waste, an example of Bong's "nature beyond repair." Yet, look again: a 2012 image reveals new landscaping of the stream.[40] The new plantings, sculptured banks, stepping-stones, waterside pathways, benches, and exercise equipment (a constant preoccupation) are part of a wider program to "bring nature back"—likewise the Cheonggyecheon reconstruction, as well as the vast Hangang riverside parks (figure 5.2).

The expressed artificiality of these landscape reconstructions, sculptural rather than fake-naturalistic, puts them in the same dramaturgical realm as Bong's deconstructive vision in *The Host*. They present for the most part a hard, unromantic nature, evoking an ironic rather than a melodramatic imagination, in the sense argued by Peter Brooks, above.[41]

Neo-Seoul

There is another apocalyptic vision of a future Seoul, also negotiating that dialectic of the melodramatic and the ironic and to be set against its engagement in *The Host*. It emerges as one of many layers of *Cloud Atlas* (2004), a novel by English author David Mitchell, subsequently adapted to a German American film (2012).[42] Nea So Copros is an immense, economically powerful, corporate nation centered on a unified Korea, where Korean-style neocapitalism has run amok in seemingly the world's last bastion of "civilization," albeit ambiguously defined. Its capital is Neo-Seoul. "Nea So Copros" is a corruption of "New East Asian (Sphere of) Co-Prosperity"—the imperial Japanese vision is finally achieved, albeit with a Korean hegemony. The land in Nea So Copros is mostly uninhabitable, rendered toxic by industrial waste and nuclear accidents (Fukushima multiplied). Society is stratified in a Confucianist apotheosis, ranging from Xecutives who appear

FIGURE 5.2 Digital Media City, 2012. This image effectively summarizes the city: the mountains had restricted the city's development to the small valleys in the era of the "Miracle on the Han" (the dreary boxlike buildings along the stream); the later, wall-like arrays of apartment towers engulf the lower slopes; most recently, the stream itself is transformed from industrial drain to overdesigned, landscaped, recreational walkway. Digital Media City claims to be the generator of an entirely new, digitally enabled age.

to control Nea So Copros as part of the *juche* (a reference to the philosophy of the Syngman Rhee regime, also to that of present North Korea) to consumers to the relict poor and down to genomed clones known as "fabricants," manufactured for specific tasks, such as serving food and cleaning up radioactive water, but kept from intellectual development.

It is Neo-Seoul and its filmic graphics that especially challenge any reading of the present city.[43] The year is 2144, and the levee walls and floodgates erected to protect Seoul from the rising sea levels have long since failed. Old Seoul has been submerged, and the abandoned metropolis is now a slum megasociety with shack dwellings growing up like a coral reef on the levee walls and immense shantytown flotillas built on and around the half-sunken skyscrapers bridged by salvaged steelwork from ancient, wrecked oil rigs. Here reside the poor, servicing the glittering Neo-Seoul sprawling up and between the mountainsides above. Even in the murk of the world's industrially destroyed atmosphere, Neo-Seoul shines brilliantly, amid holographic building "skins" and illuminated freeway ribbons; there are factory ships manufacturing fabricants, and others industrially slaughtering them to produce food for new fabricants.

Mitchell's novel has been much acclaimed; the film and its graphics have been more controversial. It has been observed that the depicted skyscrapers of Old Seoul seem more Hong Kong than Seoul; Shanghai and Midtown Manhattan also seem to be represented. Neo-Seoul is also derivative of *Blade Runner* (whose implication seems to have been that civilization had run out of new ideas and could now only pillage its past—again, an ironic comment on "old" Seoul).[44] Nea So Copros is a corporate state, and Neo-Seoul is festooned with the advertising that similarly decorates Old Seoul of the present. The advertising is in Korean, though mostly upside-down.

Two concluding points can be drawn from the fable of Neo Seoul. First, it might usefully be read as an ironic metaphor on the debates of present Korean historiography: the colonial era returns, but it is now Korea colonizing a devastated Japan; neoliberalism has gone berserk; there is democracy, but only corporations have the vote; Confucian hierarchy reigns. The upside-down script is appropriate for an inverted history. Second, this is a parable of Seoul and Seoulites, but it has been told by an English author and German filmmakers, albeit with Korean (and American) actors. The cultural colonization might bemuse the culturally colonized (as might that represented in the present book), yet it also highlights Seoul's global appropriation, always reciprocal. The intrusion of skyscrapers from Hong Kong, Shanghai, and elsewhere is itself metaphoric of the hybridizing force of globalization.

Inescapable discursus (1): Dark passages

The dark undertones running through *The Host* will draw unwelcome attention to another, darker space of Seoul, of subterranean or submarine passages of infiltration, invasion, "lines of flight," and, indeed, the terror of the next erasure. The Han River is the ever-threatening passage for feared North Korean frogmen or midget submarines. A further recurring feature of Seoulites' forebodings are the "water panics": the first was in 1986, when it was discovered that North Korea was building massive dams on the Imjin River, a tributary of the Han, giving it the potential to release massive walls of water into the Han and thereby to flood Seoul. In September 2009, floods were suddenly sent, without warning, toward Seoul (Choe Sang-hun 2009). The image of a flooded "old" Seoul in *Cloud Atlas* may express yet another level of modern Seoulite paranoia.

The Demilitarized Zone (DMZ) presents other darkly threatening passages in the form of the North Korean tunnels. The first of the infiltration tunnels was discovered in November 1974, a second in March 1975, and a third in October 1978—it is estimated that there may have been a total of seventeen tunnels. In March 1980, North Korean infiltrators were killed trying to enter via the Han River estuary; in October 1995 infiltrators were intercepted attempting to enter at the Imjin River, presumably thence *down* the Han River. Even the Seoul subway system is feared as a potential network for the dispersal of an invading force through (under) the city.

There was one (melo)dramatic moment that materialized these fears. On 21 January 1968, an elite North Korean commando unit launched the "Blue House Raid," in an attempt to assassinate President Park Chung-hee. They got within one hundred meters of the Blue House before being thwarted. They had infiltrated the DMZ by simply cutting through fencing, crossing the Imjin River, and entering Seoul, where they launched their attack. Having been defeated, they then attempted to disappear into Seoul's mountains, with their informal settlements—other dark places.[45]

So much for the subliminal messages of *The Host*. One might also suspect that there are other messages to be read in the New Wave and in the culture more widely. Are the retreat to the goodness of "family values"—even in such terrifying portrayals as *The Housemaid*—and the unquestionably devout turn to Christianity also to be seen as normal quests for reassuring certainties in an age of uncertainty?

Another cinema

There is another Korean cinema, with another great figure behind it. In September 1967, twenty-six-year-old film buff Kim Jong-il was appointed cultural arts director of North Korea's Propaganda and Agitation Department. Hollywood was young Kim's envied realm of dreams, and it was Hollywood's blockbusters that he would emulate as he took control of the cinema industry.[46] Among his oeuvre are a bloody and sentimental three-hour-long adaptation of *Sea of Blood* about the Japanese occupation of Korea, and North Korea's *Gone with the Wind*. Sensing, however, that all his achievements were trash alongside their American models, Kim conceived an extraordinary plan to bring real quality into his work. In 1978 his agents kidnapped renowned South Korean director Shin Sang-ok and his onetime wife, admired leading lady Choi Eun-hee. They were kept apart for four years, and then on 6 March 1983 reunited in a Kim-hosted banquet and "invited" to join him to collaborate on a new series of "quality" blockbusters.[47]

They made seven films together. There were typical nationalist melodramas, a light romance titled *Love, Love, My Love,* and the globally praised social-realist tragedy *Salt* (1985). Then there was the wonderfully ridiculous *Pulgasari* (1985), a *Godzilla* rip-off but presenting a terrifying monster with noble socialist sentiments. All were domestic hits beyond Kim's expectations. Shin and Choi finally escaped during a visit to Vienna in 1986; however, their subsequent careers were less stellar than Kim's.[48]

Part 2

THE KOREAN WAVE

The New Wave South Korean films are distinguished by high production values that, significantly, were transferred into the realm of Korean television. Equally significantly, Korean films were characterized by their exploration of domestic social issues, their frequent concern with family-centered values, and their often unpredictable plotting. In all these ways they presented as "Asian" and "un-Hollywood" and came to foreshadow the Korean Wave.

The Korean Wave, also called Hallyu, from the Korean pronunciation of the term, allegedly began with the export of Korean TV dramas in the 1990s, which many Asian television companies purchased because they were impressive looking but cheap. As their exposure increased, the dramas resonated with audiences, and their popularity increased. By 2000 the Korean Wave was in full swing, and soon reinforced by iconic programs such as *Jewel in the Palace* and *Winter Sonata.* Although TV dramas dominated the "wave" and accounted for the vastly greater part of its earnings, the dramas were quickly matched in the fields of cinema (the "New Wave" alluded to above) and popular music.[49] The "wave" can be seen as a function of Korea's sudden leadership in digital technology, where content—building on the long history of the struggle for freedom of expression in the cinema field—equally suddenly seized the opportunity to "fill" the new digital media. It was also a consequence of the realization of globalization and its corollary in Asian regionalism that hit Asia following the 1997 IMF crisis.

As Cho Hae-Joang (2005, 147) observes, "The global technology revolution and global capitalism prepared the system for the manufacture of cultural products and circulation within Asia, and formed the coeval space of capitalist Asia." "Korea mania" initially hit China around mid-1999; Hong Kong, Taiwan, Vietnam, and Singapore soon followed. By 2001 the phenomenon was receiving increasing critical attention and discursive engagement.

In view of the seminal role of the TV dramas in the rise and spread of the wave, these need some explanation. The sixty-six-episode TV drama *First Love* had been produced in 1996 and was aired between September 1996 and January 1997. It has been ranked the highest-rated of all Korean dramas to that time. This and a variety of other drama series from the 1990s provided a platform for yet higher production values but also contributed to the gathering myth of Korean sophistication in media content.

Winter Sonata was the second part of the TV drama series *Endless Love*, directed by Yoon Seok-Ho and reprising the lead actors from the earlier *First Love*. The series comprised four parts: *Autumn in My Heart* (2000), *Winter Sonata* (2002), *Summer Scent* (2003), and *Spring Waltz* (2006).[50] This second installment, in twenty episodes, originally aired from 14 January to 19 March 2002. The setting is the present day and the theme is the interplay of present-day Korean values. As the story alternates between Korea and the United States, however, there is an additional subtext of the nuanced differences between Korean and American values. While not reaching the domestic adulation of *First Love*, *Winter Sonata*'s appeal beyond Korea was certainly greater. The greatest international impact, however, came with *Jewel in the Palace*.

Dae Jang Geum, literally "The Great Jang Geum" but aired in the West as *Jewel in the Palace*, is a historical drama series set in Chosun Korea in the reigns of Kings Seongjong (r. 1457–1494), Yeonsan-gun (r. 1494–1506), and Jungjong (r. 1506–1544). It focuses on Jang-geum, the first female royal physician in the Chosun era, and stresses diverse themes of perseverance, the portrayal of traditional Korean culture, royal court cuisine, cultural practices, and traditional medicine. As in the tradition of Korean cinema, the presentation is characterized by high production values and the story by unpredictable twists of plot. The series was filmed in fifty-four one-hour episodes and first shown on MBC channel from 15 September 2003 to 30 March 2004. It was reputedly the highest-rating TV series in Korean history. In May 2004 it began airing in Taiwan; in September 2005, in Hong Kong and China; in October 2005, in Japan; and subsequently throughout Asia, the Middle East, Africa, the United States, and Europe.

It received high ratings throughout Asia and critical acclaim virtually everywhere.[51]

The Korean Wave is not all success. Kim Seong-kon has observed that there is a significant gap between the Korean Wave—more specifically, K-pop—and Korean literature. The success of Shin Kyung-Sook's novel *Please Take Care of Mom* (2009) stands out from a field of otherwise internationally unrecognized work. It is noteworthy that this novel is a story of family values, woman-centeredness, and motherhood—themes that elsewhere elevated the drama series to international acclaim. Kim Seong-kon's suggestion is simple but debatable: this is no longer the age of translated texts; it is now the age of the TV series.[52] This gap between genres would seem to have been tested in Shin's next novel, *I'll Be Right There* (2014), in which the foreign and the esoteric are made familiar to each other, as the interpreter of emotion and experience is led to bridge any gaps between East and West.

The Korean Wave and architecture

If we see the Korean Wave as a fusion of international appropriation (a Koreanization of American and Japanese culture) with more indigenous Korean themes and practices, then we might well ask if any similar fusion is to be observed in present Korean architecture and in a reading of Seoul urban space. While such a hybridization might well be seen to have run through the second and third periods of Kim Swoo Geun's work, reviewed in chapter 3, that was from an earlier time. So, what of the 2000s? Especially useful sources on recent Korean architecture and its provoked reactions are publications that have emerged from periodic exhibitions—notable are John Hong and Park Jinhee (2012), based on an exhibition at Harvard, and Caroline Maniaque-Benton and Jung Inha (2014), based on a small show at Malaquais School of Architecture (École nationale supérieure d'architecture Malaquais) in Paris[53]—as well as Kim Sung Hong and Peter Schmal (2008).

The reimagining (reinvention) of the culture is identifiable in both the historical dramas and the historical reconstructions in the space of the city—the rebuilding of Gyeongbokgung Palace as its most dramatic element, but also the Chosun-clad guards and reenactments at the main palaces and other sites. The hordes of children who daily visit those sites on school excursions and photograph the brilliantly colored guards and each other in these settings will be mentally rehearsing stories from both the historical dramas and their school history lessons that would seek a continuity with Chosun, thereby to erase those earlier erasures from colonization and dictatorship—to reconstruct (reinvent) memory. Thus the nostalgic aspect of the Korean Wave finds a place in a deeper historical reconstruction that is reinforced in both architecture and daily theatrical performance, as in the television dramas.

Todd Henry (2014, 217) suggests an interesting caution: by redirecting both Korean and international attention to the reimagined glories of a united peninsula under Chosun monarchs, the period immediately preceding Japanese rule, a periodization of history based on Japanese imperialist rule is privileged. The centrality of that rule and its postcolonial heritage is asserted.

There is also, however, that myth of national elegance that runs through the Korean Wave and its marketing. To walk the streets of Myeong-dong, Insadong, or Gangnam, or to visit the finer hotels, coffee shops, or tourist locales, is to have the myth confirmed—it is a city of the young, the tall, and the display of "style." (By contrast, the markets, the myriad noncentral business districts, and the subway reveal an older, shorter, clearly poorer population—relicts from those hard times of the dictatorship and the still-only-incipient economic miracle; on the Seoul Station Plaza and at many other locations, there are the homeless, seemingly always sleeping, huddled in old coats and blankets, faceless.) Architecture again reinforces the Hallyu myth: Insadong and Gangnam in particular present brilliant displays of urban elegance. It is urban design at the highest level of competence. Much of this design finesse is linked to the new precision and inventiveness that have been enabled by the computer—examples abound in the Seoul region.

In any final analysis, however, this display of "style" and elegance may carry Korean characteristics but is ultimately internationalist. Elegant young Koreans might dress in black and white more than young people elsewhere, yet such display is not uniquely Korean, nor can its genealogy point back to Korea. The power of digital technology in enabling a "more liberated" design culture, which may have been taken up vigorously in digitally focused Korea, yet its genealogy is overwhelmingly North American (most famously, architect Frank Gehry and the immense shock of Gehry's Bilbao Guggenheim Museum, venue for Paik Nam June's 2001 further shock on modernist sensibilities). In Seoul, Dongdaemun Design Plaza is the most insistent and arguably the most distinguished demonstration of the genre, albeit by Zaha Hadid, an Iraqi-British architect.

The people on the street (some streets) reinforce the Korean Wave myth. The architectural culture can do so only incidentally. There is, however, a different dimension to this culture that is certainly "Korean"—Seoul is preeminently the city of architectural "pop," to be read not so much against the force of the Korean Wave as its linked movement of K-pop.

K-pop

K-pop (Korean popular music) is commonly referred to in Korean as *inky gayo* (popular music) or simply as *gayo* (music).[54] It is a musical genre comprising elements of electronic, hip-hop, pop, rock, and R&B (rhythm and blues) music originating in the early 1990s. A turning point for Korean music was the 1992 launching of the group Seo Tai-ji and Boys. Also important was the establishment of Korea's largest talent agency, SM Entertainment.

Lee Soo-man graduated from Seoul National University in the early 1970s and pursued a career as a singer, then, in the 1990s, surveyed teenage girls on what they wanted to see in music groups. He turned music entrepreneur and founded SM Entertainment in 1989, and in 1995 the company became a public company. Lee started the boy band HOT ("High-five Of Teenagers") and girl group SES; both became successful in the late 1990s. By that time other talent agencies had also entered the market and were producing performers as fast as the public could consume them. Notable were YG Entertainment, DSP Entertainment, and JYP Entertainment (Russell 2008).

As with Korean cinema and TV, it is production values and sheer professionalism that lift K-pop above other pop movements in Asia. The talent agencies adopt a strategy of apprenticeship: solo artists, girl groups, and boy bands will be recruited, nurtured at the agencies' expense, and prepared for the opportune moment for their release. The apprenticeship might last for two years or more as trainees hone their voices, learn choreography, shape their bodies through exercise, and study multiple languages—all the while still attending school (Kim Ji-eon 2010).

The professionalism, however, has also masked exploitation, and SM Entertainment in particular became embroiled in the attendant controversies.[55] At the height of their popularity, boy band HOT came to realize that their royalties were far below industry standards. After fruitless negotiations with Lee Soo-man, three of the group's five members left the company in 2001, to the dismay of millions of teenage fans. SES disbanded a year later, in 2002, then in 2003 the very successful Shinhwa moved away from SM to new management. In 2009 the Korea Fair Trade Commission was called on to probe allegations that naïve young singers, desperate for fame, were being locked into unfair "slave contracts" that enriched their managers while the stars were left in relative penury.[56] By 2009 a variety of law cases and controversies had overtaken SM; in 2017 they continue.[57] In 2016 the Chinese Alibaba Group acquired a controlling stake in SM Entertainment.

Despite its contractual travails, SM Entertainment has subsequently thrived and diversified. SM Entertainment Japan was established in 2001. Together with SM Japan, SM Entertainment then moved to establish headquarters in both Beijing and Hong Kong. Not surprisingly, SM Entertainment located its Korean headquarters in Gangnam-gu, the upmarket neighborhood of Apgujeong-dong, then moved in 2012 to Cheongdam-dong, with its American headquarters on Los Angeles' Wilshire Boulevard. JYP Entertainment is likewise located in the area, but with its American base in New York City. Cube Entertainment is similarly in Cheongdam-dong. YG Entertainment, by contrast, declares no location (although it has headquarters in Hongdae), seeing itself instead as virtual and ubiquitous, characterized by the constant mobility of both its sponsored performances and its auditions.[58] The sites for the consumption of Seoul "cool" similarly include Gangnam and Apgujeong, as well as Samcheong and, notably, Hongdae (Russell 2014, 10).[59]

Ma Sheng-mei sees an underlying subtext of the terror of national preservation and survival—a racial substratum and the terror of "bastardy"—in the Korean Wave and its K-pop sibling. There is "a wave of nostalgia for an essentialized tradition"; tradition lives in the fear of the symbolic "bastards" who might usurp power, perhaps through contamination of the bloodline through incest. So, in the context of foreign invasions and suffering, the hermit kingdom resembles a circle that tries to keep itself intact, impervious to outside forces. Translated into the Korean Wave's TV dramas, this drive inward might turn into the tease of forbidden love, usually between lovers who mistake themselves for half-siblings, as in *Winter Sonata*. Many television dramas revolve around protagonists of lowly origin caught in the hierarchies of premodern Korea, in which the story line swings between tradition and bastardy. Even the tease of incest and bastardy, which causes pain in the Korean consciousness, Ma suggests, is not demonized as the Other. Rather, it is internalized in contrast to the Western tendency, as this duality of tradition and bastardy in the Korean Wave attracts wider Asian audiences, who find themselves ambivalently wedged between a lost tradition and a modernity of the Other (Ma Sheng-mei 2006, 132).

Park Gil-Sung (2013) offers a distinctively different critique of K-pop. While the global rise of K-pop might be attributed to the passionate support of inter-Asian audiences, its actual production, performance, and dissemination have had little to do with an Asian pop-culture system. Its dissemination has been made possible only through global social network services such as YouTube, Facebook, and Twitter, none of which is owned or operated by Asians—despite Korea's place in the global e-economy and culture. Park suggests that the "manufacturing of creativity in non-Western music," as in the case of Hallyu, involves three stages: globalization of creativity, localization of musical contents and performers, and global dissemination of musical contents through social media. The salience of the first of Park's stages reflects a general debate on the importance of inter-Asian cultural connections and hybridizations (riding on the backs of Japanese, Chinese, or Indian popular music!) in explaining K-pop's ascendance (reviewed, for example, in Iwabuchi 2013). It is an argument rejected by Park for its inability to account for K-pop's simultaneous success in Japan, China, India, Europe, and the United States, something never achieved by Indian, Chinese, or Japanese pop music. Simply, it is creativity that is globalized in cultural production, not contents.[60]

K-pop and Gangnam style

The emblematic space of Korean modernity is Gangnam; it is also the symbolic home of K-pop in both its production and its consumption. In 2012 a quite extraordinary collision of Gangnam and K-pop threw the ambivalences of Korean urban modernity into especially high relief. Park Jaesang is a Korean musician who goes by the pseudonym Psy, for psycho. His career in the K-pop scene had been relatively undistinguished, perhaps complicated by his being a Kim Jong-un look-alike and by a stage persona as a fool and court jester (Fisher 2012). On 15 July 2012 he issued a K-pop single titled "Gangnam Style." It featured quirky, absurdist, rap dancing, equally quirky music, and somewhat inane lyrics—mostly an endlessly repeated "Oppan Gangnam Style," which might be freely translated as "[I am] Big Brother Gangnam Style"—*oppa* being an expression used by Korean women to refer to an older male friend or an older brother, while "Gangnam Style" would refer to the lavish lifestyles associated with Seoul's Gangnam District (chapter 4).

Psy succeeded where the K-pop entertainment-industrial-complex and its superstars had failed: the clip broke into the American and wider global markets. By mid-September "Gangnam Style" had topped the iTunes Charts in thirty-one countries, including the United States, the United Kingdom, Australia, and Canada. By 20 September it was recognized by Guinness World Records as the "Most 'Liked' Video in YouTube History." By 25 September it had been viewed over 280 million times on YouTube; by early October it had been viewed 400 million times. On 21 December 2012 views reached one billion;

by late 2013 views were over 1.8 billion. Then, in December 2014 viewing hit (crashed through) a digital brick wall: YouTube had been designed with a counter using a computer integer that could count to 2,147,483,647, as it was unimaginable that counting would go beyond that point. "Gangnam Style," however, broke through, and YouTube (Google) had to be redesigned. By April 2017 the count was over 2.8 billion.

Psy would be an unlikely candidate for making such an impact. He is not the superbeautiful superstar favored in K-pop; at thirty-four he was relatively ancient for the genre and, unlike other performers, he writes his own music and choreographs his own videos. "Gangnam Style" was composed by Psy and Yoo Gun-hyung, a well-known producer in Seoul who had also previously collaborated with Psy. Yoo arranged the song, and Psy wrote the lyrics.

With its almost inept dance moves, seemingly meaningless lyrics, and ridiculous settings and imagery, the clip is extremely funny—albeit, in the first few seconds, it might seem so for all the wrong reasons. Yet its core is satire, as it parodies popular imaginings of the high-class, consumption-focused, swinging lifestyles of Gangnam; both Gangnam's self-important, ostentatious denizens and its envious wannabes are lampooned. Satire, however, is unusual in K-pop, which is mostly dominated by "teen" or "bubblegum" pop; hence, vacuous bubblegum pop is also lampooned—Psy's dream girl is played by Kim Hyun-a, at twenty a grand old lady of teen K-pop.[61] The video has Psy appearing in unexpected places in the Gangnam District, although, it should be noted, only two of the scenes are actually filmed in Gangnam, while the others are filmed in various places in Gyeonggi Province and in Incheon—most notably New Songdo. So, Psy appears in hedonistic relaxation on a fancy beach, which is revealed to be a children's playground sandbox; he visits a sauna not with big-time businessmen but with mobsters; he dances not in a nightclub but on a bus full of middle-aged tourists; he first meets his love interest (Hyun-a) in the subway; he struts with two models not down a red carpet but in a parking garage, trash and snow flying at them.

Max Fisher (2012) cites Adrian Hong's reaction to "Gangnam Style" and its ironic take on conspicuous consumption: important to the video's subtext, claims Hong, is South Korea's credit card debt rate. In 2010 the average household carried credit card debt of 155 percent of their disposable income (the US average just prior to the subprime crisis was 138 percent); in Korea there are nearly five credit cards for every adult. Gangnam is home to some of Korea's biggest brands (Samsung, for instance) as well as US$84 billion of its wealth or 7 percent of the entire country's GDP. Quoting Hong, "The neighborhood in Gangnam is not just a nice town or nice neighborhood. The kids that he's talking about are not Silicon Valley self-made millionaires. They're overwhelmingly trust-fund babies and princelings" (Fisher 2012). Fisher also quotes blogger Jea Kim: the video is "a satire about Gangnam itself but also it's about how people outside Gangnam pursue their dream to be one of those Gangnam residents without even realizing what it really means." However, Kim opines, that feeling is changing, and "Gangnam Style" captures people's ambivalence—the uncertainties and insecurities of the age.

So "Gangnam Style" can also be seen as a critique of the place of fashion in Seoul society and of the mechanism whereby the pressure of envious, aspiring outsiders pushes the privileged insiders to new plateaus of fashion. To quote Fernand Braudel (1992, 324), "I have always thought that fashion resulted to a large extent from the desire of the privileged to distinguish themselves, whatever the cost, from the masses that followed; to set up a barrier. . . . Pressure from followers and imitators obviously made the pace quicken. And if this was the case, it was because prosperity granted privileges to a certain number of *nouveau riches* and pushed them to the fore." Thus, indeed, Korea.

The immense popularity of what is really very sharp satire can be attributed in part to the video's lack of aggression and its humorous edge; also in part to Psy's ordinariness of persona. Overwhelmingly, however, it is the jerky rhythm and the dance moves. The song's ubiquity has triggered numerous flash mobs in many countries, as well as a turn to "Psy-inspired clothing." In Bangkok, a clash between rival flash mobs led to massive gunfire. As the video was not copyrighted, it was inevitable that it would spawn imitations, restylings, and parodies (albeit of a parody), the earliest appearing on 23 July, only eight days after the original's release.[62] Many of these were surprising, and some offensive—"Jewish Style" in Israel, for instance. There was also "Gangnam Style Hitler."[63]

The North Korean government released their own homage to "Gangnam Style" with their "I'm Yusin Style!," a nonhumorous parody of presidential candidate Park Geun-hye, mocking her as a devoted admirer of the Yusin system of her father, Park Chung-hee.[64] While the DPRK elite might express fear and loathing of the South and attempt to block its cultural impact, they clearly pay some attention to K-pop. Although "Gangnam Style" went viral in mid-August 2012, and despite Psy's unfortunate resemblance to Kim Jong-un and, more distantly, his father, it took more than a month for a "Kim Jong Style" parody to surface.[65] Here Psy dances, sings, and shakes his finger, and his people do his bidding; there are lines such as "The national pastime of the people is to be oppressed" and "work, work, work, then sleep . . . torture."

Innovate or imitate: K-pop and Samsung

The ambivalence that Ma Sheng-mei sees highlighted by the Korean Wave, and more specifically K-pop, referred to above, raises the question of sources; it also reprises the story of Samsung, from chapter 3. "To South Koreans, the legal battles the two giants [Samsung and Apple] are waging across continents have highlighted both the biggest strength and worst weakness of Samsung in particular and of their economy in general" (Choe Sang-hun 2012). A California court had imposed damages of US$1.05 billion on Samsung for violating Apple's patents for the iPhone and iPad. Choe Sang-hun quoted James Song of KDB Daewoo Securities to the effect that the ruling labels Samsung a "copycat" but also reflects on the brilliance of Samsung's move— companies such as Nokia, Motorola, and Blackberry, which did not do as Samsung did, drastically lost market shares.

Where Apple is seen as the great innovator and the world's number one company by value, pro tempore, Samsung presents as the brilliant strategist, albeit largely an imitator, and the largest technology company by sales. Samsung is seen as the quintessential, representative Korean icon. So Choe also quotes Anthony Michell (2010) on Samsung: "Koreans do things quicker than almost anyone. This allows them to change models, go from design to production faster than anyone at the present time." (It is an alacrity also mirrored in the architecture of the city.) The strategy has been to build something similar to another company's product but make it better, faster, and at lower cost; it would pounce, flooding the market with a wide range of models that would be constantly upgraded with incremental improvements that rivals could not match. In effect, the strategy was the innovation.

The story of Samsung and Apple raises the broader issue of innovation versus imitation in Korea's modern cultural history. The reconstructed palaces are simulacra, Hallyu is periodically accused of building on Japanese and American popular culture (with the Japanese, in turn, also mimicking America), and K-pop looks back to American "bubblegum pop" of the 1960s and 1970s.[66] However, cultures—including industrial cultures—are never isolated; the question is how ideas, irrespective of lineage, transform as they pass through different cultures, markets, and traditions. Modern minimalist architecture passes through the prism of Seoul back-street, boxland visual cacophony to yield the display of Paju Book City or a few of the more assured elements of Hongdae; K-pop passes through the mind of Psy to be displayed in the confidence and originality of "Gangnam Style," transforming K-pop into something seemingly extraordinary and indigenous.

K-pop and architecture

The sorts of traits running through K-pop can also be read analogously in the architecture of the city. Seoul might well be read as the city of "pop" architecture—an over-the-top architecture of signage, emblems, logos, and kitsch, albeit montaged onto the blank space of the ubiquitous boxlands, ever-changing with the changes of fashion and products. At a somewhat superficial level this manifests in places like Seoul's Lotte World, although this is no more than a children's theme park in the style of Disneyland; the earlier Songdo Resort is also in this undistinguished category. More important is the more indigenous, even vernacular evolution of a wild and distinctive visual, architectural culture. Indeed we are concerned here with nothing less than the evolution of a new vernacular; it is for the most part a story of the power of graphic design (and in sharp contrast with the ubiquitous presence of "Hello Kitty"—Japanese rather then Korean—and all its standardized marketing in Seoul space).

There is, of course, another Seoul vernacular scarcely surviving in the spaces of the city and best represented in historic enclaves such as Bukchon, Seongbuk-dong, and, more intermittently, in areas such as Insadong. Traditional houses, or *hanok,* discussed previously, are built of earth, stone, and wood, with curved black-tile roofs, mostly dating from the city's densification of the early twentieth century.[67] However, that bland housing from the 1960s and its constant elaboration in the present time is no less a vernacular and no less worthy of reflective observation.

The hard times and their austere urban fabric of the 1960s are now, in much of inner Seoul, swept away in the rush of later development or else cloaked in the skills of the graphic designer (Insadong as its paradigmatic, transforming manifestation, as in figures 4.4 and 4.5; also Itaewon in figure 4.13, and Hongdae in figure 4.15). However, these grinding, mean times are clearly represented in later districts, most typically along the Korail commuter Line 1 to Incheon (chapter 4); Bupyeong may be later, but it is clearly still in a world of "hard times" (see figure 4.23). This is typical Seoul boxland, adorned for the most part with standardized graphics and advertising logos, signage, and similar devices. At an even meaner level are the small establishments on "the wrong side of the expressway" in Chamwon-dong (Gangnam) (see figure 4.16).

The tiny shops that proliferate in the back streets and alleys are, in their "style," survivals from that earlier, harder age (even though many are of more recent provenance). They are akin, in some sense, to the endless stalls and street markets and underground galleries. They proclaim their presence with signage,—perhaps signboards, decoration, or emblems—or simply by the display of their merchandise. This is still the character of the establishments behind Jogno. The decoration might become more inventive and there will be conscious design. It is still, however, to be seen as "folk" (as in Insadong and Hongdae).

A zone like Gangnam is at an altogether higher level of affluence and entrepreneurial sophistication: Teheranno and its back streets, while evidencing the same proliferation of very small establishments, is both in competition with other entertainment zones and manifesting vigorous competition within its own economic community. While the graphics might be less standardized, frequently inventive, and often outlandish, this is still a graphic designer's architecture—it is just that the boxes are adorned more imaginatively and the effect is more spectacular.

At Hongdae, the design inventiveness becomes even more the game: proprietors, marketers, and designers take these local, "indigenous" forms and images—the boxes and their marketing adornment—and transform them into a competition for "artistic" notoriety in what would proclaim to be an artistic community. The design inventiveness becomes more self-conscious, but in a way that is far more linked to the folk origin of the genre than are the adorned boxes of Insadong, where ideas of "international" elegance are more likely to inform the competition (witness the façade war of Insadonggil, in figure 4.5).

It is good to recall the seminal *Learning from Las Vegas: The Forgotten Symbolism of Architectural Form* of Robert Venturi, Steve Izenour, and Denise Scott Brown (1977) and its designation of the predominant forms of iconography in architecture as the "Duck" and the "Decorated Shed," a gentle but telling subversion of modernism in architecture.[68] Some buildings are what they are—the ducks; others are only what they appear to be—decorated sheds. The Kim Swoo Geun searches for identity would be ducks, likewise the Zaha Hadid building's claim for universality and a small number of other monuments—they seek distinction through their own unique forms. Much of the rest—numbered towers, back-street boxlands, Hongdae, Paju Book City—present as decorated sheds. This is not a judgment, the Venturis would insist, just an observation of the modern world we exist in. In the case of Seoul, the task of architectural interpretation might be twofold: what might the decoration of the shed attempt to communicate (alternatively, to mask)? And how might the decoration be placed on some dimension of folk-to-sophisticated?

At one level, Hongdae, Itaewon, and, to a lesser extent, Gangnam are globalist—they become part of Seoul's attempt at distinctiveness to compete in the "hyperspace" by elevating the local to the level of pastiche, a caricature of itself. This is still distinctively "Seoul," however—it is decidedly not Beverley Hills and Rodeo Drive nor anything in Bangkok, Singapore, or elsewhere, although it competes with many such places.

To understand something of the logic underlying the production of places such as Hongdae or the Teheranno back streets—indeed of Seoul "back-street" space generally—one can turn again to the idea of assemblage and its logic, introduced at the end of chapter 4. In *A Thousand Plateaus,* Gilles Deleuze and Félix Guattari (1987) present the rhizome as a spatial model of logic and the acquisition of knowledge; a rhizome is described as being noncentered, ahistorical, nonhierarchical, nonsignifying, and without organizing memory or central automation. The rhizome system is made only of lines—lines that segment and stratify—as its dimensions. It breaks from the old model of logic/thought, having no beginning or end; it is coming and going rather than starting and ending (Berger 2004)—the state of metamorphosis itself.

Although Deleuze and Guattari are describing a system of logic, they employ a spatial metaphor. One can reverse that method in order to interrogate the ever-shifting state of chaotic, back-street Seoul. The rhizome system is made up of "plateaus" that are always in the middle; there is constant multiplication; it is a "multiple," an "origami" universe of constant folding, unfolding, refolding. The back street, the city, the ecosystem, the universe, cannot be reduced to some totality—these, rather, are to be conceptualized as "assemblage." The same can be said for "Gangnam Style"—an assemblage of bits, each of which somehow belongs to something (somewhere) else. The reality of the assemblage is only in its components, each of which is itself always part of some other assemblage, elsewhere (DeLanda 2006; Dovey 2011; McFarlane 2011). Because the city, the state, the culture, and society are assemblages, there are interstices between ever-multiplying elements; the destabilizing, subversive, dissenting, rhizomic infiltrations into these interstices are the mechanisms of metamorphosis. The infiltrations, in the case of back-street Seoul (Itaewon, Hongdae, even rarified Insadong), are new ideas or a new, radical, destabilizing image, from whatever source.

Where the logic of New Songdo space is in the mind of its willful creator (who is likely to be a committee more than a person), that of Hongdae or Gangnam back streets is the logic of an assemblage. Although individual designers will design specific components of that space—often very large components—it is still the product of chance activities. The urban planners/designers ultimately have very little power to "order" the disorder. There is, however, a measure of self-control—increasingly, "good taste," self-discipline, and style will be demonstrated, albeit in the name of good marketing. Yet then the rhizome inserts: the brilliant designer (graphic, architectural, urban), or even the recalcitrant marketer, disrupts what might seem to be an agreed or perhaps accidentally emerging order, and a new trajectory for the competition of ideas and images is set.

The back streets do not have the ordering attempts of the planner nor even the self-control of the well-mannered designer demonstrating a place in a global order. Here, rather, the objective of each *innovative* entrepreneur is to break any rules that can be identified.

The roots of this assemblage of back-street Seoul space (or front-street Itaewon, Hongdae, and so on) may be in the peculiar characteristics of Seoul's survival, both culturally and economically. Economic survival was necessarily fought for, in the Japanese era then in the 1950s and 1960s, in a world of grinding hardship and periodic destruction, though it was always aided by specific aspects of the survival of cultural practices. Despite the colonial-era obliteration and then the destruction of the Korean War, it was mostly "high culture" that languished. Everyday practices simply continued on, albeit "modernizing" with new technologies and new imposed institutions throughout the Japanese, Korean War, and postwar dictatorship eras. People still went to the market, worked at their small-scale production, and exercised some necessary entrepreneurial spirit. As people negotiated life in a world of disorder, they demonstrated the "Asian disorder" that stood powerfully against the order of the developmental state. It is in these dimensions of cultural survival that the distinctiveness of Seoul noncorporate space and its vernacular practices and architecture emerges.

This may be the mechanism whereby new, "modern" vernaculars arise. True vernaculars are never static. There are no master designers or key innovators—the logic of this production is that of assemblage. The force of "Gangnam Style" may be in its assembling of bits and pieces of the culture (both high and K-pop) and of the city (faux Gangnam) and reflecting them back at both the Korean and the international observer.

Vernacular as the naturalization of disorder

There is another conceptual lens through which the rise of a vernacular can be viewed. There is an interesting introduction, from Niall Kirkwood, chair of landscape architecture at the Harvard Design School, to the work of Kim Jungyoon and Park Yoonjin:

There has been recent expressions [*sic*] of interest in the phenomenon of the "Korean Wave." This term or its translation "Hallyu" references a surge of interest in Korean popular culture among other Asian popular cultures and beyond, particularly through television programs, music, movies, fashion, foods and what is identified as teen culture. This explosion of popular culture is being exported across the globe. . . . But can we attempt to place landscape architecture and site design and in particular the work of Park Kim within this cultural movement. Does the "landscape" stand timeless, removed from popular culture. . . . Some clues are offered in a recent chapter written by [Kim and Park] in the book Asian Alterity edited by William S. W. Lim based on a workshop held in Singapore in 2007. Entitled The Experience of Nature without Parks: Gangnam Alternative Nature they focus on the particular local outlook of the cultural sphere of alternative nature and detachment of experience through 5 lenses—nature revealed, spot nature, nature memory, distancing nature and interiorized nature? all of which have allowed for the absence of matching past and present, of skipping reinterpretation and producing an urbanity that is pragmatic, non-nostalgic and grounded in a contemporary set of environmental conditions—a very Korean condition.[69]

Leaving aside the inescapable rhetoric typically associated with an introductory address, the point of the observation is that the discordant, disordered, even transgressive confrontations of the everyday become *naturalized*—natural, part of a "new" nature—in the extraordinarily rapid transformation from one age to another. We return to the ideas of Walter Benjamin and "new nature." Benjamin was preoccupied with the now-possible relationships and responsibilities to external phenomena and technology that thereby enable the actualization of inner nature (culture—the eruption of the Korean Wave). This "new nature," however, is either idealized—seen as a new utopia—or else cloaked in archaic forms (nostalgia, melodrama, the reimagined palaces and Chosun-garbed guards) (Buck-Morss 1991, 116). Lionel March, writing in 1970, could observe that the existing city is mostly the shell of historic urban life (albeit very recent history in Seoul's case), but that we "fail to see the new patterns of urbanization as positive forms in their own right because we attempt to construe them in terms of our habitual assumptions derived from the past" (March 1981, 202–203).

This seems to be the point of Kirkwood's comment above. The Seoul back streets are the landscape and the architecture of the Korean Wave, even while it is the "front streets" that the wave ("Gangnam

Style") would parody; this is that "other space" that complements the regimented arrays of the residential towers. It becomes "natural" and thereby a new vernacular—the "new nature" that architects and landscape architects must now address through design. The ironic imagination can present images (designs, also "Gangnam Style") to be held up as mirrors to the urban society, thereby questioning held assumptions about the society and its urban space. Some of the more reflectively designed architectural projects considered above, and certainly the landscape designs of Park and Kim, as well as Paik Nam June Media Bridge, and including Bulwongcheon, Cheonggyecheon, and some of the other waterway projects, come some way in this.[70]

In the context of such an understanding of "new nature," there is the problem of determining what might be the task of landscape architecture in a society like Korea's that fails to recognize even such an activity and profession.

Part 3

THE KOREAN WAVE AS CULTURAL COLONIZATION

Korean pop music, especially dance music, began to gain popularity among Chinese teenagers after it was introduced in 1997 through a radio program called "Seoul Music Room" broadcast from Beijing. The decisive moment in igniting K-pop fever in China was the concert held at the Beijing Workers' Gymnasium in February 2000, featuring Korean boy band HOT. Korean news reports of the event used the term Hallyu for "Korean Wave" seemingly for the first time. The term, acknowledged in an article in *Beijing Youth Daily* as early as November 1999, began to be recognized by Koreans themselves from this point onward.[71]

Kim Hyun Mee writes of the wave's impact in Taiwan, which has led Taiwanese to view Korea "as a country of modern and urban elegance, and woman-centredness" (Kim Hyun Mee 2005, 183).[72] Kim Youna (2011) suggests that the wave's broader impact in Asia is linked to three main factors. First is emotional intensity: the Chinese, in particular, embrace the Korean ability to express emotions freely, seeing this as some manifestation of "democracy" and again of "woman-centredness."[73] Second is a sense of reflexive modernity: Korean dramas can portray an urban middle-class modernity that is accessible to an Asian imagination. While "American" things can be dreamed of and yearned for, "Korean" things—culture, language, fashion—present as an "accessible future," to be reflected upon and understood. The third factor is family: the television dramas in particular dramatize "Asian sensibilities," most notably family values. The viewer is presented with the vision of a country that has modernized yet retained its traditions—in some sense there has been no erasure.[74]

The Korean Wave is additionally seen to satisfy the tastes of the video generation by embracing creative visual imagery. Just as the Korean Wave is itself a filtering (hybridizing?) of American and Japanese popular culture—through a Korean episteme, as it were—so the wave is transformed as it weaves through other, recipient cultures. The case of Singapore may be illustrative: "[The Korean Wave in Singapore has] reinforced local 'parochial' identities structured on rigid ideas of ethnicity and race. Aside from the apparent physiological familiarities of Koreans with Chinese to Singaporean audiences, the Sinicization [naturalization] of K-pop [in Singapore] becomes evident when their products are distributed through the networks of Mandarin/Chinese based distributors, retailers, and media networks in Hong Kong, Taiwan and Singapore" (Yin and Liew 2005, 228). In the case of Singapore, packaging takes a form of Sinicization, as "Korea" slips into a global hyperspace of cultural appropriation and consumption. Yin and Liew see Korea intersecting with and challenging the predominance of "Chinese"-based popular culture in Singapore while remaining very much a form of Chinese consumption.[75]

Especially interesting has been the wave's reception in erstwhile colonizer Japan. Lee Soobum and Ju Hyejung (2011) observe that the Korean drama series have uniquely broken the effective barrier against foreign television imports, starting with *Winter Sonata* in 2003;[76] by 2008 there were ten new Korean dramas airing daily on Japanese television. They suggest that this in part relates to the tendency of younger Japanese to identify with the situations of Korean people: traditional values are strongly portrayed, family dignity is extolled, the stories do not depend on ethnic hybridity (Japanese, like Koreans, portray themselves as "pure"),[77] and there is a "pleasant nostalgia" that can resonate with the Japanese postcolonial experience. Their conclusion is that there may be some consequent transformation under way: "Behind the scenes of *Hallyu* in Japan, sensitive tensions between Korea and Japan, caused by their shared colonial history, are enormous obstacles to increasing mutual openness to media and popular culture. . . . Although the *Hallyu* phenomenon is not a foreign cultural 'invasion' in Japan, its visible influence on Japanese society cannot be ignored" (198–199). Furthermore, the opening of Japan to Korea, however ambivalently, has also had some effect in diminishing Japan's cultural barriers to other Asian media production, with a new sense of an "Asian" identity that is in sharp contrast with the Orientalist/anti-Asian sentiment of its colonizing age, recounted earlier.

Kim Ji-myung (2012) has commented on the impact of Hallyu on young girls in the Arab world: they are reported to retire to a friend's home, remove their hijab, then sing and dance to their favorite K-pop bands. Kim warns, however, that the issue is complex: when this simple, research-based observation was put to a conference on international exchange, Middle Eastern men became very uncomfortable; cultural sensitivities were at stake. While the Hallyu penetration was reported to be virtually global now, it is with the Arab Middle East that Koreans observe the vastest "mountain of misunderstanding." The mind turns to that isolation of the Itaewon mosque and the reported attacks on it. At something of a further extreme, Hallyu chic even undermines French chic: a poll by Korea Tourism Organization's Paris branch had more than 90 percent of 3,775 young respondents wanting to visit Korea and 76 percent declaring an intention to do so (though only 5 percent had already done so)—a tour with K-pop concerts ranking highest, followed by a tour to Hallyu drama-related sites.[78]

Various authors in Berry, Liscutin, and Mackintosh (2009) argue that K-pop and its inevitable impregnation of pop culture more widely has facilitated the formation of a new cultural region, focused on Seoul, effectively cutting across—perhaps even undermining—processes of globalization. By the mid-2000s the wave's impact had become so great that people from around that region were traveling to Seoul to have plastic surgery to make themselves look more like Koreans.[79] K-pop was alleged to be the main motivator for young people to learn the Korean language.[80]

Rise or fall?

In the 2010 collection *Pop Culture Formations across East Asia* are essays that suggest that the Korean Wave is now in decline (Shim, Heryanto, and Ubonrat 2010). Shim Doobo's essay, "Whither the Korean Media," suggests that overseas sales of Korean cultural products (films, TV dramas, and pop music) had been disappointing, despite the power of foreign fandom for Korean popular culture. Explanations were sought in internal factors in South Korean media industries contributing to a financial crisis in TV drama production. Ko Jeongmin examined the influence of the Korean Wave in regions such as Japan, China, Southeast Asia, and the United States. However, in a review of these essays, Brenda Chan (2011) comments that both Shim and Ko mostly focus on TV dramas and on statistics and media reports relating to them, whereas they ignore the latest trend whereby

Korean pop music (K-pop), with its boy bands and girl groups, has now replaced K-dramas at the forefront of the Korean Wave.

K-pop now reigns: Charlene Chua (2011) observes that K-pop idols attract megacrowds of besotted fans when they perform in Singapore and that many students will turn up at local auditions held by Korean talent scouts, hoping to make a name in the K-pop industry—and all that pre–"Gangnam Style." In 2011, Singapore-based StarHub TV launched two Korean channels for the burgeoning Singaporean fans—a Korean drama channel in April and a K-pop channel in October. CTC Travel organizes Korean Hallyu Dream Tours for Singaporeans to travel to Korea for K-pop concerts. It is a lucrative market and, in late 2011, two other Singapore travel agencies also announced plans to introduce tours to K-pop concerts in Seoul (Gwee 2011). Anecdotal evidence is that the wave continues to surge.[81] As Choe Youngmin (2016) argues, international tourists increasingly focus on Hallyu movie sets, filming sites, and theme parks, reinforcing the wave's sense of transnational collaboration and the region's evolving transnational politics.

While K-pop might indeed thrive, there are certainly signs of competition in the TV drama field. Although Ubonrat Siriyuvasak (in Shim, Heryanto, and Ubonrat 2010, 174), refers to the "'weaker' cultural economy in Southeast Asia" compared to that of the Northeast, she suggests that this might be changing. In 2008 the Thai TV drama series *Lued Kattiya* (The Princess) attracted a wide audience in mainland China; in 2009 the series *Battle of Angels,* also Thai, was aired in China to favorable ratings and spurring a craze for such Thai material and online fan communities for Thai actors (Parinyaporn 2011).

Parinyaporn Pajee observes, however, that the fan-favored Thai actors arc mostly part-Chinese and look Chinese (likewise, one could add, the Korean pop idols). She also suggests, "In some ways, China and Thailand share a similar culture and lifestyle, so it's easy for Chinese fans to associate with the story." There are inhibitors, however: there is an ambivalence toward gender issues in Thai culture; there will be gay characters and girl-fight scenes, all anathema to the Chinese censors, and there will be much editing. K-drama is seen as more wholesome, family-focused, and the subversion will be more subliminal.

Various explanations are offered for the popularity of the Korean Wave. Cho Uhn has suggested that it is to be seen in the nexus between the rush of globalization and a Korean turn to localization, as "a transnational culture flow that challenged Western cultural hegemony in Asia, though in different terms . . . hybrid culture that blurred the boundaries between national/indigenous and global cultures . . . the coexistence of local power, regionalization, and globalization" (Cho Uhn 2005, 144).

Cho Hae-Joang is more specific in suggesting the role of globalization: "The global technology revolution and global capitalism prepared the system for the manufacture of cultural products and circulation within Asia, and formed the coeval space of capitalist Asia" (Cho Uhn 2005, 147). The Korean Wave can be seen in part as a response to the sudden and brutal realization of globalization that came with the 1997–1998 Asian financial crisis and the humiliation of the IMF bailout. It is instructive to observe the switching of both public and corporate investment into cultural production at that time on the grounds of its high value-added nature.

At the sociocultural level, Cho suggests three "takes" often invoked to explain aspects of the wave. First, "What is Korean is international." This, however, might well be dismissed as a local delusion (Cho Hae-Joang 2005, 153). The second relates to the tension between the media culture of violence and the culture of familism—the widespread belief that Korean culture is filtered through "family values and a Confucian sensibility" to produce "a common 'Asian culture'" (154). The third popular argument is that "Anti-Japanese sentiment has helped," to which one might add anti-American sentiment in which China in particular is seen as ideologically opposed to the United States and Japan and thereby attuned to the sorts of anti-Japanese and anti-American values that might be imagined to imbue the wave. This, however, can be dismissed as a projection of Korean nationalism (155–156).[82] There is also something of a fourth "take" on the wave that is also implied in Cho's discussion: that Korea is becoming a cultural center in a globalized world, marking the retrenchment of American culture in East Asia. This too may be a delusion: Cho cites Im Jin-mo to the effect that Korean pop culture is still only a "copy" of—reflection of—US and Japanese pop culture, as observed above in the discussion of Samsung: "In fact, there are signs of East Asia becoming nothing more than a production centre and subcontracting base for Europe and America—a cultural colony. No East Asian country has been able to successfully export its culture to America or Europe" (157)—that judgment, incidentally, despite the singular success of *Jewel in the Palace,* and more recently of "Gangnam Style" and other isolated products. Yet, note: the animation for the emblematic American *The Simpsons* is sourced from Korea.

There are certainly other factors involved in the wave. With the destruction of the past, nostalgia comes in to replace lost memory (Ma Sheng-mei 2006); furthermore, South Korea is now a major economy, and its media companies are able to finance output with much higher production values than in other Asian countries. I would also argue that the long "epistemic break" of colonialism and civil war, followed by the long suppression of an avant-garde in the era of military dictatorship, and then the later flowering of video and cyber avant-gardism represented in the generation of the likes of Paik Nam June and composer Kang Sukhi, were crucial to the "enabling conditions" of the explosion. Linked to the globalization and "explosion" argument is also Jin Dal Yong's (2016) observation of the new, enabling forces of social media.

We can turn again to Nederveen Pieterse's observation of globalization's effect in increasing the available modes of organization and the hybridization of those modes consequent on the "speeding-up" of the age: "Furthermore, not only these modes of organization are important but also the informal spaces that are created in between, in the interstices. Inhabited by diasporas, migrants, exiles, refugees, nomads, these are sites of what Michael Mann . . . calls 'interstitial emergence' and identifies as important sources of social renewal" (Nederveen Pieterse 1997, 51). The interstitial nature of Korean creativity returns the attention to both the subversive effect of the Fifth Estate and the wildly dissident civil society that goes back to the student uprisings of the 1980s democratization, the *minjung* revision of history, anti-Japanese resistance, and the anarchism of the Donghak Rebellion (Abelmann 1996). Korea seems to find itself in the interstices between economies, epistemes, and ages. The manifestations of its social renewal include the outbursts of cyberart, the Fifth Estate in the political arena, and the Korean Wave, but also the threats that other Asian societies seem to perceive in the uncontrollable proliferation of "Korea" (to be explored below).

Meanwhile, within Korea itself, the "new Korea" may also be deeply subversive. Nancy Abelmann and colleagues have used an ethnographic study of contemporary Korean college students to observe how all aspire to and accept the burden of managing their personal formation in a changing world in ways that are quite new and resonant with discussions of neoliberal subjectivity. They conclude that neoliberal subjectivity, highlighting personal ability, style, and responsibility, works to obscure escalating structural inequality in urban society and in Korea more widely (Abelmann et al. 1999)—it is something of a turn back to neo-Confucianism, and to the Protestant work ethic. Within the colleges and universities, neoliberalism is expressed in the system's newfound addiction to its own assessment of itself. While the assessment system was founded on the solid ground of accelerating competition among universities and professors, it has become narrowly focused on measures and testing. The real problems of the sector—allegedly irregularity, immorality, intellectual dishonesty, and low productivity—remain unaddressed and, indeed, unable to be assailed in a neoliberal paradigm (Hong Duck-Ryul 2009).[83]

The postnation hyperspace

Jan Nederveen Pieterse draws attention to James N. Rosenau's (1990) idea of the structures of "post-international politics," "made up of two interactive worlds with overlapping memberships: a state-centric world, in which the primary actors are national, and a multi-centric world of diverse actors such as corporations, international organizations, ethnic groups, churches" (Nederveen Pieterse 1997, 50)—and, one must add, the *chaebol*. Whereas the political sphere implodes from the first (state-centric) world to the second (beyond the control of the state though still within its spatial borders), the religious (Protestant) sphere explodes, into the households/Internet cafés of China, beyond the control of either the Korean or the Chinese state: "Today, in China, South Korean missionaries are bringing Christianity with an Asian face. South Korean movies and dramas about urban professionals in Seoul, though not overtly political, present images of modern lives centering on individual happiness and sophisticated consumerism" (Onishi 2006). The fragmented, out-of-control nature of this export harkens back to the tradition of wild, antigovernment action, a dissident politics, and the fragmentation of Korean society in Donghak, as well as to the linked *minjung* culture movement of the 1970s as a rereading of history to bring hitherto marginalized people to the center of history and to become agents of history (Choi Chungmoo 1995; Wells 1995; Lee Sang Taek 1996). It is worth noting again, however, that within Korea a "citizens' movement" (*simin undong*) emerged as an alternative to the more radical and militarist *minjung,* in some response to the collapse of state socialism in Europe and to the gathering success of democratization in Korea (Shin Kwang-Yeong 2006, 6).

The Korean non-state invasion of China is far more than religious and explicitly ideological, however. Rather, it rides on the Korean Wave, thereby in large measure eluding the restrictions and the censors of the Chinese state. Kim Jeong-Nam and Ni Lan (2011) have looked at the nexus between Hallyu and soft power, arguing that the wave has been actively "used" in cultural public diplomacy—to sell Korea and to enhance the nation's weight in international affairs.[84] That may indeed be so; however, the wave is no more under control or direction of the Korean state than it is under the Chinese. As I have argued above, the logic to explain it is that of an assemblage: noncentered, ahistorical, nonhierarchical actions—albeit frequently reflecting political agendas—accumulate outside the consciously coordinating role of either state or capital, unable to be reduced to some totality. Korean Wave cultural production, K-pop insinuation, and the emerging Korean modern-vernacular architecture and urbanism follow similar logics.

Fredric Jameson (1991) has written of "the postmodern hyperspace," introduced in the preface to the present book—the stretching of space and time to accommodate the multinational global space of late capitalism—international networks of capital, communications (the Internet, the cellular phone), and travel; undifferentiated airports, hotels, and office parks; globalist products and their logos and franchises. The prefix "post-" in relation to Korea, however, must seem misplaced, for here the headlong leap into this space of the global has been in the context of the most frenetic of modernization, as well as in the context of the simultaneous and equally frenetic leap to reimagine antiquity. Each leap would seem to compel the other.

The hyperspace depends, as if by definition, on the local—on "hypertraditions" of exaggerated city and national identity—to differentiate the undifferentiated, as its wandering denizens seek ever-new difference and stimulation. In Korea's case, however, the traditions (*milieux de mémoire* in Pierre Nora's terms) are in crucial ways erased, replaced by museums, re-created set pieces, and dark memories (*lieux de mémoire*). Instead we now confront an electronic hypertraditionalism, always unstable, ephemeral, and globally disseminating (the Korean Wave, its nostalgia, and "family values" being one of its manifestations). So Korea evokes a hyperspace in which old ideas of the nation and of national culture no longer hold in ways that might still operate—in this brief historical moment—for other nation-states. We seem to face, instead, a postnation hyperspace. It is that wild profusion of the advertisement-adorned boxes and the forest of conical spires and crosses—the new vernacular suggested above—that most indelibly defines the local, far more than the reimagined palaces and their costumed guards.

Korean formal (state, corporate) space is quintessentially the hyperspace. So the National Assembly Building, by lacking specific cultural references, becomes "placeless nationalism"—a contradiction, and an expression of the demise of the salience of the nation itself, torn between "universal civilization and [the dream of] national cultures" (Ricoeur 1965). Benedict Anderson has argued that the quintessential enabling condition for the rise of nationalism was print capitalism, and that the novel is the analogue and contemporaneous parallel of the nation. Korea, however, arises in a later era of capitalist history, effectively in the postprint age, and the analogue of the nation is no longer the novel but the blog and the transpositions of video art (the cloudbursts of modern advertising, the phantasmagoria of Neo-Seoul). So while the search for an identity may be through the routinized practices of "the nation," the reality of that identity may be more in the selective imagining of a surface antiquity (nostalgia, no depth, reconstructed palaces, *Jewel in the Palace*), and in the actuality of an irresistible hyperspace.

The rise of the non-state "second world" in the sense argued by Rosenau (1990) is not unique to Korea. Witness also China or Malaysia (King 2008). What is distinctive is that Korea can rise in the vacuum of previous destruction and that it arises at a speed at which the (reimagined) past is still surviving in the present—it is "a new state with old traditions, torn between two modes of thought" (Choi Chungmoo 1997b, 27).[85] It is surprising in its absence of epistemic constraints—we see the power of erasure.

Inescapable discursus (2): The North

There is a most serious omission from the account above. There is another Korea, north of the Demilitarized Zone.[86] Kim Suk-Young (2010) has recently recounted that there, too, the media and their linked performative arts are thriving, also in the vacuum created from systemic erasure. No state is more theatrical, nor does any nation stage massive parades and collective performances on the scale of North Korea.[87] Even in the midst of chronic political and economic crises and financial collapse, massive resources are invested to sponsor overwhelming displays of patriotism and to glorify the country's leaders and the history of magnificent revolutionary struggle through state rituals that can involve hundreds of thousands of performers. Kim Suk-Young explores how sixty years of state-directed propaganda performances—public spectacles, theater, film, posters—shape everyday practices in education, the mobilization of labor, the gendering of social interactions, the organization of the national space, tourism, and human rights.[88]

In sharp contrast to the serendipitous, subversive explosion of the media in the South, the North's visual culture and performing arts were manipulated to set the course for the formation of a distinctive national identity and state legitimacy—for what Kim Suk-Young terms an "illusive utopia." *Nothing to Envy*, the title of Barbara Demick's interview-based book on "ordinary lives" in North Korea, describes one condition of possibility of North Korea's success: the utopia to be conveyed by the media is one of national glory and wonderful leaders beyond which nothing could possibly be wished—the summit of human aspirations.[89] Demick cites the ubiquitous red-lettered banners:

> *Long Live Kim Il-Sung*
> *Kim Jong-Il, Sun of the 21st century*
> *Let's live our own way*
> *We will do as the party tells us*
> *We have nothing to envy in the world.*[90]

The passing of Kim Jong-il in December 2011 and the inauguration of the third reign changed the banners but not the message. There is no distracting communication of base, desirable commodities, possessions, or of dehumanizing social difference. Everyone is equal. There is indeed no one and nothing to be envied (Demick 2010).[91] This is the perfect, ultimate society. Then from the third reign and the continuing happiness there is a new uplifting slogan, "without you, there is no us."[92]

The perfection, however, is assailed: elsewhere Kim Suk-Young recounts the story of the popular South Korean drama *Boys over Flowers* of 2009 and its hedonistic appeal to high school girls with enticing images of beautiful boys, romance, and consumerism. Defectors reported the drama's special allure in North Korea. How, then, to account for the success of a program "known for championing consumerism and hedonistic cultivation of bodily beauty . . . in a country that still, albeit nominally, opposes the decadent culture of the open market while upholding the ideals of classless society" (Kim Suk-Young 2013, 94)? There is also an industry of book publishing on great escapes from North Korea—the literature on the Shin and Choi story recounted above comes within this genre, as do Kang Hyok (2005); Kang Chol-hwan and Rigoulot (2005); Ling and Ling (2010); Kirkpatrick (2015); Harden (2012; 2015); and Park Yeonmi (2015).

One might be entitled to ask if the erosion of the individual in the brainwashing propaganda of the North is more or less destructive than the addictive online games, the PC *bangs,* and the gadgetry fetish of the South. In one, the manipulated are the victims of the state and there is no choice; in the other, they are victims of capital (of the *chaebols,* of "progress"), and, in one sense, the servitude is chosen—there is a choice, and many have escaped, to produce a society and culture of extraordinary creativity and diversity.

Part 4

SEOUL AS ASSEMBLAGE REVISITED

Returning to a theme from chapter 4, Todd Henry (2014, 52) cites an exhortatory text from Sakai Kenjiro, who was head of the colonial urban planning division in 1926: an organic metaphor is invoked to describe Seoul as analogous to the human body—with a heart, skeleton, and blood—and each component of the city is to be seen as having a meaningful existence only as part of some greater whole. Similar thinking persisted into postcolonial planning. Yet the Kenjiro text also implied a more syncretizing mode of thought that could almost prefigure late-twentieth-century discourse on the city.[93] For Gilles Deleuze and his followers, the assemblage becomes the favored mode for thinking about the city—rather than the network or the collage of fragments, it is the idea of multiplicity and the processes of assembling and of breaking apart (fragmenting) that best help make sense of the structure of the city.[94]

The idea of assemblage can enable the mind to grapple with the reality that the city's assembling and disassembling fragments make no sense outside the context of its cultural multiplicity—New York makes no sense outside the context of its ethnicities and their cultures; Los Angeles is incomprehensible without Hollywood and its multiple representations. Likewise, modern Seoul makes no sense if divorced from the realities of the wave, K-pop, and their representations of that city, variously melodramatic, ironic, amusing, and outrageous.

There are four levels at which assemblage thinking can be invoked to make sense of Seoul in the Korean Wave, and thereby of Seoul as a new form of city.

Assemblage as folding

The Korean Wave can be viewed somewhat simplistically as one assemblage of many interlinked parts, like the metro subway system or a *chaebol*. This, however, does not tell us very much, for the wave's salient characteristics are its multiplicity, immanence, and instability—coming apart and reassembling, constant becoming. In Deleuze's sense, it constantly folds, unfolds, refolds—boy groups and girl bands break up (unfold) and regroup, and identities shift with a new song or a new exploiting entrepreneur, new locations emerge, new images and new competitors enter into the assemblage, albeit negatively, although also potentially provoking new invention, as well as a new audience. Deleuze's notion of "the fold" is ambiguity-ridden—it is Deleuze's own thought folding, or doubling, into the thought of another;[95] it can also be understood as the name of one's relation to oneself; it is the self-production of one's own subjectivity. Thought, too, is a kind of fold, an instance of the "forces of the outside" that fold the inside (Deleuze 1993).

Thus Im Sang-soo produces *The Housemaid* (of 2010), folding in and out of *The Housemaid* (of 1960) and the imagination of Kim Ki-young. Im's thought doubles (folds) into that of Kim, identities and times become unstable. The eradication of the colonial memory can interweave in the viewer's imagination with the eradication of the memory of the dictatorship; the melodramatic imagination of elitist reality (*The Housemaid* of 2010) can suddenly be thrown into absurdist relief by Psy's (2012) ironic vision of a (dreamed, wannabe) reality in "Gangnam Style"; the subjectivity of the viewer (listener) enfolds new "forces of the outside."

There is another sense in which Deleuze invokes the idea of the fold. It is in the context of a critique of the German polymath Gottfried Wilhelm Leibniz (1646–1716) that he presents the idea of the "Baroque moment." "Baroque" here refers not to the so-called European Baroque era, roughly of Leibniz's time, but to "identical traits existing as constants within the most diverse environments and periods of time" (Focillon 1942, 15). Henri Focillon wrote of culture as composed of differently paced but intermingling phases: an "experimental" beginning, looking for solutions to problems that a "classical" moment then exploits, followed by a "radiating" period of increasing refinement, and then a "baroque" phase that sums up, contorts, inverts, and narrates the formulas of all the others (Conley 1993, x). It is in this sense that Deleuze sees difference coming together, "enfolding," yet without contradiction—"the criterion or operative concept of the Baroque is the Fold, everything that it includes, and in all its extensiveness" (1993, 33). The Baroque would "enfold" all the other moments that it might reflect upon—in the present instance, the Korean Wave is to be seen as a "Baroque moment." All will be swept into the cauldron: Chosun, dark memories, melodrama, and irony; Japanese *manga* are appropriated and transformed, as are Japanese pop music, American bubblegum pop, pop-art imagery, elegant minimalism, and over-the-top excess. There is no Korean Wave "style," only multiplicity. Neo-Seoul might well be viewed as the apotheosis of the baroque—all will be enfolded.

Brett Nicholls (2010, 146) observes that, in his work on Leibnitz, Deleuze is concerned with "a point upon which series converge. . . . An identity emerges in and through the convergence of a series of singularities." New possibilities are affirmed. Such indeed is the case with the Wave.

Assemblage and place

At this first level, above, assemblage thinking would seem to present as unproblematic—ideas, people, images, products, imaginings, and songs all assemble, come apart, and reassemble in both reality and the mind (thought, subjectivity). At a second, more geographical level, all these things happen in the space of the city; they assemble with places—a street, a studio, a coffee shop, a music stage, a Hongdae venue, an audition space, or a corporate boardroom.

Manuel Tironi (2010) has drawn attention to an urban space that is in some sense commensurable with aspects of Seoul space. In Santiago, Chile, there is a relatively cohesive group of young people doing avant-garde music and constituting an experimental music "scene." This comprises a variety of musical projects, from electronic to folk, *musique concrète* to hip-hop, and is seen as characterized by three main principles: hybridity, nonconventional procedures (creativity), and commercial marginalization—the first two might also describe the Korean Wave, but the third is more complex. In Korea there is more of a tension—articulation, hybridization—between inventive isolation and commercial exploitation. Tironi's most interesting assertion, however, is that the link between the stability of such a scene with its urban spaces and knowledge hinges on the concept of cluster, manifesting features such as value-added creation, economic spillovers, and horizontal/vertical linkages. Cluster theory assumes the existence of a bounded space—a definite and ontologically closed territory.

In the case of the Santiago music scene, however, this territory seems characterized more by dispersal than centrality or closure. Its participants appear as nomads, and there is constant territorializing and deterritorializing; clusters will momentarily "gel," then momentarily come apart again. So, suggests Tironi, the space of Santiago is "gelable." Seoul likewise manifests nomadism; it is a city of a plethora of "creative districts," where anecdotal evidence will refer to clustering as something passing—ephemeral. In Seoul, however, there are the territorializing forces of institutional attraction (Hongdae in the thrall of Hongik University) and capital (Gangnam and K-pop, and Heyri Art Village as a focus for film production).

Place is to be understood as assemblage—streets, buildings, monuments, and memories, but also the ebbs and flows of creativity, clustering and dispersal, territorializing forces and deterritorializing forces.

Assemblage and rhizome

There is a third and far more complex way in which the Korean Wave is to be seen as geographic—not so much "occupying" places and thereby in part defining them, however fleetingly, as destabilizing their meanings and the ideas that attach to them. The Hangang River in *The Host* is dark and forever threatening. It enters like a rhizome into other imaginings of the river.

The visitor in Gyeongbokgung Palace confronts, at the simplest level, a physical assemblage of pavilions, axes, spaces, and pathways. In the memory and imagination, however, all this flies apart: this is all simulacra, the imagination sweeps it away, and it is all empty, a tabula rasa and a seemingly obligated forgetting of the Japanese; imagining further, it is all back again, and we are in the time of King Kojong or perhaps Sejong the Great, except that, in that distant time, this is a forbidden place and we are not there, we are excluded. Other imaginings insert themselves into the reverie. There is *Jewel in the Palace,* and suddenly we are there, no longer excluded. The television series completes the destruction of the magic and mystery that the Japanese opening of the palace had begun. The Korean Wave again enters rhizomatically into the imaginary construction of place.

The wholesomeness of "family values"—and therefore of Confucian values—is destabilized by *The Housemaid*'s insertion into the socially desired space of the superrich. Psy's absurdist send-up of "Gangnam Style" destabilizes the illusion of the dreamed world of the rich and famous. The motivations that might be seen to underlie the drive of middle-class effort begin to appear as chimera.

Assemblage and the crossroads

Finally, at a fourth level, the relations of exteriority of the multiplicity that is Seoul and its culture break free of all geographic specificity, though they are still geographic—in space—whether physical, imagined, or cyberspace, or some space of the memory or perhaps of compelled forgetting. The Korean Wave enters rhizomatically into wider Asian space. Not only are "Korean values" now inserted into the imaginings of Chinese, Japanese, Singaporean, Thai, or Taiwanese, but images of the physical and social spaces of Seoul also enter those imaginings.

Such intrusions, certainly, are not novel. Hollywood long ago entered the space of Japan, Taiwan, and most likely all other national spaces—Tokyo or Beijing will be read against an imagined New York or Los Angeles. What is new here is that the intruding assemblage of images, sounds, ideas, stories, and values relates to Seoul, an Asian city. The impact of the Korean Wave is geopolitical, as Beijing and Seoul (Tokyo or Osaka and Seoul, Taipei and Seoul, Singapore and Seoul) fold into each other. Might not the imagining of Seoul be able to insinuate itself into Beijing—be acceptable to a Chinese sensibility in ways that will always be closed to alien America?

AbdouMaliq Simone (2010), in bringing an assemblage perspective to the consideration of a selection of Asian and African cities, subtitled his account *Movements at the Crossroads*; it is a further metaphor for the phenomena that "assemblage" would attempt to theorize. The Korean Wave can be seen in one sense as arising at a crossroads of Japan and America, albeit in Korean cultural space. Similarly, we can now witness Seoul and Beijing intersecting. Similar thinking runs through Marina Warner's *Fantastic Metamorphoses: Other Worlds*: "[T]ales of metamorphosis often arise in spaces (temporal, geographical, and mental) that were crossroads, crosscultural zones, points of interchange on the intricate connective tissue of communications between cultures. . . . in transitional places and at the confluence of traditions and civilizations" (Warner 2004, 17–18). Warner speculates on transformations and the underlying energies and processes whereby one motif, representation, or idea generates another. She concludes that, on the evidence of history, the transformations that mark great creativity and leaps to new modes of thought and life will most likely occur in those places and times where different cultures collide and all ideas of immutable identity come apart. Metamorphosis, or life-as-change, runs counter to any idea of the unique, singular nature of identity and its defense. Seoul as crossroads of America and Japan seems to have been a condition of possibility of Park's "invention" of modern Korea; then the intersection of that brutal vision with the dissonance and disorder of a surviving, informal, subsistence economy may be seen as a condition of possibility for the subsequent explosion of Korean creativity. The Korean Wave, in turn, arises at a multiple crossroads—popular cultures of Japan and America, the great creativity, democracy, new prosperity—the release of the spring that is perhaps symbolized in "spring" at the Cheonggyecheon.

So the question is: at the new crossroads of Seoul-Beijing (Seoul-Tokyo, Seoul-Taipei, and so on), what new transformations and energies are we to expect?

CHAPTER 6

IMAGINING THE NATION

Reinvention and Its Conditions of Possibility

A recurring theme of this book has been the dialectic of erasure and reinvention—the historical manifestation of the idea of "creative destruction" that ran through the writings of Nietzsche, Benjamin, and Schumpeter. Consequent on the distortion of Korean identity and memory in the Japanese colonial era and subsequent wartime destruction, Seoul had to be constructed as national capital in the absence of continuity in its represented past. Seemingly contingent on the absence of continuity has been an absence of epistemic constraints, albeit far from total, especially as new constraints on the construction of knowledge (thereby on the construction of the built environment) have swept in to fill the void. Thus we witness the power of erasure: Protestantism becomes indigenized and, additionally, hybridizes with old beliefs and traditions; American corporate capitalism, Japanese *zaibatsu* economy, and Korean traditions of family hybridize, thereby conditioning the economic imagination; there is that crossroads of old values (a half-remembered past) and external novelty from which the Korean Wave emerges.

It is in this context of absence and new invention that one observes not just the explosion of the tiger economy—the "Miracle of the Han"—but also the reality that the "miracle" rode on new communications technology. Furthermore, that technology is in a seemingly endless cycle of accelerating new invention and replacement, beyond anticipation or prediction. High-speed Internet is everywhere; free Wi-Fi becomes ubiquitous in the space of the city; with the universal mobile phone, interconnection is total. As interconnection becomes universal, the population paradoxically withdraws into the private space of the small apartment and the *bang*. In the Deleuzian sense of lines that segment and stratify (chapter 5), entirely new dimensions have been added to the communicative power of space in what is one of the most total of urban transformations—Seoul emerges as a radically new sort of city.

The mind returns to the arguments of Jean Baudrillard (1983; 1985) rehearsed in chapter 1. Writing in the age of television—pre-Seoul, as it were—Baudrillard sees private space transformed by that medium: the endless soapies that mimic domestic life are, in turn, mimicked by everyday life. Population simulates the media, which, in turn, hyper-simulate the population, until there is no original but only a world of simulacra, everything a copy—the replicated palaces and shrines of Seoul as simulacra. Everyday life implodes into the hyperreality of the spectacle, a world without depth or meaning. Seoul is preeminently a site where one observes yet further technologies and media inserted, successively and at accelerating speed, into the "old" media of which Baudrillard writes and which Paik Nam June invokes in the decon-struction of an earlier era; it is accordingly a site in which to observe further transformations. We can turn again to Rosenau's (1990) argu-ment on the two interactive worlds that constitute a "postinterna-tional politics": a state-centric world, in which the primary actors are national, and a multicentric world of diverse actors, such as corpora-tions, international agencies, ethnic groups, and religions. The politi-cal sphere, as observed earlier, implodes from the first (state-centric) world to the second (beyond the control of the state though still within its borders); the sphere of culture and ideas explodes into the house-holds / Internet cafés / social networking media, beyond the control of the state, whether Korean, Chinese, Taiwanese, Vietnamese, and so on. The cultural life and ideas of Seoul—or at least their hypersimulation—become ubiquitous.

Chapter 5 reported anecdotes on the Internet's effect on the 2002 Korean presidential election—a transformative event. A decade later attention had shifted from the openness of the media to new cri-tiques (its resistance to appropriation) to its openness to emptiness—to K-pop glitz. For the 2012 National Assembly elections, candidates were reported to have sought links to pop stars, Hallyu identities, and beauty contest winners.[1] Fourth estate media still manages to retain some power over contents.

The explosion of media triggers the explosion of creativity—of contents to fill those media. There is never an exact parallelism between cultural spheres—in the present case between cinema and television, on the one hand, and architecture and the design of urban space, on the other. Yet to read one against the other can provoke new uncer-tainties. We return to the provocative argument of Moon Jae-cheol (2006, 44), that the Korean New Wave cinema viewed history through a melodramatic imagination, seeking meaning in a world of destroyed values, "through the lens of nostalgia, thereby emphasising a sense of loss in the present." However, Moon suggests, there is now a post–New

Wave cinema, in which melodrama is supplanted by an ironic imagination—rather than look for hidden meaning in history, ambiguity is accepted, as is the impossibility of any positive truth. One might look at the city of ruthless progress and modernism as a manifestation of a Korean dread of the past—will the erasures of recent history recur? What of the North? Then the compensating turn to nostalgia (the replicated palaces and shrines, simulacra in place of authenticity) parallels that of the media. Irony in the media, in turn, can be seen as foreshadowed in the art of Paik Nam June; however, is this Korean or European? Paik spent much of his time in Germany, where the prevailing national sentiment, except in its right-wing, retro-Nazi fringe, has been powerfully antinostalgic and most determinedly ironic—no "true" explanation or meaning for a horrendous past can ever be found. Whereas in Germany a savage irony has ultimately been translated, uncompromisingly, into the urban design of the capital, Berlin, we look with difficulty for a similar confrontation in the urban design of Seoul—the seated girl fronting the Japanese Embassy is an exception, as is the image of Chun T'ae-il on the bridge over the Chonggyecheon; another (though possibly unintended) exception is a seemingly disdainful King Sejong alongside the US Embassy.

That said, there is a "softening" in Seoul space. There is a mission to make it more amenable and "human." To pursue Seoul space further in this sense of what might be emerging, it is necessary to consider what, so far, has made this extraordinary city possible. In the realm of ideas, where has Seoul come from?

CONDITIONS OF POSSIBILITY

Immanuel Kant wrote of "conditions of possibility" underlying our concepts and experience (Gutting 2005, 36). While Michel Foucault adopted Kantian language, he insisted that such conditions (constraints on discourse and the formation of knowledge) are always contingent on the particular historical situation, varying over times and domains of knowledge. In considering how conditions of possibility might underlie the social production of the space of the city, a starting point is the historical task of imagining the (Korean) nation.

To repeat from chapter 1, Benedict Anderson invokes Ernest Renan's observation of the obligation always already to have forgotten many things and to have remembered (imagined?) many things in the construction of the nation and national identity—a "characteristic device in the later construction of national genealogies" (Anderson 1991, 199–201, citing Renan [1882] 1947–1961). Furthermore, it is suggested, a selectively remembered and selectively forgotten antiquity may be a necessary condition for the possibility of "novelty" (Anderson 1991, xiv).

The question for present historiography is the extent to which Japanese colonization provided an "enabling violation" (Spivak 1996, 19), with its potential of freeing or enriching the "conditions of possibility" for the discourse of culture and indeed of nation. What was the nexus between the distortion and the emancipation of culture in the Japanese era—the forever contested question for chapter 1 above? The sources consulted in the writing of chapter 2, on the Japanese colonization, conveyed an almost smothering negativity toward that time. Yet, as we have seen, life continued, the sun shone, the rain fell, and writers and other artists responded to the new manifestations of modernity being experienced. More recent historiography, albeit now from the comfort of distance, is increasingly reassessing that time.

The long, subsequent half century of "erasing the erasure" implied both selective forgetting and reimagining the past while simultaneously emulating the erstwhile mutilators of that dreamed, lost past. I suggest that the present conditions of these gymnastics of the memory and the imagination can be posed in four forms. First is the obliteration, only ever partial, of a bitter bequest. Second is the reimagining, always disablingly nostalgic, of the past—a dreamed history. Third is the syncretizing and indigenizing power of the Korean "mind," the ability to draw in, "assemble," and appropriate other ideas and other cultures, or what I would call the "naturalizing of material culture." Fourth is the transposing of reality—the compression of time. Each will be considered following.

1. Obliterating the colonial memorial

While the Japanese era represented loss and humiliation, more recent histories will locate the real eradication of urban culture in the 1950–1953 Korean (Civil) War and then the ultimate national humiliation in the dictatorship and its suppression of the Korean spirit. Korea's was a serial colonization, passing through stages of tributary "semicolonialism" under the long sway of China, to national elimination under the Japanese, to colonization in the name of liberation under American self-interest and its dictatorship clientele. The significance of the shift from Japan to America, and then to what Anderson (1991, 160) describes elsewhere as a postcolonial, postrevolutionary state, is that Korea's revolution had to wait until 1987—the transition from colonialism to dictatorship might be seen as seamless. Any sense of revolution came later and was as much against liberator America as against America's client, the dictatorship with its peculiar idea of "official nationalism" ("nationalistic democracy"). Both Japanese and American oppressors presented as paradigms for resented but inescapable emulation—undoubtedly hated as much for the inability to escape (from both Japan and American modernity and their seductive dream) as for the remembered oppression.

Kang Jung In has written of the damage that Eurocentrism (Americanization?) has done to Korean academia, alleging that Koreans have Westernized their consciousnesses in dealing with issues, interpreting and thereby marginalizing Korean reality according to Western theoretical perspectives.[2] The consequent effect has been to reinforce Korean academia's dependence on the West (Kang Jung In 2004). The role of language cannot be underestimated here: English, as the language of global academic discourse, condemns Korea to a new Western subservience in the realm of ideas.[3]

In the sphere of ideas, it is the Euro-American colonization that has now to be forgotten. In a broader cultural sense, the Japanese colonization has to be selectively forgotten, for at one level the historic hatred of the Japanese stands against the material emulation of the Japanese "developmental state," and of the electronic modernity on which that state seems to stand.[4] Emancipation will be sought by pushing that modernist dream and its electric fantasy to its frenetic conclusion (the New Songdo mirage, though only for the brief moment until it, too, is bypassed by the next wave—most likely in the realms of content, creativity, and imagination—the extraordinarily creative volatility of the "Korean way").

In this realm of remembering and forgetting, there is an important realization that is brought to the fore in a variety of essays in Shin Gi-Wook's (2006) *Rethinking Historical Injustice and Reconciliation in Northeast Asia: The Korean Experience.* In all the countries in the northeast region of Asia coping with historical injustice, the Republic of Korea has the rare distinction of confronting internal and external injustices simultaneously, both as victim and as perpetrator, albeit still very tentatively. Contrast the savage confrontations of Berlin.

The difficulty, in the Korean case, is that this confrontation might indeed arise in the rarefied discourse of academia and the political discourse of newfound democracy, yet the space of the city—the historic theater of the repressions and erasures—remains empty. For the most part it persists as blank space (despite that suspected shift from a melodramatic, nostalgic imagination to an ironic imagination hinted at above—"Gangnam Style" as an extraordinary manifestation). There are other models, where the city itself is the surface on which is written both the glory and the ignominy of the society—Berlin, surely, being the paradigm. There is a need for memorials—to the Japanese

Government-General Building and the compromises and accommodations it represented to Seoul Shrine, to Seoul Station and the 1980 uprising, and the specific sites of the repressions of the dictatorship. (There are exceptions, though all too isolated: a signboard at Tapgol Park announces its role in the March First uprising.)

Yet there are signs of change, from the melodramatic to the ironic and the challenging of otherwise unquestioned "understandings." The bronze monument of the girl on the chair facing the Japanese Embassy referred to above and installed in December 2011 would be worthy of Berlin; earlier, in 2002, the cemetery of the massacred victims from the 1980 Gwangju uprising was declared a National Cemetery. This latter is especially significant, as it memorializes an atrocity by Koreans rather than by outsiders.

In the discussion of "the meaning of newness" in Korean cinema, cited in chapter 5 and again more immediately above, Moon Jae-cheol refers to Korea as "a culture that esteemed letters over images," accounting for film's difficulty in achieving a position in high culture (Moon Jae-cheol 2006, 37). Moon qualifies this first assertion with a further assertion: "Traditionally, Korean film criticism valued narrative or theme over image. Today, image and spectacle have become the staples of Korean film" (52). No evidence is presented to support the assertion of "letters over images"; nevertheless, the comment provokes thought: might some such cultural trait lie behind what is clearly an absence of representational intent in the architectural image? At the risk of essentializing, one is tempted to see architectural discourse as preoccupied with images and meanings in the Malay world (Indonesia, Malaysia) and even in Thailand (King 2008; 2011); much less so in Korea, however.

Korea faces its monsters increasingly through cinema—where, inevitably, image and narrative come together. The confrontation has yet to be translated into the built environment. Michel de Certeau and Luce Giard (1994, 204) wrote that they wanted planners to awaken "the ghosts of the city" by working with the narratives of everyday lives. The tragedy of Seoul is that so many of those narratives will be dark.

2. Dreaming antiquity

Benedict Anderson has observed that, for the first generation of nationalisms (those of the Americas of the eighteenth and early nineteenth centuries), it was newness and the break with the past that took on potency. However, for what he terms the second generation, "it was no longer possible to 'recapture / The first fine careless rapture' of their revolutionary predecessors" (Anderson 1991, 195). So identity and

authenticity are sought elsewhere, in the past, and every new nationalism has to imagine itself ancient. But Korea's forgetting of its double colonization had to include forgetting the American client state of the
dictator Park, with its own embrace of a crudely imagined past (Admiral
Yi Sun-sin, the Blue House, the curved roofs—and is this the subliminal
reason behind the King Sejong image now inserted between Admiral Yi
and the Park-sponsoring US Embassy?). Accordingly the imagined
past would now be represented most "authentically" in the simulacra of
the reimagined and reconstructed Chosun palaces. It is necessary to
travel back, in the imagination and in reinventions, across the gap of
the colonial obliteration to that dreamed, desired fantasy-past.

We can return to Pierre Nora's argument on *lieux de mémoire*,
from chapter 1, and to that range of spaces, physical and intellectual,
wherein the memories of "the nation" might be constructed, contained,
and contested. Admiral Yi Sun-sin, the Blue House, King Sejong, and
similar installations are exercises in the artificial production of *lieux
de mémoire*, which, in turn, must be reimagined to free them from
associations with military dictatorships and the American semicolo-
nization. The newly emerged simulacrum of the Gyeongbokgung with
other restorations are yet further, constructed *lieux de mémoire*. More
real, one must argue, is that cemetery in Gwangju.

These are mostly conscious, official-nationalist attempts to (re)
imagine the culture (in the dreamed palaces and shrines, as well as
the vast proliferation of museums that bestrew Seoul, contra the Japanese).[5] The ecological lessons of shrine and palace, however, and the
worldview in which they were based in the past, are to be forgotten. The
new parklands—ironic indeed in their aesthetic—are sculptural rather
than ecologically restorative. The claim on antiquity is purely visual,
not aesthetic in the Kantian sense of an expression of truthfulness.[6]

3. Naturalizing material culture

There had long been a dichotomy between the (Buddhist) contempla-
tive spiritual and the (Confucian) discipline of family, learning, duty,
and tradition. The Japanizing of Korean Buddhism (Cho Sungtaek
2005), together with the ambivalent Confucian responses to the shock
of Western culture (albeit largely via Japan), saw an increasingly mate-
rialist shift in Korean culture. Most notably, the strong, traditional
family focus translated into ways of doing business in the peculiar
forms of emerging Korean capitalism (Kim Hyuk-Rae 1998). One is
left to wonder: are "family values," in turn, a reaction against the corporate world subversion, in part via the institution of the *chaebol* and
the linked idea of the family?

As ever, the "spirit of capitalism" could be reinforced via the ethics of Protestantism, more so, it might be argued, than via Confucianism. Moreover, a material culture is to replace one founded on ideas of the (Buddhist) spiritual. The *chaebol* are the family, exploded to the scale of the absurd; Seoul is a city of exaggerated (exploded) Christian witness; the skyline is one of logos and the innumerable neon-red crosses atop red cones glowing in the night. At the same time, however, the ecological basis of Buddhism is sublimated. "Old" nature must be forgotten:

> "The city is lines." Roads were built through mountains, over rivers, and across the sea to show off modern technological progress, while subjugating nature as a plastic thing. . . . Instead of being treated as an object of reverence, nature becomes something to overcome, control, and even exploit on behalf of people.
>
> Nature has lost its spontaneous autonomy and degenerated into a visually manipulated plastic thing that requires management. (Ryu Jeh-hong 2004, 10)

One should not, however, despair: the same point was made previously in chapter 5, though from a more positive viewpoint, regarding "new" nature. The world that Ryu Jeh-hong decries is simply that of "now-possible relationships and responsibilities" to external nature and to technologies that Walter Benjamin identified as new nature—opportunities. Likewise the spatial and visual muddle of Seoul "back streets" might be decried as loss, yet, in reality, it is the space of everyday life (trade, leisure, entertainment, creativity) and, as argued above, the formation of a new urban vernacular. Both the city as lines and the city of decorated boxes are now naturalized—part of "the nature of the city."

There remains the extraordinary power of Korean syncretism and indigenizing. Buddhism, Confucianism, Christianity, shamanism—all thrive in a strange, undifferentiable state of indeterminacy. To repeat from earlier, if there is such a thing as "Asian values," it is likely to do with this acceptance of noncontradiction, the ability to believe diversely, and the immense pool of resources that such an episteme bestows—including the ability to survive in a partitioned world (the national family divided) of ever-present, dark, foreboding threat (the North, the DMZ, tunnels, the Han River—that dreadful image of *The Host*).

4. Transposing reality

The distinguishing character of Korea has to be the recentness and suddenness of its modernization and transformation: three centuries (for Europe) had to be compressed into thirty years—and with a fractured past—with the profound disorientation that such a dizzying metamorphosis must impose. More than anything else, it is this compression that enables Seoul space: "Korean society sped up modernity, such that it needs to make use and disuse of modern spectacles to rotate fast" (Ryu Jeh-hong 2004, 18).

The compression of time is matched by an explosion of space—from the Hermit Kingdom to a global diaspora. Sonia Ryang has traced the Korean presence in Japan, long assumed to be the most homogeneous of societies and both the envied and abhorred demon of modern Korean history.[7] Her *Koreans in Japan* (2000) is subtitled *Critical Voices from the Margin,* alluding to a minority that is scarcely known in either Japan or the West or, for that matter, in Korea itself. Many are victims of the displacements of (Japanese) colonization and of the subsequent postcolonial division of Korea in the Cold War. Ryang's *North Koreans in Japan* (1997) addresses an even more surprising insertion: because she was raised in this community, she brings her own knowledge to bear on this closed society, offering a rare glimpse into North Korean culture and the transmission of tradition and ideology within it. Through Chongryun, its umbrella organization, the community directs its commercial, political, social, and educational affairs, including running its own schools and teaching children about North Korea as their homeland, and Kim Il-sung and his beloved son (and subsequently, no doubt, his revered grandson) as their wonderful leaders. Although highly insulated within their community's boundaries, many in the younger generations are well integrated into Japanese society. Yet, apparently, they remain serious in their commitment to North Korea while simultaneously dedicated to their lives in Japan.

Sonia Ryang, however, is an "American" scholar, as are so many of the Korean authors cited above. They are part of the Americanization of Korea. The diaspora is expressed in American academia, as much as in the communities and culinary colonization of North America more widely. So much of North America is Korean.[8]

THE POSTNATION AND THE (OTHER) NATION

Whereas the populations of Asia may jump at the "cool" of Korea, the culturally invaded nation-states of those populations mount their resistance. Already by 2005 there was a backlash. The Vietnam government threatened to ban the broadcast of Korean programs if local shows were not given more time on Vietnamese television; Taiwan considered placing limits on Korean and other foreign content; China considered the relative merits of boycotts and limits on Korean material. Most interestingly, in Japan a comic book with a title usually translated as "Hating the Korean Wave" was launched to popular acclaim but also to charges of promoting racial hatred and proclaiming historical inaccuracies (Sakamoto and Allen, 2007)—the ultimate proof, surely, of the movement's simultaneously disintegrative and hybridizing power.

One is left to suspect that it is the nation-state (China, Vietnam, Japan, and so on) that is now "in the interstices," that the processes (though not yet the institutions) of the postnation are now hegemonic, and that the view along Seoul's Taepyeongno (Sejongno) is that of the present age, revealing the unsustainable compromises underlying the increasingly discredited claims of the nation-state.

THE IDEA OF "THE END OF HISTORY"

Gianni Vattimo (1985) has argued that new technology for the collection, transmission, and global diffusion of information vastly expands the locations where a picture (history) of human activity can be constructed. By 2016, live streaming of police shootings, murders, terrorism, and natural disasters had displaced the Fourth Estate and rendered everyone the historian-of-the-moment. Historiography breaks free. At the same time, the multiplicity of images of such activity, at the very moment of its occurrence, shifts attention from a past-to-present linear progression to a multifaceted, ever-changing, ungeneralizable present. The effect of these processes is a "dehistoricizing of experience." So the new era is characterized by the experience of the "end of history"—a new experience of time itself.[9]

The idea of the end of history arises differently in the writings of Jean Baudrillard. In the 1980s and 1990s, a common theme in Baudrillard's writings was historicity or, more specifically, how present societies utilize notions of progress and modernity in their political choices. History, he argued, had ended, or "vanished," with the collapse of the very idea of historical progress. The end of the Cold War was not caused by one ideology's triumph over the other but by the disappearance of the utopian visions that the political Right and Left shared—the ends that they had both hoped for had always been illusions. Indeed, the idea of an "end," itself, was nothing but a misguided dream (Baudrillard 1994a). Within a society subject to and ruled by fast-paced electronic communication and global information networks, he argued, the collapse of the façade of history's progress was always going to be inevitable.

If "the nation" is part of this historical imagining of ends, then does the nation as a desired end also wither to the status of a collapsed illusion—a delusion of that brief age of nationalism recounted by Anderson? Does Korean culture (not Korean nation) sow the seeds that erode the (Chinese, Japanese, Taiwanese, and so on) nation? Is this the entry, if not of the end of history, then of the end of the age of the nation?

SEOUL AT THE END OF HISTORY

We return to those questions that arose from the introduction to this chapter. Is Seoul urban space able to address an ironic, antinostalgic view of its own history? The answer is, still, in the depressing negative. It seems that the nostalgic (the dream of the reconstructed palaces, happy family excursions to mountain shrines, reimagined Chosun) and its obverse in unreflective modernism (the endlessly repeated tower blocks of everyday life) still prevail. Yet, for all that, a more positive view must be argued: in the interstices between these dichotomous urban worlds (the nostalgic vis-à-vis the modernist), one can identify destabilizing insertions that call held certainties into question—the city of lines, that new vernacular of information-adorned boxes, cones, and crosses. There is also the discordant architecture of Paju Book City (a happy theme park, yet also holding up a mirror to the culture—fun vis-à-vis the DMZ); the unsettling and disordered practices of Hongdae; the almost untraceable proliferation of art districts, museums, and galleries; the discordant discourse provoked by Cheonggyecheon and its non-nostalgic return to a Chosun past, and, at a more microscopic scale, the bronze sculpture of the little girl confronting the Japanese Embassy. There is another reason for a more positive view: although other societies may be as brilliantly creative and resilient as Korea's, none would seem more so. The ironic imagination of Paik and of post–New Wave cinema will inevitably inform the design of the city of the twenty-first century.

Modern Seoul can be understood only in the context of bitterly contested memory and the creative fragmentation (reinvention) represented most startlingly in the Korean Wave.

Appendix

BCE

2333	Legendary foundation of Gojoseon kingdom, capital in Liaoning
551	Gong Fuzi (Confucius) (551–479 BCE)
400	Gojoseon capital moves to Pyongyang
208	Gojoseon ended by Han Chinese invasion; various small states ensue
108	Baekje kingdom established (to 660), various capitals in vicinity of Greater Seoul
57	Silla kingdom established (to 935)
37	Koguryo kingdom established (to 668)
18	Baekje capital established on the Han River

CE

661	Battle of Baekgang-gu: Tang China and Silla defeat Japan and Baekje
668	Silla effects unification of Korean Peninsula; allied with Tang China
918	Goryeo (Koryo, Korea) kingdom established, ending Silla in 935
958	Confucian civil service examinations first held in Korea
992	National University founded in Gaeseong
1234	Koreans invent movable metal type printing
1243	An Hyang (1243–1306), responsible for introduction of neo-Confucianism to Korea
1390	Law to institute ancestor veneration

Chosun

1392	Yi (Chosun, Joseon) dynasty replaces Goryeo
1394	Hanyang (Seoul) established as Chosun capital
1398	Namdaemun, Great South Gate, built
1403	Metal type printing technology perfected (invented in 1234)
1407	Yeongeunmun Gate (Welcoming Gate for Obligation [to Chinese]) built
1418	King Sejong the Great reigns (to 1450)
1446	*Han-gul* Korean alphabet invented
1455	King Sejo reigns (to 1468); strengthens Buddhist practice against Confucianism

1469	King Songjong reigns (to 1494); reinforces Confucian rule
1563	Yi Su-gwang (1563–1628), *silhak* scholar; brings new Western learning from visit to Beijing (c. 1602)
1569	Ho Kyun (1569–1618), author of novel *Hong Kil-tong chon*
1592	Hideyoshi invasion of Ming and Chosun realms; Gyeongbokgung Palace destroyed
1597–1598	Second Hideyoshi invasion; defeated principally by Korean admiral Yi Sun-sin in Battle of Noryang, 16 December 1598
1598	Matteo Ricci (1552–1610), Jesuit missionary in Beijing, influence to Chosun
1737	Park Ji-won (1737–1805), *silhak* novelist and philosopher
1801	Pogrom against native Catholics
1824–1834	Kim Jeong-ho map of Seoul
1824	Ch'oe Che-u (1824–1864) formulates ideology of Donghak
1839	Second pogrom against Catholics
1846	Third pogrom against Catholics
1867	Gyeongbokgung Palace restored
1868	Meiji Restoration
1875	Japan provokes Unyo Incident against Korea
	Syngman Rhee (1875–1965)
1876	Japan establishes unequal treaty with Korea
1880	Japanese legation established in Seoul
1882	Military mutiny; Progressive (Independence) Party seeks to emulate Meiji Restoration
1884	Violent coup launched by Progressive Party

Colonization

1894	Chon Pong-jun assumes Donghak leadership; Japanese virtual annihilation of Donghak
	July: Japanese occupy palace, impose "protection" on King Kojong
	Sino-Japanese War (to 1895)
	Reform movement initiated by Korean government
1895	October: Queen Min assassinated
1896	February: King Kojong escapes to Russian legation
	Independence Club founded, principally by Seo Jae-pil; Yeongeunmun demolished
1897	February: King Kojong returns to Deoksugung Palace
	October: Great Han (Daehan) Empire proclaimed
	Tapgol (Pagoda) Park constructed
	Independence Gate replaces Yeongeunmun Gate
1898	Myeong-dong (Catholic) Cathedral
1899	Daehan Cheon-il Bank established
	Kyeongin railway links Seoul and Incheon
	Seoul's first tram, along Jongno
1902–1910	Deoksugung Palace restructured and refashioned

1904–1910	Ilchinhoe, Patriotic Enlightenment (pro-Japan) Movement
1905	Japanese protectorate established over Korea
1906	Japanese landownership legalized in Korea
1907	King Kojong deposed by Japanese Residency-General
	Keijo (Seoul) Exhibition
	Daehan Hospital built
1907–1912	Righteous armies fight against colonial rule
1909	Ahn Jung-geun assassinates Ito Hirobumi, first prime minister of Japan and first resident-general of Korea
1910	August: Korea annexed to Japan
1912	Bank of Chosun opens, designed 1907 for Japanese Dai-Ichi Bank
	Kim Il-sung (1912–1994)
1914	First formal expansion of Seoul city boundaries; first urban planning ordinance
1915	Korean Industrial Exposition
1917	Park Chung-hee (1917–1979)
1919	March First Movement
1920	Battle of Qingshanli; Koreans defeat Japanese
	Colonial antipublishing laws relaxed; Korean newspapers established
1920s	The urban *hanok* develops as an urban housing form; predominates to the 1960s
1921	Japanese measures to strengthen Korean media and literature
	Cheondogyo Central Temple built
1922	National University Movement established, unsuccessfully
	Kim Chung-up (1922–1988), architect
1924	Keijo Imperial University established (closed 1946)
1925	Japanese establish the Joseonsa Pyeonsuhoe, or Korean History Compilation Committee
	Seoul Station built
	Korean Artists Proletarian Federation founded
1926	New Seoul city plan; further plans in 1928 and 1930
	October: Government-General Building dedicated
	Death of Sunjong, last Chosun monarch
	Arirang, part of first "golden age" of Korean cinema
1929	Korean Exposition; Gyeongbokgung Palace demolished to make way for it
	Gwangju Incident
1931	Tightening military rule following Gwangju Incident
	Kim Swoo Geun (1931–1986), architect
1932	Paik Nam June (1932–2006), video artist
1934	Town Planning Act
	A Day in the Life of Novelist Kubo, novel by Pak Tae-won
1937	Sino-Japanese War (to 1945)
	Hwasin Department Store opens
1938	Foundation of Samsung

1939	Colonial education redirected to converting Koreans to loyal (Japanese) imperial subjects
1940	Korean newspapers shut down by colonial government
1942	American missionaries expelled; enforced assimilation of Koreans
	October: Korean linguists arrested, tortured
1943	Total mobilization

Dictatorship

1945	Tokyo obliterated by US firebombing
	15 August: End of World War II and of Japanese colonization
	US military government installed
1948	Syngman Rhee installed as president (to 1960); the First Republic
1951–1953	Korean War; Seoul obliterated
1953	15 August: Government returns to Seoul
1954	Rev. Sun Myung Moon establishes the Unification Church, "the Moonies"
1955–1972	Second "golden age" of Korean cinema
1958	Gimpo International Airport replaces Yeouido
1960	19 April Revolution, the Second Republic; civil society thrives
	The Housemaid, film by Kim Ki-young
1961	The 5.16 coup d'état, Park Chung-hee, the Third Republic
1962	First Five-Year Economic Development Plan
1965	Normalization treaty with Japan
1966	Basic Urban Planning for Seoul
1967	Second Five-Year Economic Development Plan
	Guro Industrial Complex founded; Daewoo founded
	Sewoon Mega Complex, Kim Swoo Geun architect
	Statue of Admiral Yi Sun-sin in Taepyeongno
1967–1971	Samil Expressway built over Chongyecheon Stream
1968	The Blue House raid
	Seoul tramway system finally closes down
1969	Seoul Plan based on 1966 Basic Urban Planning
1970	Patriot Ahn Jung-geun Memorial Hall built on site of demolished (1945) Seoul Shinto Shrine
1970s	Emergence of Hongdae art culture district
1971	National Land Development Plan
1972	Yusin (Restoration) Constitution, the Fourth Republic
	Third Five-Year Economic Development Plan
1974	First Five-Year Plan for the Revival of Culture and Arts
	Seoul subway Line 1 opens
1975	National Assembly Building
1977	Fourth Five-Year Economic Development Plan
1979	Park Chung-hee assassinated

1980	Chun Doo-hwan becomes president
	May: Gwangju uprising and massacre; Kim Dae-jung receives death sentence
	Kyung Dong Presbyterian Church, Kim Swoo Geun's masterpiece
1981	Seoul selected to host 1988 Olympic Games
1982	Fifth Five-Year Economic and Social Development Plan

Democratization

1987	Sixth Five-Year Economic and Social Development Plan
	Mass protests; Chun and Roh Tae-woo succumb to demands for democratic elections
1988	Roh Tae-woo elected president
	Seoul Olympic Games
1989	Beginning of new towns program
	SM Entertainment founded
1992	Seventh Five-Year Economic and Social Development Plan
	Seo Tai-ji and Boys pop group launches; beginning of K-pop
1993	Kim Young-sam elected president
1994	Death of Kim Il-sung; succession of Kim Jong-il
1995	15 August: Ritual demolition of Government-General Building
1996	*First Love* TV drama series
1997–1998	Asian financial crisis
1998	Kim Dae-jung elected president

The Korean Wave

2000	Korean boy band HOT in Beijing, first Korean reference to Hallyu
2001	Incheon International Airport replaces Gimpo as principal airport
	"The second Gwangju": attack on unionists at Daewoo plant, Bupyeong
2002	*Winter Sonata* TV drama series
2003	Roh Moo-hyun elected president, Internet role significant
	Decision by mayor Lee Myung-bak to demolish Samil Expressway (Cheongyecheon)
2003–2004	*Jewel in the Palace* TV drama series
2005	Cheongyecheon rehabilitation completed
	Delightful Girl Choon-Hyang, popular Korean TV drama series
	Under the Black Umbrella: Voices from Colonial Korea, 1910–1945, by Kang Hildi
2006	*The Host*, film by Bong Joon-ho
2007	May 18 Memorial Hall to commemorate 1980 Gwangju massacre
2008	Lee Myung-bak elected president
	Global financial crisis
	Destruction of Namdaemun by fire
2009	New Songdo first stage opens
	Who Ate Up All the Shinga?, novel by Park Wan-suh; *Please Take Care of Mom*, novel by Shin Kyung-Sook

2010	*The Housemaid*, film by Im Sang-soo
2011	December: Peace Monument unveiled, in front of Japanese Embassy
	December: Death of Kim Jong-il; succession of Kim Jong-un
2012	New "capital," Yeongi-Sejong, opens
	Cloud Atlas, film based on 2004 novel by David Mitchell; "Neo-Seoul"
	July: *Gangnam Style*, by Psy (Park Jaesang)
	December: "Gangnam Style" hits one billion views
2013	Park Geun-hye elected president
2014	Dongdaemun Design Plaza opens, Zaha Hadid architect
	"Gangnam Style" "hits" break the YouTube counting barrier
2015	New Songdo fails scheduled timetable
2017	Park Geun-hye impeached, Hwang Kyo-ahn acting president
	Increased North-South tension

Notes

PREFACE

1. Creative destruction, sometimes termed "Schumpeter's gale" (the gale of creative destruction), is most commonly associated with the Austrian American economist Joseph Schumpeter. See especially Schumpeter (1950).
2. While the idea of a "postmodern hyperspace" has featured in the writings of a number of historians and cultural critics of recent decades, it is especially linked to the work of Fredric Jameson, notably Jameson (1991). I would avoid the "postmodern" epithet; "late modern" or "late capitalist" would seem to better capture the intent.
3. An increasing phenomenon in Seoul is Japanese tourism. In a study of the complex decision making of Japanese- and English-speaking tourists in Seoul, Lee Hyuk-jin and Joh Chang-Hyeon (2010) have noted that Japanese tourists are mostly women, older and homemakers, with a focus on shopping. They are likely to have visited previously. English-speaking tourists are more likely to be male, younger, often business visitors and students and more interested in aesthetic and cultural touring.

CHAPTER 1: INTRODUCTION

Epigraph: Pierre Nora 1996, 18.

1. In representing Korean words in the roman alphabet, the Revised Romanization system will mostly be used except where a cited source uses the McCune-Reischauer or some other system.
2. Andre Schmid (2002) draws attention to a much earlier monument to celebrate ancient royal achievement: in 1905, Korean intellectuals greeted the discovery of a stele celebrating the territorial conquests of a Koguryo dynasty king, Kwanggaet'o (375–415). These intellectuals are often grouped together by historians as the Patriotic Enlightenment Movement. Subsequently, these debates were increasingly constrained by the colonial regime with its goal of making Koreans loyal imperial subjects.
3. On the writing of history in the Goryeo dynasty and the early stages of the Chosun dynasty, see Lee Ki-baik (1984, 166–167). This writing took an annals form and "employed the perspective of Confucian moralism to view history didactically as a mirror for government." In the thirteenth century more general accounts began to emerge, to describe ancient folkways and institutions. A more modern form of historiography arose with the *silhak* ("practical learning") movement of the late seventeenth and early eighteenth centuries (Lee Ki-baik 1984, 232–233; Eckert et al. 1990, 164–169).
4. Important in this tradition was Fukuda Tokuzo, especially his 1904 essay on Korean backwardness, "Kankoku no keizai soshiki to keizai tani" [The Economic

Organization and Economic Units of Korea], based on Karl Bucher's "economic stages" theory of economic development, and advocating "stagnation theory" to explain Korea. See Miller (2010, 4–5).

5. Em especially refers to Paek Nam-un (1933; 1937). On Paek Nam-un, also see Pang Kie-chung (2005). Lee Namhee (2013, 150–155) provides a fine critical review of Em.

6. For example, Auslander and Chong Eun Ahn (2015) report a case of comfort woman denial, proclaimed at Central Washington University to coincide with Japanese prime minister Shinzo Abe's visit to Washington and the 114th birthday of the Showa emperor (Hirohito).

7. Yoshimi Yoshiaki is especially important for having investigated the Japanese government's responsibility for the comfort women tragedy, following a 1991 event in which three Korean women filed a suit in a Tokyo district court stating that they had been forced into sexual servitude and demanding compensation. See O'Brien (1999).

8. Palmer especially cites Pak Kyong-sik (1965) as a seminal work in this tradition: Pak studied the forced mobilization of Koreans during Japan's 1937–1945 war.

9. Also, in English, attention is drawn to Eckert's *Offspring of Empire* (1991), referred to above, as well as Park Soon-won, *Colonial Industrialization and Labor in Korea* (1999) and Theodore Jun Yoo, *The Politics of Gender in Colonial Korea* (2008).

10. In this context of understanding Korean nationalism, Keith Pratt (2006, 20–24) distinguishes among political nationalism, *minjin* nationalism, and cultural nationalism.

11. It is worth noting Lee Ki-baik's recognition of the monumental achievement of An Chang-bok (1712–1791) in the *Tongsa kangmok* [Annotated Account of Korean History], written from an orthodox Confucian point of view, also of Han Ch'i-yun's (1765–1814) *Haedong yoksa* [History of Korea] in an annals-treatises format (Lee Ki-baik 1984, 237). Korean historiography has a long lineage.

12. On "voice," see Mikhail Bakhtin (1986, 99); on Bakhtin's argument, in turn, see Holquist and Emerson (1981, 434); and Wertsch (1991, 51).

13. Whereas chapters 1 through 13 might be identified as acknowledging Japanese colonial historiography, chapters 14 through 16 turn to unrelenting condemnation of the Japanese insertion. See, for example, the critique by Slantchev (2001).

14. Although Cumings' assessment of the Korean War as a civil war would now be widely accepted, recent research would question his attribution of causes. A strong critique of Cumings (2011) and its failings is by William Stueck in the *Washington Post*, 12 September 2010. The core of Stueck's criticism is that Cumings had ignored more recent research and scholarship published since his earlier books on the Korean War (1981; 1990); see William Stueck, "Bruce Cumings's 'The Korean War,'" *Washington Post*, 12 September 2010, http://www.washingtonpost.com, accessed 18 September 2015.

15. On these arguments, see De Ceunster (2001); Ahn Byung-ook (2002); and Kim Kyu Hyun (2004; 2005).

16. One must acknowledge the immense body of critical literature following the original 1966 publication of Moore's *Social Origins of Dictatorship and Democracy*. For a critical review of responses to Moore's argument in its first decade, see Jonathan Weiner (1976).

17. There has been criticism of the Atkins argument. See Aso (2012).

18. A finely researched account of the Japanese settler community and its various relations with the Government-General and with indigenous Koreans is Todd Henry (2014).

19. Kwon Nayoung Aimee (2015) would argue that there is also a "reality" of postcolonial modernity, wherein a studied amnesia would attempt to eliminate the memory of the colonial era from both Japanese and Korean memories.

20. Ryu Youngju (2015) recounts the struggle of different interpretations of the times to be heard in the dictatorship era of the "Winter Republic"—a term from a subversive poem of 1975.

21. Kim Hyung-A and Sorenson (2011, 9) summarize the present divide thus: "[A]lmost three decades after the end of the Park era. Public debate on this era and Park's role in contemporary South Korean history continues to rage between two camps—those who approve of Park-style modernization and now promote the 'advancement' (*sonjinhwa*) of South Korea, and others who insist that Park-style 'compressed' economic development inherently delayed South Korea's democratization and now promote social justice and economic equality."

22. Renan's seminal essay was a lecture delivered in 1882. Benedict Anderson (1991, 199–201) has elaborated on the consequences of this Renan utterance.

23. Ignoring the modern reconstructions, Seoul does possess fragments from its Chosun past. There are the remnants of Changdeokgung, Changgyeonggung, and Deoksugung Palaces, the Chongmyo Ancestral Shrine, the Bell Tower, remnant gates and parts of the encircling city wall, and the Bukchon *hanok* village, the last albeit mostly from the 1920s. There are royal tombs beyond the city. Arguably most significant are the surviving city walls of Suwon, the Hwaseong Fortress (c. 1796), some thirty kilometers south of Seoul and arguably grandest of all Korean monuments but also largely reconstructions (from the 1970s). The point of the present comment is that the destructions, whether by the Japanese or during the Korean War, far outweigh the survivals.

24. Meaning is conveyed by words (language) but also by "the voice" in which an utterance is delivered, as insisted upon by Mikhail Bakhtin. See especially Bakhtin (1986, 99); for a review, see King (1996, 72).

25. On the Japanese Meiji-sanctioned architectural styling, see Coaldrake (1996).

26. From conversations with academic architects in Seoul, 1999 and 2000.

27. On the *hanok* and its *ondol* floor system, see Clark (2000, 93–96).

28. Jung Inha (2013) cites Kim Ranky and Yoon Do-Geun (1989, 232).

29. On the idea of a "contra-Anderson" argument, see especially Duncan (n.d.) in Lee Hong Yung (2013, 6); and Schmid (2002). Controversially, Anderson argues that the idea of the modern nation arose not in political emergences in Enlightenment-era Europe but in the creole communities of the Americas subsequently to be translated into "old world" polities.

30. Anderson adds a footnote here to the effect that the events of the late eighteenth and nineteenth centuries that enabled the bourgeois revolutions in Europe and the creole revolutions in the Americas were not the first such incident. He quotes Febvre and Martin (1976): while a visible bourgeoisie existed in Europe by the late thirteenth century, paper did not come into use until the late fourteenth—the necessary conditions were not met for the formation of a new, shared, bourgeois identity.

31. The problematic notion of assemblage as a logic and "new social theory" underlying Korean space will be addressed in chapter 4.

32. It will be clear from Baudrillard's focus on the question of value (exchange value, sign value) that he is working in a Marxian framework. Important is his extension of Marx's argument: "Marx set forth and denounced the obscenity of the commodity, and this obscenity was linked to its equivalence, to the object principle of free circulation, beyond all use value of the object. . . . One has only to prolong this Marxist analysis, or push it to the second or third power, to grasp the transparency and obscenity of the universe of communication, which leaves far behind it those relative analyses of the universe of the commodity. All functions abolished in a single dimension, that of communication" (Baudrillard 1985, 131).

33. We will note in chapter 3 the signally important transformation in Korean society—later than in many other affluent societies—whereby economic

progress shifted from dependence on export-oriented production to dependence on a consumer economy. On this transformation, see Hart (2001).

CHAPTER 2: ERASURE AND REINVENTION

1. I take the idea of the wish image from Susan Buck-Morss (1991) and her magisterial critique of Walter Benjamin's *Passagen-Werk*.
2. Kyung Moon Hwang (2010, 18–19) makes the point that Baekje's contact was with islands to the east that were just coming together to form what we now know as Japan at the same time as the Silla unification of the peninsula (the 660s CE).
3. A useful supplement to an account of the successive and rival kingdoms of old Korea is Shin (2014), *Korean History in Maps*.
4. For a recent study of conditions enabling Silla's alliance with the Tang and of the strength of that alliance against Koguryo in the eighth century, see Kim Jong-bok (2014).
5. On the geography and geomancy of Gaeseong (Kaesong) as Goryeo capital, see Lee Ki-baik (1984, 111–112).
6. On the legends of Paektu, see Lee Ki-baik (1984, 107); and Cumings (2005, 28).
7. Cumings (2005, 30) observes that An Ho-sang, Rhee's first minister of education, produced the regime's *juche* philosophy based in Silla ideals. *Juche* is the North Korean spelling of *chuch'e*, referring to their own guiding (legitimating) ideology.
8. To be discussed following is the Japanese fantasy of the mythical (Japanese) state of Mimana as the "true" origin of (southern) Korea.
9. These principles conform with the *Rites of Zhou*, officially attributed to the semi-mythical Zhou dynasty of the Chinese Warring States period and one of the classics of Confucianism. Nylan (2001, chap. 4); Kyung Moon Hwang (2010, 63).
10. There would seem to have been further agendas underlying the siting: its proximity to the river supported trade and commerce, while both Pugaksan and Namsan were topped by defensive mountain fortresses (Lee Ki-baik 1984, 217). Naksan, close by Changdeokgung Palace, was mostly demolished in an over-hasty expansion to the east of the city during the Japanese colonial period; "Nasan Park," Korea Tourism Organization, http://visitkorea.or.kr, accessed 10 July 2012. The mountain's remnants now constitute Seoul's Naksan Park. The other defining mountains retain their integrity.
11. Jongno and its commerce in the long Chosun era, with its so-called Six Licensed Stores late in the dynasty, is well described in Eckert et al. (1990, 120). Subsequently, in 1791, a "commercial equalization enactment" abolished all special privileges granted to commercial merchants except for the Six Licensed Stores, facilitating the development of three great markets operated by private merchants: at Jongno, inside the east gate (genesis of the present Dongdaemun Market), and outside the south gate (the present Namdaemun Market) (Lee Ki-baik 1984, 230).
12. Significantly, the Ten Injunctions attributed to Wang Kon or T'aejo, the founder of the Goryeo dynasty, insisted that state-sponsored Buddhist festivals must retain worship of the shamanistic and geomantic spirits of indigenous Korean religion; Korean distinctiveness was to be preserved (Lancaster et al. 1996; Kyung Moon Hwang 2010, 37).
13. In late Goryeo, the Chogye Buddhist sect arose, drawing promising young monks away from other Buddhist sects and emphasizing a concrete gradualism. Its key figure in Goryeo was Chinul (1158–1210). Its effect was to prepare the ground for neo-Confucianism (Lee Ki-baik 1984, 132, 154).

14. An Hyang founded Seoul Munmyo (Munmyo Shrine) in 1398 in the reign of the first Chosun king, Taejo. It is Korea's primary Confucian shrine, currently located on the campus of Sungkyunkwan University in the Jongno area.

15. On the role of Confucian scholars in the tumultuous overthrow of Goryeo and the foundation of Chosun, see Kyung Moon Hwang (2010, 61–67).

16. Keum Jang-tae (2000) traces the dominant role of Confucianism in the formation of "Korean Thoughts" following the fifteenth century and persisting into the present. Other publications by Keum similarly document the role of Confucianism in the formation of a Korean epistemology. On the later trajectory of Confucianism into the colonial period, see Duncan (2000; 2007, 36).

17. The royal lecture was of ancient lineage. For its use in the Goryeo dynasty, see Breuker (2010, 66).

18. See Lee Ki-baik (1984, 173–181); Eckert et al. (1990, 107–115); Hyung Moon Hwang (2010, 49), also "Yangban," *Encyclopædia Britannica*, last updated 10 November 2016, http://www.britannica.com, accessed 4 September 2013. Lee Ki-baik explicitly defines Chosun as a "*Yangban* Society" (1984, 172).

19. Haboush brings an entirely different view to the condition of women in the Chosun era, this time at the level of royalty, in her translation of the renowned *Memoirs of Lady Hyegyong* (2015).

20. In contrast, Kyung Moon Hwang (2010, 13–23) emphasizes the high status of women in the Silla state, including queen regnant Sondok as a driving force for the Silla unification.

21. Prior to these invasions of the 1590s, there had long been waves of Japanese maritime marauders, or *waegu*, beginning during the reign of the Goryeo kingdom of King Gojong (r. 1213–1259) and intensifying after 1350. See Lee Ki-baik (1984, 162). On the real achievements of Hideyoshi, as well as his alleged delusional ambitions of world conquest, see M. E. Berry (1989); and Turnbull (2002; 2011).

22. Also on women's status and literature in the Chosun era, see Park Chan E. (2012).

23. Also titled *Sassy Girl, Choonhyang*; "Delightful Girl Choon Hyang," KoreanDrama.org, http://www.koreandrama.org, accessed 15 July 2012. The case of *Sassy Girl* will be reprised in chapter 5. More generally, Lee Ki-baik (1984, 243–245) and Eckert et al. (1990, 174–175) observe that morality tales dominated a new genre of literature in that era—good overcomes evil, also the place of women. This might well be seen as foreshadowing themes that would later run through Korean Wave literature, film, and television. While there were anti-Japanese themes, the greater preoccupation was with stories of love.

24. For an outline of the rise of *Donghak*, and for writings on Ch'oe Cheu, see Duncan (2000). There had been earlier uprisings against the Chosun dynasty, most notably the Musin Rebellion of 1728 (Jackson 2016); these, however, were mostly factional, in which one faction sought hegemony over another. The Donghak Rebellion is to be distinguished as having a social class origin.

25. On the *hwarang* and the *Hwarang Segi* (Hwarang Chronicles), see Lee Ki-baik (1984, 54–55); and McBride (2008).

26. The official government sloganeering was little different: in 1871 the Daewongun (Yi Ha-eung, the father of King Kojong and the most powerful figure in the kingdom for much of that reign) had stone markers set up on Seoul's main thoroughfare proclaiming, "Western barbarians invade our land. If we do not fight, we must then appease them. To urge appeasement is to betray the nation." Eckert et al.(1990, 197) see this stand as anachronistic and myopic, especially as China and Japan had already opened to the West in the 1840s and 1850s.

27. Korean nationalism was complex and divided (and divisive); Keith Pratt (2006, 20–24) identifies three distinctive manifestations, in political nationalism,

minjung nationalism, and cultural nationalism. For an extended treatment, see Lee Ki-baik (1984, 302–305); and Eckert et al. (1990, 232–236).

28. Adding further to the complexity of Korean relations, the Russian expansion of influence into the peninsula provoked a British response; apparently with Chinese cognizance, Britain established a naval base in 1885, occupying Komun-do off the southern coast of Cholla, to contain Russia (Lee Ki-baik 1984, 280).

29. The Gyeongbokgung had been destroyed in the Hideyoshi invasions of the 1590s, eventually to be rebuilt by the Daewongun. The Daewongun had seen that such a reconstruction was crucial to reinforcing dynastic prestige. The project began in 1865, to be completed in 1867, at great expense and inflicting both social and economic damage (Lee Ki-baik 1984, 261–262).

30. The Seokjojeon was damaged in the colonial period and then again by North Korean arson in the Korean War. Its restoration was begun in 2009

31. Seo Jae-pil is a seminal figure in the abortive 1884 coup and the 1890s reform movement. See Lee Ki-baik (1984, 302–304); Eckert et al. (1990, 232–234). Subsequently he was significant to the independence movement in the colonial period and then later as principal advisor to the post-1945 South Korean government of Syngman Rhee.

32. Yoshimi Takeuchi ([1947] 1993) is cited to the effect that "Asia" arrived at its self-consciousness thanks to "the West's" or "Europe's" colonization albeit, in part, colonization in imagination. The historical colonization of Asia is essential to the possibility called Asia.

33. Park especially cites Kwon Taeeok (2005); Omameuda (2006, 138–139).

34. As Alexis Dudden (2006) argues, there was also a legitimation in legalisms: there were always assiduously pleaded intellectual and "international law" justifications put forward to underpin Japan's imperial aspirations.

35. American Secretary of War (later president) William Howard Taft approved Japan's domination of Korea in a secret agreement with Japan's foreign minister, in exchange for Japanese quiescence about US colonization of the Philippines. This is seen by many Koreans as America's first betrayal; the second was the division of Korea agreed upon, again secretly, at the end of World War II (Oberdorfer and Carlin 2013, 4).

36. The Anglo-Japanese Alliance was renegotiated in August 1905, acknowledging Japan's right to "guide" Korea in return for Japan's recognition of British interests in China (Eckert et al. 1990, 238).

37. On the ideology and agenda of the Patriotic Enlightenment Movement, see Syngman Rhee (1904), written from a Seoul prison but not published until 1910. A partial translation into English is Kim Han-Kyo (2000, 299–305).

38. There were 58 *jingu* (Shinto shrines) in Korea, 322 smaller shrines, and 310 prayer halls; the largest, for the legendary Amaterasu, founder of Japan, and for the Meiji emperor, was Korea Shrine, or Choson Jingu, on Namsan, the sacred (to Koreans) Southern Mountain (Lautensach 1945, 391; Cumings 2005, 182; Henry 2014). Todd Henry (2014, 65–91) recounts at length the efforts of the colonial government to bring Koreans into the fold of Shinto worship.

39. I am indebted to an anonymous reviewer for this point on the role of the mission stations in creating Koreans' sense of awe toward Western modernity.

40. See Kyung Moon Hwang (2010, 167–169) on the role of women, and especially painter and radical writer Na Hyesok, in the cultural production of the 1920s. On such production in the 1930s, see Son Min-jung (2014).

41. On various aspects of the highly valued tradition of education in ancient Korea, see, for example, Lee Ki-baik (1984, 119, 130, 206–207, 222).

42. There is an extensive literature on the comfort women, who continue to haunt both Korean and Japanese memory and historiography. See, for example, C. Sarah Soh (2009); George Hicks (1997); and Yoshimi Yoshiaki (2002). The latter two look at the issues more broadly.

43. Palmer (2013, 195n2) cites Higuchi Yuichi (1992, 120, 131) and Hanil Munjae Yon'guwon (1995, 82–84).

44. On the Japanese assimilation policies and practices in Taiwan and the "devastating and transforming" effect on the Taiwanese political and socioeconomic fabric, see L. T. S. Ching (2001).

45. On the Caprio argument, see Palmer (2010). For another take on these inequalities, see Henry (2014).

46. On Reischauer, see Fujitani (2000); also Reischauer (1964).

47. Lee Young-ho (2014) provides an account of the interweaving of Japanese land reform measures with the Korean government's autonomous land reforms in the early colonial period, revealing the failure to resolve the problems of a multilayered landownership system until the Japanese Residency-General forcefully took away the rights of multilayered landowners without compensation.

48. See Hwang Insang, "The History of the Statistical System of Korea: From the Choson Period to the US Occupation Period," http://www.ier.hit-uac.jp, accessed 5 July 2015.

49. Park Chan Seung (2010, 88), citing Kim Young-geun (2002) and Kim Baek Young (2009), writes that the Japanese lived in the southern villages of Seoul south of the Cheonggyecheon Stream, with Koreans in the northern village that had been the aristocratic sector in the Chosun era. Also see Kal Hong (2011, 106); and Henry (2014).

50. The railway, it should be noted, was used very effectively by the Japanese to facilitate their 1904–1905 war with Russia for East Asian supremacy.

51. Lee Ki-baik (1984, 206–207) describes the role of private academies (*sojae*) that had existed since the end of Goryeo and had concerned themselves solely with education. Subsequently, in early Chosun another class of academy (*sowon*) proliferated, linked to the commemoration of past worthies and reinforcing the power of the neo-Confucian literati. These were state supported and performed a role akin to that of Buddhist temples in Goryeo. Many *sowon* were subsequently founded in the countryside by neo-Confucian literati who had been excluded from power in the capital (222).

52. Bartholomew (1993) gives the same statistic but in relation to Gyeongbokgung Palace. More specific is Jin Jong-Heon (2008, 40–41), stating that only thirty-six of approximately three hundred original buildings of the palace remained standing.

53. There had been an earlier, small-scale Keijo (Seoul) Exhibition in 1907. Although proclaimed as a joint venture of Japanese and Korean businessmen, it was clearly dominated by the former, held in the area of the southern (Japanese settler) village, and backed by the increasingly aggressive action of the Residency-General.

54. Kal Hong refers to "Hakurankai Iho" [Exposition Report], *Chosen* (October 1929), 325–327.

55. On the Beaux Arts predilections running through Japanese goals for their new and newly appropriated ancient cities in Manchuria (Manchukuo), under the planning control of the South Manchuria Railway Company (Mantetsu), see Jung Inha (2013, 8–9).

56. On Tokyo Station, see Coaldrake (1996). For a detailed account of the Government-General Building and its context in the array of colonial administration buildings and their architecture throughout the Japanese colonial empire, see Nishizawa (2014). Yasuhiko Nishizawa observes that, in all their colonies, the administration headquarters came late, as initial building efforts had been directed toward education, health, and other sectors to overcome backwardness —presumably to attract colonizers from Japan.

57. Also on Namsan was Seoul Shrine, founded in 1898 by Japanese settlers. Henry (2014, 62–63, 80) recounts that there was always tension between the settlers'

Seoul Shrine and the government's Korea Shrine, with the former a locus of settler opposition to the Government-General. There was also tension between
Shinto and the government's commitment to religious freedom. In 1929 indigenous deities were incorporated into Seoul Shrine, and in 1931 into Korea Shrine.

58. Henry (2014, 2) is quoting Ogasawara Shozo (1953, 73). In the vain hope of
advancing some measure of assimilation, Shozo had unsuccessfully attempted to
invoke native deities to inhabit Korea Shrine.

59. On these reforms, see Lee Ki-baik (1984, 290–292); and Eckert et al. (1990, 222–
227). The economic reforms brought profound social change, including aboli-
tion of class distinctions. Korean history began to be taught in schools, and
promising students were sent to Japan for higher study.

60. The Dai-Ichi Bank has a curious role in Korean history. It was founded in 1873 as
the first bank and first joint stock company ever established in Japan and effectively the central bank until 1883. In 1884 it negotiated with the Chosun government for its Korean branch to be the monopoly agent for tariff management. It
subsequently began issuing banknotes for Korea called Dai-Ichi Bank Tokens
and became the *de facto* central bank for Chosun Korea. Following the 1904
Japan-Korea Protectorate Treaty, it was deprived of its privileges in Korea by the
new (Japanese) colonial government.

61. This was the area of the Russian legation, protector of the dynasty in 1896–1905.
The legation was destroyed in the Korean War; its surviving main square tower is
in a Russian Renaissance Revival style.

62. On Yakhyeon Catholic Church, as well as the Catholic Church and the martyrs'
memorials in Seosomun, see http://www.visitseoul.net, accessed 31 July 2015.
On the background to the Chosun persecutions, see Cho Kwang (2004).

63. Also commemorating Catholic martyrs killed by Chosun is Saenamteo Church
in Yongsan-gu, on the site of a former military camp that served as a place of
execution of opponents of the dynasty; it holds the relics of nine Korean saints.
Though of recent construction, the church is unusual in being in a Korean style.
There were notable executions of Catholics in Seoul in 1801, 1839, 1846, and
1866.

64. The 1928 city plan (fortunately not implemented) would have obliterated Cheondogyo Temple, as well as Unhyeongung Palace (Henry 2014, 53).

65. "Old Seoul Station—Seoul, Korea," Waymarking.com, 23 June 2009, http://www
.waymarking.com, accessed 26 July 2012. On the quite extraordinary extent of
the (Japanese) Korean railway system in 1926, virtually on the eve of the Manchurian intrusion, see Uchida (2009, 118).

66. Chung J. Young, pers. comm., 10 March 2006.

67. By some accounts "only" 47 were demolished (Chung J. Young, pers. comm.,
10 March 2006); by leaving the main pavilion standing, the Japanese deformation became all the more explicit. Compare with the estimate of Jin Jong-Heon
(2008), that 36 of the approximately 300 original buildings remained standing.
It would seem that Jin's account refers to the whole palace complex plus the
ancillary buildings. Henry (2014, 98) refers to 123 palace buildings being "swept
away."

68. See also Henry (2014, 212). Henry observes, however, that the double-square
plan form has been commonly adopted by modern architects and that the
nationalistic reading by Korean critics is more recent—observers in the colonial
era seem not to have raised the issue and, in any case, would have lacked the
means to observe this symbolic calligraphy from above.

69. The City Hall, of 1926, was in a heavy-handed Art Deco—allegedly "European"
—style. Henry (2014, 50) notes the significance of City Hall's location immediately opposite Deoksugung Palace, center of the government of the erstwhile
Chosun Daehan Empire.

70. This progressive transformation of the capital, including the *de*formation of its royal and geomantic magic, is well represented in a series of maps in Jung Inha (2013, 11).

71. This "consent" was subsequently denied. In June 1965 the Treaty of Normalization with Japan repudiated the legality of the annexation and of the consequent colonization (Kyung Moon Hwang 2010, 225–226). The very idea of normalization met with widespread opposition in Korea and with student rebellion in Seoul.

72. Park Gil-ryong (1898–1943) worked initially with the Government-General's architecture department, where he designed the university main hall; he formed his own office in 1934 from which he designed the Hwasin Department Store, his masterpiece, in 1937 (Jackson and Koehler 2012; also Woo Don-Son 2014).

73. On the Mitsui and Company Building, later the USIS Building, see "Historical Japanese Architectures in Korean & Taiwan: Skylines & Photography," Skyscrapercity.com, http://www.skyscrapercity.com, accessed 3 July 2011.

74. Kang Sukhi (2007).

75. Upon its inauguration in 1900, the park was open to the public on Sundays but reserved for the royal household during the rest of the week. Citing the royal exclusiveness as illustrating Korean "backwardness," the Japanese opened the park on a daily basis in 1913. See Henry (2014, 41).

76. It is significant that the tram would traverse the commercial Jongno then, already in 1899, extend beyond the old city to the area that is now the University of Seoul campus.

77. Eckert et al. (1990, 231) observe that new Russian and US influence after 1895 enabled American businessmen to initiate the tramway, electricity generation and a city lighting plant, gold mining, and the Seoul-Incheon railway. The franchise for this last was awarded to James R. Morse, who in 1898, under some duress, sold it to a Japanese company.

78. Seoul's first electricity had been installed in 1886, to illuminate Gyeongbokgung Palace (Henry 2014, 40).

79. A fine and well-illustrated discussion of the spaces of colonial Seoul, enriched with the memories of the author's grandmother, is Jane Song (n.d. but probably 2009).

80. Henry (2014, 131–167) provides a very detailed and graphic account of hygiene and public health issues in the colonial period and of the very different policies and practices directed by the colonial authorities toward the two villages and their differentiated communities.

81. The street widening and reordering might be labeled "Haussmannization" in the manner most famously fashioned by Baron Georges-Eugène Haussmann (1809–1891) in the rebuilding of Paris. One can speculate that the Daehan would also have pursued this form of "erasure" of old Seoul if it had persisted. However, Henry (2014, 51) observes that the challenge to extend this rationalization beyond the arterial boulevards, into the internal capillaries, was never met.

82. Henry (2014, 49) suggests, however, that the expansion of the Korean quarters was a "concession" to the marginalized Korean community—effectively a sop.

83. On the land readjustment project, see Ishida and Kim Jooya (2014).

84. Henry (2014, 44–48) recounts the related story of the Keijo City Planning Research Association (KCPRA), founded in 1921 in the context of the cultural policy and following the model of the Tokyo-based Urban Research Association (URA) established in 1917. Both were extragovernmental agencies and both were divided into twelve departments to form the planning authorities of their respective cities. While the URA was mostly well resourced, it was politically constrained by powerful vested interests of the metropole; the KCPRA, by contrast, could rely on the backing of a powerful nonelected government but never had appropriate resources.

85. On the Hwasin Department Store and its much-reviled, alleged collaborator entrepreneur Park Heung Shik, see Cumings (2005, 171–172).

86. There are also the quasi-autobiographical novels and stories of Richard Kim. See especially Richard E. Kim (1988). Richard Kim recounts that when his novel *Lost Names* was translated into Korean and Japanese, both publishers translated "lost" with a word that implied "violently taken away." In subsequent editions, he asked for the removal of the unwanted implication of "the haunting shadows of victims and victimizers" (197). Both publishers had difficulty with the request.

87. Park Wan-suh (1931–2011) was one of Korea's most revered writers. Her work centered on families, family values, and biting critiques of the middle class and of strict Confucian mores; see, for example, *Three Days in that Autumn* (2001). Among her other fifteen novels, the best known would be *The Dreaming Incubator, Year of Famine in the City, Swaying Afternoon, Warm Was the Winter that Year*, and *Are You Still Dreaming?*

88. Lee Ji-Eun (2015) effectively places the rapidly evolving "modernization" of Korean women and their roles in this cultural production during the Japanese era.

89. In addition to Hwasin, there were four Japanese department stores by the end of the 1930s, all branches of department stores in Japan: Mitsukoshi, Chojiya, Minakai, and Hirata. They were part of Japanese capital's attempt to capture the Korean market, bringing both new products and fierce competition. See Oh Jin-seok and Howard Kahm, "Colonial Consumerism: Capitalist Development and the Internal Management of Department Stores in Late Colonial Korea," http://www.worldbhc.org, accessed 6 July 2015.

90. For translations of Pak's work, see Pak Tae-won (2010a; 2010b). Henry (2014, 51) observes that, in novelist Kubo's wandering in civic Seoul, there is no mention of City Hall and its plaza, alleged (by the government) to be the epicenter of civic life. Rather, it is the intense alienation of Taihei Boulevard and Seoul Station that seem most powerfully to evoke the civic spirit of Seoul.

91. Kimberley Chung (2014) has examined the New Tendency movement championed by KAPF that represented the beginning of "proletarian sensibilities" in 1920s colonial Korea. Its literature developed tropes of excess against the abject poverty of the masses, Marxist critique, descriptions of poverty, images of the body in pain, and the politics of the abject subject.

92. The contrary view, articulated earlier in this chapter, is that, especially in the cases of Ainu and Ryukyuan peoples, both policies and practices were more those of obliteration of culture than of assimilation (Caprio 2009).

93. This is dealt with by Atkins (2010), to be discussed below.

94. See Grayson (1977); Atkins (2010, 177–180); Seth (2006, 31–32). Atkins (2010, 177–180) writes that the "location, expanse, and Japaneseness of Imna/Mimana remain among the most disputed issues in East Asian historiography." Korean scholars generally interpret the claim about Mimana as a product of a nationalist, colonial Japanese historiography (Schmid 2002, 263; Kim Chun-Gil 2005, 27–29; Seth 2006, 31–32). Kim Chun-Gil refers to the "the Mimana fallacy."

95. Also see Henry (2014, 151), who cites newspaper reports of the time on the Japanese rhetoric of Keijo (Seoul) as the empire's "diseased city" and its Korean population as without "civic morality."

96. For more on Naoki Sakai's arguments on Japanese cultural nationalism, see Sakai (1992; 2008). On the origins of Japanese cultural nationalism, see Fujitani (1998).

97. On obligated forgetting and obligated remembering (imagining) in both Japanese historiography and popular culture, see the work of John Dower, notably Dower (1999; 2012).

98. Arguing similarly is Brudnoy (1970). For critiques of aspects of Atkins' study, see Aso (2012) and Dusinberre (2013).

99. A number of papers in Koh Wee Hock (2007) explore the more recent displays of Japanese ambivalence toward sexual slavery in World War II. There is Japanese prime minister Shinzo Abe's 2016 denial of forced wartime prostitution, apparently recanting a 1993 apology for the comfort women.
100. *Korea Journal* devoted a special issue to the event. See Park Chan Seung and Kim Hyun-ju (2010).
101. On the nature of that memory, see Yang Hyunah (1998). Comfort women are constructed as national virgins; the discourse of the violation of national virgins mobilizes the Korean sense of shame, which in turn serves to unify the nation. Thus the exchange value of shame for national unity is the basic capital that circulates in the symbolic economics of nationalism (Elaine H. Kim and Chungmoo 1998a.
102. This is the title of a nineteenth-century novel by Han Bangqing.
103. For different perspectives on these events in North Korea, see Armstrong (2013); and Suzy Kim (2013).

CHAPTER 3: RE-IMAG(IN)ING THE NATION

1. Paradoxically, Ahn remains an admired figure for both Koreans and Japanese. See Ippei Wakabayashi (2008). A further memorial hall to him was dedicated in Harbin, in 2014.
2. For a summary of Rhee's political corruption and manipulation, see Eckert et al. (1990, 348–352). On the atrocities of the era, especially the "Jeju 4.3 Incident" (massacre) of 1948 and on the historiography around it, see Merrill (1980; 1989); and Kim Hun Joon (2014).
3. On the Korean War, see especially Fehrenbach ([1963] 2000); Cumings (1981; 1990; 2011); and Hastings (1987).
4. *The Guest* is a novel by Hwang Sok-yong originally serialized in a South Korean newspaper in 2000, telling of a historical calamity known as the "Sinch'on Massacre," which took place in 1950 during the Korean War. Sinch'on, in Hwanghae Province, north of the 38th parallel, was a place where two historical forces collided: the landed anti-Communist Christian elites and the peasants rebelling against their masters under the authority of the Communist state (Hwang Sok-yong 2005).
5. This assessment is contested. Bruce Cumings (2005, 301) argues to the contrary, that the destruction to the North was greater. Possibly more significant, the entrepreneurial class from the North had fled to the South during the war, strengthening the human capital of the latter.
6. Midopa was at that time Seoul's largest department store.
7. The Fourth Republic was regulated by the so-called Yusin Constitution, adopted October 1972. *Yusin* in Korean means "rejuvenation" or "renewal"; it also carries connotations of the Japanese "restoration" component of the Japanese Meiji-ishin, or Meiji Restoration, alluding to the "imperial" role that Park Chung-hee saw for the presidency. There is an extensive literature on the Park era; especially useful are Kim Hyung-A (2004); Lee Byeong-cheon (2005); Kim Hyung-A and Sorenson (2011); and Byung-kook and Vogel (2011). For Park's earlier background, see Lee Chong-sik (2012).
8. Cumings begins his *The Korean War: A Modern History* (2011, xv) with the assertion that, while the Korean War was a civil war, it was mostly prosecuted by the United States and that US policy had largely underlain it. Subsequently, memory of its reality has been dismissed, even suppressed, in America. He states his intention as "to uncover truths that most Americans do not know and perhaps don't want to know." These assertions of Cumings are now somewhat questioned; see William Stueck, "Bruce Cumings's 'The Korean War,'" *Washington*

Post, 12 September 2010, http://www.washingtonpost.com, accessed 18 September 2015.

9. At the fiftieth anniversary of the normalization, deep Korean resentment was still widely reported, and was exacerbated by Japan's ongoing distortions of history in school textbooks, its territorial disputes, and its refusal to apologize for its wartime sexual slavery. See Song Sang-Ho (2015).

10. Park's charge is not without merit: the progressive Japanese intrusions into Korea were variously tolerated and lauded by Britain and even more by America. See Eckert et al. (1990, 237).

11. Lee Chong-sik, a confessed Park admirer (2012, ix), gives a good and balanced summary of the arguments for and against Park, trying to account for the origins of his manifest flaws.

12. Park Chung Hee historiography continues to grow. In the first of a projected two-part history of Park and his era, Carter Eckert (2016) traces the roots of militarism and the dictatorship to Park's background in Japanese Manchuria. Also relevant to this story are various chapters in Byung-kook and Vogel (2011); see also Lee Chong-sik (2012).

13. Cho Kapche (1998), cited in Ch'oe Yong-ho et al. (2000).

14. Woo Jung-en (1991, 44) has characterized Rhee's Korea as "a 'client' state, led nevertheless by a recalcitrant, putative nationalist . . . autocracy commingled with party politics and semifascist mobilization, thriving on a system-wide corruption." Cumings (2005, 305) adds that Kim Il-sung similarly milked the Soviet Union in the 1950s.

15. On the five-year plans and their context generally, see Hemmert (2012, 20, 28–29). For Park's own take on his planning and rationale for dictatorial rule, see Park Chung-hee (1970; 1971).

16. "Korea's experience with the First Five-Year Economic Development Plan," paper for the International Conference on the Problems of Modernization, sponsored by Asiatic Research Center, Korea University, Seoul, 28 June to 7 July, 1965, http://www.dwnam.pe.kr, accessed 7 July 2011.

17. Daewoo and Hanbo collapsed in the 1997 Asian economic crisis. An outline of the *chaebol,* their stimulation under Rhee, and their surging under Park, is in Hemmert (2012); for a brief discussion, see Cumings (2005, 327–331).

18. Hemmert (2012) provides an introduction to the story of Samsung.

19. The rise of Samsung can be contrasted with that of its Japanese competitors Sony, Matsushita, Toshiba, and so on. The mainstream view is that all rode on a government-sponsored, export-led growth policy; however, Simon Partner (2000) argues that in the Japanese cases the driver was an explosion in domestic consumer demand.

20. Posco (Pohang Iron and Steel Company) was inaugurated in 1968 as a joint venture between the Korean government and TaeguTec, beginning production in 1972. The Japanese financing followed the 1969 Third South Korea-Japan Ministerial Meeting.

21. There were also large-scale urban developments elsewhere that fundamentally changed the urban structure of Seoul: in Jamsil, Mokdong, Godeok, Gwacheon, Sanggye-dong, and so on.

22. "South Korea—The Government Role in Economic Development," US Library of Congress, http://countrystudies.us, accessed 7 July 2011.

23. "What to Do with the Chaebol?," *Korea Times,* 30 March 2012, http://www.koreatimes.co.kr, accessed 30 March 2012.

24. For a different approach to the Japanese political economy, with a focus on representation and accountability that also bears on the comparison with Korea, see Kabashima and Steel (2010); see also Kingston ([2001] 2014) on the post-1945 transformation. For a more broadly comparative study, see Wan Ming (2007). Also see Rosenbluth and Thies (2010) on more recent restructuring; and Neary

(2002) on the longer view. A further useful source is *Japanese Journal of Political Science.*

25. This understanding of "the aesthetic" relates to that implied in Immanuel Kant's third critique, the *Critique of Judgment* (Kant 2007), and even more to its development by Jürgen Habermas. See Habermas (1973); see also King (1996, 224–225). For more on Kant, see Doran (2015).

26. The reference to grafting links to the arguments of Jacques Derrida on grafting and montage, to be addressed in chapter 4. See Derrida (1981); and Ulmer (1985, 88).

27. Park Sang Mi (2010) cites *Munhwa kongbo 30 nyon* [Thirty Years of Culture and Public Information] (Seoul: Munhwa Kongbobu, 1979, 224, 226).

28. On broader issues of gender, sexuality, and labor relations in modern Korea and Japan, see Moon Seungsook (2005); Barraclough and Faison (2009); and Kyung Moon Hwang (2010, 274–277).

29. On the shift from the democracy movement to the burgeoning civil society, see various chapters in Shin Gi-Wook and Paul Chang (2011).

30. Cumings (2005, 380) argues that this was to be seen more as a mutiny within the military by Chun and his close friend Roh Tae Woo, both from the 1955 class of the Korean Military Academy.

31. For more on the Gwangju uprising, see Lee Jae Eui (1999); and Gi Wook Shin and Kyung Moon Hwang (2003).

32. In the face of the June Democracy Movement and the looming specter of the national disgrace of losing the Olympics, Chun and Roh gambled, correctly, that Roh could win in competitive elections anyway, in the absence of a well-organized opposition. Although Roh won in December, the effect was that the shift to democracy had become unstoppable.

33. On the minutiae of Gwangju, see Katsiaficas (2012).

34. The belated acknowledgment of Gwangju can be seen in part as a response to "the second Gwangju," a brutal and illegal attack by police on unionists at a Daewoo plant in Bupyeong (Incheon) in April 2001 (Kwon Jong Bum 2011).

35. On assessing Park, see Kim Hyung-A (2004); also see various papers in Kim Hyung-A and Sorenson (2011).

36. See, for example, Bell (2004); Ahn Sang Jin (2001); Song Changzoo (1999); Yang Sung Chul (1999); and Kang Wi Jo (1968).

37. Admiral Yi had, paradoxically, been popular during the colonial period, for example, in a historical naval series, *Yi Sun Sin,* by Yi Kwang-su in the *Dong a Ilbo,* 1931–1932. Yet here was stressed not so much anti-Japanese victory as the story of a principled man wrongly accused by jealous Korean associates (Kal Hong 2011, 135n2).

38. The debates over demolition or retention of the Government-General Building stretched over some forty years. See Jin Jong-Heon (2008); Henry (2014, 210–217). Henry in particular refers to Bae Changmii (2002).

39. Independence Hall of Korea, in the small southern city of Chonan and opened in 1987, was a major cultural project of President Chun Doo-hwan to capitalize on mounting anti-Japanese sentiment in the 1980s and thereby to add legitimacy to his own dictatorship (Kal Hong 2011, 101; Jung Inha 2013, 84).

40. There are numerous media reports of this event. See, for example, "Fire Ravages South Korea Landmark," BBC News, last updated 11 February 2008, http://news.bbc.co.uk, accessed 5 November 2015.

41. Equally significant, in 1938 the gate had been designated Korean treasure number one by the (Japanese) Government-General of Korea.

42. Chung J. Young, pers. comm., 10 March 2006.

43. It is noteworthy that the present information stele on the 1926 Dong-A Ilbo declares that it is an example of early Korean modernism: it "echoes the Korean

architectural trends of the 1920s" (observed 12 April 2012). There are similar, postcolonial claims for other constructions of the colonial age.

44. Among the extensive literature on Korean modernization, see, for example, Amsden (1989); Kim Hyuk-Rae (1998; 2000); and Uk and Roehrig (2010).

45. Jung Inha (2013, 53–54); also "Seoul Urban Planning and Structure," Macalester. edu, http://www.macalester.edu, accessed 12 July 2012.

46. Repeated in Seoul Metropolitan Government (2014), "The 2030 Seoul Plan," http://english.seoul.go.kr, accessed 17 July 2015.

47. An extensive presentation and discussion of the 2006 Seoul Master Plan (for target year 2020) is *Urban Planning of Seoul* (2009). This also provides both an outline of the city's history and development, and a history of its planning.

48. The nominated regional centers were Yongsan (to "absorb higher-level business function including international affairs"), Sangam-Susaek in the northwest, Magok and Gasan-Daerim in the southwest (the former for "knowledge-based industry," with bioindustry mentioned, the latter for "creative knowledge-based employment"), Cheongnyangni-Wangsimni and Changdong-Sanggye in the northeast, and Jamsil in the southeast (the last to "interface with Gangnam"). For the 2030 Seoul Plan, see "2030 Seoul Plan," LinkedIn SlideShare, 27 May 2014, http://www.slideshare.net, 41–42, accessed 17 July 2015.

49. Specifically, Magok would link to Incheon, Gasan-Daerim (now Gasan Digital Complex) to Suwon, Jamsil to Sungnam, Cheongnyangni-Wangsimni via Changdong-Sanggye to Dongducheon, and Sangnam-Susaek (now Digital Media City) to Paju. "2030 Seoul Plan," 43–44.

50. For tram views of Asia, see "Korea," Tramz.com, http://www.tramz.com, accessed 25 March 2012.

51. On the massive technological challenge confronting the metro system, see Kim Seung-Ryull (2008).

52. On metro and subway systems, see "The World's Longest Metro and Subway Systems," railway-technology.com, http://www.railway-technology.com, accessed 5 November 2015.

53. The Seoul Development Institute had originally been set up in 1971 as an autonomous think tank of the South Korean government with a social science focus. Since 1997 it has conducted the KDI (Korea Development Institute) School, now linked to the educational programs of the World Bank. See Korea Development Institute, OECD.org, http://www.oecd.org, accessed 14 July 2012.

54. On the 1928 plan and Japanese land adjustment planning generally, see Jung Inha (2013, 14, 18–19).

55. Todd Henry specifically cites *Keijo toshi keikaku chosasho* 1928, 251–252, 270–271).

56. Gelézeau argues that a "difficulty" with the new, functional, LDK (Living-Dining-Kitchen) model was that it replaced the traditional, polyfunctional, and gender-differentiated space of the *hanok*. However, the specificity of the Korean housing culture is retained through the reformulation of specific aspects of the *hanok*, such as the courtyard. On the *hanok*, see Park Nani and Pouser (2015).

57. Also see Gelézeau (2001; 2011). An excellent English review of Gelézeau's 2003 book is James E. Hoare, *Korean Studies Review*, no. 4 (2004), http://koreanstudies .com, accessed 1 October 2013.

58. "Property Investment Index by Country for 2011": South Korea's, at 1.39, was equal lowest with Taiwan's. Source http://.numbeo.com, accessed 24 June 20011. It is not clear, however, if part of this low yield is to be explained by peculiarities of the Korean *chonse* deposit system for rental property.

59. However, at least in upmarket Corbusian-style estates such as Chamwon-dong (chapter 4), even the English garden idea will be seized on, albeit translated into a more Scandinavian-style forest walk.

60. In Korea today there is a national temple-stay program, initially devised by the Korean Cultural Office as a way for foreigners coming to the 2002 FIFA World Cup to gain experience of Korean culture and Buddhism (Zitwer 2012).

61. For an extended recent discussion of present Seoul slums, see Mike Stulberg (Chincha), "On Seoul's Guryong Slum and Pushing Poverty under the Carpet," 15 July 2013, http://chincha.co.uk, accessed 2 October 2013. See also Agence France-Presse, "Seoul Slum Life in the Shadow of 'Gangnam Style,' " 22 October 2012, http://www.rappler.com; and, for a more extended analysis, Agence France-Presse, "Seoul's Poverty Lingers in the Shadows of Gangnam-style Prosperity," 23 October 2012, http://www.scmp.com, both accessed 2 October 2013.

62. "Slum Eviction: Jaegeon Community in Seoul, S. Korea," YouTube, 13 August, 2011, http://www.youtube.com, accessed 2 October 2013.

63. For a photo-essay on the slums of Seoul, derived mostly from various blogs, see Hannah Bell, "Some Pictures of Daily Life in South Korea," 1 June 2011, http://www.democraticunderground.com, accessed 2 October 2013.

64. "South Korea Slum Revamped with Arts," 17 March 2013, YouTube, http://www.youtube.com, accessed 2 October 2013.

65. Estimates relate to administrative divisions. The 2010 census counts, which are restricted to administrative city limits, can vary slightly from these estimates. Even more at variance is the count for the Seoul National Capital Area, over 25.6 million in 2012.

66. For example, the Government-General's nomination of specific buildings and artifacts as Korean Treasures, with Namdaemun heading the list. *Chosun Ilbo Japan* (in Japanese), 28 November 2005.

67. On Kim Chung-up (Kim Joong-eop), see Ahn Byung Ui (1988); and Jung Inha (2013, 85–88).

68. Many of the observations following derive from an exceptional review of Kim Swoo Geun's work, based in part on the retrospective exhibition of his work, at Culture Station 284 (Seoul Station). See especially http://www.hancinema.net, accessed 10 May 2012.

69. On Freedom Center (1964), see http://www.rjkoehler.com, accessed 5 July 2015.

70. These notes on the Asian People's Anti-Communist League Center are based on material in the exhibition of Kim Swoo Geun's work and ideas in the (Japanese era) Seoul Station Building in April 2012, viewed 18 April 2012. The following comments on Kim's work are also in part based on observations from this exhibition.

71. Exhibition panel, Seoul Station, viewed 18 April 2012.

72. Exhibition panel, Seoul Station, viewed 18 April 2012.

73. Arko Center home page quoted in http://www.rjkoehler.com, accessed 5 July 2015.

74. Takayama (b. 1910) founded the Department of Urban Engineering at the University of Tokyo, the first academic program in city planning in Japan; he is seen as a foundation figure in research-based planning in Japan. Kim had attended the Takayama Eika Research Center in 1958–1960.

75. See, for example, http://www.actakoreana.org, accessed 3 April 2007.

76. Also significant in the Japanese architectural resurgence were Kiyonori Kikutake (1928–2011) and Kisho Kurakawa (1934–2007). Toyo Ito (b. 1941) and Itsuko Hasegawa (b. 1941) were ten years younger.

77. On diverse aspects of Catholic history in Korea, see various papers in Yu Chai-shin (2004).

78. On Korean Christianity under Japanese colonization, see Choi Jai-Keum (2007).

79. On *minjung*, see Wells (1995); also Larsen (2008).

80. Comment on exhibition panel, Seoul Station, viewed 18 April 2012.

81. However, Donald Clark (2007, 185) cites a more conservative ninety-six Protestant denominations, fifty-nine of them being Presbyterian. Another source lists over one hundred Presbyterian denominations; see "Overview of the Worldwide

Reformed Church," Reformed Online, http://www.reformiert-online.net, accessed 17 September 2012. The uncertainty relates to the difficulty in deciding what degree of difference or disagreement constitutes a real division and hence a distinctive denomination.

82. In an empirical study of social groups participating in protest events in 1970–1992, Christians were the third most numerous (409 events, following 1,116 for students and 714 for laborers—and presumably there were also Christians among the student and laborer protesters) (Shin Gi-Wook et al. 2011, 23).

83. The "French" attribution to Catholicism in part relates to the role of the Paris Foreign Missions Society, whose priests arrived in Korea in 1836 to augment (control?) the indigenous priesthood.

84. For the "authorized" account, see Rev. & Mrs. Moon, "Who Is Reverend Moon?," Unification.org, http://unification.org, accessed 9 September 2012.

85. American sociologist Irving Horowitz (1980, xiii–xiv) has compared the attraction of Unification theology for young Americans in that era to the attraction of hippy and radical movements of the 1960s and 1970s.

86. For further takes on shamanism, see various essays in Yu Chai-shin and Guisso (1988).

87. Korea's recovery from the disgrace of the 1997 financial collapse was dramatic. Korea was required to repay its US$19.5 billion by May 2004 but made its final repayment in August 2001 (Rhee So-eui and Roger Yu 2001).

CHAPTER 4: ERASURE AS HERITAGE

1. This observation is akin to Jean-François Lyotard's (1984) identification of the eschewing of metanarratives as the hallmark of "the postmodern condition." In considering "the urban condition," Michael Dear (2000) translated Lyotard's argument into the intellectual realm of urban space, questioning the validity of the idea of "the city" as concept or metanarrative in the present age. Instead, Dear writes of the city as a collection of places in a space of "Keno capitalism," also of the "power of place" as the real concern of late modernist geography. While the present argument also rejects the possibility of some metanarrative to account for the city (there is no overall structure that can explain the myriad places that constitute Seoul), it will invoke assemblage theory to account for how these places form and transform, also constantly come together yet fly apart in a world of immanence and becoming. For another perspective on this phenomenon, Jameson (1991).

2. A number of papers in *Korea Journal* 47, no. 4, in 2007, approached the theme of Seoul as a patchwork of ethnic communities. See also Kim Eun Mee (2008).

3. I have previously developed the following argument in King (1996).

4. "Touristic" Seoul brings its own ambiguities: while Seoul does not present as a focus for global tourism, in 2014 it ranked tenth among global destination cities for international visitors, and sixth for visitor spending (Hendrick-Wong and Choong 2014).

5. Sir John McLeavy Brown was a lawyer in the British Customs Service, based in Canton and subsequently in Seoul to manage the Korean Customs Department. King Kojong in 1893 offered him a position as financial advisor and chief commissioner of customs. Upon the murder of Queen Min in 1895, the king fled but first handed absolute control over the Treasury to McLeavy Brown (*New York Times*, 31 August 1905).

6. The actual declaration was at the Taehwagwan Restaurant, out of fear that a declaration at the park could lead to a riot.

7. It is also symbolic of the continuing, wary glance to Japan: Jongno Tower is not Japanese in its referencing, yet architect colleagues shortly after its

1999 completion would darkly comment to me that "it's Japanese, you know"—
therefore presumably invalid as a Korean icon.

8. A site of some ambiguity: the store's reviled collaborator-entrepreneur in the
Japanese era was referred to in chapter 2.

9. Historical Seoul had always been a city of markets, marked by informal assemblage. In the specific case of Jongno, a night market had been established there in
1916 as an initiative of the Korean community following the 1915 Korean Industrial Exposition (Henry 2014, 112). This set the pattern of formal and informal
market juxtapositions that characterizes much of present Seoul commercial
space.

10. Where *bang* signifies a room, *norae* carries the meaning "singing your way to
success"; the "singing rooms," *norae bang,* therefore carry a certain ambiguity
(De Mente 2012, viii). I acknowledge my indebtedness to Jorge Almazan for
drawing my attention to the full significance of the rise of the *bang.* Jorge
Almazan, pers. comm., 23 November 2009.

11. On the *bang* and their derivation, see Song Do-Young (1998); Huhh Jun-Sok
(2008); and Oh Myung and Larson (2011, 145–146).

12. Yi Whan-woo, *Korea Times,* 4 April 2012.

13. On the role of the PC *bang,* see Kang Inkyu (2014).

14. *Soju* is a distilled beverage, akin to vodka, indigenous to Korea. A 2002 study
ranked it number one in global sale records of the diluted alcohol market;
see Han Joonhye, "Korean Soju," *TED Case Studies,* no. 756 (2004), http://www1
.american.edu, accessed 6 November 2015.

15. The origins of Chinese *manhua* "comics" can be traced back at least to the Ming
dynasty and, in their present satirical form, to Chinese newspapers of the 1870s
and to Shanghai picture books in the 1920s. Sun Yat-Sen established the Republic of China in 1911 using Hong Kong *manhua* to circulate anti-Qing propaganda. There has long been a subversive dimension to the *manhua,* albeit mostly
subliminal in recent times; similar undertones can be sought in much of the
Korean *manhwa.*

16. Unhyeongung, strictly speaking a royal residence rather than a palace, was the
residence of the Daewongun (1820–1898), the father of King Kojong. He was
regent during Kojong's minority and effective ruler of Chosun thereafter.
The residence shares much of the controversy and ambiguity that still attaches to
the Daewongun.

17. On Ssamzie, see "Company Introduction," EC21, http://ssamzie.en.ec21.com,
accessed 19 May 2011.

18. The genesis of both markets is traced by Lee Ki-baik (1984, 230).

19. SK Group is the third largest of Korea's *chaebols,* comprising ninety-two subsidiary and affiliate companies. While its business is mainly based in the chemical,
petroleum, and energy industries, it also provides services in construction, ship-
ping, marketing, and information technology. Like other *chaebols,* SK is a monarchy: its chairmanship is inherited from father to son, from its founder, the late
Chey John-hyun, to the eldest son, Chey Tae-won, who is married to the daughter of former president, Roh Tae-woo.

20. Samil (Sam-Il) refers to the March First Movement, hence Korean "self determination" and the Declaration of Independence. Also on the Cheonggyecheon, see
Kal Hong (2011, chapter 6).

21. The antirestoration debate can be seen in the context of two others: first, the
wider debate on retention of more immediate history versus restoration of an
imagined past that had especially raged around the demolition of the Jungang-cheong (chapter 3); and second, the debate over retention of existing,
vibrant communities that lined the Cheonggyecheon and on which Seoul's creativity was said to partly rest (Ryu Jeh-hong 2004).

22. In *K-pop: Popular Music, Cultural Amnesia, and Economic Innovation in South Korea,* John Lie notes that, in transforming Cheonggyecheon, Lee Myung-bak also obliterated the concatenation of used-book sellers and secondhand music dealers for the second time; the first had been with its paving in the 1960s. A slice of Korean history was thereby finally consigned to oblivion (Lie 2014, 6).

23. For further references in this debate, see Kal Hong (2011, 144–145n3).

24. The overriding rhetoric of this intended makeover relates to Seoul's 2010 designation as "World Design Capital" by the International Council of Societies of Industrial Design. It is in part the context in which Cheonggyecheon Cultural Plaza is to be read.

25. See "Shaping Change—Strategies of Development and Transformation," on the Bertelsmann Transformation Index: http://www.bertelsmann-transformation -index.de, accessed 30 July 2011; on the determinants of the Korean informal economy, Joo Donghun (2011).

26. From the extensive literature on Korean prostitutes and the US military, see Moon Seungsook (2010); and Höhn (2010).

27. In the face of strident opposition to the American presence in Korea, the garrison is (in the 2010s) being progressively moved south, out of the inner city, albeit very slowly.

28. It is worth noting that the Korea Tourism Organization describes Itaewon as "a unique place where one can meet people of diverse nationalities and cultures" as well as Seoul's first designated "Special Tourism District," and extols its "diversity of culture, shopping and entertainment experiences"; Korea Tourism Organization, "Itaewon," http://www.visitkorea.or.kr, accessed 26 January 2010. The blogs, on the other hand, stress the venality.

29. Cheil Worldwide is a global marketing and communications company and Korea's largest advertising agency. Its forerunner, Cheil Jedang (a sugar company), was founded in the 1950s by Lee Byung-chull (1910–1987), who had previously, in 1938, founded Samsung (chapter 2). Cheil is now a subsidiary of Samsung.

30. "New Master Plan for Yongsan Business Hub Unveiled," *Chosun Ilbo,* 17 December 2011, http://english.chosun.com, accessed 17 December 2011.

31. "Yongsan Apartment Design 'Conjures Images of 9/11,'" *Chosun Ilbo,* 12 December 2011, http://english.chosun.com, accessed 17 December 2011.

32. If one is to focus on avant-garde artistic production, Beijing would be seen as being ahead of Seoul. See Wu Hung (2005).

33. The spread of the Seoul Art Space program across the space of the city is well suggested in the map "Arts Space of SFAC," http://english.sfac.or.kr, accessed 29 July 2015.

34. "Seoul Art Space Geumcheon," Transit Artists, http://www.transartists.org, accessed 28 July 2015. Seoul Art Space Geumcheon is linked with the Dutch program, TransArtists.

35. The label "Gangnam" here is used somewhat broadly. The term "Gangnam area" commonly refers to the southern region of the Han River. When urban development began in the 1960s, the area was called the Yeongdong District, or "east of Yeongdeungpo," and comprised four wards, of which Gangnam was one. In 1975 Seoul City named the area Gangnam-gu. In 1979 Songpa-gu and Gangdong-gu were separated from Gangnam-gu, then in 1988 Seocho-gu was similarly separated off. So Banpo might be in the greater Gangnam area, but not in Gangnam-gu.

36. The Corbusian "perfection" of the estate cannot be overemphasized. In his plan for Ville contemporaine for three million people (1922), Le Corbusier stressed the importance of a pedestrian world separated from vehicular traffic, passing through a richly landscaped ground that provides a setting for recreation of all kinds as well as for schools, restaurants, cafés, clubs, and youth centers. It is in

Seoul that the dream seems finally to have been achieved. In this particular fragment, however, it is disturbing that the "richly landscaped" pedestrian world is right beneath the immensity of Highway 1, and that one needs to pass under Highway 1 to access the "restaurants, cafés, clubs" segregated from the Corbusian purity of identical towers and green paths. See *Le Corbusier et Pierre Jeanneret* (1935); and King (1996, 51–54).

37. "Gang Nam Seoul, South Korea," GlobalPhotos.org, http://www.globalphotos.org, accessed 12 July 2011.

38. The principal advocates of this myth, alleges Thrift, are Harvey (1989); and Virilio (1993).

39. For an extended exploration of such issues, see W. Mitchell (1995).

40. I have previously documented a similar, also distanced juxtaposition of formal-corporate and informal-entrepreneurial realms in Cyberjaya vis-à-vis Kuala Lumpur, in the case of Malaysia (King 2008).

41. "Seoul's New Solar-powered GT Tower Boasts a Mind-bending Wavy Façade," Inhabitant.com, http://inhabitat.com, accessed 30 April 2012.

42. On Seorae and its distinctive French character, see Lee Seung-ah, "French Town in Seoul Exudes Exotic Beauty," http://www.korea.net, accessed 29 July 2015.

43. Dobongsan is a three-peaked mountain in Bukhansan National Park; the station is named for it. The walking trail to its peak (at 740 meters) brings its own confrontation with the relics of obliteration: bunkers from the Korean War. It also presents Cheonchuksa Temple, the oldest in the region, and several other temples.

44. Dongducheon, like Dobongsan, also presents as a space of (potential) annihilation: it is close to the DMZ and houses the main camps of the US Second Infantry Division. However, the city also presents as emblematic of Koreans' resentment toward the US presence, as it has long been embroiled in the conflict over US retention of its bases (Rowland and Yoo Kyong Chang 2015).

45. Home Plus is a South Korean / British discount store retail chain jointly owned by Samsung and Tesco. It is the second-largest retailer in Korea, just behind Shinsegae Group, which was also previously linked to Samsung.

46. This information is from the attribution board at the shrine, placed by the Lee clan and the city of Incheon, observed 16 April 2012. It is also summarized in "Woninjae, Incheon Yeonsu-gu: The Official Mansion of Incheon Lee Lineage," Moe Girls' Korean Story, blog, http://moe-hankook.blogspot.com.au, accessed 30 July 2015.

47. The majority stake is held by Gale International, with 61 percent; Posco with 30 percent; and Morgan Stanley Real Estate with 9 percent.

48. A no-doubt bitter irony is that it will *not* be Korea's tallest building: that is the unfinished ghost of the trouble-plagued Ryugyong Hotel in Pyongyang, North Korea. Furthermore, even in South Korea, it would be exceeded by two projects in the Yongsan Business Hub—if they are ever implemented.

49. See Songdo IBD's home page, http://www.songdo.com, accessed 20 May 2011.

50. The Incheon City government had established a master plan for Songdo New City in 1992 at the time when five new towns were also being planned for Seoul. In 1997 Incheon City invited three architectural firms to submit proposals for a new master plan. From this process Rem Koolhaas' Office for Metropolitan Architecture was chosen. The Koolhaas proposal was truly revolutionary in a Korean context: there would be seven programmatic "bands"—business, media, university, culture, commercial, leisure, research—that would intersect but also leave a space of voids whose uses would evolve with the passage of time and ideas (see, for example, Jung Inha 2013, 128–129). This was abandoned, as the city wanted immediate success rather than evolution. Hence the turn to Gale International and KPF.

51. "New Songdo city: Atlantis of the Far East," *Independent,* 22 June 2009, http://www.independent.co.uk, accessed 20 May 2011.
52. Also on New Songdo as a city without people, see Arbes and Bethea (2014).
53. "Hello Kitty" is another instance of Japanese neocolonization, as an aspect of Japanese *kawaii* ("cuteness") culture targeting preadolescent females. Hello Kitty was introduced in Japan in 1975, created by Yuko Shimizu and produced by Japanese company Sanrio. The image and its products run like a rhizome through Korean urban space.
54. Kim Donyun, pers. comm., 27 August 2015.
55. Paju is the bleak, desolate urban setting for Park Chan-ok's 2009 film of that name. The much acclaimed film *Paju,* part of the Korean Wave (chapter 5), explores the political tensions around the North-South divide, the present gentrification of Korean cities, and the violence of development. Park described that, to her, Paju is always foggy and the urban expression of mystery (Park Sunyoung 2009).
56. See "Paju Book City 1," Davey Dreamnation, blog, 25 February 2011, http://daveydreamnation.com, accessed 15 June 2011.
57. The sort of urban elegance expressed through small-scale boxlike forms and found in Insadong, Paju Book City, and Heyri Art Valley (to follow), held up as a mirror to back-street, boxland Seoul, was also finely displayed in the photo exhibition of new architecture, "S(E)OUL SCAPE: Towards a new urbanity in Korea," in Florence and Barcelona in 2008. See http://www.arqchile.cl, accessed 31 May 2012.
58. Yi Ki-Ung, "City to Recover the Lost Humanity," http://www.pajubookcity.org, accessed 4 May 2012.
59. For a fine collection of images of Heyri Art Village as both theme park and fun park, see http://pilgrimwithapassport.blogspot.com, accessed 12 July 2016.
60. There is a substantial literature detailing the failure of Seoul's various new town projects; for example, see Ha Seong-Kyu (1998); Berg (2012); Jun Myung-Jin (2012); and Lee Sang Keon et al. (2015). The last of these gives a good history and assessment of Korea's various essays in new town development. The program's abandonment was announced in January 2012.
61. There is a certain temptation to impose a structuralist-Marxist ontology and critique on the first of these Deleuzean dimensions, seeing the expressive end of the axis as merely referencing the superstructure, thence to subsume assemblage thinking into critical political economy (also see McFarlane 2011, the response from Brenner et al. 2011, and the counterresponse of Dovey 2011). Instead, Deleuze seeks a distinctively different ontology, of the *becoming* of things rather than their *being;* so to see things as assemblages is to ask how are they constantly coming about, how are they working, how are they constantly becoming something else?
62. Assemblage theory is close to but not coincident with Actor Network Theory (Latour 2005; Farías and Bender 2010); it shares with ANT a preoccupation with the microscale, microeconomic, and microspatial. So the difference with structuralist-Marxist thinking is in part one of scale—the walker in the street rather than the visionary from on high (de Certeau 1984, 92–93).
63. Multiplicity also manifests in time or duration: "The other type of multiplicity appears in pure duration: It is an internal multiplicity of succession, of fusion, of organization, of heterogeneity, of qualitative discrimination, or of *difference in kind;* it is a *virtual continuous* multiplicity that cannot be reduced to numbers" (Deleuze 1988, 38). Identity shifts across various scales of duration—it is multiple (*we* are multiple). For Deleuze, assemblage thinking is part of a much broader philosophical endeavor, namely to think a radically new ontology to do with possibilities—*How might one live?* (May 2005; Boundas 2010). "The concern is

with multiplicities, possibilities, difference. . . . If things don't have strict borders of identity and if the relations among them are not reducible to natural laws, then we can no longer be sure of what a body [a city] is capable. Perhaps there is more going on in our world than is presented to us" (May 2005, 72).

64. My understanding of the ethnic minorities of Seoul and their communities (as assemblage) has been greatly assisted by discussions at the University of Melbourne with Choi Sung Jun.

CHAPTER 5: NEW CULTURE

Epigraph: Lie 2014, 166–167n1.

1. While Marx theorized the processes of accumulation and annihilation of wealth under capitalism, the "gale of creative destruction" is mostly identified with Austrian American economist Joseph Schumpeter. The notion has run through previous chapters and, following Lie (2014), will be applied in the present chapter in the field of popular culture. Also on applications in the social sciences, see Berman (1988).

2. Oh Myung held a pivotal role in the development of Korea's ICT sector as vice minister and minister of the Ministry of Information and Communication, and later as deputy prime minister. On the Oh and Larson text, see Kim Sung-Young (2014).

3. A source on broadband penetration is the annual "OECD broadband statistics update." The 2009 survey found that, with 95 percent of homes having full broadband (voice and data), South Korea ranked number one, followed by Singapore (88 percent), the Netherlands (85), Denmark (82), and Taiwan and Hong Kong (both 81). The 1917 survey revealed Korea as still being number one (109 percent), although when data-only subscriptions are added in, Japan was number one. Korea's highly urbanized population and its government's vigorous e-economy policy are to be seen as determining factors. "OECD broadband statistics update," www.oecd.org/sti/broadband/broadband-statistics-update.htm, accessed 28 April 2017.

4. "Tech Capitals of the World," *Age* (Melbourne), 18 June 2007, http://www.theage.com.au, accessed 25 June 2011.

5. "South Korea: Wifi All Over Capital," *Age* (Melbourne), 16 June 2011, 12. This and other items attributed to the *Age* were displayed in many newspapers globally; my reading of them, however, was from the *Age.*

6. The term "new ubiquitous city," for New Songdo, is used by Oh Myung and Larson (2011: 120–123).

7. The Korean Creative Content Agency (KOCCA) is an agency of the Korean government established in 2009 to support the growth of the cultural industry. It brought together a number of separate agencies previously focusing on specific creative sectors.

8. An account of architect Kim Tai Soo and the design process for the National Museum of Contemporary Art is Jung Inha (2013, 116–118).

9. Although *TV Buddha* was replicated many times in Paik's exhibitions, thereby demonstrating Baudrillard's (1994b) idea of the simulacrum, its first presentation would seem to have been in 1974. Also see "Nam June Paik 'TV-Buddha,'" Media Art Net, http://www.medienkunstnetz.de, accessed 14 August 2015.

10. "Famous Video Artist Nam June Paik Dies at 74," *Pravda,* 30 January 2006, http://newsfromrussia.com, accessed 30 March 1007.

11. Paik's own description of his program: "Marcel Duchamp achieved everything in every field except for video art. He created a large entrance and an extremely small exit. The small exit is video art. When we take the exit, we are out of the scope of influence of Marcel Duchamp." Paik's "exit" from Duchamp's aesthetic

world was by "combining electronic music and happenings." Korea Tourism Organization, "Gyeonggi-do—Yongin-si—NJP Art Centre," http://english .visitkorea.or.kr, accessed 14 August 2015.

12. Paik is generally attributed with coining the term "information superhighway"; subsequently, in 1974, he used the slightly different term "electronic super high-way" (Paik Nam June, 1974).

13. See "NJP ArtCenter," http://njpac-en.ggcf.kr, accessed 14 August 2015.

14. "Gyeonggi-do—Yongin-si—NJP Art Centre."

15. See http://www.saic.edu; see also School of the Art Institute, "News from Nowhere: Chicago Laboratory, Moon Kyungwon and Jeon Joonho, 2013," 2014, http://vimeo.com, accessed 26 October 2013.

16. "Hallyu (Korean Wave)," Korea.net, http://www.korea.net, accessed 2 August 2015.

17. On Back's *Blow Up* series in particular, see Lee Sohl (2014).

18. The installation is also based on Shostakovich's satirical opera *The Nose*, which also derives from Gogol and which Kentridge directed at New York's Metropolitan Opera.

19. Kern and Nam Sang-hui (2011, 178) observe that Korea's extraordinarily active citizen journalism movement was especially enabled by the move from narrow band to broadband Internet, which had been a singular policy of the Kim Dae-jung government; also see Oh Myung and Larson (2011, 66).

20. *StarIn Tech* was a Monday section of the *Star* daily tabloid newspaper, Malaysia. It has subsequently been renamed *StarBytz*.

21. On Korean cinema and its evolution generally, see Lee Hyangjin (2001); James and Kim (2001); Min Eung-jin et al. (2003); Kim Kyung Hyun (2004); and Shin Chi-Yun and Stringer (2005). More recent is the volume edited by Kim Do Kyun and Kim Min-Sun (2011).

22. Atkins recounts how "Arirang," a song associated with the film and "oozing with indignation towards Japanese," became a "huge hit in Japan" (Atkins 2010, 2).

23. Chung Chonghwa (2012) provides a finely detailed account of the emergence of the Korean film industry during colonial rule, in particular criticizing the staunch right-wing historiography that would deny any creative effect of the need for Korean filmmakers to negotiate with the hegemonic Japanese.

24. Theodore Hughes (2014) has argued that this early Cold War era cinema in Korea was in many ways a continuation of the war-interrupted cultural production of the colonial era. On film and fashion cultures in the 1950s, see Steven Chung (2014b).

25. Kim Byeongcheol's paper is part of a special issue of *Korea Journal* on contemporary Korean cinema.

26. Also on the "Golden Age," Kelly Jeong (2014) draws attention to the actor Kim Sung-ho as the "patriarch" of that time.

27. On such transcultural (transnational) "genre flows," see Chung Hye Seung and Diffrient (2015).

28. An extensive and wide-ranging debate on Moon's article can be followed on the blog Korean Cinema, 29 July 2009, http://kcinemaclass.blogspot.com, accessed 9 July 2011.

29. Kim Kyung Hyun has written further on Korean cinema especially in relation to the Korean Wave in Kim Kyung Hyun (2011a). With Choe Youngmin, Kim has also edited *The Korean Popular Culture Reader* (Kim Kyung Hyun and Choe Youngmin 2014).

30. Lee and Choe (1998) is especially valuable for presenting Korean cinema work chronologically through to the late 1980s. The early periods are covered in detail, together with the melodramas of the 1950s and 1960s, as well as the artistic extravaganzas of the late 1970s and early 1980s.

31. Ironic imagination is akin to the notion of dialectic image introduced in chapter 4.

32. The source of the story for *Sassy Girl* was the ancient and subversive *pansori* (song drama) *Chunhyangga* (Song of Chunhyang); see chapter 2.

33. On the New Wave Korean cinema generally, see Gateward (2007); and Choi Jin-hee (2010). Choi in particular stresses the role of corporate and venture capital support in enabling the renaissance since around 1999. Similarly, Choe Young-min (2014, ix–x) points to the 1997 financial crisis and the IMF's consequent advocacy of cultural liberalization policies that were implemented in 1998. Also in the context of the New Wave, one needs to consider the persisting theme of what Daniel Martin (2014) calls "South Korean cinema's postwar pain," the continuing thread of gender and national division in films stretching from the 1950s to the 2000s.

34. Stephanie Bunbury, "Revealing the Seoul of desperate housemaids," *Age* (Melbourne), 19 July 2010, 18.

35. On both the market and the critical impacts of *The Host,* see Jin Dal Yong (2013).

36. Bong Joon-ho (2011).

37. Naksan, the "Left Blue Dragon" of Seoul's sacred, geomantic topography, had in fact been mined (obliterated) during the Japanese colonial period in the sense referred to by Bong.

38. Also on Bong Joon-ho, particularly his fourth feature, *Mother* of 2009, see Michelle Cho (2014).

39. The 2002 Nanji Waste Dump Rehabilitation provided for both the World Cup Park and Digital Media City (Kim Dongyun 2015).

40. The Bulwongcheon reconstruction preceded the Cheonggyecheon reconstruction and is reported to have been used to develop the techniques and technologies then adopted for the latter; likewise approaches used in the development of Digital Media City are reported to have been subsequently adopted in aspects of New Songdo (Kim Donyun, pers. comm., 27 August 2015).

41. Landscape architects Park Yoonjin and Kim Jungyoon, practicing under the name PARKKIM, have since 2004 provided various significant examples, both as constructed and as competition entries, of landscape projects to reflect on Korean urban landscapes. The aesthetic is decidedly deconstructive (ironic) rather than nostalgic (melodramatic).

42. See D. Mitchell (2004); on the book's translation to cinema, see D. Mitchell (2012).

43. The film was directed by Lana and Andy Wachowski and Tom Tykwer, and featured American and Korean actors. On the film's graphics, see Anders (2012).

44. For this comment comparing Neo-Seoul with *Blade Runner,* see critic "false-prophet" in Anders (2012).

45. Thanatourism, or "dark tourism," refers to tourism to places of death, danger, and disaster—where murders, wars, battles, and atrocities have occurred. The DMZ is a very popular site of such tourism. It is also a place for nature tourism, as it presents a vast terrain that has not been disturbed for sixty years. See Bigley et al. (2010). On tourism to "dark" North Korea, see Buda and Shim (2014).

46. On the counterthread of social-realist aesthetics running through North Korean Hollywood-envy cinema, see Workman (2014).

47. This improbable story is recounted in Paul Fischer's (2015) *A Kim Jong-il Production,* in which Kim's well-known intoxication with American cinema culture is also well documented. It is based on Shin and Choi's own accounts of this story; Fischer explicitly deals with the skepticism that has long greeted those accounts (Fischer 2015, 333–337): were they kidnapped, or did they defect? For Kim Jong-il's own account of his cinematic career, see Kim Jong-il (2001a; 2001b).

48. Fischer's overdramatized 2015 book can be read as one tome in the substantial great-North-Korea-escape genre. Therefore, also see Shin Sang-Ok and Choi Eun-Hee (1988; 2001); Kang Chol-hwan and Rigoulot (2005); Shin Sang-Ok

(2007); Harden (2013; 2015); Jang Jin-sung (2015); Boynton (2016); and Kim Eunsun (2016).

49. The term "Korean Wave" is a Chinese pun that translates directly into Korean but not English: the Chinese for both "cold current" and "Korean Wave" are translated *han-liu* in Chinese, *hallyu* in Korean.

50. On *Autumn in My Heart* and the melodramatic form, see Baldacchino (2014).

51. My own viewing of *Jewel in the Palace,* admittedly intermittent, was via one of its seemingly endless repeats on Thailand's television. I also catch up on other Korean historical dramas during frequent visits to Bangkok, as well as Seoul.

52. Kim Seong-kon (2013).

53. For a review of these exhibitions and their publications, see Szacka (2014).

54. On the K-pop scene in general, see Russell (2008; 2014). *Korea Journal* 53, no. 4 (Winter 2013) was devoted to papers on K-pop. Also see Chua Beng Huat and Iwabuchi (2008); Kim Do Kyun and Kim Min-Sun (2011); Kim Youna (2013); Lie (2014); Hong Euny (2014); Choi JungBong and Maliangkay (2014); Tudor (2014); Lee Sangjoon and Nornes (2015); and Jin Dal Yong (2016). For an attempt to place the movement in a broader history of Korea, see Kim Do Kyun and Kim Se-Jin (2011). Shin Hyunjoon and Kim Pil Ho (2014) trace origins back to Korean groups on the entertainment circuit of US military clubs in the 1960s.

55. On K-pop and gendered disempowerment, see Epstein and Turnbull (2014).

56. "Show Me the Money: Are Pop Stars Underpaid?," *Time Asia,* http://205.188 .238.181/time/asia/covers/110120729/money.html, accessed 22 May 2011.

57. "SM Entertainment Announces Lawsuit against TVXQ Trio," *allkpop,* 13 April 2010; http://www.allkpop.com, accessed 22 May 2011.

58. Reprising a previous point, Kim Seong-kon (2013) has articulated an often-heard regret: that K-pop thrives globally while Korean literature languishes. Despite the success of Shin Kyung-Sook's *Please Take Care of Mom,* Korean novels have few international translations and have had little impact.

59. Russell (2014) is also a useful source of information on the geography of K-pop—where produced, where consumed; the nightspots, theaters, clubs; the ambience of different locales. A wider context for its production and consumption is developed in several papers in Kuwahara (2014).

60. It is worth noting that there had been an earlier flowering of popular culture in Japan in the 1970s, represented, for example, in the manga Showa Genroku tradition and leading in the present day into the TV anime explosion. Both the Japanese and the Korean movements can be seen as having been enabled by a confluence of new prosperity, together with new sentiments of national freedom and achievement.

61. This is also a story about K-pop. Hyun-a (b. 1992) made her debut as the main rapper of the Wonder Girls, a girl group managed by JYP Entertainment. She was also a television cohost until she left Wonder Girls in July 2007 (at the age of fifteen). In 2008 she transferred to Cube Entertainment, joining the girl group 4Minute. She has subsequently released a number of singles, attracting some controversy—her 2010 single "Change" received a 19-plus rating, to be watched only by 19+ viewers (Hyun-a was seventeen at the time), due to her provocative dancing. Her first mini-album, *Bubble Pop!,* was released in 2011, and was also flagged for racy content. In March 2012 it was announced that Hyun-a would be launching her own fashion brand, Hyuna x SPICYCOLOR. On 14 August 2012, Psy released a female version of "Gangnam Style" titled "Oppa Is Just My Style," with additional vocals by Hyun-a.

62. On the speed of Singapore's take-up of "Gangnam Style" and its transit to local parody—to "Singaporean Style" and performative acts of broader social critique—see Liew Kai Khiun (2013, 177–178). Liew also covers Singapore's abject succumbing to the onslaught of K-pop more broadly.

63. See Josh Wolford, "Gangnam Style Hitler Is the Viral Hit's Logical Conclusion," Web Pro News, 18 September 2012, http://www.webpronews.com, accessed 29 September 2012.

64. See http://www.uriminzokkiri.com, DPRK government website, accessed 29 September 2012.

65. Todd Wasserman, "Gangnam Style Goes North as Kim Jong Style," 24 September 2012, http://mashable.com, accessed 26 September 2012.

66. The "looking back" has been problematic. While Korean popular culture can readily be viewed as building on what was seen in Japanese popular culture, Roald Maliangkay (2014, 296) reminds the reader that first steps toward democratic election began in 1987, but the various ethics committees of the dictatorship era did not loosen their grip for another decade, especially in their censorship of any Japanese influence. Maliangkay cites Mun Okpae (2004).

67. Sand (2013) provides an interesting account of similarly dual vernaculars in present Tokyo and the rediscovery of their importance in the context of that city's politics. A finely illustrated presentation of *hanok* is Park Nani and Pouser (2015).

68. Robert Venturi and his future wife and architectural partner, Denise Scott Brown, were among my colleagues at the University of Pennsylvania. I remain indebted to their insights. Also see Venturi (1966).

69. "Eight Years Later: Park/Kim," introduction to lecture at Harvard Design School, 16 September 2008, http://www.parkkim.net.

70. On Paik Nam June Media Bridge, see "Paik Nam June Media Bridge by Planning Korea," *de zeen magazine,* 27 October 2010, http://www.dezeen.com, accessed 10 November 2015.

71. "Hallyu (Korean Wave)."

72. While it may be a "woman-centered" society, in Korea the reality of women's emancipation is somewhat challenged by Laurel Kendall's analysis of the still-Confucian-informed restriction on women when it comes to marriage, at a "crossroads" between tradition and modernity (Kendall 1996). Similarly, Moon Seungsook (2005) sees Korean citizenship as "gendered," consequent on its modern transformation into an industrialized and militarized nation. Also see various papers in Kim and Chungmoo (1998), notably those of Choi Chungmoo and Moon Seungsook; also see Kim Youna (2005).

73. On the wave's underground penetration of China, see Maliankay (2010).

74. Also on the wave's wider impact in Asia, see Chua Beng Huat and Koichi Iwabuchi (2008); Kim Do Kyun and Kim Min-Sun (2011); and Marinescu (2014).

75. For an analysis of Korean and Japanese pop culture and its impact on a wider, multicentered Chinese world, albeit with Singapore as the study's principal locus and a theoretical focus on the idea of soft power, see Chua Beng Huat (2012).

76. See also Atkins (2010, 1–2).

77. Contrast this, however, with the reality of Japan's history of variously colonizing and assimilating the diverse ethnicities of its own archipelago, recounted in chapter 2.

78. "9 out of 10 French Hallyu Fans Want to Visit Korea," *Korea Times,* 7 April 2012.

79. Louisa Lim, "South Korean Culture Wave Spreads across Asia," 26 March 2006, http://www.npr.org, accessed 30 March 2007.

80. Nearly 60 percent of 524 Korean language learners from sixty-five nations declared that K-pop inspired them to learn the language, according to a survey by Kyung Hee University's Institute of International Education. Yi Whan-woo, "K-pop Motivates Foreigners to Learn Korean," *Korea Times,* 4 April 2012. Similarly, Noh Hyun-gi reports on the case of Sohn Ho-min, professor of Korean language at the University of Hawaiʻi at Mānoa: of 480 students enrolled in Korean in fall semester 2011, only one had a Korean heritage; the rest gave love of K-pop as their reason for enrolling; *Korea Times,* 20 December 2011.

81. One sign of the K-pop surge is the emergence of a series of K-pop dictionaries, such as Fandom Media (2016a; 2016b).
82. Note Son Min-jung (2014) to the effect that Koreans' adoption of Western popular music in the 1930s is to be seen as resistance to Japanese-inserted culture and to still-thriving Confucianism.
83. This is a constant complaint against narrowly focused, measurement-preoccupied evaluation of academic "quality" in Australia, the United Kingdom, and elsewhere.
84. Also on soft power and the Korean Wave, see Nye and Kim Youna (2013). On K-Pop and globalization, see Fuhr (2016).
85. Also on this point, see Kim Kwang-Ok (1994); Kendall (1996, 72–73); and Bell (2004).
86. North Korea and North Koreans, however, constitute a persisting theme in Korean Hallyu cinema. See Lee Jong Hwa and Han Min Wha (2011).
87. On the continuity in policies and ideologies of the successive reigns of the Kim dynasty in North Korea, see Park Yong Soo (2014). Furthermore, on the translation of those ideologies into North Korean cinema, see Workman (2014).
88. See also "Illusive Utopia," University of Michigan Press, http://press.umich.edu, accessed 29 June 2011. On wider issues of North Korean economic and political developments, one could very usefully turn to the work of Ian Jeffries (Jeffries 2006; 2010). On the North-South divide, see Robinson (2007b); Oberdorfer and Carlin (2013); and Armstrong (2014).
89. For another take on the happiness of the perfect society, see The Great North Korean Picture Show, http://www.nfsa.gov.au, accessed 27 August 2013; see also "Hollywood Kim Jong-il Style," The Great North Korean Picture Show, http://www.thegreatnorthkoreanpictureshow.com, accessed 24 October 2013.
90. See excerpt of *Nothing to Envy* at http://nothingtoenvy.com, accessed 1 July 2011.
91. On ways in which to view North Korean culture in the context of its responses to its international environment, see Ryang (2009).
92. *Without You, There Is No Us* is the title of Kim Suki's book of 2014.
93. A central moment in this discourse was Christopher Alexander's immensely influential 1965 essay "A City Is Not a Tree." A more powerful analogy is the net, a realm of connections. Initially published in *Architectural Forum,* Alexander's essay was often republished in the 1960s and subsequently more widely in anthologies and edited works. Michael Dear (2000, 157–159), in the context of "Keno capitalism," sees the modern city as fragmented parcels coming together, seemingly randomly—"collage" might be the appropriate metaphor.
94. Deleuzean thought on the assemblage is most notably developed in Deleuze and Guattari (1987); Deleuze (1991); and Deleuze and Parnet (2002).
95. In this instance, it is Deleuze's thinking doubling into the thinking of Leibniz and Foucault (O'Sullivan 2010, 107).

CHAPTER 6: IMAGINING THE NATION

1. Park Si-soo, "Stars Spice Up Campaigns," *Korea Times,* 3 April 2012. While the political recruitment of "celebrities" might be seen as a global phenomenon, its scale in Korea's case (and its link to "family"—to actual relationships with the celebrities) would seem exceptional.
2. I have written on the same phenomenon in the case of Thailand; see King (2011, chap. 5).

3. It is instructive to observe that, in the brave new world of New Songdo, English is to be the lingua franca. Even more symbolically charged is the use of English in the new "administrative capital" of Sejong.

4. On the broader issues of the Japanese–South Korean relationship and why it matters, a useful source is the work of Marie Söderberg of the European Institute of Japanese Studies. Although Japan and South Korea are seen as natural partners, there is much distrust and suspicion between them (Söderberg 2011).

5. On the museums and their symbolic intent, see Kal Hong (2011).

6. The reference here is to the Kantian notion of the three critiques: of Pure Reason, of Practical Reason, and of Judgment. The last constitutes the critique of aesthetic judgment; Kant ([1790] 2007).

7. The assumption of Japanese homogeneity is problematic. As observed previously, Japan was always a collection of ethnicities.

8. I must add a counterobservation: in Shenyang, in China's Northeastern Liaoning Province, I have often observed the impressive presence of "Korea town," a district of expatriate (mostly North) Korean communities. Its genealogy can be traced back to the Japanese colonization of Manchuria, with its contingent Korean settlement there, as well as to the displacements of the Korean War and then refugees from Kim dynasty North Korea. So, both North America and China have their vigorous Korean diaspora communities.

9. On "the end of history" more widely, see Bellamy (1987).

Glossary

-ak	suffix for mountain (also *-san*)
ARU	Architecture Research Unit
bang	small room for karaoke, watching DVDs, etc.; see also *norae bang*
chaebol	family trust, presiding over a conglomerate or group
Changdeokgung	palace; part of the East Palace complex
Changgyeonggung	palace; part of the East Palace complex
Cheondogyo	Religion of the Heavenly Way, the religious formulation of Donghak
Cheonggyecheon	stream/rehabilitation project in downtown Seoul
Chongmyo	Chosun dynasty ancestral shrine
COEX	COnvention centers, EXhibition halls
CRC	corporate-restructuring company
Deoksugung	Seoul palace of Daehan Empire after Gyeongbokgung was abandoned
DMZ	Demilitarized Zone
Donghak	Eastern Learning (vis-à-vis Western Learning, Catholicism)
DPRK	Democratic People's Republic of (North) Korea
Gwanghwamun	ceremonial gate to Gyeongbokgung Palace
Gyeongbokgung	principal Seoul palace, currently rebuilt, axially located
Gyeongun	palace, also termed Deoksugung
han-gul	Korean alphabet
hanok	traditional Korean house form
HCIP	Heavy Chemical Industrialization Plan
ICT	information and communication technology
Ilchinhoe	Advance in Unity Society
IMF	International Monetary Fund
JGB	Jae-Gae-Bal, slum/substandard housing redevelopment program
JGC	Jae-Gun-Chuk, private-sector residential renewal program
Joseonsa Pyeonsuhoe	Korean History Compilation Committee
juche	philosophy of Syngman Rhee regime

KAPF	Korean Artists Proletarian Federation
KCPRA	Keijo City Planning Research Association
Keijo	Japanese colonial-era name for Seoul
KPF	Kohn Pedersen Fox architects
lieu de mémoire	realm or site of memory (Nora)
Meiji	Enlightened Rule (applied to Japanese imperial restoration)
milieu de mémoire	environment of memory (Nora)
minjung	the common people
MPVA	Ministry of Patriots and Veterans Affairs
Naisen Ittai	ideology of "Japan and Korea are one"
norae bang	song (karaoke) box
OECD	Organization for Economic Co-operation and Development
ondol	traditional Korean heated floor system
p'ansori	ancient song drama
Posco	Pohang Iron and Steel Company
pungsu	cosmic energy of Korean geomancy
-san	suffix for mountain
Seohojeongsa	traditional Korean house element installed in Paju Book City
SEZ	Special Economic Zone
SFAC	Seoul Foundation for Arts and Culture
silhak	practical learning movement (seventeenth and eighteenth centuries)
toyoshi	Orientalist (Japanese) historiography tradition
undongkwon	student activists
yangban	"two branches" gentry class of office-bearing aristocrats
yongyeok	people hired by government to destroy illegal premises, typically of poor occupants
Yusin	Restoration, Rejuvenation (title of Park Chung-hee constitution)
zaibatsu	Japanese conglomerate, initially family based

References

Abelmann, Nancy. 1996. *Echoes of the Past, Epics of Dissent: A South Korean Social Movement.* Berkeley: University of California Press.

———. 2003. *The Melodrama of Mobility: Women, Talk, and Class in Contemporary South Korea.* Honolulu: University of Hawai'i Press.

Abelmann, Nancy, and Kathleen McHugh, eds. 2005. *South Korean Golden Age Melodrama: Gender, Genre, and National Cinema.* Detroit: Wayne State University Press.

Abelmann, Nancy, Park So Jin, and Kim Hyunhee. 1999. "College Rank and Neoliberal Subjectivity in South Korea: The Burden of Self-development." *Inter-Asia Cultural Studies* 10 (2): 229–247.

Ahn Byung-ook. 2002. "The Significance of Settling the Past in Modern Korean History." *Korea Journal* 42 (3): 7–17.

Ahn Byung Ui. 2008. "Remembrances: Kim Chung-up." *Koreana* 22:4.

Ahn Sang Jin. 2001. *Continuity and Transformation: Religious Synthesis in East Asia.* New York: Peter Berg.

Akita, George, and Brandon Palmer. 2015. *The Japanese Colonial Legacy in Korea, 1910–1945.* Portland, ME: MerwinAsia.

Amsden, Alice H. 1989. *Asia's Next Giant: South Korea and Late Industrialization.* New York: Oxford University Press.

Anders, C. J. 2012. "An Exclusive Look at the Stunning Concept Art behind *Cloud Atlas'* Future Seoul." *Concept Art,* 26 October. http://io9.gizmodo, accessed 18 August 2015.

Anderson, Benedict. 1991. *Imagined Communities: Reflections on the Origin and Spread of Nationalism.* Rev. edn. London: Verso.

Arbes, Ross, and Charles Bethea. 2014. "Songdo, South Korea: City of the Future?" *The Atlantic* (27 September). http://www.theatlantic.com, accessed 1 August 2015.

Armstrong, Charles K. 2007. "Introduction." In *Korean Society: Civil Society, Democracy and the State,* edited by C. K. Armstrong, 1–8. 2nd ed. Abingdon, UK: Routledge.

———. 2013. *The North Korean Revolution, 1945–1950.* Ithaca, NY: Cornell University Press.

———. (2007) 2014. *The Koreas.* 2nd ed. Abingdon, UK: Routledge.

Ashin [pseud.]. 2014. "Dongdaemun Design Plaza Opens to the Public." *Arirang.* http://www.arirang.co.kr, accessed 28 February 2015.

Aso, Noriko. 2012. "*Primitive Selves: Koreana in the Japanese Colonial Gaze, 1910–1945* (Review)." *Journal of Interdisciplinary History* 42 (3): 198–199.

Atkins, Everett Taylor. 2010. *Primitive Selves: Koreana in the Japanese Colonial Gaze, 1910–1945.* Berkeley: University of California Press.

Auslander, Mark, and Chong Eun Ahn. 2015. "Responding to 'Comfort Woman' Denial at Central Washington University." *Asia-Pacific Journal: Japan Focus* 13, issue 21 (3).

Bae Changmii. 2002. "The Symbolic Landscape of National Identity: Planning, Politics, and Culture in South Korea." PhD thesis, University of Southern California.

Bakhtin, Mikhail Mikhailovich. 1986. *Speech Genres and Other Late Essays*. Edited by C. Emerson and M. Holquist. Translated by Vern W. McGee. Austin: University of Texas Press.

Baldacchino, Jean-Paul. 2014. "In Sickness and in Love? *Autumn in My Heart* and the Embodiment of Morality in Korean Television Drama." *Korea Journal* 54 (4): 5–28.

Barraclough, Ruth, and Elyssa Faison, eds. 2009. *Gender and Labour in Korea and Japan: Sexing Class*. London: Routledge.

Bartholomew, Peter. 1993. "Choson Dynasty Royal Compounds: Windows to a Lost Culture." *Transactions: Royal Asiatic Society, Korea Branch* 68:11–44.

Baudrillard, Jean. 1972. *For a Critique of the Political Economy of the Sign*. Translated by C. Levin. St. Louis, MO: Telos Press.

———. 1983. *In the Shadow of Silent Majorities, or the End of the Social*. New York: Semiotext(e).

———. 1985. "The Ecstasy of Communication." In *Postmodern Culture*, edited by H. Foster, 126–136. London: Pluto Press, 1985.

———. 1988. *America*. Translated by C. Turner. London: Verso.

———. (1976) 1993. *Symbolic Exchange and Death*. London: Sage.

———. 1994a. *The Illusion of the End*. Translated by C. Turner. Cambridge, UK: Polity Press.

———. 1994b. *Simulacra and Simulation*. Translated by S. Faria Glaser. Ann Arbor: University of Michigan Press.

Beirne, Paul. 1999. "The Eclectic Mysticism of Ch'oe Cheu." *Review of Korean Studies* 2:159–182.

Bell, Kirsten. 2004. "Cheondogyo and the Donghak Revolution: The (Un)Making of a Religion." *Korea Journal* 44 (2): 123–148.

Bellamy, Richard. 1987. "Post-modernism and the End of History." *Theory, Culture, and Society* 4: 727–733.

Benjamin, Walter. 1978. "Paris, Capital of the Nineteenth Century." In *Reflections: Essays, Aphorisms, Autobiographical Writings*, 146–162. New York: Schocken Books.

———. 1982. *Gessamelte Schriften: Das Passagen-Werk*. Vol. 5. Edited by R. Tiedemann and H. Schweppenhuser. With T. W. Adorno and G. Scholem. Frankfurt: Suhrkamp: Verlag.

Berg, Nate. 2012. "Seoul Ends Failed 'New Towns' Project." *Citylab*, (6 February). http://www.citylab.com, accessed 18 February 2016.

Berger, Jason. 2004. "Tethering the Butterfly: Revisiting Jameson's *Postmodernism and Consumer Society* and the Paradox of Resistance." *Cultural Logic: An Electronic Journal of Marxist Theory & Practice* 7.

Berman, Marshall. (1982) 1988. *All That Is Solid Melts into Air: The Experience of Modernity*. Ringwood, Aus.: Viking Penguin.

Berry, Chris. 2003. "The Documentary Production Process as Counter-public: Notes on an Inter-Asian Mode and the Example of Kim Dong Won." *Inter-Asia Cultural Studies* 4 (1): 139–144.

Berry, Chris, Nicola Liscutin, and Jonathan D. Mackintosh, eds. 2009. *Cultural Studies and Cultural Industries in Northeast Asia: What a Difference a Region Makes*. Hong Kong: Hong Kong University Press.

Berry, Mary Elizabeth. 1989. *Hideyoshi*. Cambridge, MA: Council on East Asian Studies Harvard University.

Bigley, James D., Lee Choong-Ki, Chon Jinhyung, and Yoon Yooshik. 2010. "Motivations for War-related Tourism: A Case of DMZ Visitors in Korea." *Tourism Geographies* 12 (3): 371–394.

Bloch, Ernst. 1997. "Nonsynchronism and the Obligation to Its Dialectics." *New German Critique* 11:22–38.

Blodrowski, Steve. 2007. "The Host: Monstrous Political Satire." *Hollywood Gothique—News & Notes,* 8 March. http://hollywoodgothique.bravejournal.com, accessed 14 June 2011.

Bong Joon-ho. 2011. "The Director's Statement." Hollywood Gothique, http://www.hollywoodgothique.com/host2006.html, accessed 14 June 2011.

Boundas, Constantin V. 2010. "Ontology." In *The Deleuze Dictionary,* edited by A. Parr, 196–198. Rev. ed. Edinburgh: Edinburgh University Press.

Boynton, Robert S. 2016. *The Invitation-Only Zone: The True Story of North Korea's Abduction Project.* New York: Farrar, Straus and Giroux.

Braudel, Fernand. 1992. *The Structures of Everyday Life.* Berkeley: University of California Press.

Brenner, Neil, David J. Madden, and David Wachsmuth. 2011. "Assemblage Urbanism and the Challenges of Critical Urban Theory." *City* 15 (2): 225–240.

Breuker, Remco Erik. 2010. "Writing History in Koryo: Some Early Koryo Works Reconsidered." *Korean Histories* 2 (1): 57–84.

Brooks, Peter. 1976. *The Melodramatic Imagination: Balzac, Henry James, Melodrama, and Modes of Excess.* New Haven, CT: Yale University Press.

Brudnoy, David. 1970. "Japan's Experiment in Korea." *Monumenta Nipponica* 2: 155–195.

Buck-Morss, Susan. 1991. *The Dialectics of Seeing: Walter Benjamin and the Arcades Project.* Cambridge, MA: MIT Press.

Buda, Dorina Maria, and David Shim. 2014. "Desiring the Dark: 'A Taste for the Unusual' in North Korean Tourism." *Current Issues in Tourism* 18 (1): 1–6.

Caprio, Mark E. 2009. *Japanese Assimilation Policies in Colonial Korea, 1910–1945.* Seattle: University of Washington Press.

Cha, Victor. 2013. *The Impossible State: North Korea's Past and Future.* London: Vintage Books.

Cha Myung Soo. 2010. "The Economic History of Korea." *Online Encyclopedia of Economic History.* Economic History Association. http://eh.net, accessed 5 September 2013.

Ch'ae Man-Sik. 1993. *Peace Under Heaven.* Translated by Chun Kyung-ja. Armonk, NY: M. E. Sharpe.

Chan, Brenda. 2011. "Book Review: *Pop Culture Formations across East Asia.*" *SOJOURN, Journal of Social Issues in Southeast Asia* 26 (2): 335–339.

Ching, Leo T. S. 2001. *Becoming Japanese: Colonial Taiwan and the Politics of Identity Formation.* Berkeley: University of California Press.

Cho, Michelle. 2014. "Face Value: The Star as Genre in Bong Joon-ho's *Mother.*" In *The Korean Popular Culture Reader,* edited by Kim Kyung Hyun and Choe Youngmin, 168–194. Durham, NC: Duke University Press.

Cho Hae-Joang. 2005. "Reading the 'Korean Wave' as a Sign of Global Shift." *Korea Journal* 45 (4): 147–182.

Cho Kapche. 1998. "Pak Chonghui ui saengae" [Life of Pak Chonghui (Park Chunghee)]. *Choson Ilbo,* 30 November.

Cho Kwang. 2004. "The Choson Government's Measures against Catholicism." In *The Founding of Catholic Tradition in Korea,* edited by Yu Chai-shin, 103–114. Fremont, CA: Jain.

Cho Myungrae. 2004. "Cheonggyecheon pokwon gwa bojon un hamkke halsu issulgga" [Can the Cheongye Stream Restoration and Development Come Together?]. *Tangdae pip'yong* 26: 88–104.

Cho Sungtaek. 2005. "The Formation of Modern Buddhist Scholarship: The Cases of Bak Jong-hong and Kim Dong-hwa." *Korea Journal* 45 (1): 5–28.

Cho Uhn. 2005. "Positioning the Korean Wave in the Nexus between Globalization and Localization." *Korea Journal* 45 (4): 143–146.

Ch'oe Chun-sik, Pak Chong-hun, and Pak Chun-sok. 2005. *Soul in Seoul: A Cultural Journey.* Seoul: Tong Asia.

Choe Sang-hun. 2009. "North Korea Opens Dam Flow, Sweeping Away 6 in the South." *New York Times* (Asia Pacific), 6 September.

———. 2012. "Mixed Emotions over Deft Imitator." *International Herald Tribune,* 3 September, 16.

Ch'oe Yong-ho, Peter H. Lee, and Wm. Theodore de Bary, eds. 2000. *From the Sixteenth to the Twentieth Centuries.* Vol. 2 of *Sources of Korean Tradition.* New York: Columbia University Press.

Choe Youngmin. 2014. "Preface." In *The Korean Popular Culture Reader,* edited by Kim Kyung Hyun and Choe Youngmin, ix–xi. Durham, NC: Duke University Press.

Choi Chungmoo. 1995. "The Minjung Culture Movement and the Construction of Popular Culture in Korea." In *South Korea's Minjung Movement: The Culture and Politics of Dissidence,* edited by K. M. Wells, 105–118. Honolulu: University of Hawai'i Press.

———. 1997a. "Sorcery and Modernity." Paper presented at the symposium "Unmapping the Earth," Gwangju Biennale, 1 September to 27 November 1997.

———. 1997b. "Hegemony and Sharmanism: The State, the Elite, and the Sharmans in Contemporary Korea." In *Religion and Society in Contemporary Korea,* edited by L. R. Lancaster and R. K. Payne, 19–48. Berkeley: Institute of East Asian Studies.

———. 1998. "Nationalism and Construction of Gender in Korea." In *Dangerous Women: Gender and Korean Nationalism,* edited by E. H. Kim and Choi Chungmoo, 9–32. New York: Routledge.

———. 2002. "The Politics of Gender, Aestheticism, and the Cultural Nationalism in Sopyonje and the Genealogy." In *Im Kwon-Taek: The Making of a Korean National Cinema,* edited by D. E. James and Kyung Hyun Kim, 107–133. Detroit: Wayne State University Press.

———. 2016. *Tourist Distractions: Traveling and Feeling in Transnational Hallyu Cinema.* Durham, NC: Duke University Press.

Choi Jai-Keum. 2007. *The Korean Church under Japanese Colonialism.* Seoul: Jimoondang.

Choi Jinhee. 2010. *The South Korean Film Renaissance: Local Hitmakers, Global Provocateurs.* Middletown, CT: Wesleyan University Press.

Choi Jong-deok. 2006. *Changdeokgung: The True Palace of Joseon* [in Korean]. Seoul: Nulwa.

Choi JungBong and Roald Maliangkay. 2014. *K-pop—The International Rise of the Korean Music Industry.* Abingdon, UK: Routledge.

Chua, Charlene. 2011. "Homegrown K-pop Stars." *New Paper* (Singapore), 16 April.

Chua Beng Huat. 2012. *Structure, Audience, and Soft Power in East Asian Pop Culture.* Hong Kong: Hong Kong University Press.

Chua Beng Huat and Koichi Iwabuchi, eds. 2008. *East Asian Pop Culture: Analysing the Korean Wave.* Hong Kong: Hong Kong University Press.

Chung, Kimberley. 2014. "Proletarian Sensibilities: The Body Politics of New Tendency Literature (1924–27)." *Journal of Korean Studies* 19 (1): 37–57.

Chung, Steven. 2014a. *Split Screen Korea: Shin Sang-ok and Postwar Cinema.* Minneapolis: University of Minnesota Press.

———. 2014b. "Regimes within Regimes: Film and Fashion Cultures in the Korean 1950s." In *The Korean Popular Culture Reader,* edited by Kim Kyung Hyun and Choe Youngmin, 103–125. Durham, NC: Duke University Press.

Chung Chonghwa. 2012. "Negotiating Colonial Korean Cinema in the Japanese Empire: From the Silent Era to the Talkies, 1923–1939." *Cross-Currents: East Asian History and Culture Review* 5 (December): 136–169.

Chung Hye Seung and David S. Diffrient. 2015. *Movie Migrations: Transnational Genre Flows and South Korean Cinema*. New Brunswick, NJ: Rutgers University Press.

Chung Sae Wook. 1997. "La planification de Séoul: passé, présent, futur" [The Planning of Seoul: Past, Present, and Future]. *Revue de Corée* 29 (2): 9–21.

Chung Yong-Hwa. 2006. "The Modern Transformation of Korean Identity: Enlightenment and Orientalism." *Korea Journal* 46 (1): 109–138.

Clark, Donald N., ed. 1988. *The Kwangju Uprising: Shadows over the Regime in South Korea*. Boulder, CO: Westview Press.

———. 2000. *Culture and Customs of Korea*. Westport, CT: Greenwood Press.

———. 2007. "Protestant Christianity and the State: Religious Organizations and Civil Society." In *Korean Society: Civil Society, Democracy, and the State*, edited by Charles K. Armstrong, 171–189. 2nd ed. Abingdon, UK: Routledge.

Coaldrake, William. 1996. *Architecture and Authority in Japan*. London: Routledge.

Conley, Tom. 1993. "Translator's Foreword: A Plea for Leibniz." In *The Fold: Leibniz and the Baroque,* by Gilles Deleuze, ix–xxi. Minneapolis: University of Minnesota Press.

Cumings, Bruce. 1981. *Liberation and the Emergence of Separate Regimes, 1945–1947*. Vol. 1 of *The Origins of the Korean War*. Princeton, NJ: Princeton University Press.

———. 1990. *The Roaring of the Cataract, 1947–1950*. Vol. 2 of *The Origins of the Korean War*. Princeton, NJ: Princeton University Press.

———. 2004. *North Korea: Another Country*. New York: The New Press.

———. (1997) 2005. *Korea's Place in the Sun: A Modern History*. New York: Norton.

———. 2007. "Civil Society in West and East." In *Korean Society: Civil Society, Democracy, and the State*, edited by C. K. Armstrong, 9–32. 2nd ed. Abingdon, UK: Routledge.

———. 2011. *The Korean War: A History*. New York: Modern Library.

Curley, Gregory. 2010. "Heyri Art Village: South Korea's Melting Pot of Creativity." *CNNGO*, 24 May. http://www.cnngo.com, accessed 15 June 2011.

Cyhn, Jin W. 2002. *Technology Transfer and International Production: The Development of the Electronics Industry in Korea*. Cheltenham, UK: Edward Elgar.

Dear, Michael J. 2000. *The Postmodern Urban Condition*. Oxford: Blackwell.

de Certeau, Michel. 1984. *The Practice of Everyday Life*. Translated by S. F. Rendall. Berkeley: University of California Press.

de Certeau, Michel, and Luce Giard. 1994. "Les revenants de la ville" [Ghosts of the City]. In *L'Invention du Quotidien: Arts de Faire* [The Invention of Everyday Life: The Art of Living], 187–204. Paris: Gallimard.

De Ceunster, Koen. 2001. "The Nation Excorcised: The Historiography of Collaboration in South Korea." *Korean Studies* 25 (2).

———. 2010. "When History Is Made." *Korean Histories* 2 (1): 13–33.

De Mente, Boyé Lafayette. (1998) 2012. *The Korean Mind: Understanding Contemporary Korean Culture*. Tokyo: Tuttle.

DeLanda, Manuel. 2006. *A New Philosophy of Society: Assemblage Theory and Social Complexity*. New York: Continuum.

Deleuze, Gilles. (1966) 1988. *Bergsonism*. Translated by H. Tomlinson and B. Habberjam. New York: Zone Books.

———. 1991. *Empiricism and Subjectivity*. New York: Columbia University Press.

———. 1993. *The Fold: Leibniz and the Baroque*. Translated by T. Conley. Minneapolis: University of Minnesota Press.

Deleuze, Gilles, and Félix Guattari. 1987. *A Thousand Plateaus: Capitalism and Schizophrenia*. Translated by B. Massumi. Minneapolis: University of Minnesota Press.

Deleuze, Gilles, and Claire Parnet. 2002. *Dialogues II*. New York: Columbia University Press.

Demick, Barbara. 2010. *Nothing to Envy: Ordinary Lives in North Korea.* New York: Spiegel and Grau.

Derrida, Jacques. [1971] 1977. "Signature Event Context." *Glyph,* 1.

———. 1981. *Dissemination.* Translated by B. Johnson. Chicago: University of Chicago Press.

Dignam, Larry. 2010. "Cisco's Grand Telepresence Experiment in Songdo, South Korea." *Between the Lines,* 3 June. http://www.zdnet.com, accessed 21 May 2011.

Doran, Robert. 2015. *The Theory of the Sublime from Longinus to Kant.* Cambridge: Cambridge University Press.

Dovey, Kim. 2011. "Uprooting Critical Urbanism." *City* 15 (3–4): 347–354.

Dower, John W. 1999. *Embracing Defeat: Japan in the Wake of World War II.* New York: W. W. Norton.

———. 2012. *Ways of Forgetting, Ways of Remembering: Japan in the Modern World.* New York: The New Press.

Drake, Frederick C. 1984. *The Empire of the Seas: A Biography of Rear Admiral Robert Wilson Shufeldt, USN.* Honolulu: University of Hawai'i Press.

Dudden, Alexis. 2006. *Japan's Colonization of Korea: Discourse and Power.* Honolulu: University of Hawai'i Press.

Duncan, John B. 1996. *The Origins of the Choson Dynasty.* Seattle: University of Washington Press.

———. 2000. "The Emergence of the Tonghak Religion." In *Sources of Korean Tradition: From the Sixteenth to the Twentieth Centuries,* edited by Ch'oe Yong-ho, Peter H. Lee, and William Theodore de Bary, 228–234. New York: Columbia University Press.

———. 2007. "The Problematic Modernity of Confucianism: The Question of 'Civil Society' in Chosŏn Dynasty Korea." In *Korean Society: Civil Society, Democracy, and the State,* edited by Charles Armstrong, 33–52. Abingdon, UK: Routledge.

———. N.d. "Non-Elite Perceptions of the State in the Late Choson." Unpublished paper.

Dusinberre, Martin. 2013. "Janus and the Japanese Empire." *Journal of Colonialism and Colonial History* 14 (1).

Duus, Peter. 1995. *The Abacus and the Sword: The Japanese Penetration of Korea, 1895–1910.* Berkeley: University of California Press.

———. 2003. "Review of *Colonial Modernity in Korea,* Shin Gi-Wook and M. Robinson, eds." *Monumenta Nipponica* 58 (1): 128–130.

Duus, Peter, Ramon H. Myers, and Mark R. Peattie. 1996. *The Japanese Wartime Empire, 1931–1945.* Princeton, NJ: Princeton University Press.

Eckert, Carter. (1991) 2014. *Offspring of Empire: The Koch'ang Kims and the Colonial Origins of Korean Capitalism, 1876–1945.* Seattle: University of Washington Press.

———. 2016. *Park Chung Hee and Modern Korea: The Roots of Militarism, 1866–1945.* Cambridge, MA: Belknap Press.

Eckert, Carter, Lee Ki-baik, Lew Young Ick, Michael Robinson, and Edward W. Wagner. 1990. *Korea Old and New: A History.* Seoul: Ilchokak Publishers, for Harvard University.

Em, Henry H. 2013. *The Great Enterprise: Sovereignty and Historiography in Modern Korea.* Durham, NC: Duke University Press.

Epstein, Stephen J. 1997. "The Meaning of Meaningless in Kim Sung-ok's 'Seoul: Winter 1964.'" *Korea Journal* 39 (4): 98–107.

Epstein, Stephen J., and James Turnbull. 2014. "Girls' Generation? Gender, (Dis) Empowerment, and K-pop." In *The Korean Popular Culture Reader,* edited by Kim Kyung Hyun and Choe Youngmin, 314–336. Durham, NC: Duke University Press.

Fackler, Martin. 2007. "In Korea, a Boot Camp Cure for Web Obsession." *New York Times,* 18 November.

Fandom Media. 2016a. *KPOP Dictionary: 200 Essential K-pop and K-Drama Vocabulary and Examples Every Fan Must Know.* N.c.: CreateSpace Independent Publishing Platform.

———. 2016b. *Understanding What Your Favorite Idols Are Saying.* Vol. 2 of *KPOP Dictionary.* N.c.: CreateSpace Independent Publishing Platform.

Farías, Ignacio, and Thomas Bender. 2010. *Urban Assemblages: How Actor-Network Theory Changes Urban Studies.* Abingdon, UK: Routledge.

Farris, William Wayne. 1994. "Ancient Japan's Korean Connection." *Working Papers in Asian/Pacific Studies.* Durham, NC: Duke University, Asian/Pacific Studies Institute.

Febvre, Lucien, and Henri-Jean Martin. 1976. *The Coming of the Book: The Impact of Printing, 1450–1800.* London: New Left Books. Translation of *L'Apparition du Livre.* Paris: Albin Michel, 1958.

Fehrenbach, Theodore Reed. (1963) 2000. *This Kind of War.* Washington, DC: Brasseys.

Fischer, Paul. 2015. *A Kim Jong-il Production.* London: Penguin Vintage.

Fisher, Max. 2012. "Gangnam Style, Dissected: The Subversive Message within South Korea's Music Video Sensation." *Atlantic,* August 23. http://www.theatlantic .com, accessed 27 September 2012.

Focillon, Henri. [1934] 1942. *The Life of Forms in Art.* Translated by C. B. Hogan and G. Kubler [in French]. New Haven, CT: Yale University Press.

French, Paul. 2014. *North Korea: State of Paranoia.* London: Zed Books.

Fuhr, Michael. 2016. *Globalization and Popular Music in South Korea: Sounding Out K-Pop.* Abingdon, UK: Routledge.

Fujitani, Takashi. 1998. *Splendid Monarchy: Power and Pageantry in Modern Japan.* Berkeley: University of California Press.

———. 2000. "Reischauer no kairai tenno-sei koso" [Reischauer's Design of a Puppet Emperor System]. *Sekai* (March): 137–146.

———. 2011. *Race for Empire: Koreans as Japanese and Japanese as Americans during World War II.* Berkeley: University of California Press.

Gale, James S. 1972. *History of the Korean People.* Annotated and introduced by R. Rutt. Seoul: Royal Asiatic Society. First published serially in mid-1920s.

Gateward, Frances K., ed. 2007. *Seoul Searching: Culture and Identity in Contemporary Korean Cinema.* New York: SUNY Press.

Gelézeau, Valérie. 1997. "The Street in Seoul: In Search of the Soul of Seoul." *Korea Journal* 37 (2): 71–83.

———. 2001. "La modernisation de l'habitat en Corée du Sud: Usage et image des appartements de style occidental" [Housing Modernization in South Korea: Use and Image of Western-style Apartments]. *Annales de géographie* 620: 405–424.

———. 2003. *Séoul, ville géante, cités radieuses* [Seoul, Gargantuan Town, Radiant City]. Paris: CNRS Editions.

———. 2011. *Atlas Seoul.* Paris: Atlas Megapoles.

———. 2014. "Streets and Open Spaces in Seoul (1995–2010): A Cultural Geography of Local Neighborhood." In *KNCU-Korean Studies Series, Seoul,* 162–188. Seoul: Hollym.

Gelézeau, Valérie, Koen De Ceuster, and Alain Delissen, eds. 2013. *Debordering Korea: Tangible and Intangible Legacies of the Sunshine Policy.* Abingdon, UK: Routledge.

Graham, Stephen, ed. 2004. *The Cybercities Reader.* London: Routledge.

Grayson, James H. 1977. "Mimana, a Problem in Korean Historiography." *Korea Journal* 17 (8): 65–69.

Gutting, Gary. 2005. *Foucault: A Very Short Introduction.* Oxford: Oxford University Press.

Gwee, E. 2011. "K-Pop Fans Take Flight." *Sunday Times* (Singapore), 16 October, 4–5.

Ha Seong-Kyu. 1998. "Housing Problems and New-Town Policy in the Seoul Metropolitan Region." *Third World Planning Review* 20 (4): 375–390.

Habermas, Jürgen. 1973. "Wahrheitstherien." In *Wirklichkeit und Reflexion: Walter Schulz zum 60. Geburtstag,* edited by H Fahrenbach. Pfullingen, Ger.: Neske.

Haboush, JaHyun Kim. 2003. "Versions and Subversions: Patriarchy and Polygamy in Korean Narratives." In *Women and Confucian Cultures in Premodern China, Korea, and Japan,* edited by D. Ko, JaHyun Kim Haboush, and J. R. Piggott, 279–304. Berkeley: University of California Press.

———. 2015. *The Memoirs of Lady Hyegyong: The Autobiographical Writings of a Crown Princess in Eighteenth-Century Korea.* Berkeley: University of California Press.

———. 2016. *The Great East Asian War and the Birth of the Korean Nation.* New York: Columbia University Press.

Halbwachs, Maurice. 1992. *On Collective Memory.* Chicago: University of Chicago Press.

Hanhardt, John G. 2000. *The Worlds of Nam June Paik.* New York: Guggenheim Museum.

Hanhardt, John G., and Ken Hakuta. 2012. *Nam June Paik: Global Visionary.* Washington, DC: Smithsonian American Art Museum.

Hanscom, Christopher P. 2013. *The Real Modern: Literary Modernism and the Crisis of Representation in Colonial Korea.* Harvard East Asia Monographs 357. Cambridge, MA: Harvard University Asia Center.

Harden, Blaine. 2012. *Escape from Camp 14: One Man's Remarkable Odyssey from North Korea to Freedom in the West.* New York: Penguin Books.

———. 2015. *The Great Leader and the Fighter Pilot.* New York: Viking Penguin.

Hart, Dennis. 2001. *From Tradition Consumption: Construction of a Capitalist Culture in South Korea.* Seoul: Jimoondang.

Harvey, David. 1989. *The Condition of Postmodernity: An Enquiry into the Origins of Cultural Change.* Oxford: Basil Blackwood.

Hastings, Max. 1987. *The Korean War.* New York: Simon & Schuster.

Hatada, Takashi. 1969. *A History of Korea.* Translated by W. W. Smith, Jr., and B. H. Hazard. Santa Barbara: ANC-Clio Press.

Hawley, Samuel. 2005. *The Imjin War: Japan's Sixteenth-Century Invasion of Korea and Attempt to Conquer China.* Seoul: Royal Asiatic Society Korean Branch.

Heathcote, Edwin. 2009. "A City Dedicated to Books and Print." *Design and Architecture (Financial Times)* 22 (21 August): 38. http://www.ft.com, accessed 15 June 2011.

Hemmert, Martin. 2012. *Tiger Management: Korean Companies on World Markets.* Abingdon, UK: Routledge.

Hendrick-Wong Yuwa and D. Choong. 2014. "MasterCard 2014 Global Destination Cities Index." http://newsroom.mastercard.com, accessed 6 Nov 2015.

Henry, Todd A. 2014. *Assimilating Seoul: Japanese Rule and the Politics of Public Space in Colonial Korea, 1910–1945.* Berkeley: University of California Press.

Hicks, George. (1994) 1997. *The Comfort Women: Japan's Brutal Regime of Enforced Prostitution in the Second World War.* New York: W. W. Norton.

Höhn, Maria. 2010. "The Racial Crisis of 1971 in the U.S. Military: Finding Solutions in West Germany and South Korea." In *Over There: Living with the U.S. Military Empire from World War Two to the Present,* edited by M. Höhn and Seungsook Moon, 311–336. Durham, NC: Duke University Press.

Holquist, Michael, and Caryl Emerson. 1981. "Glossary." In *The Dialogic Imagination: Four Essays by M. M. Bakhtin,* 423–434. Translated by C. Emerson and M. Holquist. Austin: University of Texas Press.

Hong, John, and Park Jinhee. 2012. *Convergent Flux: Contemporary Architecture and Urbanism in Korea.* Boston: Birkhäuser–Harvard Graduate School of Design.

Hong Duck-Ryul. 2009. "A Critical Study on the University and Academic Assessment System in Korea." *Inter-Asia Cultural Studies* 10 (2): 292–302.

Hong Euny. 2014. *The Birth of Korean Cool: How One Nation Is Conquering the World through Pop Culture.* New York: Picador.

Hong Suhn-kyoung. 1968. "Donghak in the Context of Korean Modernization." *Review of Religious Research* 10 (1): 43–51.

Hong Young-gi. 2010. "Background of Christian Democratic Movements in Korea." 2 April. http://eng.revhong.com, accessed 17 September 2012.

Hoon Shin Young. 2008. *The Royal Palaces of Korea: Six Centuries of Dynastic Grandeur.* Singapore: Stallion Press.

Horowitz, Irving Louis. 1980. *Science, Sin, and Society: The Politics of Reverend Moon and the Unification Church.* Cambridge, MA: MIT Press.

Hue-Tam Ho Tai. 2001. "Remembered Realms: Pierre Nora and French National Memory." *American Historical Review* 106 (3): 906–922.

Hughes, Theodore. 2014. *Literature and Film in Cold War South Korea: Freedom's Frontier.* New York: Columbia University Press.

Huhh Jun-Sok. 2008. "Culture and Business of PC Bangs in Korea." *Games and Culture* 3 (1): 26–37.

Hwang Jin-Tae. 2014. "Territorialized Urban Mega-Projects beyond Global Convergence: The Case of Dongdaemun Design Plaza & Park Project, Seoul." *Cities* 40 Part A: 82–89.

Hwang Sok-yong. 2005. *The Guest.* New York: Seven Stories Press.

Ishida, J., and Kim Jooya. 2014. "Colonial Modernity and Urban Space: Seoul and the 1930s Land Readjustment Project." In *Constructing the Colonized Land: Entwined Perspectives of East Asia around WWII,* edited by K. Izumi, 171–192. Farnham, UK: Ashgate.

Itoi, K. 2005. "Korea: A Tussle over Treasures." *Newsweek,* 21 February. http://www.newsweek.com, accessed 5 July 2011.

Iwabuchi, Koichi. 2013. "Korean Wave and Inter-Asian Referencing." In *The Korean Wave: Korean Media Go Global,* edited by Kim Youna, 43–57. Abingdon, UK: Routledge.

Jackson, Andrew D. 2016. *The 1728 Musin Rebellion: Politics and Plotting in Eighteenth-Century Korea.* Honolulu: University of Hawai'i Press.

Jackson, Andrew D., and Colette Balmain, eds. 2015. *Korean Screen Cultures: Interrogating Cinema, TV, Music, and Online Games.* Bern, Switz.: Peter Lang AG.

Jackson, Ben, and Robert Koehler. 2012. *Korean Architecture: Breathing with Nature.* Seoul: Seoul Selection.

Jager, Sheila Miyoshi. 2003. *Narratives of Nation Building in Korea: A Genealogy of Patriotism.* London: M. E. Sharpe.

James, David E., and Kim Kyung Hyun. 2001. *Im Kwon-Taek: The Making of a Korean National Cinema.* Detroit: Wayne State University Press.

Jameson, Fredric. 1991. *Postmodernism, or the Cultural Logic of Late Capitalism.* Durham, NC: Duke University Press.

———. 1994. "Foreword." In Karatani Kojin, *Origins of Modern Japanese Literature,* v–xx. Durham, NC: Duke University Press.

Jang Gyu-sik. 2003. "Geodae dosi 'seoul gonghwaguk'-ui myeongam'" [The Bright and Dark Sides of the Metropolis, "The Seoul Republic"]. *Yeoksa bipyeong* [Critical Review of History] 65: 75–95.

Jang Jin-sung. 2015. *Dear Leader: My Escape from North Korea.* New York: Atria.

Jang Sukman. 1999. "Protestantism in the Name of Modern Civilization." *Korea Journal* 39 (4): 187–204.

———. 2004. "Historical Currents and Characteristics of Korean Protestantism after Liberation." *Korea Journal* 44 (4): 133–156.

Jeffries, Ian. 2006. *North Korea: A Guide to Economic and Political Developments.* London: Routledge.

———. 2010. *Contemporary North Korea: A Guide to Economic and Political Developments.* London: Routledge.

Jencks, Charles. 1987. *The Language of Postmodern Architecture.* 5th ed. London: Academy Editions.

Jeong, Kelly. 2014. "The Quasi Patriarch: Kim Sung-ho and South Korean Postwar Movies." In *The Korean Popular Culture Reader,* edited by Kim Kyung Hyun and Choe Youngmin, 126–144. Durham, NC: Duke University Press.

Jin Dal Yong. 2010. *Hands On / Hands Off: The Korean State and the Market Liberalization of the Communication Industry.* Cresskill, NJ: Hampton Press.

———. 2011. *Korea's Online Gaming Empire.* Cambridge, MA: MIT Press.

———. 2013. "Hybridization of Korean Popular Culture: Films and Online Gaming." In *The Korean Wave: Korean Media Go Global,* edited by Kim Youna, 148–164. Abingdon, UK: Routledge.

———. 2014. *De-Convergence of Global Media Industries.* Abingdon, UK: Routledge.

———. 2016. *New Korean Wave: Transnational Cultural Power in the Age of Social Media.* Urbana: University of Illinois Press.

Jin Jong-Heon. 2008. "Demolishing Colony: The Demolition of the Old Government-General Building in Choson." In *Sitings: Critical Approaches to Korean Geography,* edited by T. R. Tangherlini and Sallie Yea, 39–60. Honolulu: University of Hawai'i Press.

Jones, Randall S. 1984. *The Economic Development of Colonial Korea.* Ann Arbor: University of Michigan Press.

Joo Donghun. 2011. "Determinants of the Informal Sector and Their Effects on the Economy: The Case of Korea." *Global Economic Review* 40 (1): 21–43.

Jun Myung-Jin. 2012. "The Effects of Seoul's New-Town Development on Suburbanization and Mobility: A Counterfactual Approach." *Environment and Planning A* 44 (9): 2171–2190.

Jung Inha. 1997. "L'aménagement de Yŏuido: Modèle de l'urbanisme moderniste de Séoul?" [The Planning of Youida: A Model for Korean Modernist Urbanism?]. *Revue de Corée* 29 (2): 22–45.

———. 2013. *Architecture and Urbanism in Modern Korea.* Honolulu: University of Hawai'i Press.

Jung Ji-Young. 2011. "Questions Concerning Widows' Social Status and Remarriage in Late Choson." In *Women and Confucianism in Late Choson Korea: New Perspectives,* edited by Kim Youngmin and M. J. Pettid, 109–136. Albany, NY: SUNY Press.

Kabashima, Ikuo, and Gill Steel. 2010. *Changing Politics in Japan.* Ithaca, NY: Cornell University Press.

Kal Hong. 2011. *Aesthetic Constructions of Korean Nationalism: Spectacle, Politics, and History.* Abingdon, UK: Routledge.

Kang, Hildi. (2001) 2005. *Under the Black Umbrella: Voices from Colonial Korea, 1910–1945.* Ithaca, NY: Cornell University Press.

Kang Chol-hwan and Pierre Rigoulot. [2000] 2005. *The Aquariums of Pyongyang: Ten Years in the North Korean Gulag* [in French]. Translated by Yair Reiner. New York: Basic Books.

Kang Hyok. 2005. *This Is Paradise: My North Korean Childhood.* With P. Grangereau. Translated by S. Whiteside. London: Little, Brown. Originally published in French as *Ici, C'est le Paradis: Une enfance in Corée du Nord.* 2004. M. Lafon.

Kang Hyun-kyung. 2009. "Sejong City Project Will Have Far-reaching Ramifications." *Korea Times,* 26–27 September, 2.

Kang Inkyu. 2014. "It All Started with a Bang: The Role of PC Bangs in South Korea's Cybercultures." In *The Korean Popular Culture Reader,* edited by Kim Kyung Hyun and Choe Youngmin, 55–75. Durham, NC: Duke University Press.

Kang Jung In. 2004. *Seogu jungsim juui-reul neomeoseo* [Beyond the Shadow of Eurocentrism]. Seoul: Aconet.

Kang Sukhi. 2007. "Nam June Paik as a Composer and Korea." http:/www.snc.pe.kr, accessed 30 March 2007.

Kang Wi Jo. 1968. "Belief and Political Behaviour in Chongdogyo." *Review of Religious Research* 10 (1): 38–43.

Kant, Immanuel. [1790] 2007. *Critique of Judgment* [in German]. Translated by J. C. Meredith. Oxford: Oxford University Press.

Katsiaficas, George. 2012. *South Korean Social Movements in the 20th Century.* Vol. 1 of *Asia's Unknown Uprisings.* Oakland, CA: PM Press.

Kaufmann, Walter A., ed. 1975. *Existentialism from Dostoevsky to Sartre.* New York: New American Library.

Kawashima, Ken C. 2009. *The Proletarian Gamble: Korean Workers in Interwar Japan.* Durham, NC: Duke University Press.

Keijo toshi keikaku chosasho. 1928. Keijo (Seoul): Keijofu.

Kendall, Laurel. 1996. *Getting Married in Korea: Of Gender, Morality, and Modernity.* Berkeley: University of California Press.

———. 2009. *Sharmans, Nostalgias, and the IMF: South Korean Popular Religion in Motion.* Honolulu: University of Hawai'i Press.

Kern, Thomas, and Nam Sang-hui. 2011. "Citizen Journalism: The Transformation of the Democratic Media Movement." In *South Korean Social Movements: From Democracy to Civil Society,* edited by Shin Gi-Wook and P. Y. Chang, 173–189. Abingdon, UK: Routledge.

Keum Jang-tae. 2000. *Confucianism and Korean Thoughts.* Seoul: Jimoondang.

Kim, Elaine H., and Choi Chungmoo, eds. 1998a. *Dangerous Women: Gender and Korean Nationalism.* New York: Routledge.

———. 1998b. "Introduction." In *Dangerous Women: Gender and Korean Nationalism,* edited by E. H. Kim and Choi Chungmoi, 1–8. New York: Routledge.

Kim, Richard E. 1988. *Lost Names: Scenes from a Korean Boyhood.* Berkeley: University of California Press.

Kim, Suzy. 2013. *Everyday Life in the North Korean Revolution, 1945–1950.* Ithaca, NY: Cornell University Press.

Kim Baek Young. 2009. *Colonial Rule and Space—Colonial City Seoul and Imperial Japan* [in Korean]. Seoul: Moonji Publishing.

Kim Byeongcheol. 2006 "Production and Consumption of Contemporary Korean Cinema." *Korea Journal* 46 (1): 8–35.

Kim Byung-kook and Ezra F. Vogel, eds. 2011. *The Park Chung Hee Era: The Transformation of South Korea.* Cambridge, MA: Harvard University Press.

Kim Chong un and Bruce Fulton, trans. 1998. *A Ready-Made Life: Early Masters of Korean Fiction.* Honolulu: University of Hawai'i Press.

Kim Chun-Gil. 2005. *The History of Korea.* Westport, CT: Greenwood Publishing.

Kim Do Kyun and Kim Min-Sun, eds. 2011. *Hallyu: Korean Popular Culture in Asia and Beyond.* Seoul: Seoul National University Press.

Kim Do Kyun and Kim Se-Jin. 2011. "*Hallyu* from Its Origin to Present: A Historical Overview." In *Hallyu: Influence of Korean Popular Culture in Asia and Beyond,* edited by Kim Do Kyun and Kim Min-Sun, 13–34. Seoul: Seoul National University Press.

Kim Dongyun. 2015. "Urban Regeneration for Competitive City and Sustainable City—Seoul Experience." In *New Future for Asian Cities—Innovation of City Planning,* n.p. Shanghai: Asian City Forum.

Kim Eun Mee. 2008. "Korea's Multicultural Experiment." *Koreana* 22 (2): 14–23.

Kim Eun Mee and Kang Jean S. 2007. "Seoul as a Global City with Ethnic Villages." *Korea Journal* 47 (1): 64–99.

Kim Eun-shil. 2004. "Itaewon as an Alien Space within the Nation-State and a Place in the Globalization Era." *Korea Journal* 44 (3): 34–64.

Kim Eunsun. [2012] 2016. *A Thousand Miles to Freedom: My Escape from North Korea* [in French]. Translated by D. Tan. New York: St. Martin's Press.

Kim Han-Kyo. 2000. "The Patriotic Enlightenment Movement." In *From the Sixteenth to the Twentieth Centuries,* vol. 2 of *Sources of Korean Tradition,* 295–305. New York: Columbia University Press.

Kim Hun Joon. 2014. *The Massacre at Mt. Halla: Sixty Years of Truth Seeking in South Korea.* Ithaca, NY: Cornell University Press.

Kim Hyuk-Rae. 1998. "Family Capitalism and Corporate Structure in South Korea." *Korea Focus* 6:55–67.

———. 2000. "Fragility or Continuity? Economic Governance of East Asian Capitalism." In *Politics and Markets in the Wake of the Asian Crisis,* edited by R. Robison, M. Beeson, K. Jayasuriya, and H.-R. Kim, 99–115. London: Routledge.

Kim Hyun Mee. 2005. "Korean TV Dramas in Taiwan, with an Emphasis on the Localisation Process." *Korea Journal* 45 (4): 183–205.

Kim Hyung-A. 2004. Korea's Development under Park Chung Hee. Abingdon, UK: Routledge.

Kim Hyung-A and Clark W. Sorenson, eds. 2011. *Reassessing the Park Chung Hee Era, 1961–1979.* Seattle: Center for Korean Studies, University of Washington.

Kim Jeong-Nam and Ni Lan. 2011. "The Nexus between *Hallyu* and Soft Power: Cultural Public Diplomacy in the Era of Sociological Globalism." In *Hallyu: Korean Popular Culture in Asia and Beyond,* edited by Kim Do Kyun and Kim Min-Sun, 131–154. Seoul: Seoul National University Press.

Kim Ji-eon, Cindy 2010. "The New Korean Wave: Girl Groups." 28 October. http://www.korea.net, accessed 22 May 2011.

Kim Ji-myung. 2012. "Hallyu and Mutual Respect." *Korea Times,* 14–15 April, 6.

Kim Jinwung. 2001. "From 'American Gentlemen' to 'Americans': Changing Perceptions of the United States in South Korea in Recent Years." *Korea Journal* 41 (4): 172–198.

Kim Jong-bok. 2014. "A Buffer Zone for Peace: Andong Protectorate and Diplomatic Relations between Silla, Balhae, and Tang in the 8th to 10th Centuries." *Korea Journal* 54 (3): 103–125.

Kim Jong-il. 2001a. *On the Art of the Cinema.* Honolulu: University Press of the Pacific.

———. 2001b. *On the Art of Opera.* Honolulu: University Press of the Pacific.

Kim Joo-young. 1995. "Tamyang: A Rich Literary Heritage and Great Natural Beauty." *Koreana* 9 (3): 62–69.

Kim Kwan-Joong. 1998. "New Form, Classic Problem: Pseudo-Public Residential Redevelopment in Seoul." *Built Environment* 24 (1): 235–250.

———. N.d. "Inner City Growth Management Problem in Seoul: Residential Rebuilding Boom and Its Planning Issues." Seoul Development Institute. http://up.t.u-tokyo.ac.jp, accessed 23 June 2011.

Kim Kwang-Ok. 1994. "Rituals of Resistance: The Manipulation of Sharmanism in Contemporary Korea." In *Asian Visions of Authority: Religion and the Modern States in East and Southeast Asia,* edited by C. F. Keyes, L. Kendall, and H. Hardacre, 195–220. Honolulu: University of Hawai'i Press.

Kim Kyu Hyun. 2004. "Reflections on the Problems of Colonial Modernity and 'Collaboration' in Modern Korean History." *Journal of International and Area Studies* 11 (3): 95–111.

———. 2005. "War and the Colonial Legacy in Recent South Korean Scholarship." IIAS Newsletter 38. http://www.iias.nl, accessed 22 June 2015.

Kim Kyung Hyun. 2004. *The Remasculinization of Korean Cinema.* Durham, NC: Duke University Press.

———. 2011a. *Virtual Hallyu: Korean Cinema of the Global Era.* Durham, NC: Duke University Press.

———. 2011b. "The Blockbuster Auteur in the Age of *Hallyu:* Bong Joon-ho." In *Hallyu: Korean Popular Culture in Asia and Beyond,* edited by Kim Do Kyun and Kim Min-Sun, 181–206. Seoul: Seoul National University Press.

Kim Kyung Hyun and Choe Youngmin, eds. 2014. *The Korean Popular Culture Reader.* Durham, NC: Duke University Press.

Kim Okkyun. 2000. "Memorial." In *Sources of Korean Tradition: From the Sixteenth to the Twentieth Centuries,* edited by Ch'oe Yong-ho, P. H. Lee, and W. T. de Bary, 256–258. New York: Columbia University Press.

Kim Rahn. 2008. "Seoul Plaza Suffering under Mass Rallies." *Korea Times,* 15 June. http://www.koreatimes.co.kr, accessed 10 July 2011.

Kim Ranky and Yoon Do-Geun. 1989. "Iljeha minjok geonchuk saeng-saneopja e gwanhanyeongu" [A Study of the Production of National Architecture under Japanese Colonial Rule]. *Proceeding of the National Conference of the Architectural Institute of Korea* 9 (2): 227–232.

Kim Seong-kon. 2013. "The Gulf between K-pop and Korean Literature." *Asia News Network,* 29 June.

Kim Seung-Kyung. 1997. *Class Struggle or Family Struggle: Lives of Women Factory Workers in South Korea.* New York: Cambridge University Press.

Kim Seung-Ryull. 2008. "Some Experience from the Soft Ground Tunnelling in Urban Area." The State-of-the-Art Technology and Experience on Geotechnical Engineering in Korea and Hong Kong, seminar. http://www.cedb.gov.hk, accessed 25 March 2012.

Kim Song-nyae. 2000. "P'ungsu wa singminjuui ui kiok ui erot'ik chusul." *Han'kuk chonggyo hon'gu* 2:123–157.

Kim Suki. 2014. *Without You, There Is No Us.* London: Rider.

Kim Suk-Young. 2010. *Illusive Utopia: Theater, Film, and Everyday Performance in North Korea.* Ann Arbor: University of Michigan Press.

———. 2013. "For the Eyes of North Koreans? Politics of Money and Class in *Boys Over Flowers*." In *The Korean Wave: Korean Media Go Global,* edited by Kim Youna, 93–105. Abingdon, UK: Routledge.

Kim Sung Hong and Peter Schmal, eds. 2008. *Contemporary Korean Architecture: Megacity Network.* Berlin: Jovis.

Kim Sung-Young. 2014. "Review: *Digital Development in Korea: Building an Information Society,* Myung Oh and James F. Larson." *Journal of Communication* 64 (2): E5–E9.

Kim Sunhyuk. 2007. "Civil Society and Democratization in South Korea." In *Korean Society: Civil Society, Democracy, and the State,* edited by C. K. Armstrong, 53–71. 2nd ed. Abingdon, UK: Routledge.

Kim Tong-hyung. 2010. "Yongsan Business Plans in Jeopardy." *Korea Times,* 8 August. https://www.koreatimes.co.kr, accessed 3 September 2013.

Kim Won. 1981. "Histoire de l'urbanisme à Séoul et perspectives" [History of City Planning in Seoul and Prospects]. *Revue de Corée* 13 (1): 3–25.

Kim Won Bae. 1999. "Developmentalism and Beyond: Reflections on Korean Cities." *Korean Journal* 39 (3): 5–34.

Kim Yong Choon. 1978. *The Ch'ongdogyo Concept of Man: An Essence of Korean Thought.* Seoul: Pan Korea Book Corporation.

Kim Youna. 2005. *Women, Television, and Everyday Life in Korea: Journeys of Hope.* London: Routledge.

———. 2011. "Globalization of Korean Media: Meanings and Significance." In *Hallyu: Korean Popular Culture in Asia and Beyond,* edited by Kim Do Kyun and Kim Min-Sun, 35–62. Seoul: Seoul National University Press.

———. 2013. *The Korean Wave: Korean Media Go Global.* Abingdon, UK: Routledge.

Kim Young-geun. 2002. "Changes in Social and Spatial Structure and Urban Experience in Seoul under Japan's Colonial Rule." *Seoul-hak Yeongu* [Journal of Seoul Studies] 20.

Kim Youngmin and Michael J. Pettid, eds. 2011. *Women and Confucianism in Choson Korea: New Perspectives.* Albany, NY: SUNY Press.

King, Ross J. 1996. *Emancipating Space: Geography, Architecture, and Urban Design.* New York: Guilford.

———. 2008a. "Seoul, Conditions of Possibility, and the Post-Nation Hyperspace." *Environment and Planning D: Society and Space* 27 (4): 616–632.

———. 2008b. *Kuala Lumpur and Putrajaya: Negotiating Urban Space in Malaysia.* Singapore: NUS Press.

———. 2011. *Reading Bangkok.* Singapore: NUS Press.

Kingston, Jeffrey. (2001) 2014. *Japan in Transformation, 1945–2010.* Abingdon, UK: Routledge.

Kirkpatrick, Melanie. 2015. *Escape from North Korea: The Untold Story of Asia's Underground Railroad.* New York: Encounter Books.

Kleiner, Jürgen. 2001. *Korea: A Century of Change.* Singapore: World Scientific.

Ko, Dorothy, JaHyun Kim Haboush, and Joan R. Piggott, eds. 2003. *Women and Confucian Cultures in Premodern China, Korea, and Japan.* Berkeley: University of California Press.

Koh Wee Hock, David, ed. 2007. *Legacies of World War II in South and East Asia.* Singapore: ISEAS.

Kohli, Atul. 2004. *State-Directed Development: Political Power and Industrialization in the Global Periphery.* Cambridge: Cambridge University Press.

Korean Institute of Architects. 2000. *Seoul Architecture and Urbanism.* Seoul: Seoul Metropolitan Government.

Kuroishi, Izumi, ed. 2014. *Constructing the Colonized Land: Entwined Perspectives of East Asia around WWII.* Farnham, UK: Ashgate.

Kuwahara, Yasue, ed. 2014. *The Korean Wave: Korean Popular Culture in Global Context.* New York: Palgrave Macmillan.

Kwon Jong Bum. 2011. "Exorcizing the Ghosts of Kwangju: Policing Protest in the Post-Authoritarian Era." In *South Korean Social Movements: From Democracy to Civil Society,* edited by Shin Gi-Wook and Paul Y. Chang, 58–74. Abingdon, UK: Routledge.

Kwon Nayoung Aimee, 2015. *Intimate Empire: Collaboration and Colonial Modernity in Korea and Japan.* Durham, NC: Duke University Press.

Kwon Taeeok. 2005. "The Basis of Imperial Japan's Colonial Rule." In *Structure and Nature of Japan's Colonial Rule* [in Korean]. Seoul: Kyunjin Publishing.

Kyung Moon Hwang. 2010. *A History of Korea.* New York: Palgrave Macmillan.

Lancaster, Lewis R., Suh Kikun, and Yu Chai-shin, eds. 1996. *Buddhism in Koryo: A Royal Religion.* Berkeley: Institute of East Asian Studies.

Langer, Peter. 1984. "Sociology—Four Images of Organized Diversity: Bazaar, Jungle, Organism and Machine." In *Cities of the Mind: Images and Themes of the City in the Social Sciences,* edited by L. Rodwin and R. M. Hollister, 5–34. New York: Plenum Press.

Larsen, Kirk W. 2008. "Review of *The Making of Minjung: Democracy and the Politics of Representation in South Korea* by Lee Namjee." *Journal of Korean Studies* 13 (1): 132–134.

Latour, Bruno. 2005. *Reassembling the Social: An Introduction to Actor-Network Theory.* Clarendon Lectures in Management Studies. Oxford, New York: Oxford University Press.

Lautensach, Hermann. (1945) 1988. *Korea: A Geography Based on the Author's Travels and Literature.* Translated by K. and E. Dege. Leipzig; repr., Berlin: Springer Verlag.

Le Corbusier et Pierre Jeanneret: Oeuvre complète, 1910–1929. 1935. Zurich: W. Boesiger et O. Stonorov.

Lechte, John. 1994. *Fifty Key Contemporary Thinkers: From Structuralism to Postmodernity.* London: Routledge.

Ledyard, Gari. 1971. *The Dutch Came to Korea.* Seoul: Royal Asiatic Society Korea Branch.

Lee Byeong-cheon. 2005. *Developmental Dictatorship and the Park Chung-Hee Era: The Shaping of Modernity in the Republic of Korea.* Paramus, NJ: Homa and Sekey.

Lee Chang-Moo and Ahn Kun-Hyuck. 2005. "Five New Towns in the Seoul Metropolitan Area and Their Attractions in Non-working Trips: Implications on Self-
containment of New Towns." *Habitat International* 29: 647–666.

Lee Chong-sik. 2012. *Park Chung-Hee: From Poverty to Power.* Palos Verdes, CA:
KHU Press.

Lee Eun-Jung. 2004. "E-democracy@work: The 2002 Presidential Election in Korea."
In *Asian Cyberactivism: Freedom of Expression and Media Censorship,* edited by
S. Gan, J. Gomez, and U. Johannen, 622–644. Bangkok: Friedrich Naumann
Foundation.

Lee Hong Yung. 2013. "Introduction: A Critique of 'Colonial Modernity.'" In *Colonial
Rule and Social Change in Korea, 1910–1945,* edited by Lee Hong Yung, Ha Yong
Chool, and C. W. Sorensen, 3–28. Seattle: University of Washington Press.

Lee Hong Yung, Ha Yong Chool, and Clark W. Sorensen, eds. 2013. *Colonial Rule and
Social Change in Korea, 1910–1945.* Seattle: University of Washington Press.

Lee Hoon K. 1936. *Land Utilization and Rural Economy in Korea.* Shanghai: Kelly and
Walsh.

Lee Hyangjin. 2001. *Contemporary Korean Cinema: Identity, Culture, and Politics.*
Manchester: Manchester University Press.

Lee Hyuk-jin and Joh Chang-hyeon. 2010. "Tourism Behaviour in Seoul: An Analysis
of Tourism Activity Sequence Using Multidimensional Sequence Alignments."
Tourism Geographies 12 (4): 487–504.

Lee Jae Eui. 1999. *Gwanju Diary: Beyond Death, Beyond the Darkness of the Age.* Asian
Pacific Monograph Series. Los Angeles: University of California, Los Angeles.

Lee Ji-Eun. 2015. *Women Pre-Scripted: Forging Modern Roles through Korean Print.*
Honolulu: University of Hawai'i Press.

Lee Jin Gu. 2004. "Korean Protestantism as Viewed by Netizens: A Focus on Recent
Activities of Anti-Christian Sites." *Korea Journal* 44 (4): 223–245.

Lee Jin-kyung. 2010. *Service Economies: Militarism, Sex Work, and Migrant Labor in
South Korea.* Minneapolis: University of Minnesota Press.

Lee Jong Hwa and Han Min Wha. 2011. "Transforming the Image of the Other: Rep-
resentations of North Korea/ns in *Hallyu* Cinema." In *Hallyu: Influence of
Korean Popular Culture in Asia and Beyond,* edited by Kim Do Kyun and Kim
Min-Sun, 155–180. Seoul: Seoul National University Press.

Lee Ki-baik. [1961] 1984. *A New History of Korea.* Translated by E. W. Wagner and
E. J. Schultz [in Korean]. Cambridge, MA: Harvard University Press.

Lee Ki-Suk. 1979. *A Social Geography of Greater Seoul.* Seoul: Po Chin Chai.

Lee Kyong-hee. 1997. *World Heritage in Korea.* Seoul: Hak Go Jae.

Lee Man-hoon. 1995. "Dismantling the Former Colonial Government Building to
Restore the National Spirit." *Koreana* 9 (2): 79–80.

Lee Mu-Yong. 2004. "The Landscape of Club Culture and Identity Politics: Focusing
on the Club Culture in the Hongdae Area of Seoul." *Korea Journal* 44 (3):
65–107.

Lee Myung-bak. 2005. *Cheonggyecheon un milae hulunda* [Cheonggyecheon Flows to
the Future]. Seoul: Random House Korea.

———. 2006. "Cheonggyecheon un tongbuga bijinis wa kumyung ui ch'osok" [The
Cheonggye Stream as a Foundation for the Business and Financial Hub in
Northeast Asian]. *Chach'I hengjong* (November): 16–18.

Lee Namhee. 2007. *The Making of Minjung: Democracy and the Politics of Representation in South Korea.* Ithaca, NY: Cornell University Press.

———. 2011. "From *Minjung* to *Simin*: The Discursive Shift in Korean Social Movements." In *South Korean Social Movements: From Democracy to Civil Society,*
edited by Shin Gi-Wook and P. Y. Chang, 41–57. Abingdon, UK: Routledge.

———. 2013. "The Great Enterprise: Sovereignty and Historiography in Modern
Korea, by Henry Em." Review. *Korea Journal* 55 (3): 150–155.

Lee Sang-hae. 2000. "The Historical and Natural Landscape of Seoul." In *Seoul Architecture and Urbanism,* Korean Institute of Architects, 14–19. Seoul: Seoul Metropolitan Government.

Lee Sangjoon and Abe Marcus Nornes. 2015. *Hallyu 2.0: The Korean Wave in the Age of Social Media.* Ann Arbor: University of Michigan Press.

Lee Sang Keon, You Heeyoun, and Kwon Heeseo Rain. 2015. *Korea's Pursuit for Sustainable Cities through New Town Development: Implications for LAC.* Seoul: Korea Research Institute for Human Settlements.

Lee Sang Taek. 1996. *Religion and Social Formation in Korea: Minjung and Millenarianism.* Berlin: Mouton de Gruyter.

Lee Sohl. 2014. "Seung Woo Back's *Blow Up* (2005–2007): Touristic Fantasy, Photographic Desire, and Catastrophic North Korea." In *The Korean Popular Culture Reader,* edited by Kim Kyung Hyun and Choe Youngmin, 385–406. Durham, NC: Duke University Press.

Lee Soobum and Ju Hyejung. 2011. "The Meaning of Korean Dramas in Japanese Fandom: Re-Emerging Sentiments of 'Asianness.'" In *Hallyu: Korean Popular Culture in Asia and Beyond,* edited by Kim Do Kyun and Kim Min-Sun, 273–303. Seoul: Seoul National University Press.

Lee Won Gue. 1999. "A Sociological Study on the Factors of Church Growth and Decline in Korea." *Korea Journal* 39 (4): 235–269.

Lee Yongwoo. 2006. "Technology as Art: The Legacy of Video Artist Paik Nam June." *Koreana* 20 (2): 36–39.

Lee Young-ho. 2014. "Land Reform and Colonial Land Legislation in Korea, 1894–1910." *Korea Journal* 54 (3): 126–149.

Lee Young-il and Choe Young-chol. 1998. *The History of Korean Cinema.* Seoul: Jimoondang.

Legg, Stephen. 2005. "Contesting and Surviving Memory: Space, Nation and Nostalgia in *Les lieux de mémoire.*" *Environment and Planning D: Society and Space* 23 (4): 481–504.

Leong, Anthony C. Y. 2003. *Korean Cinema: The New Hong Kong: A Guidebook to the Latest Korean New Wave.* Victoria, BC: Trafford Publishing.

Lewis, Linda S. 2002. *Laying Claim to the Memory of May: A Look Back at the 1980 Kwangju Uprising.* Honolulu: University of Hawai'i Press.

Lie, John. 2014. *K-pop: Popular Music, Cultural Amnesia, and Economic Innovation in South Korea.* Oakland: University of California Press.

Liew Kai Khiun. 2013. "K-Pop Dance Trackers and Cover Dancers: Global Cosmopolitanization and Local Spatialization." In *The Korean Wave: Korean Media Go Global,* edited by Youna Kim, 165–181. Abingdon, UK: Routledge.

Lindsay, Greg. 2010. "Cisco's Big Bet on New Songdo: Creating Cities from Scratch." *Fast Company,* 1 February. http://www.fastcompany.com, accessed 21 May 2011.

Ling, Laura, and Ling, Lisa. 2010. *Somewhere Inside.* New York: Harper.

Livesey, Graham. 2010 "Assemblage." In *The Deleuze Dictionary,* edited by A. Parr, 18–19. Rev. ed. Edinburgh: Edinburgh University Press.

Lyotard, Jean-François. 1984. *The Postmodern Condition: A Report on Knowledge.* Translated by G. Bennington and B. Massumi. Manchester: Manchester University Press.

Ma Sheng-mei. 2006. "Tradition and/of Bastards in the Korean Wave." *Korea Journal* 46 (3): 132–153.

Maliangkay, Roald. 2010. "Keep Your Enemies Closer: Protecting Korea's Pop Culture in China." *Korean Histories* 2 (1): 34–44.

———. 2014. "The Popularity of Individualism: The Seo Taiji Phenomenon in the 1990s." In *The Korean Popular Culture Reader,* edited by Kim Kyung Hyun and Choe Youngmin, 296–313. Durham, NC: Duke University Press.

Maniaque-Benton, Caroline, and Jung Inha. 2014. *Point-Contrepoint: Trajectoires de dix architects Coréens* [Point-Counterpoint: Trajectories of Ten Korean Architects]. Copenhagen: Architectural Publisher B.

Mann, Michael. 1986. *The Sources of Social Power*. Cambridge: Cambridge University Press.

March, Lionel. 1981. "An Architect in Search of Democracy: Broadacre City." In *Writings on Wright: Selected Comments on Frank Lloyd Wright*, edited by H. A. Brooks, 195–206. Cambridge, MA: MIT Press.

Marinescu, Valentina, ed. 2014 *The Global Impact of South Korean Popular Culture: Hallyu Unbound*. Lanham, MD: Lexington Books.

Martin, Daniel. 2014. "South Korean Cinema's Postwar Pain: Gender and National Division in Korean Films from the 1950s to the 2000s." *Journal of Korean Studies* 19 (1): 93–114.

Maruyama, Masao. 1974. *Nihonseiji shiso-shi kenkyu* [Intellectual History of Tokugawa Japan]. Princeton, NJ: Princeton University Press.

May, Todd. 2005. *Gilles Deleuze: An Introduction*. Cambridge: Cambridge University Press.

McBride, Richard Dewayne II. 2008. "Pak Ch'anghwa and the *Hwarang segi* Manuscripts." *Journal of Korean Studies* 13 (1): 57–88.

McFarlane, Colin. 2011. "Assemblage and Critical Urbanism." *City* 15 (2): 204–224.

McHugh, Kathleen, and Nancy Abelmann, eds. 2005. *South Korean Golden Age Melodrama: Gender, Genre, and National Cinema*. Detroit: Wayne State University Press.

Merrill, John. 1980. "The Cheju-do Rebellion." *Journal of Korean Studies* 2:139–197.

——— . 1989. *Korea: The Peninsular Origins of the Korean War*. Newark, NJ: University of Delaware Press.

Michell, Anthony. 2010. *Samsung Electronics and the Struggle for Leadership of the Electronics Industry*. Singapore: Wiley.

Miller, Owen. 2010. "The Idea of Stagnation in Korean Historiography: From Fukuda Tokuzo to the New Right." *Korean Histories* 2 (1): 3–12.

Min Eungjun, Joo Jinsook, and Kwak HanJu. 2003. *Korean Film: History, Resistance, and Democratic Imagination*. Westport, CT: Praeger Publishers.

Mitchell, David. 2004. *Cloud Atlas: A Novel*. New York: Random House.

——— . 2012. "Translating 'Cloud Atlas' into the Language of Film." *Wall Street Journal*, 19 October. http://www.wsj.com, accessed 19 August 2015.

Mitchell, William J. 1995. *City of Bits: Space, Place, and the Infobahn*. Cambridge, MA: MIT Press.

——— . 1999. *E-Topia: Urban Life Jim, but Not as We Know It*. Cambridge, MA: MIT Press.

Moon Hyung-Sun, Katharine. 1997. *Sex among Allies: Military Prostitution in U.S.-Korea Relations*. New York: Columbia University Press.

Moon Jae-cheol. 2006. "The Meaning of Newness in Korean Cinema: Korean New Wave and After." *Korea Journal* 46 (1): 36–59.

Moon Seungsook. 1998. "Begetting the Nation: The Androcentric Discourse of National History and Tradition in South Korea." In *Dangerous Women: Gender and Korean Nationalism*, edited by E. H. Kim and Choi Chungmoo, 33–66. New York: Routledge.

——— . 2005. *Militarized Modernity and Gendered Citizenship in South Korea*. Durham, NC: Duke University Press.

——— . 2010. "Regulating Desire, Managing the Empire: U.S. Military Prostitution in South Korea, 1945–1970." In *Over There: Living with the U.S. Military Empire from World War Two to the Present*, edited by M. Höhn and Moon Seungsook, 39–77. Durham, NC: Duke University Press.

Moon So-young. 2009. "Something Alluring Stays on Art Street." *Korea JoongAng Daily*, 10 March. http://joongangdaily.joins.com, accessed 18 May 2011.

Moon Yumi. 2013. *Populist Collaborators: The Ilchinhoe and the Japanese Colonization of Korea, 1896–1910*. Ithaca, NY: Cornell University Press.

Moore, Barrington. (1966) 1993. *Social Origins of Dictatorship and Democracy: Lord and Peasant in the Making of the Modern World*. Boston: Beacon Press.

Mun Okpae. 2004. *Han'guk kumjigog-ui sahoe sa* [A Social History of Censored Korean Music]. Seoul: Yesol.

Nahm, Andrew C. 1988. *Korea: Tradition and Transformation: A History of the Korean People*. Elizabeth, NJ: Hollym.

——. 1993. *Introduction to Korean History and Culture*. Seoul: Hollym.

——. 1996. *Korea: A History of the Korean People*. 2nd ed. Seoul: Hollym.

Nam Tae-je and Yi Jin-pil. 2003. "Independent Documentary Born from Combustion of Reality." In *Korean Independent Documentaries*, edited by Independent Documentary Research Group [in Korean]. Seoul: Yedam.

Naoto, Namiki. 1997. "Shokuminchi koki Chosen ni okeru minshu togo no ichidan: Souru no jirei o chushin toshite." In *Chosen shakai no shiteki tenkai to higashi ajia*, edited by Takeda Yukio. Tokyo: Yamakawa shuppan-sha.

Neary, Ian. 2002. *The State and Politics in Japan*. Cambridge, UK: Polity Press.

Nederveen Pieterse, Jan P. 1997. "Globalization as Hybridisation." In *Global Modernities*, edited by M. Featherstone, S. Lash, and R. Robertson, 45–68. London: Sage.

Nicholls, Brett. 2010. "Leibnitz, Gottfried Wilhelm von (1646–1716)." In *The Deleuze Dictionary*, edited by A. Parr, 145–146. Rev. ed. Edinburgh: Edinburgh University Press.

Nishizawa, Yasuhiko. 2014. "A Study of Japanese Colonial Architecture in East Asia." In *Constructing the Colonized Land: Entwined Perspectives of East Asia around WWII*, edited by I. Kuroishi, 11–42. Farnham, UK: Ashgate.

Nora, Pierre. 1986. *Les lieux de mémoire* [Realms of Memory]. Vol. 2, *La Nation*. Paris: Gallimard.

——. 1989. "Between Memory and History: Les lieux de mémoire." *Representations* 26: 7–25.

——. 1996. *Realms of Memory: Rethinking the French Past*. Vol. 1, *Conflicts and Divisions*. Translated by A. Goldhammer. New York: Columbia University Press.

Nye, Joseph, and Kim Youna. 2013. "Soft Power and the Korean Wave." In *The Korean Wave: Korean Media Go Global*, edited by Kim Youna, 31–42. Abingdon, UK: Routledge.

Nylan, Michael. 2001. *The Five "Confucian" Classics*. New Haven, CT: Yale University Press.

Oberdorfer, Don, and Robert Carlin. 2013. *The Two Koreas: A Contemporary History*. New York: Basic Books.

O'Brien, Suzanne. 1999. "Translator's Introduction." In *Comfort Women*, by Yoshimi Yoshiaki, 1–21. New York: Columbia University.

Oh Myung and James F. Larson. 2011. *Digital Development in Korea: Building an Information Society*. Abingdon, UK: Routledge.

Oliver, Robert T. 1993. *A History of the Korean People in Modern Times: 1800 to the Present*. Newark: University of Delaware Press.

Omameuda, M. 2006. *Contemporary History of Rice and Food* [in Japanese]. Tokyo: Yoshikawa Kobunkan.

Onishi, Norimitsu. 2006. "A Rising Korean Wave: If Seoul Sells It, China Craves It." *International Herald Tribune*, 10 January.

O'Sullivan, Simon. 2010. "Fold." In *The Deleuze Dictionary*, edited by A. Parr, 107–108. Rev. ed. Edinburgh: Edinburgh University Press.

Paek Nam-un. 1933. *Chosen shakai keizaishi*. Tokyo: Kaizosha.

——. 1937. *Chosen hoken shakai keizaishi*. Tokyo: Kaizosha.

Paik Nam June. 1974. "Media Planning for the Postindustrial Society—The 21st Century Is Now Only 26 Years Away." *Media Art Net*. http://www.medienkunstnetz .de, accessed 14 August 2015.

———. 2003. "Cybernated Art." In *The New Media Reader,* edited by N. Wardrip-Fruin and N. Montfort, 227–230. Cambridge, MA: MIT Press.

Pak Kyong-sik. 1965. *Chosenjin kyosei renko no kiroku* [A Record of the Forced Displacement of Koreans]. Tokyo: Miraisha.

Pak Tae-won. 2010a. *A Day in the Life of Kubo the Novelist: "On the Eve of the Uprising" and Other Stories from Colonial Korea.* Translated by Park Sunyoung with J. J. A. Gatrall. Ithaca, NY: Cornell University East Asia Program.

———. 2010b. *Scenes from Ch'ŏnggye Stream.* Translated by Chang Ok Young Kim. Singapore: Stallion Press.

Palmer, Brandon. 2007. "Imperial Japan's Preparations to Conscript Koreans as Soldiers, 1942–1945." *Korean Studies* 31: 63–79.

———. 2010. "Japanese Assimilation Policies in Colonial Korea, 1910–1945 (Review)." *Korean Studies* 34: 157–159.

———. 2013. *Fighting for the Enemy: Koreans in Japan's War, 1937–1945.* Seattle: University of Washington Press.

Pang Kie-chung. 2005. "Paek Namun and Marxist Scholarship during the Colonial Period." In *Landlords, Peasants, and Intellectuals in Modern Korea,* edited by Pang Kie-chung and M. D. Shin, 245–308. Ithaca, NY: Cornell East Asia Series.

Parinyaporn Pajee. 2011. "The People's Television." *Nation* (Bangkok), 19 February. http://www.nationmultimedia.com, accessed 4 December 2011.

Park, Albert L. 2015. *Building a Heaven on Earth: Religion, Activism, and Protest in Japanese Occupied Korea.* Honolulu: University of Hawai'i Press.

Park Chan E. 2012. "Flow and Irony: Locating Literary Modernity in Hahn Moo-Sook's Retrospective Gazes." *Korean Studies* 36.

Park Chan Seung. 2010. "Japanese Rule and Colonial Dual Society in Korea." *Korea Journal* 50 (4): 69–98.

Park Chan Seung and Kim Hyun-ju. 2010. "The Centennial of Japan's Annexation of Korea: Rethinking Annexation and Postcolonial Legacy." *Korea Journal* 50 (4): 5–12.

Park Chung-hee. 1970. *Our Nation's Path: Ideology of Social Reconstruction.* 2nd ed. Seoul: Hollym. Originally published as *Uri minjok-ui nagal gil: sahoe jaegeon-ui inyeom.* Seoul: Donga Chulpansa, 1962.

———. 1971. *To Build a Nation.* Washington, DC: Acropolis Books.

Park Eun-jee. 2013. "SUNY Stony Brook Brings Math and Science Expertise to Songdo Campus." *Korea JoongAng Daily,* 19 March. http://koreajoongangdaily.joins .com, accessed 1 August 2015.

Park Gil-Sung. 2013. "Manufacturing Creativity: Production, Performance, and Dissemination of K-Pop." *Korea Journal* 53 (4): 14–33.

Park Ji-won. 2011. *The Novels of Park Jiwon: Translation of Overlooked Worlds.* Translation and introduction by Emanuel Pastreich. Seoul: Seoul National University Press.

Park Kil-Dong. N.d. "Cheonggyecheon Restoration Project." Seoul Metropolitan Government. http://www.wfeo.org, accessed 28 December 2010.

Park Nani and Robert J. Pouser. 2015. *Hanok: The Korean House.* Tokyo: Tuttle.

Park Sang Mi. 2010. "The Paradox of Postcolonial Korean Nationalism: State-Sponsored Cultural Policy in South Korea, 1965–present." *Journal of Korean Studies* 15, no. 1 (2010): 67–93.

Park Soon-won. 1999. *Colonial Industrialization and Labor in Korea: The Onoda Cement Factory.* Cambridge, MA: Harvard University Asia Center.

Park Sun-young. 2009. "An Illicit Love Affair Mixed with Mystery." *Korea JoongAng Daily,* 16 October. http://koreajoongangdaily.joins.com, accessed 2 August 2015.

Park Wan-suh. 2001. *Three Days in That Autumn.* Translated by Ryu Sukhee. Korea: Jimoondang.

———. [1992] 2009. *Who Ate Up All the Shinga?: An Autobiographical Novel* [in Korean]. Translated by Yu Young-nan and S. Epstein. New York: Columbia University Press.

Park Yeonmi. 2015. *In Order to Live: A North Korean Girl's Journey to Freedom.* With Maryanne Vollers. New York: Penguin Press.

Park Yong Soo. 2014. "Policies and Ideologies of the Kim Jong-un Regime in North Korea: Theoretical Implications." *Asian Studies Review* 38 (1): 1–14.

Park Young-a. 2011. "New Activist Cultural Production: Independent Filmmakers, the Post-Authoritarian State, and New Capital Flows in South Korea." In *South Korean Social Movements: From Democracy to Civil Society,* edited by Shin Gi-Wook and P. Y. Chang, 190–205. Abingdon, UK: Routledge.

Partner, Simon. 2000. *Assembled in Japan: Electronic Goods and the Making of the Japanese Consumer.* Berkeley: University of California Press.

Pempel, T. J. 1998. *Regime Shift: Comparative Dynamics of the Japanese Political Economy.* Ithaca, NY: Cornell University Press.

Pratt, Keith. 2006. *Everlasting Flower: A History of Korea.* London: Reaktion Books.

Reischauer, Edwin Oldfather. (1946) 1964. *Japan, Past and Present.* London: Duckworth.

Renan, Ernest. (1882) 1947–1961. "Qu'est-ce qu'une nation?" [What Is a Nation?]. In *Oeuvres Complètes,* 1: 887–906. Paris: Calmann-Lévy.

Rhee So-eui and Roger Yu. 2001. "South Korea Repays IMF for Loans." *Asian Wall Street Journal,* 24–26 August, 4.

Rhee Syngman. [1904] 1910. *Tongnip chongsin* [The Spirit of Independence]. Los Angeles: Taedong sinogwan.

Ricoeur, Paul. 1965. "Universal Civilization and National Cultures." In *History and Truth,* 271–284. Translated by C. A. Kelbley. Evanston, WI: Northwestern University Press.

Robinson, Michael E. 1988. *Cultural Nationalism in Colonial Korea.* University of Washington Press.

———. 2007a. *The Japanese Colonial Empire: 1895–1945.* Edited by R. H. Myers and M. R. Peattie. Princeton, NJ: Princeton University Press.

———. 2007b. *Korea's Twentieth-Century Odyssey: A Short History.* Honolulu: University of Hawai'i Press.

Rosenau, James N. 1990. *Turbulence in World Politics: A Theory of Change and Continuity.* Princeton, NJ: Princeton University Press.

Rosenberg, Max. 2013. "This $28 Billion Korean Real Estate Project Is on the Verge of Collapse." *Business Insider Australia,* 15 March. http://www.businessinsider.com.au, accessed 3 September 2013.

Rosenbluth, Frances McCall, and Michael F. Thies. 2010. *Japan Transformed: Political Change and Economic Restructuring.* Princeton, NJ: Princeton University Press.

Rowland, Ashley, and Chang Yoo Kyong. 2015. "Korean City Irked by Slow Handover of Vacated US Base." *Stars and Stripes,* 16 January. http://www.stripes.com, accessed 30 July 2015.

Russell, Mark J. 2008. *Pop Goes Korea: Behind the Revolution in Movies, Music, and Internet Culture.* Berkeley: Stone Bridge Press.

———. 2014. *K-POP Now: The Korean Music Revolution.* Tokyo: Tuttle.

Ryang, Sonia. 1997. *North Koreans in Japan: Language, Ideology, and Identity.* Boulder, CO: Westview Press.

———, ed. 2000. *Koreans in Japan: Critical Voices from the Margin.* London: Routledge.

———. 2009. *North Korea: Toward a Better Understanding.* Lanham, MD: Lexington Books.

Ryu Jeh-hong. 2004. "Naturalizing Landscapes and the Politics of Hybridity: Gwanghuamun to Cheonggyecheon." *Korea Journal* 44 (3): 8–33.

Ryu Je-Hun. 2012. "Postcolonial Urbanization and Changes of Vernacular Toponyms around Bupyeong-gu, Incheon: A Critical Perspective." *Korea Journal* 52 (1): 140–170.

Ryu Youngju. 2015. *Writers of the Winter Republic: Literature and Resistance in Park Chung Hee's Korea.* Honolulu: University of Hawai'i Press.

Sakai, Naoki. 1992. *Voices of the Past: The Status of Language in Eighteenth-Century Japanese Discourse.* Ithaca, NY: Cornell University Press.

———. 2000. "'You Asians': On the Historical Role of the West and Asia Binary." *South Atlantic Quarterly* 99 (4): 789–817.

———. (1997) 2008. *Translation and Subjectivity: On Japan and Cultural Nationalism.* Minneapolis: University of Minnesota Press.

Sakamoto, Rumi, and Matthew Allen. 2007. "'Hating The Korean Wave' Comic Books: A Sign of New Nationalism in Japan?" *Asia-Pacific Journal: Japan Focus* (October): n.p.

Sand, Jordan. 2013. *Tokyo Vernacular: Common Spaces, Local Histories, Found Objects.* Berkeley: University of California Press.

Savada, Andrea Matles, and William Shaw, eds. 1990. *A Country Study: South Korea, the Japanese Role in Korea's Economic Development.* Washington, DC: Federal Research Division, Library of Congress.

Schmid, Andre. 2002. *Korea between Empires, 1895–1919.* New York: Columbia University Press.

Schumpeter, Joseph A. (1942) 1950. *Capitalism, Socialism, and Democracy.* New York: Harper and Row.

Seo J.-I. 2008. *Types of House Stocks in South Korea in 2005.* Seoul: Ministry of Land Transport and Marine Affairs.

Seth, Michael J. 2002. *Education Fever: Society, Politics, and the Pursuit of Schooling in South Korea.* Honolulu: University of Hawai'i Press.

———. 2006. *A Concise History of Korea: From the Neolithic Period through the Nineteenth Century.* Lanham, MD: Rowman and Littlefield.

———. 2009. *A Concise History of Modern Korea: From the Late Nineteenth Century to the Present.* Lanham, MD: Rowman and Littlefield.

———. 2011. *A History of Korea: From Antiquity to the Present.* Lanham, MD: Rowman and Littlefield.

Shim Doobo, Ariel Herianto, and Ubonrat Siriyuvasak, eds. 2010. *Pop Culture Formations across East Asia.* Seoul: Jimoondang.

Shim Youn-ja, T., Kim Min-Sun, and Judith N. Martin. 2008. *Changing Korea: Understanding Culture and Communication.* New York: Peter Lang.

Shim Youn-ja, T., and John P. Daly. 2010. *Korean Entrepreneurship: The Foundation of the Korean Economy.* Basingstoke, UK: Palgrave Macmillan.

Shin, Michael D., ed. 2014. *Korean History in Maps: From Prehistory to the Twenty-First Century.* Cambridge: University of Cambridge Press.

Shin Chi-Yun and J. Stringer, eds. 2005. *New Korean Cinema.* Edinburgh: Edinburgh University Press.

Shin Gi-Wook, ed. 2006. *Rethinking Historical Injustice and Reconciliation in Northeast Asia: The Korean Experience.* London: Routledge.

Shin Gi-Wook and Paul J. Chang, eds. 2011. *South Korean Social Movements: From Democracy to Civil Society.* Abingdon, UK: Routledge.

Shin Gi-Wook, Paul J. Chang, Lee Jung-eun, and Kim Sookyung. 2011. "The Korean Democracy Movement: An Empirical Overview." In *South Korean Social Movements: From Democracy to Civil Society,* edited by Shin Gi-Wook and Paul J. Chang, 21–40. Abingdon, UK: Routledge.

Shin Gi-Wook and Hwang Kyung Moon, eds. 2003. *Contentious Kwangju: The May 18 Uprising in Korea's Past and Present.* Boulder, CO: Rowman and Littlefield.

Shin Gi-Wook and Michael Robinson, eds. 1999. *Colonial Modernity in Korea.* Cambridge, MA: Harvard University Press.

Shin Hyunjoon and Kim Pil Ho. 2014. "Birth, Death, and Resurrection of Group Sound Rock." In *The Korean Popular Culture Reader,* edited by Kim Kyung Hyun and Choe Youngmin, 275–295. Durham, NC: Duke University Press.

Shin Kwang-Yeong. 2006. "The Citizens' Movement in Korea." *Korea Journal* 46 (2): 5–34.

Shin Kyung-sook. [2009] 2012. *Please Look After Mom* [in Korean]. New York: Vintage. Originally published titled *Please Take Care of Mom.*

———. [2010] 2014. *I'll Be Right There* [in Korean]. Translated by Sora Kim-Russell. New York: Other Press.

Shin Sang-Ok. 2007. *I Was a Film.* Seoul: Random House Korea.

Shin Sang-Ok and Choi Eun-Hee. 1988. *The Kingdom of Kim Jong-Il.* Seoul: Tonga Il-bosa.

———. 2001. *We Haven't Escaped Yet.* Seoul: Wolgan Chosonsa, 2001.

Shozo, Ogasawara. 1953. *Kaigai jinjashi (jokan).* Tokyo: Kaigai jinjashi hensankai.

Simone, AbdouMaliq. 2010. *City Life from Jakarta to Dakar: Movement at the Crossroads.* New York: Routledge.

Slantchev, Branislav L. 2001. "Review: *A New History of Korea (Han'guksa sillon)*." http://www.gotterdamerung.org, accessed 13 September 2015.

Smith, Hazel. 2015. *North Korea: Markets and Military Rule.* Cambridge: Cambridge University Press.

Söderberg, Marie. 2011. *Changing Power Relations in Northeast Asia: Implications for Relations between Japan and South Korea.* London: Routledge.

Soh, C. Sarah. 2008. *The Comfort Women: Sexual Violence and Postcolonial Memory in Korea and Japan.* Chicago: University of Chicago Press.

Son Min-jung. 2014. "Young Musical Love in the 1930s." In *The Korean Popular Culture Reader,* edited by Kim Kyung Hyun and Choe Youngmin, 255–274. Durham, NC: Duke University Press.

Song, Jane. N.d. "Moving Gyeongseong: Korean Reaction to Changes in the Urban Landscape of Colonial Seoul in the 1920s." Thesis, Tufts University. http://dl.tufts.edu, accessed 20 October 2015.

Song, K. 2003. "Just One Size Doesn't Fit All." *Far Eastern Economic Review,* 8 May, 42–45.

Song Changzoo. 1999. "The Contending Discourses of Nationalism in Post-Colonial Korea and Nationalism as an Oppressive and Anti-democratic Force." PhD thesis, University of Hawai'i.

Song Do-Young. 1998. "*Noraebang:* A Case Study of Cultural Industry and Mode of Cultural Consumption." *Korean Social Science Journal* 25 (1): 97–125.

Song Jesook. 2006. "Historicization of Homeless Spaces: The Seoul Train Station Square and the House of Freedom." *Anthropological Quarterly* 79 (2): 193–223.

———. 2009. *South Koreans in the Debt Crisis: The Creation of a Neoliberal Welfare Society.* Durham, NC: Duke University Press.

Song Sang-Ho. 2015. "History's Shadow Eclipses Korea-Japan Trust-Building." *Korea Herald / Asia News Network,* 24 June.

Spivak, Gayatri Chakravorty. 1996. "Bonding in Difference: Interview with Alfred Arteaga." In *The Spivak Reader,* edited by D. Landry and G. McLean, 15–28. London: Routledge.

Stevens, Quentin. 2009. "Artificial Waterfronts." *Urban Design International* 14 (1): 3–22.

Steward, Susan. 1984. *On Longing: Narratives of the Miniature, the Gigantic, the Souvenir, the Collection.* Baltimore, MD: Johns Hopkins University Press.

Szacka, Léa-Catherine. 2014. "Trajectories of Ten Korean Architects." *Domus* (March). http://www.domusweb.it, accessed 17 March 2016.

Takeuchi, Yoshimi. (1947) 1993. "Chugoku no kindai to nihon no kindai" [Chinese Modernity and Japanese Modernity]. In *Nihon to Ajia* [Japan and Asia]. Tokyo.

Taylor, Charles. 1991. *The Ethics of Authenticity.* Cambridge, MA: Harvard University Press.

Thrift, Nigel. 1997. "Cities without Modernity, Cities with Magic." *Scottish Geographical Magazine* 113 (3): 138–149.

Tironi, Manuel. 2010. "Gelleable Spaces, Eventful Geographies: The Case of Santiago's Experimental Music Scene." In *Urban Assemblages: How Actor-Network Theory Changes Urban Studies,* edited by I. Farías and T. Bender, 27–52. Abingdon, UK: Routledge.

Trilling, Lionel. 1972. *Sincerity and Authenticity.* London: Oxford University Press.

Tu Weiming. 1994. *China in Transformation.* Cambridge, MA: Harvard University Press.

Tudor, Daniel. 2014. *A Geek in Korea: Discovering Asia's New Kingdom of Cool.* Tokyo: Tuttle.

Turnbull, Stephen. 2002. *War in Japan, 1467–1615.* Oxford: Osprey Publishing.

———. 2011. *Toyotomi Hideyoshi.* Oxford: Osprey Publishing.

Uchida, Jun. 2009. "'A Scramble for Freight': The Politics of Collaboration along and across the Railway Tracks of Korea under Japanese Rule." *Comparative Studies in Society and History* 51 (1): 117–150.

———. 2011a. *Brokers of Empire: Japanese Settler Colonialism in Korea, 1876–1945.* Cambridge, MA: Harvard East Asia Monographs.

———. 2011b. "A Sentimental Journal: Mapping the Interior Frontier of Japanese Settlers in Colonial Korea." *Journal of Asian Studies* 70 (3): 706–729.

———. 2013. "The Public Sphere in Colonial Life: Residents' Movements in Korea under Japanese Rule." *Past & Present* 220: 217–248.

Uk Heo and Terence Roehrig. 2010. *South Korea since 1980.* Cambridge: Cambridge University Press.

Ulmer, Gregory L. 1985 "The Object of Post-criticism." In *Postmodern Culture,* edited by Hal Foster, 83–110. London: Pluto Press.

Urban Planning of Seoul. 2009. Seoul: Seoul Metropolitan Government.

Vattimo, Gianni. 1985. *La fine della modernita: Nichilismo ed ermeneutica nella cultura post-moderna* [The End of Modernity: Nihilism and Hermeneutics in Postmodern Culture]. Milan: Aldo Garzanti.

Venturi, Robert. 1966. *Complexity and Contradiction in Architecture.* New York: Museum of Modern Art.

Venturi, Robert, Steve Izenour, and Denise Scott Brown. (1972) 1977. *Learning from Las Vegas: The Forgotten Symbolism of Architectural Form.* Rev. ed. Cambridge, MA: MIT Press.

Virilio, Paul. 1986. *Speed and Politics.* Translated by M. Polizzotti. New York: Semiotext(e).

———. 1993. "The Third Interval: A Critical Transition." In *Rethinking Technologies,* edited by V. A. Conley, 3–12. Minneapolis: University of Minnesota Press.

Wakabayashi, Ippei. 2007. "Dialectic of Culture and Politics: Ahn Jung-geun as a Medium of Reconciliation." *Journal of the Faculty of International Studies, Bunkyo University* 18 (1): 131–138.

Walsh, Kelly. 2011. "The 'Modernology' of Pak Tae-won: Glimpses of 1930s Seoul." *Situations* 5: 19–47.

Wan Ming. 2007. *The Political Economy of East Asia: Striving for Wealth and Power.* Washington, DC: CQ Press.

Wardrip-Fruin, Noah, and Nick Montfort, eds. 2003. *The New Media Reader.* Cambridge, MA: MIT Press.

Warner, Marina. 2004. *Fantastic Metamorphoses, Other Worlds: Ways of Telling the Self.* Oxford: Oxford University Press.

Weems, Benjamin. 1964. *Reform, Rebellion, and the Heavenly Way.* Tucson: University of Arizona Press.

Weiner, Jonathan. 1976. "Review of Reviews: *Social Origins of Dictatorship and Democracy* [Barrington Moore]." *History and Theory* 15 (2): 146–175.

Wells Kenneth. 1995. *South Korea's Minjung Movement: The Culture and Politics of Dissidence.* Honolulu: University of Hawai'i Press.

Wertsch, James V. 1991. *Voices of the Mind: A Sociological Approach to Mediated Action.* Cambridge, MA: Harvard University Press.

Woo Don-Son. 2014. "On Park Kil-ryong's Discovery, Understanding, and Designing of Korean Architecture." In *Constructing the Colonized Land: Entwined Perspectives of East Asia around WWII,* edited by I. Kuroishi, 193–214. Farnham, UK: Ashgate.

Woo Jung-en. 1991. *Race to the Swift: State and Finance in the Industrialization of Korea.* New York: Columbia University Press.

Workman, Travis. 2014. "The Partisan, the Worker, and the Hidden Hero: Popular Icons in North Korean Cinema." In *The Korean Popular Culture Reader,* edited by Kim Kyung Hyun and Choe Youngmin, 145–167. Durham, NC: Duke University Press.

Wu Hung. 2005. *Remaking Beijing: Tiananmen Square and the Creation of a Political Space.* London: Reaktion Books.

Yang Hyunah. 1998. "Re-membering the Korean Military Comfort Women: Nationalism, Sexuality and Silencing." In *Dangerous Women: Gender and Korean Nationalism,* edited by Elaine H. Kim and Choi Chungmoo, 123–140. New York: Routledge.

Yang Sung Chul. 1999. *The North and South Korean Political Systems: A Comparative Analysis.* Rev. ed. Seoul: Hollym.

Yi In-hwa. 2006. "Korea, the Everlasting Empire of the Online World." *Korea Focus* 14 (3): 74–76. Originally published in *JoonAng Ilbo,* 20 July 2006.

Yin Kelly Fu Su and Kai Khiun Liew. 2005. "*Hallyu* in Singapore: Korean Cosmopolitanism or the Consumption of Chineseness." *Korea Journal* 45 (4): 206–232.

Yon'guwon, Hanil Munjae. 1995. *Ppaeakkin choguk kkullyogan saramdul: Ch'ilpaengman Chosonin kangje tongwon ui yoksa* [Stolen Country, Taken-away People: A History of Seven Million Koreans' Forced Mobilization]. Seoul: Asia Munhwasa.

Yoo, Theodore Jun. 2008. *The Politics of Gender in Colonial Korea: Education, Labor, and Health, 1910–1945.* Berkeley: University of California Press.

Yoo Mi-rim. 2006. "King Sejong's Leadership and the Politics of Inventing the Korean Alphabet." *Review of Korean Studies* 9 (3): 7–38.

Yoon Ja-young. 2012. "Two Thirds of Internet Cafes Suffering Deficit." *Korea Times,* 14–15 April, 8.

Yoshiaki, Yoshimi. [1995] 2002. *Comfort Women* [in Japanese]. Translated by S. O'Brien. New York: Columbia University Press.

Young, Carl F. 2014. *Eastern Learning and the Heavenly Way: The Tonghak and Ch'ondogyo Movements and the Twilight of Korean Independence.* Honolulu: University of Hawai'i Press.

Yu Chai-shin, ed. 2004. *The Founding of Catholic Tradition in Korea.* Fremont, CA: Jain.

Yu Chai-shin and Richard W. L. Guisso, eds. 1988. *Sharmanism: The Spirit World of Korea.* Berkeley, CA: Asian Humanities Press.

Yuichi, Higuchi. 1992. *Kogun heishi ni sareta Chosenjin: 15nen Sensoka nosodoin taisei nokenkyu* [Koreans Who Were Forced to Be Imperial Soldiers: Study on the General Mobilization System during the Fifteen-Year War]. Tokyo: Shakai Hyoronsha.

Yun Haedong. 2006. *Haebang chonhusa ui chaeinsik* [A Rediscovery of History before and since Liberation]. N.p.

———. 2007. *Singminji kundae ui p'aerodoksu* [The Paradox of Colonial Modernity]. Seoul: Hyumonisut'u.

Yun Haedong et al., eds. 2006. *Kundae rul tasi ingnunda: Han'guk kundae insik ui saeroun p'aerodaim ul wihayo* [Another Reckoning of Modern Times: For the Realization of a New Paradigm in Modern Korea]. Seoul: Yoksa Pip'yongsa.

Yun Seongyi. 2003. "The Internet and the 2002 Presidential Election in South Korea." *Korea Journal* 43 (2): 209–229.

———. 2006. "Electronic Democracy Elbowing Out Representative Democracy." *Korea Focus* 14 (3): 54–57. Originally published in *Weekly Chosun,* 21 July 2006.

Yun Young Min. 2003. "An Analysis of Cyber-Electioneering: Focusing on the 2002 Presidential Election in Korea." *Korea Journal* 43 (3): 141–164.

Zitwer, B. 2012. "Sermons on the Mount." *Age* (Melbourne) *Traveller,* 12 May, 14–15.

Index

About the Author

Ross King is Professorial Fellow in the Faculty of Architecture, Building and Planning at the University of Melbourne, Australia. As a frequent visitor to East and Southeast Asia, he has written extensively on the cities and communities of that region. His research deals with contested identities in Asian cities and the ways in which architecture, urban design, urban planning, and newer media are mobilized (manipulated, distorted) in such contests. He also publishes extensively on the phenomenon of informal settlements in Asian cities and on formality and informality as processes. He is the author of *Emancipating Space: Geography, Architecture, and Urban Design; Kuala Lumpur and Putrajaya: Negotiating Urban Space in Malaysia;* and *Reading Bangkok.*

Printed in the United States
By Bookmasters